THE CLASSICS
OF **WESTERN**
SPIRITUALITY

THE CLASSICS OF WESTERN SPIRITUALITY
A Library of the Great Spiritual Masters

President and Publisher
Mark-David Janus, CSP

EDITORIAL BOARD

Bishop Kallistos of Diokleia—Fellow of Pembroke College, Oxford, Spalding Lecturer in Eastern Orthodox Studies, Oxford University, England

Azim Nanji—Director, The Institute of Ismaili Studies, London, England

Seyyed Hossein Nasr—Professor of Islamic Studies, George Washington University, Washington, DC

Sandra M. Schneiders—Professor of New Testament Studies and Spirituality, Jesuit School of Theology, Berkeley, CA

Michael A. Sells—John Henry Barrows Professor of Islamic History and Literature, University of Chicago Divinity School

Huston Smith—Thomas J. Watson Professor of Religion Emeritus, Syracuse University, Syracuse, NY

John R. Sommerfeldt—Professor of History, University of Dallas, Irving, TX

David Steindl-Rast—Spiritual Author, Benedictine Grange, West Redding, CT

David Tracy—Greeley Professor of Roman Catholic Studies, Divinity School, University of Chicago, Chicago, IL

The Most Rev. and Rt. Hon. Rowan D. Williams—Archbishop of Canterbury

JEANNE GUYON

Selected Writings

TRANSLATED, EDITED, AND INTRODUCED BY
DIANNE GUENIN-LELLE AND RONNEY MOURAD

PAULIST PRESS
NEW YORK • MAHWAH, NJ

Cover Art: Rich Matts / iStockphoto

Cover and caseside design by Cynthia Dunne, www.bluefarmdesign.com
Book design by Sharyn Banks

Library of Congress Cataloging-in-Publication Data

Guyon, Jeanne Marie Bouvier de La Motte, 1648–1717.
    [Selections. English. 2012]
    Jeanne Guyon : selected writings / translated, edited, and introduced by Dianne Guenin-Lelle and Ronney Mourad.
        p. cm. — (The classics of Western spirituality)
    Includes bibliographical references (p.   ) and index.
    ISBN 978-0-8091-4718-2 (alk. paper) — ISBN 978-0-8091-0595-3 (alk. paper)
1. Guyon, Jeanne Marie Bouvier de La Motte, 1648–1717. 2. Catholics—France—Biography. 3. Mysticism—Catholic Church. 4. Quietism. 5. Spirituality—Catholic Church. 6. Spiritual life—Catholic Church. I. Guenin-Lelle, Dianne. II. Mourad, Ronney. III. Title. IV. Title: Selected writings.
    BX4705.G8A3 2012b
    282.092—dc23
    [B]
                                                                    2011023652

Published by Paulist Press
997 Macarthur Boulevard
Mahwah, NJ 07430

www.paulistpress.com

Printed and bound in the
United States of America

CONTENTS

Translator-Editors of this Volume

DIANNE GUENIN-LELLE teaches in the Modern Languages and Cultures Department at Albion College. She received her Ph.D. in seventeenth-century French literature from Louisiana State University. Her research interests include seventeenth-century French narrative and cultural production in French Louisiana. Besides having published on Jeanne Guyon's legacy, she has also written about the French comic novel as metafiction, on the importance of poetry, music festivals, and the Mardi Gras as cultural artifacts in French Louisiana, and on multicultural pedagogy.

RONNEY MOURAD teaches in the Religious Studies Department at Albion College. He received his Ph.D. from the University of Chicago Divinity School. His research focuses on the philosophy of religion and Christian theology. He has previously written about religious experience and Christian mysticism, religious uses of transcendental arguments, Reformed epistemology, and the ethics of belief.

PREFACE

This volume of selected writings by Jeanne-Marie Bouvier de la Mothe Guyon (1648–1717) presents several texts that are historically, theologically, and culturally important. Historians commonly include many of the people who surrounded Guyon, both friends and enemies, among the theological and literary giants of seventeenth-century France. Until recently, however, they have largely relegated Guyon herself to secondary status. Interestingly, the neglect or even deprecation of her work in eighteenth- and nineteenth-century French scholarship has been paralleled by a longstanding popular interest in and appreciation for it among English-speaking audiences. This divided reception history has its origins in the final years of Guyon's life and persists in some ways up to the present. A new generation of French scholars informed by interdisciplinary approaches to women's studies has begun to reexamine Guyon's historical importance and to produce critical editions of her work, and the efforts of these scholars have contributed a great deal to this volume. Among English speakers, however, Guyon's audience continues to be primarily non-scholarly. She was extraordinarily prolific, especially when one considers that with little formal education she wrote nearly forty volumes in several genres, ranging from her autobiography to biblical analyses, spiritual instruction manuals, letters, poems, and justifications of her writings addressed to the most powerful leaders at Court and in the church. Century-old English translations of her major works are regularly reprinted by evangelical Protestant presses and continue to interest readers seeking spiritual inspiration. These translations can sometimes sound antiquated to contemporary ears, though, and they leave out significant parts of the texts discovered by recent archival work and critical scholarship. A scholarly English translation of some of her most important texts is, therefore, long past due.

The texts included here have been newly translated from the French. These English translations aim to stay as close as possible to the original French, respecting Guyon's wording, her sentence structure, and ultimately, her voice. This approach stands in contrast to most other English translations, which too often have not followed Guyon's original texts faithfully. Of course, every translation must make accommodations of various kinds, and this one is no exception. As is typical in much seventeenth-century French prose, Guyon often writes in extremely long, complex sentences that defy the stylistic expectations of contemporary English speakers. In many cases the preservation of her syntax seemed too high a price to pay for the awkwardness of the resulting English translations. Nonetheless, we have tried whenever possible to find a middle way that respects Guyon's texts while producing readable English versions. A close reading of these newly translated works should bring fresh issues to light for English-speaking audiences relating to her role as a woman writing her own story, her contributions to mystical theology, her relationship to the Catholic Church, and her place in French history and literature.

Guyon's theological writings, represented here by *A Short and Easy Method of Prayer* and the *Commentary on the Song of Songs of Solomon* present Guyon's conception of the contemplative tradition in Christianity and reveal how this understanding was informed by her life experiences in seventeenth-century France. These texts also indicate Guyon's conceptualization of spiritual practice based on her consciousness of God and God's relationships to human beings. Guyon's *The Life of Madame J. M. B. de la Motte Guyon Written by Herself* (*Life*) provides fascinating insight into her spiritual and theological development and into some of the important events in her life that shaped and reflected her theology. The *Life* also presents Guyon's own historically valuable perspective on how she is implicated in the Quietist Affair and how her persecution stemmed primarily from political motives. While her explanation of this episode was political, her reaction to it was theological and remained quite consistent with her mystical convictions. Her writings present a model of resistance based on a spiritual practice that inculcates an indifference to or even a valorization of suffering and an absolute devotion to the will of God. By these means she was able to maintain her integrity and sanity during long periods of imprisonment in a way that inspired her friends and confounded her persecutors.

ACKNOWLEDGMENTS

Thanks are due to a number of people for their help with this book. We have depended on Dominique Tronc's excellent critical editions of Guyon's *Life* in preparing the translations, notes, and introduction for this volume. Marie-Louise Gondal's edition of the *Short and Easy Method* and her *Récits de captivité* were also very helpful. The project as a whole has benefited at every stage, from conception to completion, from Bernard McGinn's detailed feedback. We also appreciate the editorial work and support of the staff at Paulist Press. Albion College provided sabbatical funding that made some of the work possible.

Many people offered useful suggestions regarding the translations, including Emmanuel Yehwah, Mark Soileau, Nicolas Replumaz, Alexis Julian-Laferrière, Sophie Gérard, Melanie Galley, Marine Ridoux, Maury and Helen Branch, and David Begg. In addition to those already mentioned, we are grateful to have other terrific colleagues in the Modern Languages and Cultures Department and the Religious Studies Department at Albion who offered personal encouragement for this project, including Selva Raj, Jocelyn McWhirter, Nancy Weatherwax, Perry Myers, Cathie Grimm, Julia Medina, Kalen Oswald, and Linda Clawson. We would like to thank Albion College's president, Donna Randall, and provost, Susan Conner, for their interest in and encouragement of this project. Thanks, also, to our friends in Noisy-le-Roi and Bailly, France, for their eagerness to learn more about this book.

Finally, we wish to thank our families and friends for their support and encouragement, Dianne is particularly grateful to her husband, Mark Lelle, for his limitless love and patience, as well as to Connie Whitener, Bruce Guenin, and Janet Guenin-Oliva for their ongoing interest in their sister's work. She is grateful to Sophie Gérard, Carlos Valcárcel, Philipp Cronenberg, and Alejandro

Mercado for their understanding during those many days when their American host mom was unavailable to share in their international experience. Finally, she is grateful to her children, Hannah and Austin Lelle, for their understanding, their patience, and their willingness to "keep the volume down" during those long days, too numerous to mention, when their mom needed quiet to decipher Guyon's words. Ron would like to thank his wife, Emily Kuo, for her love and support, as well as Walid and Najat Mourad, Greg and Diana Mourad, and Nawal Mourad for their encouragement and interest in the project. He would also like to thank his sons, Peter and Luke Mourad, for helping him better understand Guyon's views on self-annihilation and, more important, pure love.

INTRODUCTION

The life of Jeanne-Marie Bouvier de La Mothe Guyon was full of remarkable contrasts that are not easily reconciled. This is in part because Guyon does not fit neatly into the social or religious fabric of her time. She was a noblewoman, a mystic, an itinerant spiritual teacher, a lay person, a mother, a writer, a social activist, a devout Catholic, and for many years an enemy of the state. She believed that the path she followed was laid out for her by God and not principally by the church, her family, or any other social institution. Not surprisingly, the differences between the notions about what a woman (especially a woman engaged in spiritual teaching and writing) should be in seventeenth-century France and how Guyon lived her life often put her at odds with the clergy in power around her. As Marie-Louise Gondal points out, "The 'establishment' of priests, confessors, superiors and bishops is at the same time drawn to and disconcerted by this woman who did not follow the traditional paths and sometimes dared to say 'no.'"[1]

Guyon is a fascinating transitional figure in many ways. At the end of the seventeenth century, Catholic mysticism in France was transformed from a fairly mainstream theoretical and practical discipline to a marginalized and suspect esoteric tradition, and Guyon witnessed and suffered from this transformation. The possibilities for female agency were changing quickly around her, with new educational opportunities and more open forms of monastic life for women emerging against a backdrop of severe constraints and oppressive gender stereotypes, and Guyon's life reflected the resulting ambiguities. She negotiated the increasing epistemological tension between theological and naturalistic explanations of human experience emerging from the scientific revolutions of the seventeenth century. Her *Life* in some ways anticipates the literary turn from confessional and spiritual narrative to modern autobiography. Her evolving concep-

1

tion of apostolic mission reflects a shift from Reformation-era antagonism between Catholics and Protestants to a model of coexistence, tolerance, and dialogue that was ahead of its time.

This Introduction touches on several of these aspects of Guyon's place in history. It begins with a biographical sketch and then presents a brief summary of the larger historical context of her life, focusing especially on events, people, and institutions relevant to the Quietist Affair, the conflict resulting in Guyon's long imprisonment. The next two sections treat the theological context in which she wrote and summarize some of her main influences and her central claims about mysticism, prayer, and the spiritual life. It concludes with some historiographical observations and some brief comments about the individual texts translated in this volume.

1. BRIEF BIOGRAPHY

Jeanne-Marie Bouvier de La Mothe was born in Montargis, in central France, on April 13, 1648. Her parents secured an intermittent education for her, beginning at the age of two and a half, in various convents that offered boarding schools for girls. Much of her childhood was spent with the Ursulines, who were particularly involved in the education of the daughters of noble Catholic families in seventeenth-century France. She writes in her *Life* that during those periods when she lived at home with her family, she suffered from her brother's cruelty and her mother's indifference. Her half-sisters were in a convent and provided her with experiences and lessons that helped satisfy some of her spiritual longings, even at an early age. Her father, while loving and indulgent toward her, had decidedly worldly ambitions for his daughter and was very hostile to the idea that she might pledge herself to a religious community. As a young woman she was not granted the kind of spiritual education she longed for, though she reports reading and being deeply influenced by the *Introduction to the Devout Life* by Francis de Sales and the *Life of St. Jane Frances de Chantal*. First in adolescence, then again later as a widow, Chantal became a model for her life as she sought a life of spiritual contemplation and service outside the cloistered convent system.

INTRODUCTION

Throughout her life, even as a very young child, Guyon's health was frail, and she was prone to illness. Perhaps because of her own compromised health, from an early age she engaged in continual acts of charity in a concerted attempt to relieve the suffering of others around her. Many of the historical claims about Guyon's childhood rely on her own autobiographical narrative, which colors the facts she reports with the literary tropes of confessional autobiography. Diseases and physical suffering are typically given great significance and interpreted as forms of divine communication in Guyon's *Life*, as was quite conventional in biographical descriptions of the lives of earlier ascetics and contemplatives, particularly women. Nonetheless, in a society with an average life expectancy of around twenty-five years, there is little reason to doubt that she suffered the frequent and sometimes debilitating illnesses she reports.[2]

In adolescence she blossomed, and her mother's attitude toward her changed radically. She reports that her mother became proud of her beauty and the many admirers she attracted, including members of Louis XIV's court. She was married at age fifteen in 1664 to Jacques Guyon du Chesnoy, who was twenty-two years her senior and had several children from a previous marriage. This marriage was arranged by her father. It was certainly a disappointment to her, but it was also apparently not her family's first choice and may have been necessitated by financial considerations, as her new husband possessed an enormous fortune. After one year of marriage, in 1665, she gave birth to her first child, Jacques Guyon. She went on to bear four more children during a marriage characterized by continuous psychological abuse and profound unhappiness. During virtually her entire marriage, she was ostracized and criticized by her husband and her mother-in-law.

At the age of nineteen she met the Duchess of Charost, daughter of the disgraced finance minister Fouquet, who took refuge at Guyon's father's house when the duchess was exiled from Paris. Through this relationship with Charost, who was schooled in seventeenth-century mystical practice, Guyon became acquainted with the teachings of Jacques Bertot, who was a disciple of Jean de Bernières, and Guyon became a part of a group of mystics faithful to these teachings. Soon afterward she met the Franciscan monk Archange Enguerrand, who helped her grow in her understanding and experience of contemplative prayer, and who was responsible for introducing her to Geneviève Granger, the mother superior of the local Benedictine convent. In her *Life* she reports a new interior awareness of God in this period, and she began to embrace several ascetic disciplines in accord with her evolving spiritual beliefs. During this time her second son, Armand-Claude (1668–70) was born, and in the next year her daughter Marie-Anne (1669–72) was born. She contracted smallpox in 1670, along with her three children. Her younger son died from the disease, and she and her older son received lifelong scars from it.

In 1671, her half-brother Dominique La Mothe introduced her to the Barnabite Friar François La Combe, who played an instrumental role in her spiritual formation and eventually became a central figure in the first round of persecution that she suffered. Later that same year Granger personally introduced her to Bertot, who became her spiritual director. She also made numerous pilgrimages during this time and began attempting to convert others to the spiritual life as she understood it. In 1672 she lost both her father and her daughter, Marie-Anne, at virtually the same time, and in 1674 her fourth child, Jean-Baptiste-Denys, was born. Bertot sent the family a tutor to teach Latin to Guyon's older son. The tutor also taught Latin to Guyon, which seems to be the only instance of formal classical education she received in her lifetime.

Beginning in 1675 Guyon developed a two-and-a-half-year relationship with a Jansenist priest. While she claims in her *Life* that this relationship was never physically intimate, she describes an inappropriate desire for his company and a resulting sense of spiritual conflict that drove a permanent wedge between her and Bertot. The next year, 1676, Guyon's fifth and last child, Jeanne-Marie, was born. Just before her husband's death that same year after twelve years of marriage, their relationship was somewhat transformed, and he increasingly concerned himself with her welfare and future. Upon his death, he left her with a comfortable fortune, and in 1678 she became independent, living in a house adjoining that of her mother-in-law.

After some troubling times in her personal and religious life, which she later characterized as a time of purifying interior dryness, in 1680 she experienced a profound spiritual transformation.

Around this same time Bertot accused her publicly of improper behavior. She began to dream of traveling and serving the church by converting Protestants. The next year she made the difficult decision to leave home and set out for Geneva in service of this spiritual calling, following the model of Jane de Chantal. This meant putting her financial affairs under the care of her husband's cousin. Remarkably, she and her mother-in-law reconciled, despite their earlier conflicts, and Guyon left her in charge of the older children. Soon thereafter, she left home with her daughter and traveled to Corbeil, Annecy, Gex, and Thonon, where she committed her daughter to the care of the Ursulines.

She was joined by La Combe at various points during these travels. Their relationship had grown deeper over the years during frequent visits and through their ongoing correspondence. Their close relationship was bound to cause negative gossip. The stereotype of the lecherous priest pretending to be the spiritual guide of a wealthy, devout widow as he ultimately seeks only to profit from her physical and financial favors was common in seventeenth-century France. Such gossip drew strength from popular anti-clerical sentiments that were grounded in the real, widespread corruption inherent to the commendatory system for appointing and compensating clergy. Guyon's refusal to conduct her spiritual exercises within the confines of a cloister, her category-defying apostolic aspirations, and her association with a circle of mystically inclined French nobility with powerful enemies subjected her to accusations of hypocritical piety and vice. The currency of this stereotype in Guyon's time is well illustrated by the cultural resonance and impact of Molière's *Tartuffe*, written and first performed in 1664. Indeed, her brother, who had introduced her to La Combe, openly criticized his sister's behavior. Nonetheless, she was still supported at this time by Jean d'Arenthon d'Alex, the bishop of Geneva, who even made La Combe her official spiritual director. There was never any evidence other than the testimony of their enemies that the relationship between Guyon and La Combe was sexual in nature. She consistently presents it as a deep friendship based on mutual affection and shared spiritual conviction. In Thonon a fall from a horse caused her to have visions that she attributed to the devil. From Thonon her family called her back to Paris; she therefore never arrived in Geneva, her intended destination.

In 1682, she again left her children in the care of her mother-in-law and returned to the Ursuline convent in Thonon, where she renounced much of her wealth and wrote her first book, entitled *Spiritual Torrents*, while still under La Combe's direction. She also finished the first edition of her *Life*. Trouble was coming, however, between her and the bishop of Geneva, who had begun to pressure her to become prioress of the New Catholics in Gex. In this post Guyon's remaining income (which was still considerable) would have been largely under the control of the bishop. The New Catholics were a religious community dedicated to the conversion of Protestants. Guyon had come to feel a deep aversion to the methods of this community and refused the offer, thereby making an enemy of the bishop until his death (in 1695).

Soon afterward, several powerful church leaders began to take unfavorable notice of her actions. The rumors of an improper relationship between her and La Combe took on new life after her break with the bishop of Geneva. As a result, La Combe was censored by the church and certain letters between Guyon and La Combe were intercepted. Throughout this time, and in spite of the growing accusations, Guyon continued to travel, to serve the poor, and to pursue her increasingly well-defined apostolic mission. She established a hospital, taught others about prayer and the interior life, suffered many illnesses, and traveled to various places, including the Savoy region of France and the Piedmont region of Italy. In Grenoble, in the region of Savoy, she wrote her *Short and Easy Method of Prayer*, which was published in 1685. She gained followers in several communities in Savoy, while she also wrote her extensive, multi-volume *Explanation of the Holy Scripture*. This undertaking was extremely unusual for a woman at the time. Her resulting familiarity with the Bible gave her an advantage over many of her male clerical contemporaries who lacked it. Despite partially successful efforts to reform the educational system of the French clergy earlier in the century, nobility and influence were still more important than erudition as qualifications for the priesthood. Her *Commentary on the Song of Songs*, written in 1684, was first published without her other biblical commentaries in 1688.

After she became a controversial figure in Grenoble due to her spiritual teaching, the bishop there asked her to leave. She traveled to Marseilles in March 1685, and her daughter remained at the Ursuline convent in Grenoble. Confronted with charges of witchcraft and impropriety later the same year, she took refuge in Turin at the invitation of the marchioness of Prunai, a wealthy widow and patron of mystical theology. After a falling out with the marchioness, Guyon needed to move again. Not surprisingly, given their earlier conflicts, the bishop of Geneva refused to allow her to settle in his diocese when she requested to do so in 1685.

She returned to Paris in 1686 after a long absence to find herself under attack by her half-brother Dominique La Mothe regarding certain financial matters of interest to him and regarding the nature of her relationship with La Combe. This tension with La Mothe continued unresolved until, after living in Paris for a year and a half, she was accused of sharing the heretical views of Miguel de Molinos, a Spanish priest, spiritual director, and author living in Rome. In 1687 Pope Innocent XI had signed a bull entitled *Coelestis Pastor*, which condemned sixty-eight propositions attributed to Molinos as heretical. Molinos's opponents began to refer to his position as Quietism, a term apparently derived from his emphasis on the centrality of the prayer of quiet in mystical practice, but eventually coming to signify, at least in its most technical sense, the conjunction of the propositions condemned in *Coelestis Pastor*. This document was a powerful weapon in the hands of Guyon's enemies, who used it as a template for seeking out heretical claims in her writings and in those of La Combe. They first secured La Combe's imprisonment on charges of Quietism in October 1687. La Combe remained in prison for the rest of his life, persecuted mercilessly by powerful figures in the church until he finally lost his sanity.

In November of the same year, the bishop of Geneva took advantage of the recent papal bull and the increasingly anti-mystical climate to publish a pastoral letter condemning Guyon's *Short and Easy Method*. Partly in consequence of this letter and partly for personal reasons, Guyon was confined in Paris at the convent of the Visitation Sainte Marie under suspicion of heresy on the authority of François de Harlay de Champvallon, the archbishop of Paris. At this time Guyon's daughter was being pressured to marry the archbishop's nephew, contrary to the wishes of both mother and daughter. Guyon claims that her captors tried to bribe her with the promise of release if she would allow the marriage. Ultimately she refused, and the marriage of her daughter did not take place, but Guyon remained confined in the Visitation convent for seven months.

Her fortunes took a turn for the better due to the intercession of powerful friends, particularly Madame de Maintenon, Louis XIV's second wife and the uncrowned queen of France. At Maintenon's request, the king ordered her release from confinement, acknowledging that the basis of the accusation against her was a false letter. Not long after her release, she was befriended by Maintenon. Beginning in 1688, Guyon was invited to educate young noblewomen at Maintenon's school in Saint-Cyr, near Versailles. She remained involved in this school for several years and earned the respect of many, including her future nemesis Jacques-Bénigne Bossuet, the bishop of Meaux. In 1688 she also became the friend and mystical interlocutor of François de Salignac de La Mothe-Fénelon. At the time, Fénelon was a Sulpician priest, a respected theologian, and an increasingly influential figure in Madame de Maintenon's circle. Guyon and Fénelon engaged in a long, secret correspondence, during which time Fénelon was named the preceptor for the duke of Bourgogne, an extremely important position indicating his escalating status at court. Regarding family matters, in 1689 Guyon's son Jacques was severely injured, and her daughter, Jeanne-Marie, married Louis-Nicolas Fouquet, the youngest brother of her good friend the duchess of Charost.

In the early 1690s the tide at court shifted politically and theologically, and those associated with Quietism were ostracized more than ever. Guyon was quite aware of the growing suspicion of her practices by others, to the point that she was convinced that she had been secretly poisoned. Not surprisingly, at Saint-Cyr the advocacy of contemplative prayer and other practices suspected of Quietist influence became a liability. This stemmed not only from outside forces, but also from the fact that some of Guyon's students at Saint-Cyr used the spiritual practices that they learned from Guyon as an excuse for improper behavior, arguing that in some cases socially unacceptable behavior was permitted in the eyes of God. All of this led to Guyon's release from her duties at the school in 1693.

This marks the year when she lost the favor of the French royal family and entered into her long, painful period of persecution and imprisonment. Guyon was not the only one implicated in this manner. Since Fénelon was seen as being influenced by Guyon, and he would not denounce her, he eventually began to lose his standing in the court as well. On the surface it might appear that this persecution took place because Guyon's teachings had led young girls who were under the tutelage of the queen astray, or perhaps because her writings still evoked the ire of church officials. Without downplaying the sincere theological disagreements between Guyon and her anti-mystical opponents, it is hard to avoid the conclusion that this persecution was engineered primarily for political reasons by powerful enemies attempting to manipulate Guyon and distort her words and actions. She presents the conflict this way herself in her autobiography, and her interpretation is confirmed by the timing of subsequent events and the largely polemical, satirical, and ad hominem tactics of her opponents. Initially, Guyon is the primary target, as Maintenon denounces her to distance herself from increasingly controversial mystical ideas and thereby protect her influence at court. Later, Guyon's connection to Fénelon made her an important political pawn owing to the fact that Bossuet and Fénelon were the two most powerful members of the church in France at that time, and Fénelon was a rising star at court. Bossuet's concerns regarding Quietist beliefs and practices and his personal concerns for self-preservation led him to see Fénelon as a rival. Unable or unwilling to attack Fénelon directly, he discredited Guyon by all available means in order also to discredit Fénelon by implication. Thus it happened that Guyon suffered a long, ongoing period of disgrace and persecution at Bossuet's hands. With Maintenon backing Bossuet in the persecution of Guyon and, when he would not turn against her, of Fénelon too, their fate was sealed. There was no escape from the combined power of the church and the crown.

After Madame de Maintenon dismissed her from her position at Saint-Cyr in 1693, Guyon began to search for theological allies. She asked several influential theologians, including Bossuet, to examine her work. Determined to discredit Guyon, however, Maintenon initiated a formal doctrinal inquiry into her writing at Issy in 1694, with three examiners: Bossuet, Louis-Antoine de Noailles (then bishop of Châlons and later archbishop of Paris), and Louis Tronson (the superior of Saint-Sulpice). Starting in February 1695, Fénelon joined in the deliberations. During the Issy Conference, Guyon sought refuge from her old enemy, Archbishop de Champvallon of Paris, who formally condemned her *Short and Easy Method* and her *Commentary on the Song of Songs* late in 1694. She consented to confinement and further examination at the convent of St. Marie in Bossuet's diocese of Meaux. Bossuet continued to interrogate and to harass her there until, in March 1695, the *Articles of Issy* was published. This document sought to articulate thirty-four properly orthodox pronouncements concerning contested mystical matters. Bossuet interpreted them as inconsistent with Guyon's *Short and Easy Method* and wrote a pastoral letter condemning this text in his diocese. Guyon signed an attestation submitting to the *Articles* and agreeing not to teach her method of prayer, but she would not sign any attestation of heresy. Bossuet let her leave Meaux, but later, under pressure from Maintenon, tried again to secure her admission of heresy, which she refused by letter.

A warrant for Guyon's arrest was issued. She hid under assumed names in Paris until being discovered and arrested in December 1695. She was transferred to prison in Vincennes for the next period of internment. The interrogations continued, becoming more aggressive and more intense. At this point the Quietist controversy in France was still largely centered on Guyon, and Fénelon still had the king's favor. The king had, in fact, appointed him archbishop of Cambrai earlier in 1695. Fénelon, the duke and duchess of Chevreuse, and others worked tirelessly to obtain Guyon's release, but even their powerful influence did little to change the course of events. Guyon's situation became more precarious when she was moved yet again to a very small, decrepit convent house in Vaugirard for ongoing imprisonment. There she suffered constant harassment and mistreatment, not only by officials, but also by the nuns who served as her wardens. It would appear that these nuns were led to believe that Guyon was a dangerous, wicked woman not worthy of human treatment. It followed that they feared her, sought personal profit by stealing from her, and, she claims in the fourth part of her *Life*, even tried to kill her.

In the public arena during this time the debates between Fénelon and Bossuet continued to focus on Quietism. In February 1697 Fénelon published his *Explanations of the Maxims of the Saints on the Interior Life*, which attempted to situate many of the mystical views then under attack in a long tradition of thought and offered a reading of the *Articles of Issy* favorable to Guyon's position. Bossuet published his *Instruction on the States of Prayer* one month later, advocating discursive and imaginative forms of prayer against the apophatic and passive types he regarded as the consequences of very rare and supernatural acts of grace, inaccessible and unaffected by any human method of prayer. His *Account of Quietism*, published the following year, substituted ridicule and slanderous insinuations about Guyon and Fénelon for theological argument.

Madame de Maintenon continued to wield influence and was involved not only in Guyon's ongoing imprisonment but also in the persecution that was expanding to include a focus on Fénelon. He ultimately lost royal favor and was stripped of his title as preceptor of the Duke de Bourgogne. In 1697 he was banished from the court of Louis XIV at Versailles and ordered to return to his diocese in Cambrai. The case against his *Maxims of the Saints* was taken up in Rome. Guyon's fate was then tied to the political and legal wrangling in Rome between Fénelon's advocates (especially the Jesuits and even Pope Innocent XII) and his opponents (especially Bossuet and King Louis XIV, who pressured the examining commission to find against Fénelon).

Guyon's situation continued to deteriorate. Ultimately, in 1698, she was sent to the Bastille based on a forged letter supposedly written by Father La Combe that suggested a physical relationship between the two. The strategy of the anti-mystical faction was to compromise Fénelon indirectly by slandering and mocking Guyon, and this strategy was ultimately successful—at least in part. In 1699 the pope issued a brief entitled *Cum alias* that condemned twenty-three propositions associated with Fénelon's *Maxims of the Saints*. However, both the form of the pope's statement (a brief rather than a bull) and the content (which condemned the *Maxims* in very gentle terms) disappointed Bossuet's hopes for a formal declaration of heresy against Fénelon. The outcome of the conflict became even more inconclusive when Fénelon submitted to the brief and, in a clear sign of the pope's support (despite the earlier papal concession to pressure from King Louis XIV), was eventually made a cardinal.[3] Although Fénelon's legal case was resolved in 1699, Guyon remained in prison without facing any formal charges. In the Bastille, Guyon continued to be subjected to interrogations that would last for hours and to treatment by servants and interrogators that were inhumane and sadistic, some of which almost killed her. She was also the target of all sorts of false accusations, ranging from the lascivious to the diabolical, which were used as the pretext for keeping her in the dreaded prison fortress for five long years. All the while Guyon pleaded to be given a formal trial, but, needless to say, this never happened. When she became convinced that her imprisonment was serving primarily political purposes, she began to request that her case be transferred to Parliament so she could have due process regarding the accusations against her, but did this did not happen either.

By 1703 the tide at the court was once again changing, this time in Guyon's favor. She had remained in prison for so long that the Quietest Affair had faded in importance and had been eclipsed by more pressing events, so that she no longer served the political interests of those who had sought her imprisonment. She was also growing old and remained, as ever, prone to illness. Her children were finally allowed to visit her, although the reunion was not a pleasant experience for Guyon. For reasons that are easy to imagine, Guyon's relationship with her children was not warm. She was not only a liability to the family, but also in many ways a stranger to her children, who had their own lives and their own families. In spite of all this, Guyon was finally released that year in the care of her eldest son, who had to accept formal legal responsibility for his mother.

Thankfully for Guyon, after Bossuet's death in 1704 she was relatively free to cultivate her understanding of the interior life and to continue her theological, mystical, and autobiographical writing. She received permission to live independently of her son, with whom she did not get along well. Thus, for her last twelve years she lived in her own residence in Blois, where she continued to cultivate her spiritual life, to teach others, and to write a variety of works, including poetry, letters, and her autobiography, completed in 1709. During this last period of her life she developed an ecumenical and international group of disciples who published and spread many of her writings outside France. Through these disciples she particularly influenced German Pietists, British Methodists, and American Quakers. She continued to enjoy discreet communications with Fénelon, who died in 1715, and with other members of her former mystical circle in Paris. Guyon died in 1717. Her body was exhumed after the Revolution and moved to Orléans, where it remains today.

2. GUYON'S PLACE IN FRENCH HISTORY, ESPECIALLY IN THE QUIETIST AFFAIR

Why did Guyon rise to the pinnacle of royal favor in between her periods of imprisonment? In part, the explanation lies in the fact that the religious and political world around her in the last half of the seventeenth century was changing fast, and incompatible theological visions were still vying for supremacy in an unresolved struggle. Close relatives of the spiritual practices that led to the canonization of Teresa of Ávila in 1622 and Francis de Sales in 1665 came to be seen as heretical a few decades later both by the Vatican and by the Catholic Church in France. In particular, contemplative practices associated with apophatic mysticism came to be viewed with deep suspicion during the reign of Louis XIV, when the French church became for all practical purposes an arm of the crown and operated at times independently of the Vatican. This politicizing and nationalizing of religion made any teaching of how to cultivate the inner life—that part of one's existence beyond the sociopolitical control of the state—an object of deep suspicion, calling into question one's loyalty to the crown.

The reign of Louis XIV is considered to be the culminating moment in the history of the French monarchy, a time of glory, power, and courtly sumptuousness. His reign was exceptionally long, beginning in 1638, when he was still a small child, and ending upon his death in 1715, when he was succeeded by his great-grandson. His legacy dominates historical treatments of the seventeenth century in France, which is often referred to as the *Grand Siècle*, the "Splendid Century," because of the majesty of his reign. During this time French hegemony in Europe was established, extending into the New World, with France being the unparalleled leader not only in the political arena, but also in the arts and literature. Versailles was literally and figuratively the center of this power. Louis XIV's emblem of Apollo the Sun King was apt, because he sought to surround himself with individuals whose lives revolved around his, as they served his wishes effectively and enthusiastically. Indeed, everything was fashioned to revolve around the Sun King: the court, the military, the rest of Europe, even the New World, with Louisiana owing its name to this monarch.

One of the results of the centralization of power in the court at Versailles was that politics, art, and religion became inextricably linked as perhaps never before to reinforce the glory of France and the absolute power of the king, bringing about shifts in virtually all realms of life. With respect to religion, these shifts culminated in the Quietist Affair, whose main characters, as we have already seen, were Guyon, Bossuet, Fénelon, and Maintenon. In the late seventeenth century Gallicanism, a movement advocating the administrative autonomy of the French Catholic Church from Rome, was growing. Just as the state was growing in power, the branch of the Catholic Church rooted in that state was more and more intertwined with the sociopolitical realities of the French court, where the king was absolute. As a consequence, any transgression on theological grounds could also be considered a transgression on political grounds, with the reverse also being true.[4]

In the Quietist Affair, besides these primary characters, there were many players involved both in France and Italy, including ambitious nobles in Louis XIV's court, powerful clergy both in France and Rome, and the Holy See. The core of the controversy, however, pitted Guyon and Fénelon, by many accounts the second-most-important cleric in France at that time, against Bossuet, the most-important French cleric at the time, and Madame de Maintenon, who had carved out her role at Versailles as the champion of public morality and strict piety.

Fénelon by all accounts was a complex individual, a mixture of characteristics. In many ways, apart from his involvement in the Quietist Affair, he fit the seventeenth-century model of the *honnête homme*, a well-bred, articulate, and intelligent man of wide experience. With his noble upbringing, he was easily assimilated to Versailles, where he was recognized early as a brilliant theologian, interested in the mystical tradition, and a rising star politically. Bossuet was a very different type of person in both social standing and temperament. He was an ambitious man from a bourgeois family, and although he had received a thorough education in philosophy, classics, and the Scholastic and positive theology of his day, he had neither an understanding of nor patience for mystical theology and practice.

Early in their relationship Bossuet and Fénelon enjoyed a friendship at Versailles. As Fénelon became increasingly influenced by Guyon, however, a rift developed. This rift was very public and was deepened by the emergence of factions at court. The *Féneloniens* were composed primarily of Guyon and the Chevreuses, the Beauvilliers, and the Montemarts—all prestigious noble families sympathetic to the possibilities of mystical consciousness and individual spiritual insight. In contrast, according to de Certeau's analysis, the *Bossuetistes* represented those who believed in the power of the state, accepted the view that theological doctrines should reflect and reinforce the society producing them, understood religious practice as primarily a social activity, and believed that the church's ultimate role was to serve public order.[5] The Quietists, whom they came to associate with the *Féneloniens*, threatened to subvert this order because a spirituality of abandonment and passivity became more foreign and uncontrollable in proportion to its interiority.

The advocates of the consolidation of religious power in the state, represented paradigmatically in the figure of Bossuet, found anti-mystical allies in the increasingly naturalistic concepts of human experience influenced by the scientific revolution and the development of Jesuit moral psychology. Psychological processes, unlike mystical awareness, could be described in "law-like" generalizations and hence categorized and controlled. Thus, the end of mainstream mystical practices in France resulted partly from the condemnation of Quietism, but also from a sweeping epistemological shift that favored analysis and introspection, with a focus on moral problems.

Let us not forget that Guyon, the spiritual leader whose views initiated the Quietist conflict in France, was also a woman. Bossuet considered Guyon a psychologically unstable woman with an excitable imagination, and his portrayal of her in the *Account of Quietism* is quite evidently misogynistic.[6] Perhaps the surprisingly harsh treatment she received, especially in comparison to Fénelon, is largely explained by the implicit danger she posed to established gender roles both in the church and at court. Marie-Florine Bruneau argues that Guyon "did not owe her persecution to a lack of orthodoxy or to the fact that the implications of her doctrine were different from those of accepted mystics, but rather to her refusal to cower to institutional authority," an especially egregious crime for a woman at the time.[7] Elizabeth Goldsmith examines the relation between Bossuet's anti-mystical tendencies and his misogyny, focusing on his distaste for Guyon's apostolic claims of spiritual motherhood, especially concerning Fénelon: "Outlining his objections to and repugnance for Guyon's unusual methods of proselytizing and her manner of describing them, Bossuet deflects his criticism away from Fénelon and addresses himself instead to establishing the heterodoxy of the woman who had managed to infantilize his colleague.…Guyon's maternal metaphor is inverted by her enemies and she becomes a bad mother-figure from whose clutches Fénelon, the young heirs to the French throne, and indeed all good Catholics needed to be rescued."[8]

The person with the most power over morality and dogma at court was not Bossuet, however, but Madame de Maintenon, due to her influence on the king. Secretly married to Louis XIV in 1683, she represented a change in the court of Versailles, a turning away from worldliness and splendor toward a new form of morality and piety. Born Françoise d'Aubigné, she was an unlikely player at court, with her grandfather being a famous Protestant poet of the Renaissance, Agrippa d'Aubigné. Her religious upbringing was influenced by both her family's Protestant heritage and, later, its complete conversion to Catholicism. She knew poverty, abandonment, and displacement (having spent some of her youth in the

French West Indies), and she developed an ability to cater to and please the more powerful people around her. She was married to the much older and disabled Paul Scarron, a famous novelist, and their marriage lasted many years. After his death she was able to negotiate a place for herself in privileged circles as a governess, eventually caring for the children Louis XIV had with his longtime mistress, the Marquise de Montespan. It was in that role that Louis XIV developed a relationship with her, one that would eventually lead to their secret marriage after Queen Marie-Thérèse died. At this stage in Louis XIV's life it appears as though the king's philandering was replaced with a concern for his own salvation and for a more stable life at Versailles. His behavior consequently became more sober and pious. Françoise d'Aubigné Scarron became known as Madame de Maintenon, as she took the helm of this process of court reform.

This newfound piety at Versailles and the new role scripted for Maintenon at court affected Guyon's fate just as much as Bossuet's dogmatic vehemence. As was mentioned above, Guyon was released from her first period of confinement due to Maintenon's intervention. At that time Maintenon frequented a circle of mystics comprised principally by the Chevreuse, the Beauvillier, and the Mortemart families—the same circle to which Guyon, and later Fénelon, belonged. Both Madame Chevreuse and Madame Mortemart were daughters of Louis XIV's influential finance minister, Jean-Baptiste Colbert. Maintenon deeply admired this group, especially Fénelon. Her relationship with this group of mystics seems somewhat conflicted because she does not appear to have had a mystical bent and focused her religious life on conventional morality and piety. Françoise Mallet-Joris paints an evocative portrait of Madame de Maintenon in this period. She claims that upon obtaining Guyon's release from prison, Maintenon saw Guyon as her last chance for spiritual transformation and for escaping a personal situation characterized by enormous challenges of life at court and incessant demands placed on her by Louis XIV. Maintenon invested in the form of spirituality that Guyon and her dear Fénelon proposed to her in hopes of finally obtaining the joy and serenity that she so desired, but she was disappointed. She had expected a virtual miracle from this new spirituality, "a magical transformation of her personality, of her spiritual dryness, of her problems, of her dissatisfaction."[9] It is no surprise, then, that when this magical transformation did not happen, she felt a sense of profound despondency, leading to rage and eventually to the persecution of Guyon and Fénelon. The relentless interrogations, the calumnies, and the harsh conditions—culminating in Guyon's five years of captivity at the Bastille—were not only supported by Maintenon, but indeed perpetuated by her.

3. THEOLOGICAL CONTEXT

The French Catholic Church in Guyon's time was a patchwork of different theological and political alliances. Some of these alliances were institutionally defined, such as those constituting monastic orders, seminaries, and regionally organized branches of church governance. Some of them were organized around competing political positions. And some alliances were organized around conflicting theological schools of thought, doctrinal positions, or preferences for certain types of liturgical or spiritual practice. The interactions of these different alliances contributed in complex ways to Guyon's intellectual formation and, eventually, to her persecution. The theological conflict most determinative of Guyon's work, however, concerned the nature and orthodoxy of mystical theology and practice. This conflict escalated as the seventeenth century progressed and ultimately culminated in the Quietist Affair.

This conflict in France was largely internal to the Catholic Church, but its backdrop was colored by the Protestant Reformation and the Catholic Counter-Reformation. In 1598 the Edict of Nantes established modest legal rights for French Protestants, or Huguenots, amounting to a policy of tolerance. Since the Edict of Nantes was not revoked until 1685, by Louis XIV, the development of the Catholic mystical tradition in seventeenth-century France took place alongside new Protestant forms of piety. As a result, the church was eager to support appropriately orthodox movements of spiritual revival that would compete with Protestant forms of lay spirituality, but it was simultaneously suspicious of spiritual practices that might lend support to Protestantism by questioning the authority of the priesthood or the necessity of the sacraments for salvation or sanctification.

In *The Mystic Fable* Michel de Certeau argues that the late sixteenth and seventeenth centuries produced a new science, which its French proponents called *la mystique*. The term is not well translated by the English word *mysticism*, which has its own separate French parallel. Michael B. Smith, de Certeau's translator, opts for *mystics* (his italics), intending to echo the grammatical form of terms such as *physics* or *optics*.[10] De Certeau argues that *mystics*, as a science independent of traditional theology, emerged as a reaction against criticisms of spiritual practices associated with mystical contemplation. Its proponents developed several rhetorical strategies to justify its legitimacy. De Certeau places Guyon at the end of this long process of historical development, and, although he does not discuss Guyon's work in detail, his analysis of the development of *mystics* in Spain and France provides an illuminating framework for doing so here. According to de Certeau, the term *mystics* came to name a space for discourse and practice that was largely independent of traditional theology and was primarily defined by its development of rules, methods, or "manners of speaking." In this new science, he writes, "a manner of using received language *differently* becomes objectified in a set of delimitations and processes."[11] The centrality of terminology and methodology to the development of *mystics* derived, in part, from the impossibility of defining the "object" of this new science, since that object transcended all conceptual distinctions and terms.[12]

The proponents of *mystics* in the sixteenth and seventeenth centuries reinterpreted, and in some cases faithfully perpetuated, several medieval spiritual theories and practices. Perhaps the single most important authority common to medieval spirituality and Counter-Reformation mysticism was Pseudo-Dionysius, the unknown sixth-century author of several theological texts characterizing God's essential nature as beyond names and concepts, but complementing this "negative" view with a "positive" view of God's trinitarian and hierarchical self-manifestation. The great fourteenth- and fifteenth-century German and Flemish mystics were also well known to many seventeenth-century French mystics.[13] The works of Henry Suso, Johannes Tauler, Jan van Ruusbroec, and

19

Hendrik Herp provided foundational material for *mystics*, an important part of its proponents' attempt to legitimize this new science through the establishment of a traditional canon for it. Despite their many differences, these authors all aim to theorize the nature and possibility of the soul's unmediated union with God, using metaphors such as "nakedness...annihilation, self-abasement, extinction, [and] nihility."[14] This spiritual path is commonly called negative, apophatic, or abstract. French translations of the most famous works by German and Flemish mystics became available early in the seventeenth century. Translations were also published of many sixteenth-century Spanish and Italian writers influenced by the apophatic tradition. Of these, perhaps the most influential in France were Teresa of Ávila, John of the Cross, and Catherine of Genoa.

Alongside these theoretical and negative forms of contemplation, several forms of medieval visionary and somatic spirituality also influenced the seventeenth-century discourse about mysticism. Such spiritual practices were especially prominent among female contemplatives between the twelfth and fourteenth centuries and were known to the seventeenth century through the works of some of their most famous representatives, such as the Beguines Mechthild of Magdeburg and Hadewijch of Antwerp, the German Benedictines Hildegard of Bingen and Gertrude of Helfta, and the Italian Dominican Catherine of Siena. These works were popularized in France by their inclusion in the sixteenth-century spiritual anthologies of Louis de Blois. Many mystics of the sixteenth and seventeenth centuries, including Guyon, continued to experience visions and physical manifestations of their contemplative states and to interpret instances of physical pain as participation in the incarnate suffering of Jesus.

Several types of French mysticism, influenced by the sources just discussed but forging new paths, took shape in the early part of the seventeenth century. Louis Cognet distinguishes three major traditions.[15] First, the Abstract School was influenced particularly by French translations of German and Flemish texts and by the work of Pseudo-Dionysius. This type of mysticism emphasized the unmediated union of God and the soul brought about by the annihilation of the will. The most important founding author in this tradition was the Capuchin monk Benet de Canfield. Guyon was well acquainted with his *Rule of Perfection*. Second, the French School of spirituality owes its origins to Pierre de Bérulle. Bérulle's mysticism was decidedly christocentric, and although he insisted on the importance of self-abasement and self-annihilation in the spiritual life, he argued that these goals were only accessible to human beings through "adherence" to the "interior states" of Jesus, especially and ultimately his state of self-surrender on the cross. This emphasis on the meaning of the incarnation for mystical experience is represented in many of Guyon's works.

The third major type of seventeenth-century French mysticism stems from the work of Francis de Sales and Jane de Chantal. The universality of the call to prayer in de Sales's work and the simplicity of de Chantal's "methodless" contemplation are prominent influences in Guyon's *Short and Easy Method*.

Although it is impossible to describe these schools and the work of their many proponents more fully here, there were three particularly important and controversial topics with regard to which these schools adopted broadly different positions. The theological tensions that resulted in Guyon's persecution were therefore not only present between mystics and anti-mystics but were also internal to the increasingly complex mystical tradition. The first controversial topic concerned the nature of the highest stages of contemplation. Several questions arose here. What was the relation of the higher and lower spiritual states? How did discursive meditation relate to mystical contemplation? At what point did contemplation become "infused" by God's grace rather than "acquired" by human effort? Could humans freely resist the grace of infused contemplation? Could the highest state of contemplation be sustained in duration? Was this state completely passive or did it require an act of will? The second topic concerned the relations among incarnation, atonement, sanctification, and the mystical life. Again, several questions arose. Did the mystic bypass Christ by achieving union with God, or was such a union always mediated by Christ? How did the Christ event make spiritual life possible? In what ways should the mystical life parallel the interior life of Christ himself? Is "adherence" to the interior states of Christ a psychological matter or a metaphysical one? The third topic concerned the relation between the mystical life and Christian ethics, particularly the virtue of love. Were all Christian virtues summed up by the virtue of love? What were the different types of love? Did the purest form of love require complete disinterestedness, a loss of all personal preferences? Was such a disinterest compatible with the everyday performance of petitionary prayer and the sacraments, and with hoping for one's own salvation? What was the relation between active striving for the good and passive submission to God in an ethics of pure love? Since these questions were genuinely open in seventeenth-century mysticism, Guyon would have been sensitive to their controversial character, and indeed her writing does adopt nuanced positions regarding them. As a result, they provide a useful interpretive framework for considering her mysticism.

All three of the types of French mysticism just discussed as well as the German, Flemish, Spanish, and Italian spiritual classics widely available in the seventeenth century contributed to Guyon's views. In some cases Guyon was familiar with these ideas from primary sources. In other cases she knew them as they had been filtered and interpreted by their proponents later in the seventeenth century. The question of Guyon's influences will be discussed in greater detail below. Before turning more carefully to this question, however, it is necessary to discuss the opponents of these forms of mysticism and some of their most important theological views.

Many of the opponents of the "new mystics" in France were trained in mainstream university theology. As Cognet has argued, although there were creative mainstream theological contributions in this period, the curriculum in most schools emphasized a form of dogmatic theology constituted by the explication and systematization of orthodox doctrines, as derived from the pronouncements of ecumenical church councils. This conservative form of theological education resulted from a Counter-Reformation sensitivity to and rejection of purported "novelties" in Christian practice. Theology curricula included a similarly conservative form of positive theology primarily focused on orthodox interpretations of biblical texts. Seminarians also studied important Scholastic texts, an ahistorical and deductive form of moral theology, and Patristics.[16] Mysticism was considered new and strange by many of the clergy educated this way, and a steady stream of anti-mystical publications and persecutions accompanied its development in the seventeenth century as a result.

The anti-mystical views most directly relevant to Guyon's work are neatly summarized in *Coelestis Pastor*, the papal bull issued in 1687 that condemned sixty-eight propositions attributed to Miguel de Molinos. Several distinct themes emerge in *Coelestis Pastor*. It is particularly concerned to denounce the possibility of complete annihilation of the individual's will (the loss of "activity") and complete submission to the divine will (the acquisition of "passivity"). It also traces several implications of this possibility and rejects them explicitly. First, it rejects the idea that a person in this state should neither hope for reward in paradise nor fear an eternity of damnation (either of which would seem to imply personal desires or preferences, and therefore also to imply a ground for active willing). Second, it rejects the idea that such a person should avoid asking or thanking God for anything (which also seems to imply personal preferences). Third, it denounces the idea that such people could excuse apparent sins or ignore moral doubts or temptations, on the grounds that their complete union with God's will would guarantee the rightness of their behavior. Fourth, it rejects the idea that such people should deviate in various ways from ordinary ritual practices because parts of those practices would no longer be appropriate to their state of self-annihilation. Fifth, it rejects the claim that the mystic could ever become permanently incapable of sin—or indeed incapable of any choice incompatible with the divine will. Apart from these consequences of a complete loss of individual will, *Coelestis Pastor* also rejects the superiority of negative, distinctionless, or unselfconscious forms of prayer in comparison to other spiritual practices relying on moral conscience, imagination, intellect, or special illuminations. It also denounces the possibility of a self-annihilation so complete that it implies the deification of the individual or his or her oneness with the divine essence.

The existence of this robust anti-mystical tradition in seventeenth-century France is central to understanding Guyon's work. It implies Guyon's awareness of the controversial character of her writings and the powerful constituencies inclined to oppose it. She makes this awareness explicit in Part 3 of her *Life*, where she presents and responds to some of the criticisms (both theological and personal) of her opponents, but it is present in her earlier writings as well. Many of her views in these writings can be fruitfully interpreted in their historical context as subtle replies to objections that would have been apparent to her informed contemporaries. We turn now to that task.

4. GUYON'S INFLUENCES AND THEOLOGY

Influences

During the summer and fall of 1694, while Guyon was being examined at the Issy Conference, she wrote a three-volume defense of her own mysticism entitled *The Justifications of J. M. B. de La Mothe Guyon, Written by Herself.* In this work she quotes or cites authoritative sources from the mystical tradition to support her own teachings. Guyon has, therefore, already done some of the work of identifying her influences. Using the *Justifications* as a basis to infer those influences has at least three limits, though. First, the fact that she referenced certain works to justify her orthodoxy in the face of challenges does not necessarily demonstrate that those works were a genetic influence in her writing. It is certainly possible that in some cases she scoured these works upon being accused of heresy only to prove her orthodoxy after the fact. However, the speed with which Guyon produced the *Justifications* renders this claim somewhat implausible. Her ability to marshal appropriate support for her position from so many sources shows that she was at least conversant with an impressive range of Christian mystical writings and capable of showing their relation to her own claims. A second, more serious limitation is that it would not have been helpful for Guyon to reference influences that were themselves under suspicion of heresy or novelty, given the defensive purpose of her text. For example, Jean de Bernières might be absent from the *Justifications* because his *Interior Christian* had been placed on the *Index of Prohibited Books* in 1689 or because of his historical proximity to her own time, even if he was a significant influence on her work. A third, related, limitation is that Guyon may have privileged references to certain sources out of proportion to their influence on her views because she thought that their status or antiquity would help to demonstrate her orthodoxy. With these limits in mind, a brief analysis of the *Justifications* is a useful starting point.

Guyon sometimes merely cites a source in defense of her views in the *Justifications*, while at other times she quotes passages. She cites certain authors, such as Hendrik Herp and Henry Suso, several times without quoting at significant length from their work, probably seeking to invoke their authority even if the passage she cites does not support her position very closely. For many authors, though, the number of citations and the total amount of quoted material correspond fairly well. These authors would seem to constitute her most important sources, as presented in the *Justifications*. The seven authors she cites most often are, in descending order of frequency, John of Saint-Samson, John of the Cross, Teresa of Ávila, Pseudo-Dionysius, Francis de Sales, Catherine of Genoa, and Nicholas of Jesus-Maria. The seven authors she quotes at the greatest length, again in descending order, are John of the Cross, John of Saint-Samson, Nicholas of Jesus-Maria, Catherine of Genoa, Teresa of Ávila, Francis de Sales, and Pseudo-Dionysius. Although the order is different on these two lists, the names are the same. Most of the names on the list have already been discussed above in Section 3, but John of Saint-Samson and Nicholas of Jesus-Maria bear mention here.

John of Saint-Samson was one of the spiritual leaders of a movement among French Carmelites in the early seventeenth century called the Touraine Reform. He dictated several works on prayer and spirituality. His understanding of contemplation was strongly influenced by Ruusbroec and Herp, but more than these authors he emphasizes the role of spiritual love, poured out in "prayers of aspiration," as the engine of the soul's progress toward union with God. He describes a process of gradual purification of the will toward increasingly "naked" and "passive" love, eventually resulting in spiritual states devoid of sensible affection or distinct thoughts. He belongs, therefore, to the apophatic tradition, but he also addresses distinctly seventeenth-century concerns about the role of the will in the highest spiritual states. Guyon draws from his focus on the transformation of the will, on the role of love in mystical contemplation, and on the simplicity of prayer to authorize similar conceptions in her own writings.

The Discalced Carmelite Nicholas of Jesus-Maria was an apologist for John of the Cross and one of the early contributors to a new genre, the spiritual anthology, which accompanied the development of *mystics* as an independent science in the late sixteenth century. Guyon's *Justifications* are themselves an example of this genre. De Certeau argues that such spiritual anthologies were used primarily to authorize mystical "manners of speaking" by compiling evidence for the long and distinguished tradition of their usage. The anthology of Nicholas of Jesus-Maria was entitled *Elucidatio phrasium mysticae theologiae*, and after 1639 it was published along with editions of the collected works of John of the Cross. As de Certeau points out, "This *Elucidatio*, translated into French by Cyprian of the Nativity, will again be exploited, like a mine of authoritativeness, by Madame Guyon, then by Bossuet, under the shortened and revealing title of treatise *'des phrases mystiques.'*"[17]

In fact, Guyon used several spiritual anthologies of this type in writing the *Justifications*, and probably in her larger study of mysticism. Along with Nicholas of Jesus-Maria, she quotes at length from the *Mystical Day* of the Capuchin Pierre de Poitiers, who was primarily influenced by Canfield and John of the Cross, and the *Mystical Conferences* of the Premonstratensian abbot Epiphane Louys. Guyon may have known some of the authors she cites only through anthologized passages from their work, making it unclear how fully she had read the original texts. Her partial reliance on the thematic structure and historical synthesis in these earlier anthologies helps explain the speed with which she produced her own *Justifications*. Her knowledge of this genre also helps explain the puzzlement she expresses at various points in the *Life* about her persecution. While Guyon is well aware that *mystics* as a whole had its opponents, she seems to presuppose that there was agreement among the classic authors in its tradition on certain central teachings, to which she saw herself as faithful. When she was accused of heresy, then, her first response was to seek examiners familiar with and sympathetic to this tradition. She was certainly correct that many of her opponents objected to the tradition as a whole, but she may have underestimated the differences internal to the tradition, which eventually allowed the opponents of Quietism to drive a wedge between the officially authorized teachings of some spiritual authors (such as the canonized Teresa of Ávila and Francis de Sales) and the teachings of the Quietists. Perhaps her historical milieu, coming as it did at the high point in the development of *mystics*, also helps explain the relative scarcity of explicit, systematic presentations of her terminology. She is able to assume the existence of a tradition that authorizes various mystical "manners of speaking," and her contribution is not, therefore, intended to reiterate or to define these.

De Certeau's characterization of *mystics* as defined by its methods and manner of speaking fits Guyon well, as she insisted on her orthodoxy and submission to Catholic authority but admitted that her use of certain vague terms could have caused the objections to her work.[18] Guyon repeats arguments similar to the following one in several passages of the *Life*: "I have tried to take away the abuse [of meaning], which succeeded in making an exaggeration of my terms....As for what concerns the core of doctrine, I profess my ignorance. I have believed that my director would take away bad terms, and that he would correct what he did not believe good."[19] Here, her defensive strategy is to make *doctrine* the appropriate category for the application of judgments concerning orthodoxy or heresy and *terminology* or *ways of speaking* secondary concerns that could be simply clarified or corrected so as to conform to orthodox doctrine. In the Quietist Affair, Guyon's opponents in the French church rejected this distinction and the rhetorical strategy that accompanied it, but they lacked the appropriate legal categories for condemning problematic or vague terminology when accompanied by the doctrinal submission of its author. This ambiguity produced a legal limbo for Guyon, in which her punishment was ultimately chosen without the application of any rule of law and enforced by agents of the king.

The clues about Guyon's theological influences provided by her *Justifications* and her use of mystical anthologies can be supplemented by the direct references she makes in her other writings. Her strongest influence, at least judging by the frequency with which she cites it, is the Bible itself. Guyon was deeply conversant

27

with both the Old Testament and the New Testament, having written extensive biblical commentaries deploying an allegorical hermeneutics. Her synthesis of biblical teaching with the mystical authors she had read is probably the most important source of her originality. Bossuet's objections to Guyon's writings focused in many cases on her biblical interpretations, and this is one indication of their novelty. After the Bible, Guyon cites Pseudo-Dionysius more than any other source, but she also frequently refers to the work of Canfield, de Chantal, de Sales, Augustine, and John of the Cross, among others. Based on the pattern of quotation and citation in the *Justifications* and the sources she used in her other writings, therefore, her form of negative mysticism seems most influenced by sixteenth- and seventeenth-century French and Spanish sources combined with her own interpretations of the Bible and of Pseudo-Dionysius. Although she was acquainted at some level with many of the German and Flemish authors who developed systems of apophatic contemplation in the thirteenth through fifteenth centuries, their influence on her writing seems largely mediated through later interpreters and anthologizers.

Apart from the sources she cites explicitly, several other influences are present in her work. Perhaps in some cases she did not know the origin of some of the ideas she incorporated into her writing but encountered them through conversations with her spiritual directors or her many mystically inclined friends. One such influence is Juan Falconi de Bustamente, a Spanish mystic of the early seventeenth century and a major authority for Molinos's work. Falconi's *Primer for Learning How to Read in Christ* was placed on the *Index of Prohibited Books* in 1688, probably due to its influence on Molinos, and Bossuet presents him as a precursor to Guyon in his *Instruction on the States of Prayer*.[20] Falconi argued that the highest spiritual state of infused contemplation was constituted by one continuous act. Guyon does not cite Falconi directly, but she adopts a similar position and terminology as a strategy for addressing criticisms of excessive passivity in the most advanced spiritual state. Without denying the "passivity" of this state, she presents it in the *Short and Easy Method*, like Falconi, as a kind of "simple," and "direct" *act* of submitting to God's will. Unlike other types of acts, the "simple act" is extended in duration and the agent is unaware of its performance.

The only prominent follower of the French School cited by Guyon in the *Justifications* is Jean-Jacques Olier, but the influence of other Bérullians is broadly apparent in her writing. One example is Jean de Bernières-Louvigny, a lay man and cofounder of the Hermitage retreat house in Caen. Bernières's mysticism synthesized a Bérullian emphasis on adherence to the interior suffering and victim states of Christ with a more negative and passive conception of the final union between the soul and God that is reminiscent of Canfield. One of Bernières's disciples was Jacques Bertot, who was Guyon's spiritual director, and this intellectual heritage clearly shapes Guyon's writing. Other well-known Bérullian mystics influenced her as well. The idea for the *Short and Easy Method* and its content are reminiscent of *The Conduct of Mental Prayer for Souls Who Have No Facility in It* by Claude Seguenot. Her identification of the "heart" with the deepest part of the soul probably owes something to John Eudes's popularization of this terminology. More generally, Guyon accepts the idea that mystical transformation involves adherence to Christ's interior states, which is central for all of these authors. For her, as for Olier, the mystical adoption of Christ's states can bring about a destruction of the self so thoroughgoing that it excludes even the possibility of self-awareness. As a result, Guyon presents Christ's role in the mystical ascent to God as metaphysically, but not psychologically, central in her system. In other words, her system of prayer does not focus on intellectual or imagistic meditation on Christ's nature, but the soul's largely passive, apophatic, and unselfconscious transformation is nonetheless made possible by the life, death, and resurrection of Jesus. The following passage is typical of her view: "To bear all the states of Jesus Christ is much greater than only to consider the states of Jesus Christ. Saint Paul bore the states of Jesus Christ on his body. 'I bear,' he says, 'the marks of the Lord Jesus in my body' (Gal 6:17), but he did not say that he was reasoning about this."[21]

One final possible influence is François Malaval, a lay mystic and poet from Marseilles. In 1664 Malaval wrote a brief work entitled *Easy Method for Raising the Soul to Contemplation* that could have influenced Guyon's *Short and Easy Method*. In this text Malaval champions the "prayer of simple regard," a form of acquired contemplation that, he argues, makes possible some of the most exalted spiritual states. Like Falconi and Guyon, he argues for the possibility of one such state characterized by the soul's continual, unchanging act of gazing upon God's presence. Malaval's work was placed on the *Index of Prohibited Books* in 1688, and he was linked with Quietism. Interestingly, Guyon reports in the *Life* that Malaval gave an insulting opinion of her to the bishop of Marseilles while she was traveling there, suggesting at least that she wished to distance herself from any association with him.[22] This negative portrayal of Malaval is unsurprising, given that she was writing this section of her autobiography just months after the official condemnation of his work, and does not rule out the possibility of his influence on her mysticism.

Theology

Before examining Guyon's central theological claims, some general comments about her rhetorical approach and her terminology may be helpful. Guyon's writing often exhibits a reactionary awareness of the epistemological shifts of her time. It defends a primarily apophatic form of mysticism emphasizing passive contemplation, self-annihilation, and pure love in the face of increasing challenges from advocates of Cartesian rationalism, anti-mysticism, and alternative systems of spiritual practice. In her later works, especially Parts 3 and 4 of her *Life*, the apologetic character of her writing is apparent. However, she wrote several works before the papal condemnation of Quietism in 1687, including the *Spiritual Torrents*, *A Short and Easy Method*, and the *Commentaries on the Holy Scripture*. In these earlier works one of her overarching strategies for addressing the critics of her mysticism is to weaken its claims to universal applicability by shifting the debate away from doctrinal matters and toward individual experience. Guyon often locates the authority of her mystical teaching in its pragmatic effectiveness, rather than in a systematic account of God's relationship with human beings. As a result, her teaching is typically framed by three underlying characteristics, which she occasionally makes explicit: its experiential authorization, its inclusivism, and its fallibilism. She relies on this strategy, unsuccessfully in the end, to defend herself from critics.

Guyon emphasizes experimentation in the spiritual life as well as an open flexibility in discerning and responding to God's will that she calls "suppleness." The emphasis on experimentation is very evident, for example, in the following passage from the *Short and Easy Method*: "Let those who might have difficulty believing that is easy to find God this way not believe what they are told, but let them have the experience and judge it for themselves."[23] This "try it and see" attitude pervades her work, with its emphasis on the simplicity of prayer and the universal accessibility of God. Such experimentation must be accompanied by an uncritical and receptive spirit, however. Along these lines she writes: "It is necessary to have faithfulness and an infinite suppleness in order to follow (the inclination) of grace. Without this extreme suppleness, you will always maintain the human will, however deadened it might appear to you."[24]

The experiential ground for mystical authority in Guyon's writing makes her theology essentially inclusivistic. No one system of spiritual practice should be fixed as the single dogmatically correct one, she believes, since God is an agent with different paths for each person. Hence, Guyon writes: "No one else's guidance is condemned here. On the contrary, what others believe is respected."[25] She often expresses the view that God uses many different, legitimate spiritual paths in different people. Even those she regarded as likeminded mystics, such as La Combe and Fénelon, had individually distinctive challenges and gifts in their spiritual lives. And despite the universalism of her call to prayer in the *Short and Easy Method*, she recognizes that few souls are meant to experience the most exalted spiritual states in this earthly life: "Nearly all souls belong to mercy, and there are plenty of this type. But to belong to divine Justice, oh, how rare, but how great this is!"[26] If God's treatment of each soul cannot be described in absolute generalizations, then it can only be ascertained by each individual. Still, the evidential primacy of "experience" for the justification of mystical claims points to the value of a simple, non-discursive inward "turning" in pursuit of God's presence in the individual's spiritual path, according to Guyon. In other words, the universalism of her position is primarily one of form (how to look for God) rather than substance (what everyone will find). Furthermore, although she is open to the legitimacy of alternative spiritual paths, she clearly describes the one she teaches as the easiest and most direct path to union with God.

Based as it is on individual experience (even if it is experience grounded in a tradition), Guyon's mysticism acknowledges the possibility of error or deception, produced by the imagination or the devil, in spiritual matters.[27] As a result, she repeatedly avows her submission to church authorities in correcting her teaching.[28] Nonetheless, as Bruneau points out, she was also sometimes more explicit in her criticisms of those authorities than other mystics of her time.[29] Perhaps her controversial statements about the flaws of spiritual directors and confessors help to explain why her formal submission failed to satisfy her theological opponents.

Guyon uses a variety of terms that were pervasive in the mystical writing of her time but may be unfamiliar to many readers today. A good place to start is with Guyon's frequent use of the terms interior (intérieur) and exterior (extérieur), along with their various inflections. Nicholas Paige's characterization of these terms is very appropriate to Guyon's usage. In the seventeenth century, he argues, these terms ceased to refer to "the Augustinian distinction between exterior man (homo exterior—that is, the part of man also shared by animals, such as faculties of perception) and inner man (homo interior—a term designating faculties animals did not have, such as reason). Instead 'interior' came to designate a vague psychological space to which logic, reason, and even language were foreign, indeed, 'exterior.'"[30] A similar shift took place regarding the term heart (coeur), which came to designate "a spontaneity of our being, not subject to logical rational and discursive modes," and "the site par excellence of non-discursive contemplation."[31] Notably, these terms became defined by what they excluded— reason, discourse, and language. They came to be widely used, therefore, to designate the "location" of the types of interior awareness cultivated in negative mysticism, and Guyon's usage is consistent with this larger semantic shift. She uses these two terms, along with the term depths (fond), almost synonymously throughout her writing for this purpose.

Two other sets of terms in Guyon's writing require some clarification for contemporary readers. First, when Guyon wants to make the Augustinian distinction described above by Paige, she most often does so by distinguishing the three "powers of the soul" (will, intellect, and memory) from the "senses."[32] Second, as was common in her milieu, Guyon distinguishes *orison* (*oraison*) from *meditation* (*méditation*). For Guyon, *orison* is the form of prayer associated with negative mysticism. It aims to clear reasoning, distinct thoughts, language, or self-awareness from consciousness. Since *orison* is a relatively unfamiliar term today, we translate Guyon's *oraison* with the term *contemplative prayer* or occasionally just *prayer*. She uses *meditation*, in contrast, to refer to forms of spiritual practice that used reasoning, imagination, or moral awareness as means for achieving insight and personal transformation. With these preliminary remarks complete, we turn now to a discussion of some of Guyon's major theological themes.

Despite having written a book presenting her *Short and Easy Method of Prayer*, Guyon's views on the various stages of prayer and their relation to the highest contemplative state are not always easy to discern. Complicating matters is the fact that she wrote the *Short and Easy Method* "for beginners" and therefore declines to "pursue the infinite degrees to follow" between the early stages with which she begins and the "divine union" promised in the final chapter.[33] Furthermore, in other works, without defining her terms, she sometimes uses schemata that are not present in the *Short and Easy Method* to characterize the stages of spiritual life, making the relation of the various writings unclear. Nonetheless, a charitable interpretation synthesizing her various writings on this subject is possible.

The basic framework of the *Short and Easy Method* begins with simple, minimally discursive forms of meditation. The content of the meditation can be derived from short spiritual readings or from the text of liturgical prayers. At this stage the individual is conscious of words and propositions, but "the direct and principal focus must be on the vision of God's presence."[34] Meditation therefore constitutes basic practice in metal focus and introspection in her system. She turns quickly to the "second degree of contemplative prayer," which she calls "the prayer of simplicity." Here individuals focus on

God by faith alone, without the mediation of words or propositions, but deploying "tender affections" toward God to "stir up" their awareness of the divine presence when necessary.[35] Thus far, then, this form of contemplation is actively acquired. Further spiritual progress, indeed "the key to inner life," depends on a gradual trans-formation of the will away from self-love and toward a completely pure love of God. She calls this a transformation toward "abandon-ment."[36] This process is difficult and painful because it requires the "destruction" of the individual's fallen and selfish human nature. God brings about this transformation by removing the perceptible divine presence from the soul, causing "spiritual dryness," and through the suffering and "crosses" that are a natural and inevitable part of life. Guyon advises individuals at this stage to continue to seek God by focusing inward despite the sense of divine absence and to embrace their suffering intentionally. In this way they culti-vate a thoroughgoing indifference to the personal consequences of all states of affairs. Eventually, individuals become "converted" to God as they feel themselves drawn, increasingly passively, toward the divine presence in the "depths" of their souls and away from created things.[37] The individual's role in this process is simply to focus inward and to submit to divine grace. Through this act of cooperation the individual arrives at the "contemplation of the sim-ple presence of God," the only state Guyon describes as "infused," in Chapter 12. In this state interior focus becomes habitual and continuous, the soul feels possessed by God, and consciousness is characterized by "silence."[38] Although this state depends on God's grace, it is the "natural" outcome of the preceding efforts for Guyon, and it is the highest spiritual state discussed in the book.[39] Chapters 13 through 24 of the *Short and Easy Method* address con-troversial implications of this conception of prayer rather than elab-orating the stages of contemplation in more detail. For example, Guyon addresses the issue of silence during prayer in Chapter 14 and the issue of making requests to God, despite one's loss of self-interest, in Chapter 17.

Several distinctions from Guyon's other works can be incorpo-rated into this presentation of the stages of prayer from the *Short and Easy Method*, although Guyon does not do so herself. First, Guyon sometimes distinguishes three forms of faith: luminous,

savory, and naked.[40] Other times—and apparently inconsistently—
she distinguishes souls that are "led by faith" (or sometimes, synonymously, "led by blindness") from those that are "led by
assurance" (or sometimes, synonymously, "led by illumination").[41]
As she uses the term, *assurances* are associated with special, perceptible spiritual gifts such as visions and revelations, in contrast to the
path of naked faith.[42] Those who are "led by illumination," therefore, seem to correspond to those who adopt "luminous faith," and
those who are "led by faith" seem to correspond to those who adopt
"naked faith." Savory faith is excluded from the binary form of the
distinction, but it refers for Guyon to the path of those whose
awareness of God's presence is accompanied by pleasant spiritual
sensations, or "sweetness."

Another distinction related to the stages of spiritual growth is
most fully articulated in her *Commentary on the Song of Songs*. There,
she focuses on the soul's transition from the "union of the powers"
to the "essential union."[43] The three "powers of the soul" are will,
intellect, and memory, and it is possible to experience divine union
with one, two, or all three of these powers, according to Guyon.
The union of the powers is associated with the metaphors of partial
union, God's presence within the soul, and spiritual betrothal. Self-
awareness is still present in this state. The essential union is associated with metaphors of complete and permanent union, vastness,
absence of location, self-annihilation, and spiritual marriage. Self-
awareness is absent in this state.

Based on her uses of these various terms, and her descriptions
of the various stages of prayer in the *Short and Easy Method*, it would
seem that savory faith corresponds well to the first and second
degrees of contemplation, when God's presence is still distinct and
spiritually perceptible in the soul. Naked faith corresponds well to
the state of abandonment, characterized as it is by spiritual suffering and dryness rather than by spiritual sweetness, and to the states
of conversion and infused contemplation, which are increasingly
free from distinct perceptions of any kind. The "union of the powers" seems similar to the state of "conversion" in Chapter 11 of the
Short and Easy Method, and the "essential union" seems similar to
the "contemplation of the simple presence of God" in Chapter 12.
The usefulness of this distinction in the earlier stages of prayer is a

bit unclear, although she does discuss the role of "the annihilation of the powers" in the early development of abandonment. She suggests that God temporarily annihilates one or more of the powers of the soul at this stage to help turn it away from its interest in itself and other created things.[44] The following table summarizes the preceding synthesis of Guyon's various conceptions of spiritual stages.

Spiritual Stages in the *Short and Easy Method*	Types of Faith	Types of Union
Meditation	Savory Faith	None
Prayer of Simplicity	Savory Faith	Partial Union of the Powers?
Beginning of Abandonment (through dryness and suffering)	Naked Faith	Partial Union of the Powers
Conversion	Naked Faith	Union of the Powers
Contemplation of the Simple Presence of God	Naked Faith	Essential Union

Such a table gives an artificially systematic impression of Guyon's work. Although this interpretation may be helpful in relating Guyon's different comments on prayer, the reader should bear in mind that Guyon did not present them this way herself. To all appearances, she developed some new typologies that she found congenial to her teaching in the years between 1685 and 1688, but she did not create a framework connecting the new with the old.

This synthesis leaves unresolved the relation between "luminous faith" or "illumination" and the spiritual schema in the *Short and Easy Method*. Such illuminations are simply not discussed in the latter work, and they cannot therefore be associated with particular stages of spiritual development, as in the system of Teresa of Ávila, for example. In fact, this is a broader difficulty in interpreting Guyon's mysticism. She clearly denigrates the value and reliability of illuminations such as visions and raptures in the *Life* and recommends naked faith as the preferable spiritual path.[45] However, she reports receiving some of these special illuminations herself, not only in the early stages of contemplation or meditation, but also after having achieved a profound union with God.

Although the initial formation of abandonment is listed above as a stage of the spiritual life, it is more properly presented as an ongoing process of purification that leads gradually toward increasingly perfect union with God in the higher stages of prayer. The soul's development of indifference, abandonment, equanimity, and self-annihilation is not accomplished once and for all, independent of God's ongoing activity within it. Guyon's *Commentary on the Song of Songs* helps especially to clarify this point. This text presents the soul's journey from spiritual betrothal to spiritual marriage as a slow transformation characterized by alternating periods of divine absence and presence, and of suffering and joy. Guyon seems, therefore, to envision two parallel processes in the spiritual life: an ethical one and a contemplative one. The ethical process is constituted of an increasing transformation of the soul away from self-interest and toward the pure love of God. This transformation is characterized ultimately by a submission to the divine will so thorough that it requires complete indifference to the personal consequences of acting in accord with God's guidance. The contemplative process involves the soul's increasing awareness of God's presence, leading ultimately to essential union with God. This contemplative transformation moves through states of consciousness that exclude awareness of created things in increasing degrees, until even sensations of spiritual sweetness and self-awareness disappear. These two processes exist in a dialectical relationship. Growth in the soul's awareness of God is inhibited by the intrusion of its self-interest or self-awareness and therefore requires the ethical transformation. However, the destruction of the self cannot be brought about by direct human effort but requires passive cooperation with God's grace facilitated by a mental focus that "turns" toward the divine presence.

The dialectical relationship of the ethical and contemplative transformations leads Guyon to focus strongly on the means by which God purifies the soul. This focus is consistent throughout her work, although it receives a wide variety of phenomenological descriptions. In addition to the spiritual dryness and everyday suffering (such as that caused by illness) mentioned above, God sometimes annihilates self-interest in the soul by special forms of direct, purely spiritual suffering. She describes this suffering as "an interior burning and a secret fire that, coming from God himself, purifies the fault and does not cease to cause extreme pain until the fault is entirely purified. It is like a bone dislocated from its normal place, which does not cease to cause extreme pain until it is entirely relocated. This pain is so awful that the soul places itself in a hundred different positions in order to satisfy God for its fault. It would like to rip itself apart rather than suffer such torment."[46] Guyon sees the mystical life in continuity with the afterlife, and she relates this form of passive spiritual purification to the pain of souls in purgatory.[47]

Guyon's claims about the complete annihilation of self-interest and self-awareness touch on some of the most controversial theological issues of her time. As mentioned above, the papal bull condemning Molinos focused on the ethical implications of his teachings, and these same issues were central in Guyon's own conflict with Bossuet in 1694–95. Guyon presents pure love, the completely disinterested pursuit of God's will, as the culmination of the ethical transformation necessary for spiritual growth. Following this position to its logical conclusions, she derives implications that are close to the propositions condemned in *Coelestis Pastor* but also distinct from them in subtle ways. In most cases she aims to articulate interpretations of pure love consistent with orthodox teachings on virtuous self-interest.

Her positions on petitionary prayer, the active pursuit of virtue, and concern about personal salvation are noteworthy in this regard. Guyon argues that if the individual's will has been completely purified of self-interest, it can become more difficult to make prayerful requests to God, and yet such prayers seem central to ordinary Christian piety, as indicated, for example, by the Lord's Prayer. Her solution to this tension is to argue (citing Paul in Romans 8:26–27) that although the disinterested soul cannot actively initiate certain requests, the Holy Spirit supplies the appropriate prayers, and the individual must simply submit to its activity in the soul.[48] She makes a very similar argument concerning the active pursuit of virtue. Exterior virtue is important, but true virtue only follows from submission to God's activity in the soul brought about by spiritual self-annihilation. Given the anti-mystics' polemical association of Quietism with sexual antinomianism, though, Guyon is careful to say that the truly advanced soul becomes almost incapable of exterior vice.[49] The presence of such vice therefore becomes evidence that the mystic has deceived herself regarding her degree of submission to God.[50] In addressing the issue of indifference to one's own salvation, Guyon writes, "what one calls consenting to the loss of its eternity—this is when the soul in this state of trial believes this certain and then, without any view but its own unhappiness and its own pain, makes the complete sacrifice of its eternal loss, even thinking that its God will be neither less glorious nor less happy."[51] In sum, her position seems to be that the process of spiritual suffering and ethical transformation can make the soul consent to its own eternal damnation by making it aware of its sinfulness to the point of despair, but such a consenting to self-sacrifice is made out of love for God, in order to satisfy the demands of divine justice. She also presents this willingness for self-sacrifice as a temporary outcome of the extreme trials of the soul undergoing purification. In retrospect, the soul acknowledges this willingness to be "folly" once it realizes it can "convert itself" and thereby become pleasing to God without sacrificing itself eternally.[52]

A closely related topic is the extent of passivity and activity in the various stages of spiritual development. In the early stages of prayer Guyon emphasizes human effort and activity, especially regarding the development of mental focus and the cultivation of affection for God. Such efforts prepare the soul to receive and cooperate with God's grace in contemplation. As the subsequent dialectic between ethical transformation and contemplative transformation progresses, though, her teaching increasingly recommends the soul's passive submission to the effects of God's grace. Divine activity in the soul becomes increasingly pronounced. The highest spiritual state consists of the sustained "simple act" or "direct act" of infused contemplation of God and continual submission to the divine will.[53] The influence of Falconi, and perhaps Malaval, on Guyon's view here has already been discussed. By affirming the presence of a form of human activity during essential union (even if it is a type of act that is habitual, sustained, and indiscernible), Guyon implies that freedom is never completely eliminated by spiritual transformation, even in its highest stages.

Nonetheless, despite the possibility in principle of the soul's free departure from the essential union, she claims, "after a union of this nature, it would be from the most extreme ingratitude and infidelity that she would ever want that."[54] Even when the soul has reached complete abandonment to God in the highest stages of mystical contemplation, exterior activity in service of God's will in the world never ceases, according to Guyon. In fact, those who surrender completely to God in their interior depths become completely free to act virtuously in the world precisely because their own desires have been conquered. This theme—of interior passive submission to God's control combined with exterior activity—recurs in several places in Guyon's writing.[55]

In many of her other works Guyon discusses another spiritual state that is absent from the *Short and Easy Method*; she calls it the "apostolic state." She claims in the *Life* to have received this state herself, and the resulting implication of her own authority was an important factor in her subsequent persecution. In the apostolic state the soul departs from the peace and happiness of essential union in order to help bring about the transformation of others by teaching them, communicating divine grace to them, and even suffering on their behalf. Such souls undertake this task out of pure submission to interior divine guidance. They expect no personal glory from their role. On the contrary, they expect persecution, resistance, and trials. In describing her ascent to this state, Guyon imagines the voice of Christ saying: "I was happy; I possessed glory; I was God, but I left all that. I was subjected to pain, to scorn, to ignominy, to torment. I became man to save man. If you want to finish what is missing from my passion and for me to extend my quality of redeemer into you, you must consent to lose the happiness that you enjoy to be subjected to miseries, to weaknesses, to carry the languor of those with whom I charge you, to pay their debts, and finally to be exposed not only to all the interior pain from which you yourself have been delivered, but to all of the strongest persecutions."[56]

The controversial implications of this claim derive from the fact that the apostolic state results from spiritual advancement and conformity to God's will, and not from ordination. Her teaching on this point therefore threatens to establish a mystical authority complementary to the authority of the visible church hierarchy. Furthermore, since the apostolic state derives solely from personal transformation and divine grace, it can be extended to women or the poor. Such a view threatened prevailing gender and class privileges among the clergy. She also claims that to facilitate her apostolic purpose, God gave her the ability to communicate spiritually with those she is called to teach. She calls this the "communication of the blessed spirits" and claims to have experienced it with both La Combe and Fénelon.[57]

Finally, Guyon presents several eschatological views in the *Life* related to her apostolic calling that played a significant role in the persecutions that followed the Issy Conference. She presents a controversial trinitarian view of salvation history that situates her own time at the brink of a coming "reign of the Holy Spirit," with herself and her mystical contemporaries as its martyrs.[58] This eschatological vision is complemented by other remarks (which are absent from the Oxford Manuscript of the *Life*) that Bossuet interpreted as deeply offensive messianic pretensions. Guyon writes: "It seems to me that [God] has chosen me in this century to destroy human reason and to make the wisdom of God reign over the debris of human wisdom and reason itself....He will establish the reigns of his empire in me, and the nations will recognize his sovereign power. His spirit will be widespread in all flesh; my sons and my daughters will prophesize, and the Lord will put his sweetness in them....What I bind will be bound; what I loose will be loosed."[59]

5. HISTORICAL AND CONTEMPORARY TREATMENTS OF GUYON

When the Quietist Affair is judged in historical terms, there were clear winners and losers. Louis XIV's power was not compromised by influences either stemming from the Vatican or from within his own court over this particular episode. History has judged him severely for other actions associated with his reign, such as his military expansionism, his religious intolerance in revoking the Edict of Nantes, and the excesses of his court. The Quietist Affair, however, remains a side note in his reign, one which in no real way diminished his legacy. Historians have judged Bossuet more critically, as he was considered by some to have been too harsh of an enemy of the Quietists.[60] Ultimately though, his reputation remains intertwined with the glory of Louis XIV's reign. This association with the power of the court, coupled with his being the most famous author of funeral orations in French history, has assured his reputation as a celebrated figure in seventeenth-century France. History has also judged Fénelon in a positive light, although this judgment is not based primarily on his theological texts but rather on one work of narrative fiction, *Telemachus* (1699). *Telemachus* is a novel critical of the monarchy for its abuse of power and its neglect in serving its people, and it presents a position on just governance that would gain prominence in France in the eighteenth century and culminate in the French Revolution of 1789. This work became very famous soon after its publication and is still considered an important part of the French literary canon today. For her part, Madame de Maintenon continues to be understood as an important woman in French history due to her thirty-year marriage to Louis XIV. Although the marriage was never made public, her role as queen in the most important court in Europe has been thoroughly scrutinized and continues to be a source of interest for historians. With respect to her religious influence, she is generally recognized as a stabilizing force in Louis XIV's life and a voice of moderation at court, in spite of her role in the Quietist Affair.

From the perspective of French history, Jeanne Guyon would clearly be considered the loser in this controversy, as she was all but forgotten until the twentieth century. When her name has been mentioned in this chapter of French history, it has primarily been to repeat calumnies that were perpetuated by her enemies at court, in French society, and in the church, which were most often misogynistic in nature. Specifically, this means that she has been presented as a hysterical woman with troubling messianic tendencies, all the more inappropriate since they were manifested by a lay widow. In the eighteenth century Voltaire criticized her at length, calling her "a woman without worth, without really any intellect, and who only had an excitable imagination."[61] For two centuries she was marginalized in historical treatments of the Quietist Affair, and this episode was typically presented as a struggle between the two men involved—

that is, as a polemical war of words between Bossuet and Fénelon, with Guyon situated as a secondary actor in this drama when she was mentioned at all. The following quotation from an 1850 thesis entitled *Sur la Controverse de Bossuet et de Fénelon sur le Quiétisme* is typical of how scholars represented Guyon:

> Near the end of the year 1687, a woman [Guyon] who still had traces of youth and beauty, and a name associated with wealth, and who even held on to alliances and relationships to all of the most illustrious at the court of France, was arrested in Paris by the order of the King and accused of a correspondence with the head of the Quietists, and of holding gatherings where she preached this new doctrine, after having sought to spread it through small published texts, and through writings passed from hand to hand with a mystery that only made them more dangerous. We must not commit the offense of ignoring a woman who was able to keep the esteem and friendship of Fénelon, who in turn was able to ignore for a few years the judgment of Bossuet, in the history of the Quietist Controversy. But neither must we do her the honor of delving into her writings and looking for a doctrine, a system, there.[62]

But beginning in the early twentieth century there have been critics from France who have rediscovered Guyon and have reached very different conclusions than the one just cited. These critics, the most important and ambitious of whom have been Marie-Louise Gondal and Dominque Tronc, have reconsidered Guyon's texts, as well as her place in French history and the verdicts of Bossuet concerning the Quietist Affair. Rather than concurring with Bossuet and the received notions of Guyon painted by historians, these scholars have cast Guyon in a very different light—as a powerful writer and as a fearless teacher. Through their understanding of the importance of her life and her works, these critics view her as a pioneering voice in women's literature, theology, and French history. Bruneau states:

> The task of reopening the Quietist Affair and of unraveling its complicated intrigues was undertaken in this cen-

tury by such historians as...[Henri] Brémond (1910), Louis Cognet (1958), and Jean Orcibal (1951–1975). The work of Georges Gusdorf added a European dimension to the significance and influence of Guyon's writing. Very recently, the thorough and inspiring work of Marie-Louise Gondal on the life and spirituality of Madame Guyon, as well as her publication of several unpublished documents written by Guyon, give her indeed a new profile. Dispelling the shroud of ignominy and mystery surrounding Madame Guyon, these diverse studies recognize her influence on the thought and spirituality of Fénelon. Thanks to these new works, not only does Guyon emerge cleansed of over two centuries of calumnies, but she also stands out as a powerful spiritual teacher and writer, a woman of courage, intelligence, and determination who did not let herself be intimidated by the institution of the church and the unjust punishment she was made to suffer.[63]

Although Guyon was disgraced in the French Catholic Church, her influence was significant outside of France, as has been stated above, among European Protestants who represented some of the earliest disciples in her ecumenical group. Knox states succinctly, "At the end of her life, when she lived in retirement at Blois, Madame Guyon seems to have been visited by admirers from England and Germany, and thus took rank, after her death, as a kind of honorary Protestant."[64] In considering some of the methods of this Protestant appropriation of her legacy, we can begin by considering her name. Instead of the formal Jeanne-Marie Bouvier de La Mothe Guyon du Chesnoy, she is most often referred to as Madame Guyon or Jeanne Guyon, which evokes a persona more appropriate for Protestant sensibilities. Her being called simply Jeanne Guyon allows her devotees to obscure her national and aristocratic identities and substitutes a cosmopolitan figure without clear markers of social class. This semantic choice also distances her from her own place in French history, a concern that appears to have been decidedly secondary to the preservation of her spiritual authority among English-speaking biographers and publishers. This appropriation of Guyon, this making her into "a kind of honorary Protestant," allows her work to become a kind of palimpsest onto which a wide range of religious beliefs have been inscribed, especially in the process of translation.

Let us consider her legacy among Protestants more closely. First, Guyon's works have been widely read in Germany, England, and the United States. Ward explains: "Through intermediaries and the rapid translation of her writings, she quickly became both a martyr figure and an authority on spirituality among Pietists, Quakers, Methodists, and other such movements of the time. Madame Guyon's works have been read in North America since the mid-eighteenth century, first by early Protestant immigrants from groups outside established churches, then by adherents of nineteenth-century revivalism, and finally by members of cross-denominational movements stressing the 'inner' or 'deeper' Christian life."[65] Guyon's influence seems to have been strongest on Quakers during her life and until the beginning of the nineteenth century. In her writings, rightly or wrongly, Quakers found many of the mystical principles they expounded: that God can be understood as "the Light within"; that there is "that of God" in each person; that each person can experience God directly, without the need for intermediaries such as paid clergy; and that this experience of God happens best in silent worship.

Regarding Guyon's writings, their first English translations were done by Quakers; furthermore, an only slightly revised version of her *Short and Easy Method* was found in almost every Quaker household in the nineteenth century with the misleading title *A Guide to True Peace or the Excellency of Inward and Spiritual Prayer, compiled chiefly from the writings of Fénelon, Mme Guyon and Molinos.* Even as late as 1900 we find prominent Quakers claiming that "there is no Society that has been so influenced by Guyon as the Quakers have been. If we ever had as a Society a mother-in-grace it is she."[66]

More recently Guyon has become a model for those, as Ward stated above, who are "members of cross-denominational movements stressing the 'inner' or 'deeper' Christian life." There are several Christian presses that continue to publish translations of a dozen or so of Guyon's texts, most often for readers who identify as evangelical or charismatic Christians. In these translations there is, therefore, a focus on those parts of Guyon's work that appeal to the theological interests of these audiences, including cultivating a personal relationship with Jesus Christ and undergoing deeply painful trials to arrive at a state of rebirth and transformation by the Holy Spirit. Generally speaking, the works produced by these presses take extensive liberties in the process of translation. For example, Gene Edwards, the editor of a 1989 edition of the *Spiritual Torrents*, explains in his introduction that Guyon used the word *soul* often, so in order to avoid repetition he decided to substitute "the words 'devotee,' 'believer,' or 'Christian' in those places where no damage would be done to the original meaning."[67] These translations also paint a portrait of Guyon as mirroring Anglophone attitudes and anti-Catholic sentiments. For example, in the preface to a 1984 edition of her *Short and Easy Method*, France is referred to only as a "degraded society."[68] In the introduction to an edition of her autobiography, Guyon's France was referred to only as "a nation marked with degeneracy," and the editor negotiates the fact that Guyon herself was not an evangelical Christian (according to contemporary American usage) by concluding his tribute to Guyon as follows: "We offer no apology for publishing, in the Autobiography of Madame Guyon, those expressions of devotion to her church, that found vent in her writings. She was a true Catholic when Protestantism was in its infancy."[69] Similarly, Edwards writes, "Guyon might have been the most evangelical Roman Catholic to write a book in her time, but Catholic she was."[70] In two recent editions the title of her *Short and Easy Method of Prayer* has been translated *Experiencing the Depths of Jesus Christ* and *Experiencing God Through Prayer*, titles presumably meant to be more appealing to contemporary evangelicals.[71] In spite of having to assuage Protestant sensibilities in publishing Guyon's writings, the editors usually extol the depths of her spiritual understanding and her inexhaustible faith in following God's will.

6. BRIEF INTRODUCTION TO THE TEXTS

The texts included here were chosen from Guyon's extensive body of work for several reasons. Two of them were published during the 1680s and were the primary textual sources for the inquiry into her theological views at Issy: *Short and Easy Method of Prayer* and *Commentary on the Song of Songs*. Although these published texts were the official basis for the ecclesiastical condemnations that followed the Issy Conference, Part 1, Part 2, and some of Part 3 of her *Life* were probably an even more important unofficial one. Guyon shared her unpublished autobiography with Bossuet under the seal of confession before she realized that he was hostile to her cause. Bossuet interpreted the *Life* as evidence of Guyon's pride and visionary madness and broke his promise of secrecy to use it against her. He ridiculed it privately, in his discussions with other powerful members of the clergy, as well as publicly, in his *Account of Quietism*. These texts are therefore central to understanding the historical situation leading to the Quietist Affair. They also constitute some of the best-known presentations of Guyon's theological views and, as instances of three different genres of spiritual writing, of her literary range.

Our efforts have relied heavily and gratefully on Dominique Tronc's recently published critical editions of Guyon's works. These editions have served as the source for some of these translations, and on the rare occasions when we have diverged from her text, we have included a footnote explaining our reasons. Tronc is also the source of some of the explanatory information in the footnotes for the *Life*. One systematic divergence from the French editions used in preparing these translations concerns Guyon's biblical quotations. In most cases Guyon quotes from a seventeenth-century French translation of the Latin Vulgate. Simply translating from Guyon's French into contemporary English sometimes resulted in quotations that would be difficult to recognize for contemporary English-speaking audiences. However, contemporary English translations of the Bible were sometimes too different from Guyon's French to make sense of her interpretations. We therefore chose to use the Douay-Rheims Bible, an English translation of the Vulgate first published, in separate parts, in 1582 and 1610, as the basis for our renderings of Guyon's biblical quotations. We have updated archaic usages in the Douay-Rheims, however, and we have occasionally changed the text to reflect Guyon's French more closely when the logic of her interpretation seemed to demand it. In the rare cases where Guyon quotes in Latin from the Bible or Catholic liturgy, we kept the Latin in the main body of the text and included an English translation in a note.

A Short and Easy Method of Prayer

The first text, *A Short and Easy Method of Prayer*, was written at the request of Guyon's followers, who wanted a simple, clear statement of her teachings on prayer. It was first published in Grenoble in 1685 and was popular enough to merit several subsequent additional printings. This work was placed on the *Index of Prohibited Books* in 1689, in the aftermath of Molinos's trial in Rome, and was the primary focus of her interrogations at Issy by Bossuet, Noailles, and Tronson. Written for a popular audience and avoiding many of the technical distinctions then current in mystical writing, *A Short and Easy Method of Prayer* became Guyon's best-known work in her lifetime. It is included here in its entirety.

Guyon says in the Preface to this work that she aims to present "a little method without a method," and this description is very apt. She also insists that "no one else's guidance is condemned here. On the contrary, what others believe is respected."[72] As mentioned above, some of her critics have deprecated her writing for its unsystematic character, but here Guyon presents the simplicity, experimental nature and inclusivism of her approach as intentional. In these emphases, a self-consciously modern mysticism, aware of the doubts and challenges posed by an increasingly anti-mystical era, can be discerned.

The central teaching in the text is that a form of contemplative prayer, which she calls a "prayer of the heart,"[73] is possible without elaborate mental exercises or education and can be achieved by eliminating sensory and mental distractions and simply focusing on God's presence in the depths of the soul. She also counsels patience and humility in enduring God's absence in prayer. The aim of this practice of prayer is gradual progress toward the complete abandonment of the individual's will to the will of God, developed initially by the intentional cultivation of indifference toward all personal desire or suffering. Guyon presents the soul's progress through several distinct stages of prayer in Chapters 1 through 12.

Chapters 13 through 24 deal with apparent tensions between the types of prayer she has outlined and the demands of traditional piety and morality. Her treatment of virtue in this work is one of its more controversial aspects. Since the third century, at least, the Christian contemplative tradition typically presented spiritual growth toward God as a three-stage process moving from purgation to illumination to union. Accordingly, moral virtues, or even ascetic disciplines, were often presented as preconditions for ascension to higher stages of contemplation. Guyon inverts this process, making union with God through the prayer of the heart the precondition for acquiring true virtue. This way of speaking about the acquisition of virtue raised red flags for her opponents. *Coelestis Pastor* condemned the view that morality or true virtue was the result of passive mystical transformation rather than active moral and introspective effort, and Guyon's position here could be interpreted as lending support to such views.

Given that one of the central accusations against the Quietists involved their teachings on the annihilation of the will, it is worth noting that Guyon touches on this theme in several places throughout *A Short and Easy Method of Prayer*. Guyon teaches that as the soul progresses in its practice of prayer, God begins to infuse its contemplation with divine grace, and it begins increasingly to submit to God's will. While her emphasis is on God's activity and human passivity in these stages of spiritual growth, she holds consistently to the freedom of the human partner in submitting to and participating in God's grace. Her awareness of the controversial nature of her teaching on the will is reflected by the length of Chapters 21 and 22, which treat this topic, and by her adoption of a more apologetic tone and technical vocabulary for expressing her position. She advances a twofold strategy against criticisms of excessive passivity in her teachings. First, she argues that active and self-conscious effort is necessary and appropriate in the early stages of prayer and insists that the more passive stages of the spiritual life only concern "advanced" souls. Second, regarding souls in these more advanced stages, she elaborates a typology of acts and defends a kind of cooperation with God's activity in the soul with the notion of the "simple act," a free, though unreflective and unselfconscious, "turning" toward God, by which a continuous awareness of and conformity to God's will becomes possible. This simple act is effort-less, she claims, because it consists of a submission to God's action in the soul.

Commentary on the Song of Songs

Guyon claims in her autobiography that she wrote this text in a day and a half as part of a larger commentary on the Bible, while also receiving visits from her followers. She adds that her writing was directly inspired by the Holy Spirit and was done in a com-pletely unreflective manner. Bruneau notes that such claims were common rhetorical devices used by mystics (especially female mys-tics) to protect themselves from charges of heresy by denying authorial intent and thereby blunting their responsibility for what they wrote. She criticizes historians who accepted Guyon's claim at face value and "chose to see in her a rare case of automatic writing," a position that "went along with the image of Guyon as a hysteric, conjured up in the nineteenth century."[74] Bruneau points to multi-ple, edited archival copies of the *Life* as evidence that Guyon worked gradually and carefully on that text. This evidence does not disprove Guyon's claims regarding the *Commentary on the Song of Songs*, however. Whatever the truth of the matter, the length and scope of her biblical commentary is certainly impressive, given the time frame for its composition between 1684 and 1685, while she was still living in Grenoble. Her *Commentary on the Song of Songs* was published in 1688 in Lyons. Although it was not placed on the *Index of Prohibited Books*, like her *Method*, it was condemned in a pas-toral letter by the archbishop of Paris, Harlay de Champvallon, in 1694. We include the complete text here.

Guyon's commentary stands in a long tradition of mystical interpretation of the *Song of Songs* stretching back to the patristic author Origen. Guyon, like Origen and many other Christian authors, interprets this biblical dialogue between Bride and Bridegroom as an allegory for the soul's relationship to God. She finds fertile ground for the scriptural authorization of her mysti-cism in its poetic and sometimes obscure language (often derived from problematic Vulgate translations of the original Hebrew). Stylistically, unlike her more didactic presentation in the *Short and*

Easy Method, her writing in this text inclines more toward the lyrical and evocative.

The themes of the gradual annihilation of individual will, accomplished by alternating experiences of God's joyful and "savory" presence, God's "crucifying" presence, and the painful "dryness" of God's absence, as well as the largely passive transformation of the soul toward an ethics of pure (completely disinterested) love are all prominent in the text. Of special note is the lengthy treatment of the first verse, in which the influence of Teresa of Ávila on the distinction between spiritual betrothal and spiritual marriage is evident, and Guyon presents a more systematic typology of spiritual states that is typical in her other writings. Here, she describes the divine union with the three powers of the soul—intellect, memory, and will—and correlates these powers with the activity of the three persons of the Trinity. The same typology of the soul's powers recurs throughout this commentary and elsewhere in her writing, where she correlates the powers to the three theological virtues of faith, hope, and love.[75] Still, the dominant concern of the commentary is the transcendence of the "union of the powers" and the achievement of "essential union," brought about by voluntary submission to God's purifying and transforming grace.

Two claims in her treatment of the final verse were particularly troublesome to her examiners at Issy. First, she claims that the apostolic authority to offer spiritual teaching can be given to individuals who have achieved a complete conformity to the divine will. Implying as it does the possibility of religious authority outside the church hierarchy, this teaching on the "apostolic state" was bound to be controversial. Second, speaking of the fully annihilated soul, Guyon writes, "Death and life are the same to her, and although her love is incomparably stronger than it ever has been, she cannot, however, desire Paradise." The claim that individuals should seek an indifference so thoroughgoing that they lose all individual desires (including virtuous desires such as the hope of salvation) in a complete forgetfulness of the self had been condemned in Article 12 of *Coelestis Pastor*. Although Guyon's claim in this text is descriptive (that certain souls *cannot* desire Paradise), and Article 12 condemns a prescriptive claim (that individuals *should* seek such indifference), it was not difficult for Guyon's examiners to infer a prescriptive preference for the state she describes from her larger mystical system.

Life, Parts 1–3

In Tronc's critical edition Guyon's *Life* extends to more than eight hundred pages. It therefore could not be included here unabridged. However, given its importance, the text could not simply be excluded from an introduction to Guyon's writings. It became one of her best-known works after being published in French in 1720 and in abridged English and German translations shortly thereafter. The *Life* alternates consistently between a narrative concerning the "exterior" events of her life and a parallel narrative concerning her "interior" spiritual growth, complemented by instructional asides and reflections on mystical theology. While she clearly intends each narrative to inform the interpretation of the other, we have been able to include only those parts of the "interior" narrative and its complementary theological reflections that we judged to be most important or otherwise unrepresented in the other writings included here. Guyon wrote her autobiography in three stages. She wrote the first version in Thonon in 1682, then added new material while confined in the Visitation Sainte Marie of Paris in 1688. The final parts presenting her persecution during the Quietist Affair were written during her exile in Blois in 1709. She added some of the new material from 1709 to the 1688 text to form a complete version of the *Life* intended for the public, but she kept private most of the story of her imprisonment between 1695 and 1703. Parts 1–3, abridged here, constitute the edition intended for the public (as redacted by Tronc from several manuscript versions).

The *Life* has proven to be Guyon's most attractive text for scholars in women's and literary studies. For example, Bruneau detects in it an ambivalence and even inconsistency regarding bodily manifestations of the spiritual life. The *Life* includes some of the clearest formal statements of Guyon's preference for apophatic spiritual states devoid of concepts, images, or distinctions rather than "illuminations" and "gifts" such as visions, interior locutions, dreams, prophecies, ecstasies and raptures, especially in Part 1, Chapter 9. She even denigrates such "less pure graces" as "very dangerous," subject to demonic deception and "very prone to illusions" in this chapter. She nonetheless reports several of her own dreams, visions, prophecies, and supernatural communications throughout the *Life* and treats them as authoritative. Bruneau discusses the relevance of gendered notions of mystical practice to this tension.[76] Nicholas Paige points out the stylistic changes in each phase of Guyon's autobiographical writing. He argues that she begins in the early sections with a confidence in the spiritually evocative and didactic power of the autobiographical genre—a "faith in language"— but shifts to a strictly narrative and legally precise record of events in the later sections. This shift reflects her increasing awareness of an openness and ambiguity of the genre that makes it unsuitable and even dangerous as a means for spiritual instruction. He speculates that the uncharitable interpretations of her writings given by her examiners at Issy and Bossuet's use of the early parts of the *Life* against her in his *Account of Quietism* may have been partly responsible for this change.[77]

The *Life* touches on many of Guyon's central mystical concerns (such as prayer, human freedom, suffering and the destruction of the self, and union with God) and offers some of the clearest statements about them anywhere in her writing. It also defends several of her views against charges of Quietism. In her presentation of her discussions with Bossuet she again denies any teaching on the complete passivity of will and, in 3.14.10–11 she expands her teaching on the "direct act without reflection," discussed above concerning the *Short and Easy Method*. She also defends the orthodoxy of her view on the spiritually advanced soul's inability to offer petitionary prayers in 3.14.12–13 and on its indifference to its own salvation or damnation in 3.17.3–8.

Several additional claims in her autobiography regarding authority and eschatology particularly galled her opponents in the Quietist Affair. Among these is the recurrence of her claim (in 2.8 and 2.22, and again in 3.10) of the authority to communicate divine grace to others and to offer spiritual guidance as a result of God having called her to the "apostolic state." She does not claim this authority *despite* her gender, but rather *privileges* the "humility" and "weakness" of women as more naturally conducive to the self-annihilation that necessarily precedes the apostolic state, reversing the consequences of this commonly held misogynistic view (though not openly rejecting the view itself). Her claims about the new generation of martyrs who will inaugurate the "reign of Holy Spirit" are in 3.7. Her predictions about her own status in this new era assume operatic proportions in 3.10, leading Bossuet to ridicule them as the height of pride.

A Short and Easy Method of Prayer Which All Can Practice Very Easily and Through Which All Can Arrive in a Short Time to a High Perfection

PREFACE

We were not thinking in the least of giving this little work, which had been conceived in great simplicity, to the public. It had been written for a few specific people who wanted to love God with all their heart. But many people asked for copies of it, due to the usefulness that they derived from reading this little treatise; they wished to have it printed for their own satisfaction, without any aim other than that.

We left it in its natural simplicity. No one else's guidance is condemned here. On the contrary, what others believe is respected. We even submit all that it contains to the censure of people with experience and doctrinal expertise. We only ask that each one not stop at the surface but penetrate the design of the person who wrote it, which is nothing other than to impel everyone to love God and to serve him with more pleasure and success, being able to do this in a simple and easy manner suitable to the little ones who are not capable of extraordinary or learned things but who truly want to give themselves to God for good. Those who read it are asked to read it without prejudice, and they will discover under very common expressions a hidden unction that will impel them to seek a happiness that they should all hope to possess.

We use the word *facility*, saying that perfection is easy because it is easy to find God. This passage can be invoked: "You shall seek me, and shall not find me" (John 7:34). However, this should not cause any difficulty because the same God, who can never contradict himself, has said: "Seek, and you shall find" (Matt 7:7). The one who seeks God without wanting to leave sin does not find him because he looks for him where he is not. This is why it is added: "You will die in your sin" (John 8:24). But he who truly takes pains to look for him in his heart, by sincerely leaving sin in order to approach him, will find him infallibly.

A number of people have imagined devotion to be so horrible and contemplative prayer to be so extraordinary that they have not wanted to work toward their acquisition, in desperation of ever getting to the end. But since making something difficult for oneself causes a despair of being able to succeed at it and takes away the desire to undertake it at the same time, and when one proposes something to oneself as if it were advantageous and easy to obtain one gives oneself to it with pleasure and pursues it with enthusiasm, this is what obliges us to show both the advantage and the facility of this path.

Oh, if we were persuaded of the goodness of God for his poor creatures and of the desire that he has to communicate himself to them! One would not make monsters for oneself, and one would not despair so easily about obtaining a good that he fervently wishes to give us. And after he has given us "his own Son, but delivered him up for us all" (Rom 8:32), could he refuse us anything? Assuredly not. Only a little courage and perseverance are necessary. One has so much of these for little temporal interests, and one has none of them for the "one thing" that "is necessary" (Luke 10:42). Let those who might have difficulty believing that it is easy to find God this way not believe what they are told, but let them have the experience and judge it for themselves. And they will see that they were told quite little about it in comparison with what is there.

Very dear reader, read this little work with a simple and sincere heart, with smallness of spirit, without wanting to criticize scrupulously. And you will see that you will truly find yourself in it. Receive it in the same spirit in which it is given to you, which is none other than to impel you entirely to God without reserve, and which is not to cause you to value or esteem something, but to encourage the simple and the children to go to their Father, who loves their humble confidence and who is greatly displeased by defiance. Do not look for anything other than the love of God and have the simple desire for your own salvation, and you will find it assuredly following this little method without a method.

We do not claim at all to raise our manner of thinking above that of others, but we speak sincerely about the experience that we have had, as much through ourselves as through other souls, and about the advantage of using this simple and naive manner in order to go to God.

If we are not talking here about a variety of things that we esteem, but only about the *Short and Easy Method of Prayer*, it cannot address other things, only having been written for this. I am assured that if one reads it in the same spirit in which it has been written one will find nothing shocking. One will be yet more certain of the truth that it contains if one wants to experiment with it.

It is for you, O Holy Child Jesus, who loved simplicity and innocence and whose "delights were to be with the children of men" (Prov 8:31), meaning with those among men who want to become children, it is for you, I say, to prize and to give value to this little work, imprinting it in the heart and impelling those who will read it to look for you inside themselves, where you rest as in a manger where you desire to receive the signs of their love and to give them your testimonies. They deprive themselves of these goods through their fault. This is your work, O Child God, O uncreated Love, O mute and abridged Word, to make you loved, tasted, and understood! You can, and, if I dare say, you must do this through this little work, which is all to you and all for you.

I. EVERYONE IS CALLED TO INWARD PRAYER

1. Everyone is capable of inward contemplative prayer, and it is a terrible shame that almost all people have it in their heads not to do it. We are all called to this prayer as we are all called to eternal life. Contemplative prayer is nothing more than heartfelt affection and love. What is necessary is to love God and to focus on him. Saint Paul orders us to "pray without ceasing" (1 Thess 5:17). Our

Lord says, "And what I say to you, I say to all: Watch" (Mark 13:33–37). Everyone can, therefore, perform contemplative prayer and must do so. But I understand that not everyone can meditate, and very few are ready for it. Therefore, it is not this type of contemplative prayer that God asks of us or that is desirable for you.

2. Whoever you might be, wanting to be saved, come and practice inward prayer. You should live for contemplative prayer as you live for love. "I counsel you to buy from me gold tried in the fire, that you may be made rich" (Rev 3:18). It is very easy to have these kinds of riches, and even more than you can possibly imagine. "And he that thirsts, let him come; and he that will, let him take the water of life, freely" (Rev 22:17), and do not amuse yourselves by digging "cisterns, broken cisterns, that can hold no water" (Jer 2:13). Come, weakened hearts who find nothing to make you happy, and you will be filled. Come, you who are overwhelmed with pain and suffering; you will be relieved. Come, you who are sick, and do not fear approaching him because you are filled with disease. Show him your hurt, and you will be relieved. Come, children, to your Father; he will receive you with loving arms. Come, poor lambs who have strayed and are lost; come to your shepherd. Come, you who are uneducated and simple; you are all ready for contemplative prayer because you who believe yourselves incapable are indeed the most ready. Come all without exception. Jesus Christ calls all of you. Let those without a heart not come because it takes a heart to love. But who is truly without a heart? Oh, come and give this heart to God and learn how to pray this way.

3. All who want to experience contemplative prayer can do so. It is the key to perfection and ultimate happiness, to eliminating vice and acquiring virtue, because there is one simple thing to do: walk in the presence of God in order to be perfect. God told us so: "Walk before me, and be perfect" (Gen 17:1). Contemplation alone can afford you this presence and give it to you continually.

4. It is therefore necessary to learn how to pray contemplatively, which can be done at any time, and which does not depend on any particular walk of life. This includes princes, kings, clergy, priests, lawyers, soldiers, children, craftsmen, workers, women, and the sick; indeed, everyone can perform this type of worship, my dear friends.

This is not a prayer stemming from the mind, but a prayer stemming from the heart. This cannot be a mental prayer, friends, because the mind is so limited that if it is thinking about one thing, it cannot think of another at the same time. However, prayer of the heart is not interrupted by the rumblings of the mind. Nothing can interrupt prayer of the heart but uncontrollable feelings because once we have tasted God and the sweetness of his love, it is impossible to taste anything but him.

5. Nothing is easier than experiencing God and tasting him. He is more a part of us than we are of ourselves. He has a stronger desire to give himself to us than we have to possess him. The only way to look for him is as easy and natural as breathing the air and is no more than that.

Yes, you who are so coarse, who believe that you are not good at anything, you can live in prayer and in God himself as easily and continually as you live from the air you breathe. Would you then not be a criminal if you did not do this? You will undoubtedly want to learn how, and learning how is the easiest thing in the world.

II. THE WAY TO PRAY

There are two ways to introduce souls to contemplative prayer, which one can and must use for a time. One is meditation and the other is meditative reading.

1. Meditative reading is nothing more than taking some strong truths about theory and practice, with the latter being preferable, and to read for that end. Take whatever truth you like. Then read two or three lines about it, digesting the words and tasting them, trying to take the nectar and stay focused on the passage that you are reading as long as you feel like it, focusing on this passage until it no longer inspires you. Afterward, take another passage and do the same thing, reading no more than one-half a page at a time.

It is not the amount you read, but the way you read that counts. People who rush through will not really profit. They are like bees that can only draw the nectar of flowers while at rest and not while moving around them. To read a lot is for intellectual pursuits rather than mystical ones. In order to profit by reading spiritual books, you must read them in this way. And I am convinced that once one learns how to read this way, one will get used to it and will be very comfortable with it.

2. The other way of prayer is informal meditation, which is done at an appointed hour and not at the time of the meditative reading. I believe it will be good to undertake it this way. After having put oneself in the presence of God by an act of living faith, it is necessary to read something of substance and to stop gently on it, not to reflect, but only as a means of focusing the spirit, observing that the principal task must be to cultivate the presence of God and that the topic must be sufficient to focus the spirit rather than exercise it through reasoning.

This supposes that the living faith, from the bottom of our hearts, in a present God impels us to focus on our inner being, bringing all of our focus inward rather than on external things. One important consideration from the very beginning is to liberate ourselves from a great many distractions or external stimuli in order to find God, who can only be found inside of us and in our depth, which is the inner sanctum where he lives. He even promises us that "if anyone loves me, he will keep my word, and my Father will love him, and we will come to him, and will make our abode with him" (John 14:23). Saint Augustine feels guilty for all the time he lost not looking for God in this way.

3. Once we are centered within ourselves and are profoundly penetrated by God in our depths, once our senses are all gathered up and drawn inward from the circumference to the depths (which is a bit more difficult at the beginning than after a time, I will say), once the soul is so gathered into itself, then it can focus gently and sweetly on the truth that is read, not through reasoning a lot about it, but through savoring it, exciting our will through our feelings rather than by our understanding. When we are moved to leave it, we should remain gently in peace, swallowing what was tasted. Like a person chewing an excellent piece of meat, although savoring the taste, it is not until she stops for a moment to swallow that she is nourished. It is the same thing when we feel moved in the Spirit. To continue moving forward would be to extinguish the Spirit's fire and take away food for the soul. It is necessary to swallow that which the individual has chewed and tasted, through a small loving pause, full of respect and confidence. This method is quite neces-

sary and will help the soul more and in less time than with other ways taking many years.

4. But, as I have already said, the direct and principal focus must be on the vision of God's presence. We must be most faithful in recalling this truth when we begin to lose our focus.

This is a simple and effective way to combat distractions because if we try to combat distractions directly, we will in fact irritate the situation, making it worse. Instead, we should focus more deeply on a vision of the present God and very simply recollect. Therefore, we combat these distractions indirectly and without thinking, which is a very effective method.

Let me warn newcomers not to run from truth to truth, from subject to subject, but to stay with one thought for as long as they are so moved. This is the way to penetrate these truths easily, to taste them, and to have them make their impression.

I say that it is difficult in the beginning to focus inward and recollect because of our habit of focusing outward. But when a person gets used to this violence that one does to oneself through practice, it becomes very easy, as much because the person develops the habit as because God, whose only desire is to be in direct contact with his creation, sends the person abundant grace and a desire to experience his presence quite easily.

III. FOR THOSE WHO CANNOT READ

1. Those who cannot read are not deprived of the chance for contemplative prayer. Jesus Christ is the great book, written on both the inside and the outside, which will teach all things. Those who cannot read must practice this method.

First, they must learn a fundamental truth, which is that "the kingdom of God is within you" (Luke 17:21), and it is there they must look. Pastors should teach contemplative prayer to their parishioners just as they teach them the catechism. Their parishioners were created for this end, and they are not taught to enjoy their end. They need to have this method taught to them.

Let them begin by a deep act of adoration and emptying themselves before God, and, after that, let them attempt to close the eyes of the body and to open the eyes of the soul as they focus inward. And by directly focusing on the presence of God by the living faith that God is in them, without drawing from their outside strength or senses, let them be held so tightly in this prayer that they are captive.

2. In this way let them pray the Our Father, perhaps understanding little of what they are saying, but thinking that God is within them and wants to be their Father. In this state let them make their little requests to him, and, after having pronounced this word *Father*, let them remain for a moment in deeply respectful silence, waiting for God to let them know his will. At other times, seeing themselves as children, dirty and spoiled by their shortcomings, having the force neither to sustain themselves nor to cleanse themselves, let them present themselves to their Father in a humble and confused manner, mixing together words of love and pain, then resting in silence.

After the Our Father, praying to this king of glory to reign in them, abandoning themselves to him to the point that they give up some of the rights they hold for themselves, they should then remain in silence. Afterward, they can continue with another request. If they feel inclined to peace and silence, let them not continue but remain in this state as long as they are so moved, after which they continue on to the second request, that "your will be done on earth as it is in heaven." Thus, they will desire that God's will be done in them and through them. They give their will and their freedom to God, so as to be his instrument. Then, seeing that the main object of their will must be to love, they will want to love and will ask God for his love—but in a gentle and peaceful way. They continue with the rest of the Our Father, with the help of clergy to instruct them. They should not attempt to recite much of the Our Father or the Ave, but when they do recite it, they should recite it well.

3. At other times they should be like sheep with their shepherd and ask him for their true food. O Shepherd, you give the nourishment of yourself, and it is daily bread. They could also pray for their family's needs, but this should be done through this perspective of direct and essential faith that God is in us. God is nothing like what one imagines him to be, but a living faith in his presence suffices. They should not form any image of God in their minds, although

one can do so of Jesus Christ, looking at him crucified, or as a child, or in another state or mystery, provided that the soul is still searching for it.

At other times they should look at him like a doctor and show him their ills so that he can heal them. But they should always do this without effort and with a bit of silence from time to time, in order that there is more and more silence rather than action, so that in the end, by giving more and more over to God's ways, they will profit, as I will explain in the following passage.

4. When the presence of God is given and the soul begins gradually to taste silence and rest, this experiential taste of God's presence introduces the soul to the second degree of contemplative prayer, after having started at the first degree appropriate for those who can read and for those who cannot, as already mentioned.

IV. THE SECOND DEGREE OF CONTEMPLATIVE PRAYER

1. The second degree is called by some *contemplation* and by others the *prayer of simplicity*. This latter term might be more appropriate than *contemplation*, which is more refined and done by others.

When the soul has been engaged in the way we have seen, after a period of time it feels, little by little, that it is given a facility with becoming attached to God. It begins to recollect more easily. Inward prayer becomes effortless, sweet, and pleasant. The soul knows the path to finding God. It smells the scent of his perfumes. Thus, now it is necessary to change the method so that the soul, through fidelity and courage, does what I am about to explain without being surprised at what will be required.

2. First, as soon as the soul finds itself in the presence of God through faith and focuses inward, let it stay for a moment like this in respectful silence. If, from the beginning, while performing this act of faith, it has a small inkling of the presence of God, let the soul stay in that place as long as this feeling remains, without being troubled or trying to move beyond this point, and let it keep what was given to it for as long as it remains. If this feeling leaves, let the soul stir up its will by some tender affection. And if from this first affec-

tion the soul finds itself back in gentle peace, let it remain there. Likewise, it is necessary to blow upon the fire gently and, as soon as it is lit, to stop blowing, because to continue to blow would be to extinguish the fire.

3. I ask that you never perform contemplative prayer without remaining in respectful silence for a time at the end.

It is of great consequence that the soul approach contemplative prayer with courage, that it carry with it pure and unselfish love. Let the soul never approach this type of worship in order to get something from God, but instead to please him and do his will. For a servant who only serves if he is rewarded does not deserve to be rewarded.

Approach contemplative prayer not in order to feel good but in order to be with God as he wishes. This means that you will be the same, as much in times of dryness as in times of abundance, and that you will be surprised neither by God's silence nor by periods of dryness.

V. DRYNESS

1. As God has no desire other than to give himself to a loving soul who wants to search for him, he often hides himself in order to reveal the soul's laziness and to force it to look for him with love and steadfastness. But with what goodness is the steadfastness of the beloved rewarded! And how many apparent absences are rewarded with loving caresses! You might believe that it is a mark of utmost steadfastness and love to look for our Beloved by exerting your mind, strength, or action to make him return. No, believe me, dear souls, that is not the way of this method. It is necessary to have loving patience, humble, lowered eyes, a frequent but peaceful affection, and a respectful silence as you wait for the return of your Beloved.

2. You will show him by this way of acting that it is him alone whom you love and whom you want to please, not the pleasure that you will experience through loving him. That is why it is said: "Humble your heart, and endure: incline your ear, and receive the words of understanding: and do not be impatient in the time of obscurity. Wait on God with patience: join yourself to God, and

endure, that your life may be increased in the latter end. Take all that is brought upon you: and in your sorrow endure, and in your humiliation keep patience" (Ecclus 2:2–6). Be patient in inward prayer. And have nothing else in your life other than waiting for the return of your Beloved in patience with a humble, abandoned, resigned and joyful spirit. Oh, excellent contemplative prayer! You can mix loving pleadings into it. Oh, how this procedure charms the heart of God and obliges him to return more than any other.

VI. ABANDONMENT

1. Giving all of oneself and all that one possesses begins here. All we need is to convince ourselves strongly that all that happens to us from moment to moment represents the order and the will of God. This conviction will make us content with all things and will make us see all that happens to us as coming from God and not from his creatures. I entreat you, my dear brothers and sisters wanting to give yourselves to God, whoever you might be, not to take yourself back once you have given yourself to him, and to think that once this is given it is no longer at your disposal.

2. Abandonment is what really matters on this path, and it is the key to inner life. The one who knows how to abandon himself will soon be perfect. It is then necessary to hold firm to this commitment without listening to reason and without thinking about it. Great faith makes for great abandonment. It is necessary to trust in God, "believing in hope against hope" (Rom 4:18).

3. Abandonment is giving up all care for ourselves in order to leave ourselves entirely to God's way. All Christians are exhorted to give themselves up to God because for everyone it is said, "Be not therefore solicitous for tomorrow; for tomorrow will be solicitous for itself" (Matt 6:34). "Lay open your works to the Lord: and your thoughts will be directed" (Prov 16:3). "Commit your way to the Lord, and trust in him, and he will do it" (Ps 37:5). Abandonment to God's will must be, as much on the outside as on the inside, a total surrendering and putting of your life into God's hands, forgetting yourself and thinking only of God. In this way the heart remains always free, joyous, and detached.

4. In practice, lose all of your own will unceasingly in the will of God and renounce all specific inclinations, however good they might appear. As soon as you feel them begin, make yourself indifferent and only desire what God has desired from the beginning of time. Be indifferent to all things, whether for the body or for temporal and eternal goods. Let the past be forgotten, leave the future to providence, and give the present to God. Let us be happy in the present moment, carrying in it the eternal order of God for us. The moment is an infallible declaration to us of the will of God, being inevitable and shared by all. Do not attribute any part of what happens to the world, but look at all things through God and look at them as infallibly coming from his hand, with the exception of our own sin.

Let yourselves, then, be led to God as he pleases, either through the interior or through the exterior.

VII. SUFFERING

1. Be happy about all that God will make us suffer. If you love him, you must love him on Calvary just as on Mount Tabor, since it is the place where he makes love most evident. Do not be like those people who give of themselves one moment and then take themselves back at another. They give themselves in order to be caressed and take themselves back when they are crucified, or they look to the world for consolation.

2. No, you will not find any consolation there, dear souls, but only in the love of the cross and in giving yourselves totally to God. Oh, the person who does not have any inclination to follow the cross has no inclination to follow God! It is impossible to love God without loving the cross, and a heart having a taste for the cross will find the bitterest things sweet, joyful, and pleasurable. "A soul that is full shall tread upon the honeycomb: and a soul that is hungry shall take even bitter for sweet" (Prov 27:7) because the soul finds itself as famished for its God as it is famished for the cross. The cross allows for God, and God allows for the cross. True relinquishing of control and the cross go hand in hand.

3. As soon as you find something that discourages you and brings on suffering, first offer it up to God, and then give yourself

up as a sacrifice. You will see that when the cross comes, it will not be as heavy as you would have thought. This does not mean that you will not feel its weight. Some imagine that the only suffering is that of the cross. But actually to feel suffering is one of the very principles of suffering. Jesus Christ wanted to suffer in the most painful way.

Sometimes we carry the cross with weakness, at other times with strength. All should be equal.

VIII. MYSTERIES

1. Some might criticize me that in this method we do not focus on God's mystery. It is quite the opposite. Mysteries are a given to the soul. Jesus Christ, to whom we relinquish ourselves, whom we follow as the *way,* to whom we listen as the *truth,* and who loves us like *life* (John 14:6), imprints himself on our soul and makes it bear all his states in it. To bear all the states of Jesus Christ is much greater than only to consider the states of Jesus Christ. Saint Paul bore the states of Jesus Christ on his body. "I bear," he says, "the marks of the Lord Jesus in my body" (Gal 6:17), but he did not say that he was reasoning about this.

2. Often in this state of abandonment Jesus Christ gives us views of his states in a very particular way. It is necessary to receive them and apply them wherever God desires. Choosing nothing for ourselves other than to stay with him, we should receive equally, wherever it pleases God, to love him or to deny ourselves before him, as we also receive all that he gives us: light or darkness, facility or sterility, strength or weakness, sweetness or bitterness, temptation or distraction. Pain, troubles, uncertainties, none of it should stop us.

3. There are people whom God calls for years at a time to taste one of his mysteries. Simply the sight or thought of this mystery puts them in a contemplative mode. Let them be faithful to it. But when God takes it away from them, let them allow themselves to be deprived of it. Others suffer at having no revelation of God's mystery. Inclination for mystery and love of God are incorporated in this particular kind of devotion. The person who loves God loves all that comes from him.

IX. VIRTUE

1. This is the short and sure way to acquire virtue; since God is the principle of all virtue, all virtue comes from possessing God. The closer we come to possessing this, the higher our degree of virtue.

Moreover, I say that all virtue not coming from within is a mask of virtue, like clothing that falls apart and does not last. But virtue emanating from the depths is essential, true, and permanent. "All the glory of the king's daughter comes from within" (Ps 45:13). Of all souls, there is none practicing a stronger virtue than these, although they do not particularly think about it as virtue. God, to whom they are held united, makes them practice it in many forms. He does not allow them anything; he does not permit them the least pleasure.

2. What hunger these loving souls have for suffering! How many austerities they undertake if left to their own desires! They only think about pleasing their beloved God, and they start to neglect themselves and love themselves less. The more they love God, the more they despise themselves and the more disgust they have for creatures.

3. Oh, if we would learn this method, so simple that it is right for us all, from the most coarse and ignorant to the most educated, how easily the whole church of God would be reformed! We only have to love. "Love and do what you will" (Saint Augustine).[1] For when we love, we cannot want to do anything that might displease our Beloved.

X. MORTIFICATION

1. I will say once more that it is impossible ever to arrive at perfect mortification of the senses and of the passions by any other way. The very natural reason is that it is the soul that gives strength and vigor to the senses, just as it is the senses that irritate or incite the passions. A dead person has neither sensations nor passions because of the separation existing between the soul and the senses. All the work done on the exterior always impels the soul outwardly toward the things on which it concentrates its efforts. The soul pours itself into them. Having directly applied austerity outwardly,

it is fully turned in that direction; thus, far from deadening the senses, it actually invigorates them.

The senses can only be invigorated by the application of the soul, which communicates more life to them to the extent that it is more in them. This life of the senses, far from extinguishing passions, agitates and irritates them. Austerity can weaken the body but never deadens the effect of the passions or their strength, for the reasons I have just given.

2. The single thing that can accomplish this is the soul turning inward, in order to focus on God, present there. If the soul turns all its strength and force inward, it separates itself from the senses by this single action, and, employing all its force and its strength within, it leaves the senses without strength. And the more it advances and approaches God, the more it is separated from itself. That is what happens to people for whom divine grace has a strong attraction; they become weak on the outside and are often incapacitated.

3. I do not mean by this that mortification is not necessary. However, mortification must always be accompanied by contemplation and be done according to strengths, the individual's state, and obedience. But I say that one's principal concern must not be mortification; neither should one become fixated on one austerity or another, but only follow one's inward leading and concern in the presence of God, without focusing on mortification in particular. God causes all sorts of them, and he does not give any relief whatsoever to souls who are faithful in giving themselves up to him, so as to mortify all there is to mortify in them. All that is necessary is to stay attentive to God and everything happens perfectly. Not everyone is capable of outward austerity, but everyone is capable of this.

There are two senses that one cannot mortify enough, sight and hearing, because these are the ones that produce all the forms of thought. God makes this happen; we only have to follow his spirit.

4. The soul enjoys a double advantage through this conduct; in the same measure that it is pulled away from the outside, it approaches God. In approaching God, apart from the fact that a secret strength and virtue are communicated to it, support it, and preserve it, the soul distances itself all the more from sin while approaching God and enjoys ongoing conversion.

XI. CONVERSION

1. "Return as you had deeply revolted, O children of Israel" (Isa 31:6). Conversion is nothing more than turning from the world in order to return to God. Conversion is only half perfect, albeit good and valuable for salvation, when it is simply turning from sin to grace. To be complete, there must be a turning away from the outside and a turning inward.

The soul, once turned toward God, has a great capacity to stay converted to God. The longer it stays converted, the more it moves toward God and becomes attached to him. And the more it moves toward God, the more it necessarily moves away from the creature, which is opposed to God. So much is the soul fortified in this conversion that the act of conversion becomes normal and natural.

We must know, however, that this does not happen by a violent exertion by the creature. The only exertion that it could or should make is through grace, making an effort to turn and recollect itself inwardly, after which a person only has to live turned toward God in continual adherence.

2. God has an attractive virtue, which always pulls the soul more strongly toward him and which, by pulling the soul in this way, purifies it, just as we see the sun draw a thick vapor up toward itself, until gradually the sun pervades it and purifies it, without any effort on the part of the vapor other than to let itself be drawn up while approaching the sun and leaving itself. There is, however, this difference, that vapor is not drawn freely and does not voluntarily follow, as the soul does. This way of turning inward is very easy and advances the soul quite naturally, without effort, because God is our depths. The depths always have a very strong attractive virtue. The more the depths are eminent and spiritual, the more their attraction is violent and impetuous, unable to be stopped.

3. More than the attractive virtue of the depths, all worldly creatures are given a strong inclination to reconnect with their depths in such a way that the most spiritual and perfect have this leading more strongly. As soon as a thing is turned toward its depths, unless some strong and vigorous force stops it, it moves in that direction with force. A stone thrown into the air is no sooner let go then it turns toward the earth that pulls it there by its own

weight, as toward its depths. It is the same with water and fire which, being left alone, move incessantly toward their depths.

But I say that the soul, by the effort that it puts forth to focus inwardly, turned toward the central leaning, falls toward its depths without any other effort than the weight of love. And the longer it remains peaceful and still, without any inner movement, the more it advances with speed because it gives a place to this attractive and central virtue in order to be drawn forcefully.

4. All our care, then, should be to focus inwardly as much as possible, not being surprised at the effort that we might need to do this exercise. It soon will be rewarded by remarkable cooperation on the part of God, who will make it easy, provided that we are faithful, bringing our hearts gently and sweetly through a small, gentle, and calm returning and through tender and peaceful affection when our soul is troubled by distractions and preoccupations. When passions rise, a gentle turning back to God, who is present, will easily put them out. All other resistance irritates these passions.

XII. ON CONTEMPLATION OF THE SIMPLE PRESENCE OF GOD

1. As we have seen, the soul faithful to this exercise through affection and love of its God is completely astonished that gradually it feels that he takes total possession of the soul itself. His presence becomes so easy that the soul enjoys it continuously. It receives it by habit, as well as through the act of contemplation. The soul feels the calm gradually take hold all by itself. Silence constitutes all its contemplative prayer. And God infuses it, which is the beginning of ineffable happiness. Oh, if I could pursue the infinite degrees to follow! But I must stop here, since this is only for beginners, while waiting for God to bring forth what could be useful to all the states.

2. We need to be satisfied, saying that it is of utmost importance to stop individual action and agency in order to let God operate. "Be still and see that I am God" (Ps 46:10), God himself told us through David.

But the creature is so in love with what it does that it believes that it is not doing anything if it cannot feel, know, or recognize its operation. It cannot see that the speed of its race does not allow the individual steps to be seen, and that the work of God, becoming more abundant, absorbs the work of the creature, just as we see the sun, as it rises, absorb bit by bit the light of the stars, which were quite visible before sunrise. It is not from a lack of light that we cannot see the stars anymore, but rather from an excess of light. The same is true here. The creature no longer distinguishes its operation because a strong, general light absorbs all the individual, small lights and makes them completely fade away because the excessive light surpasses all.

3. In the same way, those who criticize contemplation as being an act of laziness are making a big mistake. And it is through lack of experience that they say such a thing. Oh, if they would make an effort! In a little time they would be experienced and knowledgeable.

I say then that this lack of action does not come from deficiency, but from abundance. A person with experience would know that. This person will know that it is not a barren silence caused by deficiency, but a silence full and devoted, caused by abundance. David felt it when he said: "For he is my God and my savior: he is my protector, I shall be moved no more. In God alone there is rest for my soul" (Ps 62:2).

4. Two different kinds of people are quiet: the one from having nothing to say, and the other from having too much to say. It is the same here. We keep quiet because of excess, not lack.

Water causes two different kinds of death. One person dies of thirst; the other drowns. The one dies from scarcity, the other from abundance. Here, abundance causes certain operations to stop. It is therefore important to stay silent in this way for as long as one can, just as a small child attached to his mother's breast shows us sensibly. He starts to move his little lips to cause the milk to come. But when the milk comes in abundance, he is content to drink it with no more movement. If he does move, it will stop the process. He will cause the milk to spill and will have to stop. In this same way, in contemplative prayer we need to move our lips through affection. But when the milk of grace flows, there is nothing more to do than to stay at rest, swallowing gently, and when the milk stops coming, we must stir up a little affection, as the child moves his lips. The person who does differently will not profit from this grace.

5. What will happen to this child who drinks the milk gently in peace without moving? Who would believe that he is getting nourishment in this way? The more he nurses in peace, however, the more the milk will do him good. What happens to this child? He will fall asleep at his mother's breast. While in inward prayer the peaceful soul can often fall into mystical sleep, wherein all the powers are quiet until they enter by their state into that which is fleetingly given to them. You see that the soul is led here naturally without any discomfort, without thought, without artifice.

The interior is not a stronghold taken by the cannon, but instead by love. Thus, gently following this process in this manner, natural inward prayer will soon occur. God does not ask anything extraordinary or too difficult. On the contrary, a very simple and childlike procedure will please him extremely.

6. All the greatest things in religion are the easiest. The most necessary sacraments are the simplest. It is the same with natural things. Would you like to go to the sea? Get on a river and without noticing and without effort you will arrive there. Would you like to go to God? Take this sweet path, so easy, and in a little while you will arrive in a way that will amaze you.

Oh, if you would just try this! You would soon see that very little has been said about the experience and that your experience goes well beyond where people said it would. What are you afraid of? Let yourself be thrown promptly into the arms of Love, who stretched them out on the cross just to be able to receive you! What risk can there be in trusting God and giving yourself to him? It will not trick you but is a pleasant way, giving you much more than you expected. But those who have expected everything from themselves might hear this reproach that God makes through Isaiah, "You have been wearied by the multitude of your ways: yet you did not say: I will rest" (Isa 57:10).

XIII. REST

1. The soul having arrived at this point needs no preparation other than rest. Because it is here that the continual presence of God, the fruit of contemplation, begins to be infused almost continually. The soul enjoys, in its innermost self, an inestimable hap-

piness. It finds that God is more in the soul than the soul is itself. It only has to do one thing to find this presence: to look inward. As soon as a person closes his eyes, he will be taken up and engaged in contemplative prayer. The soul is amazed at this great gift and thus begins a conversation that the exterior does not interrupt.

2. We can say the same thing about contemplative prayer that the Book of Wisdom says: "Now all good things came to me together with her" (Wis 7:11). For virtues run joyfully in this soul that practices in a manner so easy that it seems to be completely natural. This way carries a seed of life and fertility, nourishing the soul in all that is good and rendering it insensitive to all that is bad.

Let the soul stay constantly in this state, guarding itself against looking for a method other than simple rest, whether it is in confession, communion, action, or contemplation. There is nothing more to do than let oneself be filled with a divine infusion.

I do not mean to speak of the formal preparation to take the sacraments, but only of the necessary internal disposition in taking them.

XIV. SILENCE

1. "Be subject to the Lord and pray to him" (Ps 37:7). The reason that inward silence is necessary is that the Word, being eternal and essential, needs the soul to have its same disposition in order for the soul to receive it. But it is certain that to receive the word we must lend an ear and listen. Hearing is the sense made to receive the word communicated to it. Hearing is a passive sense and not an active one, receiving and not communicating. The soul must be attentive to the Word communicating to it and reviving it.

2. This is why there are so many examples from scripture exhorting us to listen to God and to be attentive to his voice. We can cite many passages. Let us limit ourselves to the following:

"Listen to me, O my people, and give ear to me." (Isa 51:4)

"Listen to me, O house of Jacob, all the remnant of the house of Israel, who are carried by my bowels, are borne up by my womb." (Isa 46:3)

"Listen, O daughter, and see, and incline your ear: and forget your people and your father's house. And the king shall greatly desire your beauty." (Ps 45:10-11)

It is necessary to listen to God and to be attentive to him, forgetting oneself and all interest in other things. These two actions—or rather "passions," since they are completely passive—attract the love of beauty that he himself communicates. Listen and be attentive; forget yourself. Outward silence is quite necessary for the cultivation of inner silence, and it is impossible to become inward without loving silence and retreating. God tells us by the mouth of his prophet, "I will allure her, and will lead her into the wilderness: and I will speak to her heart" (Hos 2:14). How to be focused on God and be preoccupied with a thousand trifles? That is impossible. When weakness impels you to be busy on the outside, you need to make a little detour back inside. We need to remember to do this in all times of distraction and inattention. This means engaging in a little bit of contemplative prayer and focusing inward for one-half hour or one hour, if one does not remain continually in an attitude of devotion and in contemplative prayer during the whole day.

XV. CONFESSION AND SELF-EXAMINATION

1. Self-examination must always precede confession, but it must conform to the state of the soul. Those performing this act must show themselves before God, who will not fail to enlighten them and make them know the nature of their faults. This self-examination must necessarily be done in peace and tranquility, expecting more of God than of our own efforts in understanding our sins.

When we examine ourselves with our own effort, we misunderstand ourselves easily. We believe that good is bad and bad is good. And egotistical love easily tricks us. But when we stay exposed to God's eyes, it is like the sun exposing the smallest particles. It is therefore necessary to give oneself up to God often, as much for self-examination as for confession.

2. As soon as one is engaged in this type of contemplative prayer, God does not fail to admonish the soul for all of its faults. As soon as the soul has committed a fault, it feels a burning. This is an examination that God does, letting nothing escape. And the soul only has to turn itself to God, suffering the pain and correction that he brings about.

Since this examination is continual on God's part, the soul can no longer examine itself. It faithfully abandons itself to God and will be better examined by his light than by all of its own efforts. And the experience makes him know it well.

3. Regarding confession, be warned of one thing; that is, inward-looking people will often be surprised that while approaching the confessional and confessing their sins, instead of feeling the accustomed regret and contrition, they feel a sweet and tranquil love emanating from their heart.

Those who are not instructed want to get an act of contrition out of this because they have heard that this is necessary, which is true. But they will not see that they are losing a true act of contrition, which is innate love, infinitely greater than an act they could perform by themselves. They have a substantial act, although they do not have the formal one. Let them not be burdened trying to do this, when God does it in them, by them, and for them. To hate sin in this way is to hate it as God hates it. It is the purest love that God uses in this way, such that the soul does not hurry to act but remains just as it is, in the words of the sage, "trust in God, and stay in your place" (Ecclus 11:22).

4. The soul will also be amazed that it will forget its faults and that it will have trouble remembering them. This should not cause worry for two reasons. The first is that this forgetting is a mark of purification from the fault. It is best to forget ourselves, so as only to remember God. The second reason is that when it is confession time, God does not miss showing the soul its biggest shortcomings. So God himself makes the examination, and the soul will see that it will come out all the better than it would by its own best efforts.

5. This does not work for those in earlier stages of instruction, where the soul, being outwardly focused, must use its own efforts to

do all things, according to its stage of advancement. For souls at this degree, let them hold on to what they are told and not change their simple preoccupations.

It is the same for communion. Souls should let God act and remain silent. God cannot be better received than through God.

XVI. READING AND SPOKEN PRAYER

1. The way to read contemplatively is when the reader feels a little inward tug, this person should stop reading and wait peacefully, reading little and not continuing, unless feeling drawn to it.

2. The soul is not called into interior silence through taking up vocal prayers but instead by saying little. And when it says these prayers, if it finds it difficult and feels drawn to silence, let the soul stay there and let it not make any effort unless the prayers are required; in that case it would be necessary to continue. But if they are not necessary, then it feels itself drawn away and it has trouble saying them. Let the soul not be bothered and not be bound to them, but let the soul be drawn to the Spirit of God, which will satisfy all obligations in a very complete manner.

XVII. REQUESTS

1. The soul will find itself incapable of making prayer requests as it did so easily before. This should not be surprising, because "likewise the Spirit also helps our infirmity. For we know not what we should pray for as we ought; but the Spirit himself asks for us with unspeakable groanings" (Rom 8:26–27).

Let me say more; it is necessary to support God's plans, which are to empty the soul of its own operations in order to replace them with his will.

2. Let this happen. And do not let yourself be bound to anything. Although it seems good for you, it is not because it takes you away from God's will. Indeed, God's will is preferable to all other good. Practice detachment from the world and live to give yourself up to God and faith. It is here that faith begins to operate excellently in the soul.

XVIII. FAULTS

1. As soon as a person experiences a fault or a turning away from God it is necessary to focus inward, because this fault has turned us away from God, and as soon as possible we must turn ourselves to him and suffer any penance he gives us.

It is very important not to become concerned by these faults, because this concern comes from a secret pride and a love of ourselves as special. We are hurt by sensing what we are. If we feel discouraged, we further weaken ourselves. And thinking about a fault brings us greater distress than the fault itself did.

2. A truly humble soul is not surprised by its own shortcomings. The more it sees itself as miserable, the more it gives itself to God and tries to stay with him, understanding how much it needs God's help. We should follow this way, moreover, because God himself told us to do so; "I will give you understanding, and I will instruct you in this way, in which you will go: I will fix my eyes upon you" (Ps 32:8).

XIX. DISTRACTIONS AND TEMPTATIONS

1. Regarding distraction or temptations, instead of fighting them directly, which will only augment the problem and draw the soul away from its adherence to God's will, which must be our main concern, the soul must simply turn its gaze and move closer and closer to God, like a child who, seeing a monster, tries neither to fight it nor to look at it, but only turns to his mother's bosom where he finds comfort. "God is in the midst of it, it shall not be moved: God will help it in the morning early" (Ps 46:5).

2. Doing otherwise because we are weak and think that we are attacking our enemies, we often find ourselves wounded instead, or even utterly defeated. But remaining in the simple presence of God, we find ourselves instantly strengthened. It was that way with David; "I set," he said, "the Lord always in my sight: for he is at my right hand, that I shall not be moved. Therefore my heart has been glad, and my tongue has rejoiced" (Ps 16:8–9). It is said in Exodus, "The Lord will fight for you, and you will hold your peace" (Exod 14:14).

XX. PRAYER

1. Prayer must be both contemplation and sacrifice. Inward prayer, according to John's observation, is like incense whose smoke rises to God. That is why it is said in Revelation, "And the smoke of the incense of the prayers of the saints ascended up before God from the hand of the angel" (Rev 8:4).

Prayer is a pouring out of the heart in God's presence. "I have poured out my soul before the Lord," said the mother of Samuel (1 Sam 1:15). That is why the prayer of the Magi in the stable was represented by the incense they offered as gifts.

2. Prayer is simply the warmth of the love of God melting and dissolving the soul, making it soft, and causing it to rise up to God. As it melts, it sends up its odor, which comes from the charity that burns it.

This is what the bride meant when she remarked, "While the king was at his repose, my spikenard sent forth its odor" (Song 1:12). The place of repose is the depth of the soul. When God is present, and the person knows he lives in her and feels his presence, this presence of God melts and dissolves little by little the hardness of this soul, and while melting it, it gives off its perfume. That is why the bridegroom, seeing that his bride "opened to love," asked her, "Who is she that goes up by the desert, as a pillar of smoke of aromatic spices, of myrrh, and frankincense, and of all the powders of the perfumer?" (Song 3:6).

3. In the same way, this soul rises up to its God. But in order for that to happen it must let itself be destroyed and annihilated by the force of love. This is a state of essential sacrifice in the Christian religion by which the soul lets itself be destroyed and annihilated in order to pay homage to the sovereignty of God. As it is written, "For great is the power of God alone, and he is honored by the humble" (Ecclus 3:20). It is necessary to cease to be in order that the spirit of the word can be in us. But in order for the spirit to come it is necessary to give up our lives and die to ourselves, in order that he live in us.

Jesus Christ, in the holy sacrament of the altar, is the model for the mystical state. As soon as he is made present through the words of the priest, it necessary that the substance of the bread give up its place to Christ, with only simple outer appearance remaining. In the same way, it is necessary for us to give ourselves up to Jesus Christ and to give up our lives so that he lives in us, "For you are dead; and your life is hidden with Christ in God" (Col 3:3). "Come over to me," says God, "all you who desire me" (Ecclus 24:19). How to enter into God? It can only happen if we go outside of ourselves in order to lose ourselves in him; this can only happen through self-effacement. True prayer gives to God, "to the Lamb, benediction, and honor, and glory, and power, for ever and ever" (Rev 5:13).

4. This prayer is the prayer of truth. It is to "adore the Father in spirit and in truth" (John 4:23). It is to worship *in spirit* because we are drawn away from our human and carnal manner of acting to enter into the pureness of the spirit that prays for us. And it is to worship *in truth* because the soul enters into the truth that God is all and the creature is nothing.

There are only two truths, all and nothing. All the rest is a lie. We can only honor the all of God by denying ourselves. And through this denial God fills us up with himself.

Oh, if we only knew the good coming to the soul from contemplative prayer, we would not do anything else. It is "the precious pearl;" it is the "hidden treasure." When he "had found one pearl of great price," he "went his way, and sold all that he had, and bought it" (Matt 13:46). It is the "rivers of living water springing up into eternal life" (John 7:38). It is "to worship God in spirit and in truth" (John 4:23). It is to practice the purest maxims of the Bible.

5. Does Jesus Christ not assure us that "the kingdom of God is within you" (Luke 17:21)? This kingdom can be understood in two ways. The first is when God is so strong a force in us that we no longer resist him, and thus our inner being is truly his kingdom. The other way is that, possessing God who is the Sovereign Good, we possess the kingdom of God, which represents the ultimate happiness and the end for which we were created. Thus it is said: to serve God is to reign. The end for which we were created is to find joy in God in this life, and we do not even realize it!

XXI. THAT WE ACT MORE STRONGLY AND NOBLY BY CONTEMPLATIVE PRAYER THAN ANY OTHER WAY

1. When some people hear of silence in contemplative prayer, they are mistakenly persuaded that the soul remains dull, dead, and inactive. No, be assured it acts more nobly and strongly. It is transformed and acts by the Spirit of God. Paul wants us to be "led by the Spirit of God" (Rom 8:14).

We do not say that one cannot act, but it is necessary to do so according to the inspiration of grace. This is a focal point of Ezekiel. The prophet, seeing this, says, "For the spirit of life was in the wheels" and "When those went these went, and when those stood these stood, and when those were lifted up from the earth, the wheels also were lifted up together, and followed them: for the spirit of life was in the wheels" (Ezek 1:19-21). The soul must be like this. It must let itself be moved and acted upon by the life-giving spirit that is in it, following only the movement of this action and no other. But this movement is never called to go back, meaning to reflect on the world, but to always go forward, advancing incessantly toward its end.

2. This action of the soul is an action full of rest. When the soul acts by itself, it acts with effort. This is why the soul knows when it is in action. But when it acts by the spirit of grace, its action is so free, so easy, so natural, that it seems as though it is doing nothing. "And he brought me forth into a large place: he saved me, because he was well pleased with me" (Ps 18:19).

The moment the soul is leaning toward its depths, meaning that it is turned toward itself through recollecting, it is pulled to these depths with a force infinitely surpassing the speed of all other action, nothing equaling the speed of the leading toward the depths.

It is therefore an action, but an action so noble, so peaceful, so tranquil, that it seems to the soul that it is not acting because it moves completely naturally. When a wheel is only moving at half speed, we notice it. But when it moves at full speed, we no long notice anything about it. The soul resting in peace with God has a noble and exalted action but is also very peaceful. The more the

81

soul is at peace, the more it moves with greater speed because it is dwelling in the Spirit, which propels it and which causes it to go.

3. This spirit is nothing other than God who attracts us and in attracting us makes us run to him, as the divine lover knew when she said, "Draw me: we will run" (Song 1:4). Draw me, my divine depth, from the deepest part of myself. Let my powers and senses run to you through this attraction! Only this attraction can be an unguent that heals and a perfume that draws. "We run," she says "to the odor of your ointments." It is a virtue that attracts, but a virtue the soul follows very freely. It is both strong and sweet; it attracts by its strength and elevates by its sweetness. The bride says, "Draw me." She is talking to herself about herself. "*Draw me*" refers to the unity in the depths that attracts. "*Let us run*" refers to the interdependence and the path of all the powers and senses following the attraction to the depths of the soul.

4. It is therefore not a question of idleness, but of acting by dependence on the Spirit of God who must love us, since it is "in him we live, and move, and are" (Acts 17:28). This dependence on the Spirit of God is absolutely necessary and makes the soul, in a short time, arrive at the simplicity and unity for which it was created.

It was created one and simple, like God. It is necessary to leave the multiplicity of our actions in order to arrive at the goal of its creation, in order to enter into simplicity and unity with God, "and God created man in his own image" (Gen 1:27). God is one and multiple, and his unity does not prevent his multiplicity. We are one when we are united in his Spirit, sharing the same Spirit as him. And we can be very active outwardly when we continue to follow his will and not depart from this unity. The result is that we act much more with God acting infinitely and with us letting ourselves be moved by God's Spirit than we do by our own individual action.

It is necessary that we let ourselves be driven by Wisdom. This Wisdom "is more active than all active things" (Wis 7:24). Let us remain dependent on his action, acting very strongly.

5. "All things were made by him: and without him was made nothing that was made" (John 1:3). God, in creating us, created us in his "image and likeness" (Gen 1:26). He inspired the spirit of the word in us by this "breath of life" he gave us when we were created

in the image of God through the participation of this life in the Word, who is the image of his father. But this life is one, simple, pure, intimate, always abundant.

The devil, having spoiled and disfigured this beautiful image through sin, caused the Word, whose spirit inspired us in creating us, to come and repair this image. It had to be him because he is the image of his Father, and the image is not repaired through action but through suffering the action of the one who came to repair it.

Our action must be to put ourselves in a state of suffering God's action, wherein the Word retraces his image in us. An image that constantly moves prevents the painter from painting it. All movement we make by our own spirit prevents this admirable painter from doing his work and causes false strokes. Thus, we need to remain at peace and to move only when he moves us. This was David's sentiment and his practice; "But as for me," he said, "I will appear before your sight in justice: I shall be satisfied when your glory shall appear" (Ps 17:15). Jesus Christ has "life in himself" (John 5:26). And he must communicate life to all things.

This is the spirit of the church, the spirit of divine motion. Is the church idle, sterile, and barren? It acts, but it acts by dependence on the Spirit of God, who moves it and governs it. The spirit of the church must not be different from that of its members, who represent it. Therefore, it is necessary for its members to operate in the spirit of the church through the Spirit of divine action.

6. That this action is more noble is incontestable. It is certain that things only have value insofar as the spring from which they arise is noble, grand, and uplifting. Actions accomplished through the divine principle are divine actions, whereas the actions of the creature, however good they might appear, remain human actions and only become virtuous when they are performed through grace.

Jesus Christ says that he is life. All other beings are only borrowed life, but the Word has life in himself. And since his nature is a communicative one, he desires to communicate to humans. It is necessary then to give a place to this life, which can only happen through the cleaning out and the loss of the life of Adam and of our own action. As Paul assures us, "If then any be in Christ a new creature, the old things are passed away, behold all things are made new" (2 Cor 5:17). This can only happen through the death of ourselves and of our own actions, so that the action of God is substituted in its place.

One does not claim not to act, but only to act through a dependence on the Spirit of God, in order to give room to his own action to take the place of the creature's action. This can only happen with human consent. And humans only give this consent by modifying their actions in order gradually to let the action of God take over.

7. Jesus Christ, in the Bible, makes us see this way of being. Martha did good works, but because she did them only by her own will, Jesus admonishes her for it. The spirit of man is turbulent and troubled. That is why it accomplishes little, although it appears to do a lot. "Martha," said Jesus, "Martha, you are filled with care and troubled about many things. But one thing is necessary. Mary has chosen the best part, which shall not be taken away from her" (Luke 10:41–42). What did Mary Magdalene choose? Peace, tranquility, and rest. She stopped her apparent actions in order to leave the movement to the spirit of Jesus Christ. She stops living so that Jesus Christ lives in her.

That is why renouncing ourselves and our own operations is so necessary in following Jesus Christ, because we can only follow Christ if his spirit animates us. But for the spirit of Jesus Christ to come into us, we must give it space within us. "But he who is joined to the Lord," says Paul, "is one spirit" (1 Cor 6:17). And David said, "It is good for me to adhere to my God, to put my hope in the Lord God" (Ps 73:28). What is this attachment? It is the beginning of a union.

8. The union begins, continues, finishes, and is consumed. The beginning of the union comes by way of a leaning. When the soul is turned in toward itself, as we have seen, it has a leaning toward its depths and has a strong tendency toward union. This tendency is the beginning. Then, it attaches as it approaches more closely to God. Afterward, it is united. And then it becomes one, which means becoming one in spirit with him. That is when this spirit, having sprung from God, returns to its end.

9. It is then necessary to enter into this path, which is divine motion and the spirit of Jesus Christ. Saint Paul says, "Now if any man does not have the Spirit of Christ, he is none of his" (Rom 8:9).

In order to be in Jesus Christ, it is necessary for us to fill ourselves with his spirit and to be empty of ourselves; we must be thoroughly purged. Paul, in the same passage, proves to us the necessity of this divine motion. "For whoever is led," he says, "by the Spirit of God, they are the sons of God" (Rom 8:14). The spirit of this divine heritage is the spirit of divine motion. That is why the same apostle continues, "For you have not received the spirit of bondage again in fear; but you have received the spirit of adoption of sons, whereby we cry: Abba (Father)" (Rom 8:15). This spirit by which we participate in this inheritance is none other than the spirit of Jesus Christ. "For the Spirit himself gives testimony to our spirit, that we are the sons of God" (Rom 8:16).

As soon as the soul lets itself be moved by the spirit of God, it feels in itself the evidence of this divine heritage. And this is the evidence that fills it all the more with joy, so that it makes it know better that it is "called to the freedom of the children of God" (cf. Gal 5:13; Rom 8:21) and that "the spirit that it has received is not a spirit of servitude but of freedom." The soul feels then that it acts freely and gently, although forcefully and infallibly.

10. The spirit of divine motion is so necessary for all things that Saint Paul assures us in the same passage of this necessity, which he even justifies concerning our ignorance about things that we request. "Likewise the Spirit" he says, "also helps our infirmity. For we know not what we should pray for as we ought; but the Spirit himself asks for us with unspeakable groanings" (Rom 8:26). This is positive; if we do not know what we need or how we should ask for what we need, and the spirit which is in us, through the motion to which we abandon ourselves, asks it for us, should we not let this happen? He does this with ineffable groans.

This is the spirit of the Word, which is always answered as he says himself; "I knew that you hear me always" (John 11:42). If we let ourselves ask and pray through this spirit in us, we will always be answered. And why is that? Teach it to us, grand apostle, mystical doctor, and master of the interior. "He that searches the hearts," says Paul, "knows what the Spirit desires; because he asks for the saints according to God" (Rom 8:27). That is to say that this spirit only asks for what conforms to God's will. The will of God is that we be saved and that we be perfect. He then asks for what is necessary for our perfection.

11. Why, after that, overwhelm ourselves with superfluous cares and make us to be "wearied in the multitude of [our] ways: yet…[saying] not: I will rest" (Isa 57:10)? And he complains in Isaiah with inconceivable goodness about how we use the forces of the soul, which are our riches and treasure, in a thousand outward things, seeing that there is so little to do in order to enjoy the good things that we search after; "Why," says God, "do you spend money for that which is not bread, and your labor for that which does not satisfy you? Listen diligently to me, and eat that which is good, and your soul shall be delighted in fatness" (Isa 55:2).

Oh, if we only knew the happiness there is in listening to God in this way and how much the soul would be filled! "Let all flesh be silent at the presence of the Lord" (Zech 2:13). It is necessary that everything cease as soon as he appears. God, in order to make us abandon ourselves to him without reserve, assures us in Isaiah that we should fear nothing in abandoning ourselves to him because he cares for each of us individually. "Can a woman forget her infant," says God, "so as not to have pity on the son of her womb? and if she should forget, yet I will not forget you" (Isa 49:15). Oh, words full of consolation! After this who will fear to abandon himself to the will of God?

XXII. OF THE ACT

1. The act is an action that is good, useless, or criminal. There are external acts and internal acts. External acts are those that appear on the outside, relating to a sensible object and bearing goodness or moral malice only as a result of the interior principle from which they are sprung. This is not what I want to talk about. That is an exterior act. The inward act is an action of the soul turning itself toward the object from which it is turned away.

2. If I am turned toward God and if I want to perform an act, I turn myself away from God and I turn myself more or less to the things of the world, making my action more or less strong accordingly. If I am turned toward the world, it is necessary for me to perform an act by turning myself away from the world and turning

myself to God. The more perfect the act is, the more complete the conversion with God is.

Until the point that I am perfectly converted, I need to perform the act of turning myself toward God. Certain people do it all at once, others little by little. My act must bring me to turn myself toward God, using all the force of my soul for this act, following the advice of Ecclesiasticus: "In all your works regard your soul in faith" (Ecclus 32:23), and acting as David did: "I will keep my strength to you" (Ps 59:9), which refers to returning inward to oneself, as the scripture says: "Return, you transgressors, to the heart" (Isa 46:8).

Because we are removed from our hearts due to sin, it is necessary to return to our hearts. God only asks for our hearts: "My son, give me your heart: and let your eyes keep my ways" (Prov 23:26). To give one's heart to God and always to have the gaze, the strength, the vigor of the soul attached to him so as to follow his wishes is what is meant by the act. The act makes us turn toward God. It is necessary to remain turned there as soon as one is so turned. Thus, if I perform acts, then I turn myself away from him.

But how light the spirit of humans is and how easily the soul, accustomed to being turned outward, dissipates itself and turns itself away. As soon as it notices that it has turned itself away to exterior things, it is necessary by a simple act to return to God. Then its act subsists as long as its conversion continues, by virtue of returning to God through a simple and sincere returning.[2]

3. As many repeated acts become routine, the soul takes on the routine of conversion. As a result, the act becomes habitual and not isolated. The soul does not have to begin this act formally because the act is ongoing. And the soul will not be able to find the act there without much difficulty. It even finds that it would leave its state in order to do so, which it must never do, because the act subsists habitually. Then it is in a state of habitual conversion and love. Thus, the formal act cannot always subsist and must give way to the habitual.

One will notice that at certain times one will particularly enjoy doing certain acts, but it is simply a sign that one has taken a detour. One returns to the heart from which one had strayed. But one stays there in peace when one has returned there. This is to understand the acts on which all others depend, because when one says that it is wrong to perform acts, one is mistaken, but one must only perform them according to one's degree.

In order to shed light on this point that causes the most spiritual difficulty, due to lack of understanding, it is necessary to know that there are formal acts, which are individual and distinct, and substantial acts, which are continual, direct acts, and reflected acts. Not all can do formal acts and not all are in a state to do the others.

4. Formal acts are necessary for people who are turned away from God. They turn by a distinct act, more or less forcefully in proportion to how strong their relationship to God is. Thus, a simple act suffices if the distance from God is small.

5. There are substantial acts where the soul is always turned toward God by a direct act, which, unless interrupted, is not renewed and yet endures. The soul, if I may say, is in charity and remains there. "And he that abides in charity, abides in God" (1 John 4:16). Thus, the soul is in the routine of performing this type of action, remaining in this same act.

But its rest is not idle. For an act is always occurring that is entirely in God, with God attracting the soul always more strongly. And the soul, following this very strong attraction while staying in love and in charity, goes ever deeper into this love and has an action infinitely stronger, more vigorous, and swifter than the act that represents a turning away from God.

6. But the soul, being completely turned toward its God during this profound and strong act, does not notice this act because it is direct and performed without reflection. Thus, a person in this state, not explaining the situation well, says, "I do not perform any act." But, this person is mistaken, because he cannot do any more or any better. He should have said, "I no longer distinguish acts," instead of "I do not perform any act."

The soul does not perform these acts by itself, I agree, but it is drawn and follows what draws it. Love is the weight that pulls it, as a person falling into the sea would get pulled farther and farther down to infinity, if the sea were indeed infinite, and would descend to this most profound space at an incredible speed without noticing this plunging.

It is erroneous to say that we do not perform acts. Everyone performs acts, but not everyone performs them in the same way, and the mistake comes when those who know and understand that they perform acts want to do them formally. That cannot be done. Formal ones are for beginners, and the others are for advanced souls. To stop at the acts for beginners, which are weak and advance a person little, means to deprive oneself of the latter ones. In the same way, those who want to do the latter ones before having passed by the first cannot, and that results in another type of mistake.

7. It is necessary that "all things have their season" (Eccles 3:1). Each state has its beginning, its development, and its end. If a person always wants to stop at the beginning, it shows contempt of self. There is no art without its own progress. At the beginning, a person needs to put forth a lot of effort, but later this person will be able to enjoy the fruit of this labor.

When a boat is at port, sailors have to work hard at launching it. But then they easily turn it to where they want it to go. When the soul is still in sin and preoccupied with worldly things, it takes a lot of effort to draw the soul away from this port, and the lines attaching it to the world must be untied. Then, returning through strong and vigorous acts, trying to attract the soul to the inside and distancing it little by little from its own port, one turns it inside, by the very act of distancing it, to the place where one desires to travel.

8. When the boat is turned in this way, as it advances out to sea, it goes farther and farther from land. The farther it is from land, the less effort it takes to move along. Finally, we start to sail very gently, and the boat moves so swiftly that we can stop working the oars because they are useless. What does a captain do then? He is happy to spread the sails and to be at the helm.

To spread the sails means to do the simple, inward prayer of exposing yourself to God, to be transformed by his spirit. *To be at the helm* means to prevent our heart from straying from the right way, steering it gently, and leading it according to the movement of the Spirit of God, who gradually fills this heart, as the wind comes gradually to fill the sails and push the boat. As long as the boat has the wind aft, the captain and the sailors rest from their work. What progress is made without growing tired! They make more progress in one hour while resting in this way and letting the boat be guided by the wind than they made with all of their preliminary efforts. If they did want to keep rowing, besides causing fatigue, their efforts would also be useless, actually retarding the progress of the boat.

That is the guidance that we must maintain for our inner self, and, by acting in this way, we will advance more in a short time by divine motion than by our best efforts. If one takes this route, one will find it the easiest in the world.

9. When there is a crosswind, if the wind and the storm are strong, we must toss the anchor in the sea to stop the boat. This *anchor* is nothing more than confidence in God and the hope in his goodness, waiting in patience for the calm after the storm and for a favorable wind to return, as David did. "With expectation I have waited," he said, "for the Lord, and he was attentive to me" (Ps 40:1). It is then necessary to abandon ourselves to the spirit of God and to let ourselves be led by his movements.

XXIII. PREACHERS AND PASTORS

1. If all those who work on the conquest of souls tried to win them over by the heart, engaging them first in inward prayer, it would make conversions infinitely more durable. But insomuch as they focus only on outward acts and, instead of drawing souls to Jesus Christ by preoccupying the heart with him, those people are only charged with a thousand precepts for exterior exercises, this yields little fruit and does not endure.

If the country clerics had the zeal to instruct their parishioners like this, the shepherds guarding their sheep would have the spirit of the ancient contemplatives, and the workers, in leading the base of the plow, would get along happily with God. The manual laborers who are consumed with work would focus on working for eternal fruit. All vices would be banished in a short amount of time, and all parishioners would become spiritual.

2. Oh, when the heart is won, all the rest corrects itself easily. That is why God asks foremost for the heart. Through this, one would eliminate the drunkenness, blasphemy, imprudence, hostilities, and larceny that ordinarily reign over people in all countries. Jesus Christ would reign peacefully everywhere, and the face of the church would be renewed at every juncture.

Heresies have entered into the world by the loss of the inner life. If the interior were reestablished, heresies would soon be ruined. Oh, inestimable losses created by neglecting the inner life! Oh, what number of persons who are charged with souls would not have to seek God's forgiveness for not having shared this hidden treasure through their ministry of the word!

3. One makes the excuse that there is danger in this way or that simple people are incapable of spiritual things. The oracle of truth assures us that the contrary is true: "They that deal faithfully," he says, "please him" (Prov 12:22). But what danger can there be in walking in the unique way of Jesus Christ, giving oneself to him, looking at him ceaselessly, putting all confidence in his grace, and holding on with all our strength to his pure love?

4. Far from simple people being incapable of this perfection, they are far more capable of it. Because they are more docile, more humble, more innocent, and by not relying on reason, they are not misguided by their own egos. Moreover, not being well educated, they are more easily moved by the spirit of God, while others are affected or blinded by their own sense of self-reliance and resist divine inspiration much more.

Also, God tells us that "the declaration of your words gives light: and gives understanding to little ones" (Ps 119:130). He assures us again that "his communication is with the simple" (Prov 3:32). "The Lord is the keeper of little ones: I was little and he delivered me" (Ps 116:6). Let the fathers of souls not prevent the little children from going to Jesus Christ. "Suffer the little children," he says to his apostles, "and do not forbid them to come to me: for the kingdom of heaven is for such" (Matt 19:14). Jesus Christ only tells this to his apostles because they wanted to prevent children from coming to him.

5. Often one applies a remedy to the body when the illness is in the heart. The reason that one succeeds so little in reforming people, especially those who work, is that one focuses on external things, and all that one can do there happens immediately. But if one gives them first the key to inner life, the outside will then transform itself with a natural ease.

But this is very easy. Teach them to look for God in their hearts, to think about him, to return there when distracted, to do everything and to suffer everything with the goal of pleasing him, that is, to affix them to the source of all grace and to help them find all that is necessary for their sanctification.

6. You are entreated, O all who serve souls, to put them first in the way, which is Jesus Christ, and it is he whom you should entreat by all the blood he shed for these souls put under your care. "Speak to the heart of Jerusalem" (Isa 40:2). O dispensers of his graces! O preachers of his Word! O ministers of his sacraments! Establish his kingdom! And to establish it truly, make it reign in their hearts! For since it is only the heart that opposes his empire, it is by the subjection of the heart that one most honors his sovereignty. "Sanctify the Lord of hosts himself...and he shall be a sanctification to you" (Isa 8:13–14). Do specific lessons on contemplative prayer, not through reason or through a method (simple people not being capable of it), but a prayer of the heart and not the head, a prayer of the spirit of God and not the invention of man.

7. Alas! One wants to perform studied prayers. And by wanting to refine too much, one makes them impossible. One has taken children from the best of all fathers in order to have them learn a language that is too polite. Go, poor children, speak to your celestial Father in your natural language; however barbarous and uneducated it might be, it is not so for him. A father prefers a discourse disordered by love and respect because he sees that these words come from the heart more than a dry speech, vain and sterile, however educated it might be. Oh, how certain glances of love charm and ravish! They express infinitely more than all language and reasoning.

8. Alas, for having wanted to learn this love without measure through a method, we have lost the love! Oh, it is not necessary to learn the art of loving! The language of love is barbarous to those who do not love. But it is very natural to the one who loves. And a person does not learn to love God any better than through the act of loving him. In this work, often those least educated become the most adept because they come to it more simply and easily. The Spirit of God does not need these refinements. When he wants, he can take shepherds and make prophets of them. And far from closing the palace to the inward prayer of someone simple, as we are imagining, on the contrary he leaves all the doors open to everyone,

and wisdom is commanded to cry out in public places: "Whoever is a little one, let him come to me," and "to the unwise she said: Come, eat my bread, and drink the wine which I have mingled for you" (Prov 9:4–5). Does Jesus Christ not thank his Father for hiding "these things from the wise and prudent, and…reveal[ing] them to the little ones" (Matt 11:25)?

XXIV. WHAT IS THE SUREST WAY OF ARRIVING AT DIVINE UNION?

1. It is impossible to arrive at divine union only by way of meditation for several reasons, some of which I will address.

First, according to scripture, "You cannot see my face: for man shall not see me and live" (Exod 33:30). But all practice of spoken contemplative prayer or active contemplation, seen as an end and not as a disposition to passivity, are living practices by which we cannot see God, meaning being united with him. It is necessary for all that comes from man and his own industry to die, however noble and elevated it might be.

Saint John reports "there was silence in heaven" (Rev 8:1). Heaven represents the base and the depths of the soul where it is necessary that everything be silent so that the majesty of God appears. It is necessary that all efforts of the self and the sense of self be destroyed. For nothing is more opposed to God then a sense of self, and all the malignancy of man is in this sense of self that is so identified with it. In this way, the more the soul loses this sense of self the more it becomes pure. And what would be a flaw in a soul living for itself is not in this one because of the purity and the innocence acquired when it lost its sense of self, which would cause dissimilarity between the soul and God.

2. But only God can unify two such opposite things as his purity and the impurity of the creature, the simplicity of God and the multiplicity of man. This can never happen by the efforts of the creature, because two things can only be united if there is a resemblance, just as an impure metal will never fuse with pure and refined gold.

3. What does God do then? He sends his own wisdom before him, like a fire coming to earth to consume all that is impure by its

activity. Fire consumes all things, and nothing that it consumes resists it. It is the same way with wisdom. It consumes all impurity in the creature in order to open it up to God's union.

This impurity so opposed to the union is sense of self and activity. Sense of self: because it is the source of real impurity, which can never be allied with essential purity, just as the sunbeam can touch the mud, but not be unified with it. Activity: because God being in infinite rest, the soul must be in rest before being unified with him. Without this, union can never occur because of dissimilarity. Then, in order to unite these two things, they must be in proportional rest.

This is why the soul only arrives at divine union through the resting of its will. And it can only be united with God if it is in a central rest and in the purity of its creation.

4. In order to purify the soul God uses Wisdom in the same way that fire purifies gold. Certainly gold can only be purified by fire that gradually consumes all of the earthen and foreign materials and separates them from the gold. The gold cannot change the earth into gold. It is necessary moreover that the fire melt and dissolve the gold in order to take from the substance all that remains that is foreign and earthen. And this gold is put in the fire so many times that it loses all impurity and all capacity to be purified. The goldsmith no longer finds a mixture because of this perfect state of purity and simplicity, and the fire can no longer act on this gold. And it would not be any more pure a century later, and it would not be diminished. Thus, it is ready to make the most excellent pieces of work.

And if this gold is impure afterward, I say that the impurity is dirt picked up through contact with foreign bodies. But there is this difference—that this impurity is only superficial and does not prevent it from being useful. In contrast, the other impurity was hidden in the depths, as if identified with the gold's nature. However, people who do not know any better will be less impressed seeing pure gold covered with dirt on the outside than with a tainted gold piece that is very impure but has a polished exterior.

5. Moreover, you will notice that the gold with an inferior degree of purity cannot bond with that of superior purity. It is necessary that the one either be infected by the impurity of the other,

or that the latter participate in the purity of the former. To put purified gold with a lesser gold is something a goldsmith would never
do. What would he do? He would rid the gold of earthen admixture
by firing it so as to be able to bond it to the pure gold. And that is
what Saint Paul says, "Every man's work will be manifest; for the
day of the Lord will declare it, because it will be revealed in fire; and
the fire will try every man's work, of what sort it is" (1 Cor 3:13–15).
He adds, "If any man's work burn, he shall suffer loss; but he himself will be saved, yet so as by fire." This means that there are some
welcome works that are acceptable. But in order for the ones who
did them to become pure, it is necessary that they pass through the
fire so that the sense of self is taken away. And that has the same
meaning as when God will examine and "will judge justices" (Ps
75:2). For humans will never be "sanctified by the works of the law"
but by "the justice of God, by faith of Jesus Christ, unto all and
upon all them that believe in him" (Rom 3:22).

6. Given this, let me say that for man to be united to God, it
is necessary that his Wisdom accompany divine Justice, as an
unpitying, devouring fire takes from the soul all that there is of a
sense of self, of earthliness, of the carnal, and of the active. And
once he has taken all of this from the soul, he unites with it. This is
never done through the willing efforts of the creature; indeed, it
suffers regret because, as I said, man loves his sense of self and fears
its destruction so much that if God did not take up the task himself,
man would never agree to do it.

7. One might respond to all this by saying that God never
takes freedom away from man, and as such he can always resist God,
and that I should never say God takes over absolutely without the
consent of man. Let me explain myself and say that a passive consent suffices for man to have complete and full freedom because,
having given himself to God from the beginning, in order that God
do all that God wants in and through him, he consents actively and
implicitly to all that God might do. But when God destroys, burns,
and purifies, the soul does not see the advantages. Quite the contrary. Just as the fire at the beginning dirties the gold, this operation
seems to take away the soul's purity, so that if the soul needed to
give active and explicit consent to this process, it would not give it.

All that the soul does is consent passively, doing its best to undergo this operation that it neither can nor wants to prevent.

8. God, therefore, purifies this soul so much from its own distinct, noticeable, multiple operations, which cause very great disparity, that in the end he makes it conform little by little and finally makes it uniform, raising up the passive capacity of the creature, enlarging it and ennobling it in a hidden and unknown way, which is why it is called mystical. But it is necessary that all of the soul's operations function passively.

It is true that before getting to this point, it is necessary that it act more at the beginning. Then in the same measure that the operation of God becomes stronger, it is necessary little by little and successively that the soul surrender to him until he absorbs it completely. But this takes a long time.[3]

9. That is why we do not say, then, as some have believed, that we must not do this through action, because, on the contrary, that is actually the door. But we only say that one should not remain there, understanding that people must keep working toward the end of perfection and that it can only be reached by leaving the first steps, which were necessary as an introduction to the way, and which will obliterate the person afterward if they are still adhered to stubbornly, preventing the person from reaching the end. That is what Saint Paul did; "forgetting the things that are behind, and stretching forth myself to those that are before, I press toward the mark" (Phil 3:13–14).

And would one not say that a person would seem to have lost her mind if, while taking a trip, she decided to remain at the first hotel because of others' assurance that many have passed by there, some have stayed there, and the owners remain the same? Therefore, what one wants for these souls is for them to advance on their journey, for them to take the shortest, easiest route, and for them not to stop at their first juncture and to follow Saint Paul's advice: "For all who are led by the Spirit of God" (Rom 8:14) are led to the end for which they were created, which is to enjoy God.

10. Knowing that we were created only for this end and that each soul who does not arrive at divine union and at the purity of its creation in this life will burn in purgatory in order to acquire this purity, it is strange that we do not tolerate God's leading us there in

this life—as if that which leads us to perfection in glory must cause harm and imperfection in this mortal life.

11. No one can ignore the sovereign Good that is God, that the essential beatitude is union with God and that the saints are more or less saintly according to how perfect this union is. This union cannot be a result of any of the soul's activity, since God only communicates with the soul insomuch as its passivity is great, noble, and wide. No one can be united with God without passivity and simplicity. And this union being the beatitude itself, this way that carries us cannot be bad. On the contrary it is the best of all ways.

12. All can proceed there just as all are called to the beatitude; all are called to enjoy God both in this life and in the other. I say this is from God himself and not from his gifts, which cannot bring about the essential beatitude and are not able to satisfy the soul fully. And the soul is so noble and so great that all the most precious gifts of God would not be able to make the soul as happy as if God gave of himself. God's whole desire is to give himself to his creature, according to the capacity that he accorded it, and yet we still fear to give ourselves to God. Are we afraid to possess him and have divine union at our disposal?

13. One might say we must never put ourselves in that position. I agree. And I say that none of God's creatures can ever find itself in that position, since no creature in the world can be united with God by its own efforts; it is necessary that God unite himself with it. If we alone cannot unite ourselves with God, then when we cry out against such creatures who try to do this themselves, we are really crying out against imaginary monsters!

One might say that a person could feign this union. But I say that this cannot be feigned, since one who is dying of hunger cannot pretend to be well fed over a long period of time. There will always be a certain desire or envy that will escape and will show that this person is far from his pretended end.

Since no one can arrive at this end by pure will, it is not a question of introducing anyone to it, but of showing the path that leads there and insisting that one does not hold on to or stay attached to refuges or practices that one must leave when the signal is given, such as is known by the experienced guide who shows the living water and who tries to introduce it to others. And would it not be punishable cruelty to show the spring to a thirsty person and then to keep her tied up and prevented from going there, leaving her instead to die of thirst?

14. That is what we do today. Let us all agree on the way and agree to follow it to the end, which cannot be doubted. The way has its beginning, its progression, and its end. The more we advance toward the end, the more we necessarily leave the beginning behind. And it is impossible to arrive by going only a little distance away or by passing through a door to a faraway place without passing through the middle. This is incontestable.

If the end is indeed good, holy, and necessary, and if the door is good, then why would the path coming from the door and leading straight to the end be bad? Oh, how blindly most men boast of their knowledge and intelligence! Oh, it is true, my God, that you have "hidden your secrets from the learned and the clever, to reveal them to the little children" (Luke 10:21)!

COMMENTARY ON THE
SONG OF SONGS OF SOLOMON
Interpreted According to the Mystical Sense
and the True Representation of Inner States

CHAPTER 1

Let him kiss me with the kiss of his mouth: for your breasts are better than wine. (1:1)[1]

The kiss that the soul requests from her God is essential union, or real, lasting, and permanent possession, coming from the divine object; this is spiritual marriage. In order to understand this, it is necessary to explain the difference between the union of powers and the essential union. Both of these unions can be either passing (only lasting a few moments) or permanent and lasting. The union of powers is the one by which God unites very superficially with the soul; he is touching it rather than uniting with it. It is, however, united with the persons in the Trinity, according to the different effects that are appropriate to them, but always as distinct persons and by a mediated operation. This operation serves here as both a means and an end, in that the soul rests in this union that it feels, not believing that it should go any further. This union is accomplished in a certain order, in each of the powers of the soul, and at any given time the soul may notice it in one or two of them, according to God's design, and at other times in all three together. This makes the soul relate to the Holy Trinity as distinct persons. When this union is in the intellect only, it is the union of pure knowing and is attributed to the Word, as a distinct person. When the union is in the memory, which happens by the absorption of the soul in God and a profound forgetting of creatures, it is attributed to the Father, as a distinct person. And when it takes place in the will alone, by a loving pleasure, without either seeing or distinctly understanding, it is the union of love, attributed to the Holy Spirit, as a distinct person. And this is the most perfect of all because it approaches more than any other the essential union, and it is principally by this way that the soul arrives there. All these unions are divine embraces, but the point has not yet come for the kiss on the mouth.

There are two types of unions: one is fleeting, which only lasts a very short time, and the other is permanent, which is sustained by a continual presence of God and by sweet and tranquil love abiding in everything. Here, in a few words, is what constitutes the union of powers; it is a union of the betrothed and has much of the heart's affection and the caresses and the reciprocal presents of fiancées, but it does not yet have the perfect pleasure of the object.

The essential union and the kiss on the mouth is the spiritual marriage, where there is a union of essence to essence and communication of substances and where God takes the soul for his Bride and unites with it, no longer personally or by any act or means, but immediately, reducing all into unity and possessing it in the unity itself. It is therefore the kiss of the mouth, and the real and perfect possession. It is a pleasure not at all sterile or fruitless, since it signifies nothing less than the communication of the Word of God to the soul.

It is necessary to know that God is all mouth, just as he is all word, and that the application of this divine mouth to the soul is perfect pleasure and the consummation of the marriage, by which the communication of God himself and his Word happens in this soul. It is what we can call the apostolic state, by which the soul is not only married, but also fertile, because God, as the mouth, is united for some time to this soul before rendering it fertile through his own fecundity.

There are those who say this union can only happen in the next life. But I hold for certain that it can happen in this one here, with the difference being that in this life we cannot see what we possess and in the other we can see what we possess. I say, however, that, although the vision of God is an advantage of glory, which is necessary for consummation, it is nevertheless not the essential beatitude, since we are happy from the moment we possess the sovereign good, and we can enjoy it and possess it without seeing it. Here we enjoy it in the night of faith, where we have the happiness of this pleasure without having the pleasure of seeing it, whereas in the next life we will have a clear vision of God along with the happiness of possessing him. But this blindness does not prevent either the true possession or the real pleasure of the object, or the consummation of divine marriage, or even the real communication of the Word to the soul. This is very real and will be witnessed by everyone with this experience.

It is now possible to resolve the spiritual difficulty of certain people who do not want the soul, having arrived in God (which is the state of essential union), to be able to speak of Jesus Christ and of his inner states, saying that, for such a soul, this state has already passed. I agree with them that the union with Jesus Christ precedes by far the essential union, since the union with Jesus Christ as a divine person is perceived in the union of powers. And I agree that the union with Jesus Christ, as the God-man, is the first of all, and that it happens at the beginning of the illuminated life. But as regards the communication of the Word to the soul, I say that it is necessary for this soul to arrive in God alone, and that it must be established there by essential union and by spiritual marriage before this divine communication can be made with it, as the fruits and the products of marriage are only made after it is consummated.

This is more real than we can say; and God possesses the soul without interruption, which indicates the difference between the union with God himself and other unions, in that within unions with created beings, the object can only be possessed for a few moments because creatures are outside of us. But the enjoyment of God is permanent and durable because it is within us, and since God is our ultimate end, the soul can pour without ceasing into him, since its end and its depths are mixed there and transformed without ever coming out. Similarly, a river, which is composed of water that came from the sea but is very distinct from the sea, finding itself outside of its origins, tries by various agitations to approach the sea again, until, at the moment of having met it again, it loses itself and mixes with it, as it had been lost and mixed before leaving from there, and it can no longer be distinguished from it.

It must be mentioned again that God gave us, by creating us, a participation in his being, a readiness to be reunited with him, while at the same time giving us a tendency toward this union. He gave something similar to the human body with regard to humans in the innocent state, drawing this man's body itself so as to give him this tendency toward a union, as at his origin. But being between these very material bodies, this union can only be material and very limited since it is between solid and impenetrable bodies. In order better to understand this, we can draw a comparison with a metal that can be joined to another of a different sort. But although they are melted to unite them, they cannot be perfectly alloyed because they are of dissimilar natures. This process works better with the mixing of one metal with another of the same nature. Or else it is like one kind of water poured into another, which can be so mixed together that we can no longer notice any distinction whatsoever. Such is the soul; being of a completely spiritual nature, it is ready to be united, mixed, and transformed within its God.

One can be united without being mixed. That is the union of the powers. However, the mixing is the essential union, and this union is totally complete, being made from all in all. It is only God to whom the soul can be united in this way because it was created from an essence that allows it to be mixed with its God. This is what Saint Paul calls transformation, and Jesus Christ called unity, sameness, and consummation (2 Cor 3:8; John 17:11, 21). But this only happens when the soul loses its own consistency in order to live uniquely in God. This is what is known mystically as the loss of self and as a loving and perfect recollecting of the soul to God—and not as the real detachment of the intimate subsistence, which is necessary for the hypostatic union. But it is like a drop of water that loses its material consistency when it is put in a barrel of wine, where it is, materially speaking, changed to wine, although its being and its material remain forever distinct, so that an angel, if willed by God, would be able to divide them.[2] In the same way, this soul can always be separated from its God, although that thing is very difficult.

It is therefore this high and intimate union that the Bride asks of her Bridegroom with such insistence. She asks it of him as though speaking to another person. It is an impetuous leap of love, which, without looking upon the person addressed, gives flight to the passion. *Let him kiss me*, she says, since he can do it, but *with a kiss from his mouth*. Any other union cannot make me happy; this one alone can satisfy all desires and is the one for which I ask.

For your breasts are better than wine, Smelling sweet of the best ointments. (1:1–2)

The breasts, O God, with which you nourish souls just beginning are so sweet and so agreeable that they render your children, and even your children who still need to nurse, stronger than the most robust men who drink wine. They are so fragrant that, by their charming odor, they draw souls who are fortunate enough to smell them. They are also like a precious balm that heals all inner wounds. If this is the kind of thing found in the first approaches, how many delights will there be with the marriage kiss, a kiss of his mouth?

At the beginning of this Song, it proposes how it must end, with the recompense and perfect consummation of the Bride, because it is natural that the vision of and the desire for the end precede the choice of the means. Then the means to arrive there are described in order, beginning with spiritual infancy. It was the vision of this same end that drove the Bride to ask first for the kiss of his mouth, although this is the last thing that should be accorded her, which she will only receive after having paid the price with a large quantity of trials and work.

Your name is as oil poured out: therefore young maidens have loved you. (1:2)

Perceptible grace, which is expressed here by the name of the Bridegroom, so strongly penetrates the soul with the sweetness by which God advises the hearts that he wants to engage in his love that it is truly like a balm poured out, spreading out and accumulating unperceived, until the point where it covers so much, with a perfume so excellent, that the soul finds itself completely penetrated with its force and gentleness. This is done without violence and with such pleasure that the soul, still young and weak, lets itself be taken by its innocent charms. This is how God causes himself to be loved by those young hearts who only yet know how to love because of the sweetness they taste while loving. It was by pouring out this oil of joy that God the Father anointed his son above all others, who will participate in his glory (Ps 45:7).

Draw me: we will run after you to the odor of your ointments. (1:3)

This young Lover begs the Bridegroom to take her to the depths of her soul, as if she is not satisfied by the sweetness of this balm spread throughout her powers, because she already penetrates—by the grace of her Bridegroom, who attracts her always more strongly—that there is an enjoyment of himself more noble and more intimate than the one that she presently tastes. This is the door to making this request to her Bridegroom. Take me, she says, into the most intimate part of my depths, so that my powers and my senses also run to you by this most profound, although less perceptible, path. Take me, I say, O my divine Lover! And we will run to you by a contemplation that makes us feel this divine force by which you draw us to yourself. While running we will follow a certain scent that your attraction makes us smell. This is the odor of the balm that you have already poured out to heal the evil that sin has caused in the powers and to purify the senses from the corruption that slid in there. We will even bypass this odor to get to you, as if to the center of our happiness. This excellent perfume causes the prayer of recollection because the senses as well as the powers run after its odor, which makes them taste with exaltation how sweet the Lord is.

The king has brought me into his storerooms: we will be glad and rejoice in you, remembering your breasts more than wine: the righteous love you. (1:3)

As soon as the Lover has shown her God the desire she had to pass beyond everything in order to run to him alone, in order to compensate her for this already partly purified love, he has her enter his divine storerooms. This is a grace much greater than those he has already accorded her, because it is a passing union in the powers.

When the heart of man is faithful enough to want to bypass all the gifts of God, so as only to stop at God himself, God takes pleasure in bestowing on it these same gifts that it did not seek—in the same way that he indignantly takes them away from those who prefer them to seeking him alone. It was this understanding that obliged the Prophet King to invite all men to seek the Lord continually, especially to seek his face—as if meaning, without stopping at the graces or at the gifts of God, which are like rays coming out of his face but are, nonetheless, not him (Ps 105:4). Go up to his throne and look for him there; look unceasingly for his face, until you are fortunate enough to have found it. Then, says the Bride, we will be completely transported by joy at the ineffable secret that is manifested for us, and being in you, O my God, will fill us with joy; we will even tremble with happiness while remembering your breasts better than wine, meaning that the memory of the preference, which the Bride had for her Bridegroom over all else, will be the height of her happiness and pleasure. She had already preferred the sweetness of his milk over the wine of the pleasures of the century; that is why she says, we will remember your breasts better than wine. Here she prefers her God to his spiritual consolations and to the sweetness of the grace that she would experience while sucking the milk from his breasts. She adds, *the righteous love you*, to indicate that the true, right way, which leads the soul to bypass all earthly pleasures and all sweetness from heaven in order to lose itself in its God, is what constitutes pure and perfect love. Oh truly, my God, only those who are righteous in this way love you as you should be loved.

I am black but beautiful, O you daughters of Jerusalem, as the tents of Cedar, as the curtains of Solomon. (1:4)

As the greatest graces of God lead always to a deeper understanding of what we are, and as they would not be from him if they did not give, according to their degree, a kind of painful experience to the creature, this soul has only just left the cellars of her Bridegroom when she finds herself black. What is the blackness, O incomparable Lover? We say to her: we beseech you. She says, I am black because, thanks to my divine Sun, I perceived so many faults of which I had been ignorant until now; I am black because I am not at all purified of my self-ness. But in any case I do not cease to be beautiful, and beautiful like the tents of Cedar, because this experimental understanding of who I am is extremely pleasing to my Bridegroom and encourages him to come into me, as into a state of rest. I am beautiful because, having absolutely no voluntary stain, my Bridegroom makes me beautiful from his beauty. The blacker I am in my eyes, the more beautiful I am in his. I am beautiful, also, like the curtains of Solomon. The curtains of the divine Solomon are the holy humanity that covers from within the Word of God made flesh. I am beautiful, she says, like the curtains because he made me a participant in his beauty, in that, just as the holy humanity covers the divinity, so too my apparent blackness hides the grandeur of God's operations in my soul. I am still black from the crosses and the persecutions that come to me from the outside. But I am beautiful like the curtains of Solomon, since these crosses and this blackness make me like him. I am black because weaknesses appear on my exterior, but I am beautiful because I am free of malice inside.

Do not consider me that I am brown, because the sun has altered my color: the sons of my mother have fought against me, they have made me the keeper in the vineyards: my vineyard I have not kept. (1:5)

Why does the Bride ask that no one look at her in her blackness? It is that the soul, beginning to enter into the state of faith and of detachment from perceptible graces, loses little by little this sweet vigor that let it perform the good with ease and made it outwardly beautiful. And no longer being able to be fulfilled by its former practices, because God wants other things from it, it seems as if the soul has fallen into its natural state. It seems this way to those who are not enlightened. This is why she says, I implore you, my other companions who have not yet attained such a level in the inner life, you who are only at the beginning of the spiritual life, do not judge me by my brown color, which I wear on the outside, or by my exterior faults, real or apparent, because these do not come, as in souls just beginning, from the lack of love and courage. This is how my divine Sun, by his continuous, ardent, and burning gaze, discolored me. He took away my natural color, in order to leave me only with one that his ardor would give me. It is the force of love that dries my skin and tans it, and not being at a distance from love. This blackness is an advancement and not a defect, but an advancement that you should not consider, you who are still young and too tender to imitate it, because the blackness that you would give yourself would be a defect. In order to be good it must come only from the Sun of Justice, which, for its glory and the greatest good of the soul, eats and devours this brilliant outward color with which the soul blinded itself, though making itself admirable to others, to the detriment of the glory of the Bridegroom.

My brothers, seeing me black like this, wanted to make me return to my active life and to keep up appearances without applying myself to making the interior passions die; I fought for a long time against them, but finally, no longer able to resist them, I did what they wanted and applied myself to keeping up appearances regarding things that are foreign to me. I did not keep up my vineyard, which is my interior, where my God lives. This is my only concern and the only vineyard I need to tend, and when I did not tend my own, when I was not attentive to my God, I tended the others even less. This is the torment ordinarily inflicted upon souls when it is seen that the great preoccupation with their interior makes them neglect something on the outside, and because of this, the soul all closed up inside is no longer able to apply itself to certain little defects that the Bridegroom will correct at another time.

Show me, O you whom my soul loves, where you feed, where you lie in the midday, lest I begin to wander after the flocks of your companions. (1:6)

O you whom my soul loves, says this poor Lover, whom they force to depart from the sweet occupation with the inside so that she might apply herself to exterior things that are truly lowly; O you whom I love all the more because I see my love thwarted! Alas, show me where you let your flocks feed and with which food you satiate the souls that are so fortunate as to be under your guidance! We know that while you were on the earth, your meat was to do the will of your father; and now your food is that your friends do your will (John 4:34). You let your lovers graze on you, letting them discover your infinite perfections, so that they love you more ardently. And the more you manifest yourself to them, the more they ask to know you, so that they can always love you more.

Show me also, adds the Lover, *where you rest at noon!* She understands, by this figure, the burning of pure charity, desiring to learn, from the one who is her author and master, of what it consists, from the fear that, given some unfortunate human guidance, although covered with the cloak of spirituality, she might not undertake change and only satisfy self-love, even when she thinks she is focusing on pure love and the glory of God alone. She fears, rightly so, a mistake of such great consequence, which is only too frequent among the flocks of the church. This is what happens when they are guided by directors whom Jesus Christ has truly made his companions, associating himself with them for the governing of souls, but who, not being dead to themselves or crucified to the world with Jesus Christ, do not teach their pupils to renounce themselves, to crucify themselves, and to die to everything, so as to live in God alone, so that Jesus Christ might live in them. From this it happens that, both of these being in a very natural and unmortified life, their guidance is also very human and consequently prone to stray here and there, changing practices and guides often, without arriving at anything that is solid. And since this erring takes place because the maxims and the examples of Jesus Christ are not consulted enough, and because we do not address him enough by prayer to obtain what he alone can give us, this Lover, already well instructed, asks him insistently for knowledge of the Word with which he nourishes souls and the fidelity to follow his examples, knowing that this alone, upheld by grace, can prevent her from straying. We stop too often at the created means, however pious; God alone can teach us to do his will because he alone is our God (Ps 143:10). She also asks the Word to lead her to his Father, since he is the way that must lead her there. The bosom of his Father being the place where he rests in the noon of his glory and in the full day of eternity, she desires to lose herself in God with Jesus his son, to be hidden there, and to rest there forever. And although she does not say this so clearly, she lets him know it, because she says the following: *So that I no longer wander here and there*, as I have been, I will be in complete assurance there. I will no longer deceive myself, and furthermore, I will no longer sin.

If you know not yourself, O fairest among women, go forth, and follow after the steps of the flocks, and feed your kids beside the tents of the shepherds. (1:7)

The Bridegroom responds to his Lover, and to prepare her for the graces that he wants to give her as well as to teach her to put to good use those which she has received, he gives her an excellent bit of advice: *If you do not know yourself,* he says, *go forth.* He means that she will not know the divine object of her love, although she desires it so passionately, unless she also knows herself, since the nothingness of the creature helps in understanding the all of God. But since the light needed to discover the abyss of nothingness in the creature is in the all of God, he orders her to go forth. And from where? From herself. How? By renunciation and by the faithfulness to pursue it in all things, without permitting herself any natural satisfaction, and without having life in herself or in any other created thing. And to go where? So as to enter into God by a perfect abandonment of herself, where, discovering *that he is all in all things,* she consequently sees her nothingness, and that of all creatures (cf. Col 1:17). But the nothingness does not merit any esteem, since it has no good at all. Neither does it merit any love, since it is nothing. On the contrary, it is only worthy of scorn and hatred because of the self-esteem and self-love, entirely opposed to God, that sin has slid in there. It is therefore necessary that the creature who aspires to the divine union, being well persuaded of the all of God and of its own nothingness, go forth from itself, having only scorn and hatred of self, so as to keep all its esteem and its love for God; and in the same way, it will be admitted into his union. This going forth from the self, by the continual renunciation of all self-interest, is the interior exercise that the celestial Lover counsels to the souls who sigh after the kiss of his mouth, as he lets his Lover understand by this single expression, *go forth,* which suffices to order her interior.

But as for the exterior, he does not want her to neglect anything at all that is her duty, in the state in which he has put her. This includes infinitely more than all the details that could be given about it. Furthermore, since she must follow the attraction of the Holy Spirit in all freedom concerning all that is from her interior, he also wants her to conform herself to the customs of the church and to the orders of her superiors in everything concerning her exterior, which is well indicated by *follow after the steps of the flocks*, which means in the common way, for the exterior, and also by *feed your kids beside the tents of the shepherds.*

To my company of horsemen, in Pharaoh's chariots, have I likened you, O my love. (1:8)

The Bridegroom, knowing that the compliments that he gives to his Lover annihilate her all the more, instead of rendering her vain, gives her magnificent ones, so as to augment her love. He tells her: *I have likened you, my Beloved, to my company of horsemen.* This means that I want from you a course toward me so strong and so quick that, for this reason, I liken you alone to a large quantity of souls who run to me with extreme speed. I have compared you to my angels, and I want you to have the same honor as them, which is always to contemplate my face (Matt 18:10). However, so as to hide such great things while you live on the earth, *I likened you* on the outside *to the Pharaoh's chariots.* Those who see you running with so much speed, and as if without order, believe that you run after pleasures, vanities, and the multiple distractions of Egypt, or else that you are searching for yourself in your great haste. But you are running toward me, and your race will end in me alone, without anything being able to prevent you from arriving there, because of the force of the fidelity that I have provided you.

Your cheeks are beautiful as the turtledove's, your neck as jewels. (1:9)

These cheeks signify the interior and the exterior; they are beautiful as the turtledove's. The turtledove is notable because, when one of a pair dies, the one that survives remains alone for the rest of its days, without mating with another. In the same way the soul that finds itself separated from its God cannot take pleasure in another living creature, either on the outside or on the inside. In its interior it finds itself reduced to a solitude all the more strange, in that, not finding its Bridegroom, it cannot apply itself to anything at all. On the exterior, all is dead for it; it is this separation from everything created and all that is not in the least God that makes this soul beautiful in the eyes of the Bridegroom; her neck represents her pure charity, which is the greatest support left to her. But although she appears then in her ultimate nakedness, she is nonetheless enriched by the practice of many of virtues, which, like a string of pearls of great price, serve her as an ornament (Matt 13:45–46). But without this ornament, charity alone would make her perfectly beautiful, so that the neck of the Bride, although without pearls, does not stop being very beautiful.

We will make you chains of gold, inlaid with silver. (1:10)

Although you are already very beautiful in your nakedness, which marks a pure heart and an unpretentious charity, we will give you what it takes to set off your beauty by adding precious ornaments to it. These ornaments will be chains, as a sign of your perfect submission to every will of the King of Glory, but they will be of gold, in order to represent that, acting only by a very purified love, you have only the simple and pure regard for the good pleasure and the glory of God in all that you do or suffer for him. They will nevertheless be inlaid with silver, because, however simple and pure the charity might be in itself, it must produce and manifest itself externally by the practice of good works and of the most excellent virtues. It is necessary to remark that the divine Master in many passages takes particular care to instruct his beloved disciple in the sovereign purity that he asks for in the love of his wives and in their fidelity to neglect nothing at all regarding the service of the beloved or the assistance of others.

While the king was at his repose, my spikenard sent forth its odor. (1:11)

The Lover is not yet so denuded that she does not receive from time to time some visits from her Beloved. But why do I say a visit? It is, rather, a manifestation that he makes of himself, an experience of his deep and central presence. The sacred Bridegroom is always in the depths of the soul that is faithful to him, but he often lives there so hidden that the one who possesses this happiness almost always does not know it, except at certain moments when it pleases him to make himself felt in the amorous soul, which then discovers him in itself in an intimate and profound manner. He makes use of this now toward the purest of his lovers, as attested by her saying: When my King, the one who governs me and leads me as a Sovereign, was at his repose, which is the bottom and depths of my soul, where he takes his rest, my spikenard, which is my faithfulness, sent forth its odor in such a sweet and such an agreeable manner that it made him manifest himself to me. Then I recognized that he was resting in me, as if in his royal bed, which I had not known before because, although he was there, I did not see him there.

A bundle of myrrh is my beloved to me, he shall abide between my breasts. (1:12)

When the Bride, or rather the Lover (because she is not yet the Spouse) finds the Bridegroom, she is so transported with joy that she would first like to unite herself with him. But the continual, joyful union has not yet arrived. He is mine, she says; I cannot doubt that he is giving himself to me at this moment, since I feel it, but he is mine like a bundle of myrrh. He is not yet like a bridegroom whom I may embrace in his nuptial bed, but only like a bundle of crosses, of pains and of mortification, like a bridegroom of blood and a lover crucified who wants to test my fidelity by giving me a good dose of his sufferings. For this is how he gives to the soul. In order to mark the progress of this already heroic soul, however, she does not say, my Beloved will give me a bundle of the cross, but rather, this bundle will be himself, because all my exterior crosses will be those of my Beloved. The bundle will be between my breasts, in order to mark that he must be a bridegroom of bitterness to me, for the outside as well as for the inside. The exterior crosses are trifles when they are not accompanied by the interior ones, and the interior ones are made much more painful by the accompaniment of the external ones. But although the soul only perceives the cross everywhere, it is, nonetheless, her Beloved who is himself this cross, and he is never more present to her than in this bitterness, during which he lives in the middle of her heart.

A cluster of cypress my love is to me, in the vineyards of Engaddi. (1:13)

My Beloved, continues this Lover, *is to me like a cluster of cypress.* She only explains the half of it. It is as if she were saying, He is only close to me, for I do not have the honor of the intimate union by which he would be completely in me, and I completely in him. He is nonetheless close to me, but he is there like a cluster of cypress (this is the bush that produces a very fragrant balm), since it is he who gives the good odor and all value to that which is done by his lovers. This cluster of cypress grows in the vineyards of Engaddi, which are very beautiful and the grapes of which are excellent. The Lover compares her Beloved to the good odor and the rare virtue of the balm and to the delight and the strength of the wine in order to express with these figures that those who, by the interior taste of God, learned to please themselves in him cannot find pleasure in any other thing, and that if one looks for other delights, one loses the divine ones.

Behold you are fair, O my love, behold you are fair, your eyes are as those of doves. (1:14)

The Beloved, seeing the docility of his Lover in letting herself be crucified and instructed by him, is charmed by the brilliance of the beauties that he put into her. This is why he caresses her and compliments her, calling her beautiful and his Beloved. *Behold you are fair*, he says to her, *my love, behold you are fair!* O sweet word! He speaks to her of a double beauty, one interior and the other exterior. But he wants her to know it, as if meaning, now that your beauty is already formed in the depths, although not yet perfected, know also that in a short while you will be perfectly beautiful on the outside, when I will have consumed you and drawn you away from your weaknesses.

This compliment is accompanied by the promise of a more complete beauty, the hope for which must give a lot of courage to this soul and hold her in humility by the knowledge of what she is missing. But why tell her that she will soon be doubly beautiful? It is because her eyes and her expressions are already like those of doves, in that she is simple inside, not turning away at all from the view of her God, and outside, in all her words and actions, which are without guile. This dovelike simplicity is the surest mark of the advancement of a soul, because no longer using detours or artifices, she is guided by the Spirit of God. The Bride concedes from the beginning the necessity of simplicity and righteous perfection when she says, *the righteous love you,* putting the perfection of love in its own simplicity and righteousness.

Behold you are fair, my beloved, and comely. Our bed is flourishing. (1:15)

The Lover's soul, seeing that her Bridegroom has complimented her on having a double beauty, and not wanting to attribute any of this to herself, says to him also: *Behold you are fair, my beloved, and comely.* She gives him all the compliments she has received from him and gives some very great ones for her turn. No good being ours, no compliment, no glory, and no pleasure should arrest itself in us; all must be returned to the one who is the author and the basis of all good. The Bride in all this discourse teaches us this important practice, glorifying the Lord everywhere, for all he has put in her. If I am beautiful, she says to him, it is with your own beauty. It is you who are beautiful in me, with this double beauty for which you compliment me. Our bed, she adds, this depth where you live in me, which I call ours in order to invite you to come give me there the nuptial kiss, which I first requested of you and which is my end, our bed, I say, is prepared and decorated by the flowers of a thousand virtues.

The beams of our houses are of cedar, our rafters of cypress trees. (1:16)

The Bridegroom, hidden in the depths and the center of the soul (as was already said), takes pleasure in sending, from this sanctuary where he lives, some effusions of his perceptible graces, which produce so many different virtues on the exterior of the Bride.

These are so much like beautiful flowers that she appears adorned with them; surprised and charmed as she is, or else by lack of experience, she believes that her interior is nearly completed. The roofing, she says, is already put on; the beams, which are the practice of exterior virtues, are of cedar wood. It seems to me that they have an agreeable odor and that I can practice them with as much strength as ease. The regulation of the senses appears to me in an order as correct as the well-crafted rafters, made of exquisite wood. But, O Lover, that only seems so to you because this bed is flowered and the state is sweet, agreeable, and pleasant. What you feel on the inside makes you believe that you have acquired everything on the outside, but consider that the rafters are of cypress, and that cypress represents death, and what you see as so beautiful and so adorned is only the preparation for death.

CHAPTER 2

I am the flower of the field, and the lily of the valleys. (2:1)

O God, you take your Bride agreeably back from what she wanted, as soon as she was settled in a well-flowered bed, before laying her down, like you, on the sorrowful bed of the cross. I am, you say, the flower of the field, a flower that you do not pick while resting on a bed, but in the field of combat, of work, and of suffering. I am the lily of the valleys that only grows in annihilated souls, so that if you want me to draw you from your earth and take up life in you, you must be in the last stages of annihilation. And if you want to find me, you must enter into combat and suffering.

As the lily among thorns, so is my love among the daughters. (2:2)

The Bridegroom, by these words, gives notice of the progress of his Lover, who is like a lily, very pure, very agreeable, and with a nice fragrance before him, while the other girls, instead of being supple and pliable and letting themselves be led by his spirit, are like thorny bushes that prickle and sting those who want to approach them. Such are the selfish souls who are attached to their own wills, who do not want to let themselves be led by God. And it is there that a soul, well-abandoned to its God, suffers among those that are unlike itself, because the others do everything they can to take her off her path. But in the same way that the lily keeps both its purity and its odor among the thorns without being in the least damaged, so also these souls are kept by their Bridegroom in the middle of the vexations they must suffer from those who only love to lead themselves and to multiply themselves in their own practices, having no docility whatsoever in following the movement of grace.

As the apple tree among the trees of the woods, so is my beloved among the sons. I sat down under the shadow of him whom I desired: and his fruit was sweet to my palate. (2:3)

This comparison is very naive—the Lover, seeing herself persecuted by the spiritual people who are not on her path, tells them, while addressing them and her Beloved at the same time, that as the apple tree among the trees of the forest, so is my Beloved among the sons. This means among those, whether they are the saints in heaven or the righteous of the earth, who are the most agreeable to God. Do not be surprised, then, if I sit down under his shadow and if I remain at rest under his protection. I am only under the shadow of the wings of the one whom I have so desired to possess; but although I have not yet arrived at such a good, I can say nonetheless that his fruit, which is the cross, sorrow, and abjection, is sweet to my palate. It is not sweet to the mouth of flesh because the inferior part finds it rough and very unrefined, but it is sweet to the mouth of the heart, after I have swallowed it. And for me, what has the taste of my Beloved is preferable to all other tastes.

He brought me into the cellars of wine, he set in order charity in me. (2:4)

The beloved of the king, leaving the sweet meeting she just had with him, appears to her friends to be drunk and not at all herself. She is so in effect, since, having drunk the most excellent wine of the Bridegroom, she could do no less than be embraced by the strongest fervor. Also, being well aware of it herself, she asks her companions not to be surprised to see her in such an extraordinary state. My drunkenness, she tells them, is completely forgivable, since my king brought me into his divine cellars of wine. It is there that he ordered charity in me. The first time he accorded me such a singular grace, I was still such a child that I would have voluntarily preferred the sweetness of the divine breasts to the strength of excellent wine. Furthermore, the Bridegroom was happy to show me the effect of this wine, while only giving me very little to drink. But today, now that my experience and his grace have made me stronger and better instructed, I will no longer act the same way; I drank with such abandon from his pure and strong wine that he rearranged the charity in me.

What is this order that God puts in charity? O love! Charity God! You alone can reveal it! It is that he makes this soul, which by a movement of charity wanted all possible good for itself, by rapport with God, to forget itself completely in order to think only of her Beloved. She forgets all self-interest—in salvation, in perfection, in joy, in consolation—in order to think only about her God. She no longer thinks of enjoying his embraces but about suffering for him. She no longer asks anything for herself but only that God be glorified. She enters into the interests of divine justice, consenting with all her heart to all that it will do with her, whether in time or in eternity. She can only love, either in herself or in another creature, what is for God and of God, and not what is in her or for her, however important and necessary it might appear. Here is the order of charity that God puts in this soul. Her love has become perfectly chaste. All creatures are nothing to her; she wants them all for her God and does not want any single one for herself. Oh, what strength this order of charity gives for the terrible states that it will be necessary to pass through! But it cannot be known or tasted by those who are not there yet, for not yet having drunk the wine of the Bridegroom.

Stay me up with flowers, compass me about with apples: because I languish with love. (2:5)

The Bridegroom has no sooner ordered this sort of charity in the soul than he gives it a single grace to prepare it for the sufferings that must follow. He gives it his passing union in the depths, which spreads from there into the powers and the senses, and as the soul is not yet very strong, this union becomes like a suspension or an absorption of the senses, which forces it to cry out, stay me up with flowers, help me with some little things that I might practice on the exterior. Or else compass me about with the apples of some exercise in charity, so that I do not die in such a strong attraction, because I feel that I languish with love. O poor Lover, what do you say? Why do you rely on flowers and on fruits, on exterior consolations, on trifles? You do not know what you ask; pardon me if I say this to you. If you succumb to this weakness, you will only fall into the arms of your Bridegroom. Ah, how happy you would be to expire there! But it is not yet time.

His left hand is under my head, and his right hand shall embrace me. (2:6)

She is beginning to understand the mystery; this is why, as if she was repenting from the outside help that she had requested, she says: *His left hand is under my head.* He supports me with a singular protection since he has honored me with his union in the powers of my soul; what do I have to do with flowers or with fruits, with still desiring to seek sensible and human things, while divine things are communicated to me? He will do something even more in the future, uniting me to him essentially, and then I will be fertile, and I will produce for my Bridegroom fruits incomparably more beautiful than those that I requested. This is because *his right hand will embrace me*, which is his omnipotence accompanied by his love, the chaste embraces of which produce in the soul its perfect joy, which is none other than essential union.

It is true that in the beginning this embrace of the right hand is truly the engagement of the soul but not yet the marriage. *He will embrace me*, she says; he will unite me to him first by this link of engagement that makes me hope that he will honor me one day in marriage. And at that time he will embrace me and will unite himself to me so strongly that I will not fear any failure at all, because the particularity of the essential union is to reinforce the soul so that it can no longer have these failures that happen to beginning souls, in which grace, still being weak, makes them feel eclipses and still have down-falls. But by this union the soul is confirmed (if one can use this term) in charity since it abides in God. And he that abides in charity abides in God, and God in him, because God is charity (1 John 4:16).

I adjure you, O you daughters of Jerusalem, by the roes, and the harts of the fields, that you stir not up, nor make the beloved to awake, till she please. (2:7)

The soul in this sweet embrace of betrothal falls into a mystical slumber, in which she tastes a sacred rest that she had never tasted. In the other moments of rest she had been well-seated in the shadow of her Beloved, by faith, but she had never gone to sleep on his breast or in his arms. It is a strange thing that creatures, even spiritual ones, hurry to wake the soul from this sweet sleep. The daughters of Jerusalem are charitable and troublesome souls who hurry so much to draw her away from there, although under the most beautiful pretexts. But she is in such a deep slumber that she cannot leave her sleep. The Bridegroom therefore speaks for her, and, holding her tightly in his arms, he asks these persons and even charges them by all they value most, which is the practice of the strongest and most active virtues, not to wake up his Beloved at all, and not to take her out of her repose in any way, because she pleases him more in this rest than in anything else she might do outside of it. Do not wake her up at all, he tells them, directly or indirectly, using the different methods that you have planned, until she herself truly desires it, because she will only want it when I want it.

The voice of my beloved, behold he comes leaping upon the mountains, skipping over the hills. (2:8)

This soul, who is asleep to all else, is more attentive to the voice of her Beloved. She hears it and distinguishes it first. *The voice of my Beloved*, she says; I know it, I hear it, and the effect that it has in me does not permit any doubt. But what do you say, O Lover? The love is making you dream perhaps that you are sleeping in the arms of your Beloved; however, you say that it comes from the mountains and that it passes through the hills! Oh, how well all this fits together!

The Bridegroom embraces his Lover, and he is in her; he surrounds her on the outside, and he penetrates her on the inside. She feels that in this mystical sleep he goes into her, that he unifies with her, not only as before, merely by the powers (which are the hills), but more than that; passing over the hills, he comes onto the mountain (that is, the center), and here he truly touches her with his immediate union. She truly feels that this touch is different from the one of the powers and that it causes very great effects in her, although it is a passing touch, which is not yet the permanent and durable union.

My beloved is like a roe, or a young hart. Behold he stands behind our wall, looking through the windows, looking through the lattices. (2:9)

When the soul enjoys the sweet embraces of her Bridegroom, she believes that they must always endure, but if they are the pledges of his love, then they are also the mark of its flight. Hardly does the soul taste the sweetness of this union before the Bridegroom completely disappears. Seeing therefore a flight so prompt, she compares him to a roe or a young hart because of the lightness and the speed of his running. And complaining lovingly about him, after such a strange abandonment, when she believes him very far away, she notices him very close. He had only hidden himself to test her faith and her confidence; however, he did not cease to look upon her from above, because he is protecting her more particularly than ever, being even more united with her by the new alliance that he just made and that he had never made before that time. But although he looks at her incessantly, she does not always see him. She only sees him for a few moments, so that she might not be ignorant of this regard and might teach it to others one day. It is necessary to notice that the Bridegroom is standing because it is not time to rest or to stay seated, but to run. He is standing, as if ready to walk.

Behold my beloved speaks to me: Arise, make haste, my love, my dove, my beautiful one, and come. (2:10)

God, having entirely turned the soul into herself and having led her to her depths, after having made her enjoy his chaste embraces to prepare her for the spiritual marriage, makes her take a route that seems completely contrary; he makes her go outside of herself by the mystical death. The Beloved, just having spoken to this soul, invites her to go promptly out; he no longer tells her to rest. On the contrary, he commands her to arise from her rest. This is a very different manner from the one he had before; he had forbade that anyone should wake her, and now he wants her to arise promptly. He calls her in such a sweet and strong way that, when she will no longer be so passionate to obey him as she is now, she will not be able to refuse to do so. *Arise, my Beloved,* whom I have chosen to be my Bride, and *my beautiful one,* because I find you beautiful to my eyes, remarking in you a thousand traits of my beauty. *My dove,* simple and faithful, arise and come out, since you have all the qualities necessary for going outside yourself. Having attracted you to the interior, I go, so to speak, outside of you so as to make you come out from there in following me.

This going out is very different from the one spoken about above[3] and much more advanced, because the first one was a departure from natural satisfactions, in order to be able to please the Beloved, but this one is a departure from the possession of the self, so as to be possessed only by God, and so that, no longer noticing herself within her, she only finds herself within him. This is a transporting of the creature to its origin, such as will be described later.

For winter is now past, the rain is over and gone. (2:11)

It is necessary to know that there are two winters, the exterior one and the interior one, and the two of them are inversely proportionate. When winter is outside, summer is inside, which impels the soul to go further inside itself by an effect of grace that brings about a profound recollection. And when winter is inside, it is summer outside, which forces the soul to leave itself by the expansion that is caused by a more extensive grace of abandonment. The winter of which the Bridegroom speaks, saying that it is past, is the exterior winter, during which the soul could have been frozen by the forces of the cold, assailed by the rains, and overtaken by those storms and snows of sins and imperfections that are so easily found in the business of creatures. The soul that has found its depths becomes so fortified that there is nothing for it to fear on the outside; all the rains are wiped away, and it is impossible for it, unless from the blackest infidelity that ever was, to take any pleasure whatsoever in exterior things. What is more, this phrase, *the winter is past*, means that just as winter brings death to everything, in the same way, for this soul, death has come to all exterior things, so that none of them can satisfy it any longer. If something still appears to do so, this is a renewal of innocence that no longer has any of the malevolence of before. The rains of winter have also passed, so she can go out without any more to fear from winter, and with this advantage—that the winter destroyed and caused the death of what had been before alive for her, which would have made her die herself, as the power of winter purges the earth of insects.

The flowers have appeared in our land, the time of pruning is come: the voice of the turtledove is heard in our land. (2:12)

So as to make her come, he makes her understand that he wants to take her to his land; he calls it *our land* because he acquired it for her by her redemption and because it belongs to him for her, and to her through him. He says that the flowers have already started to appear in that place, but flowers that never dry out, flowers that never shrivel, flowers that no longer dread the approach of winter. *The time*, he says, *to prune the vines has come*. It is necessary that his Beloved, who had herself been compared to the vine, be pruned, that she be cut back, cut away, and destroyed. The voice of the turtledove of my humanity invites you to come lose yourself and hide yourself with it in the bosom of my Father; you will hear this voice better when you will be in the land to which I call you, which at present is not known to you. This voice of my simplicity and of my innocence, with which I want to gratify you, is very different from your own.

The fig tree has put forth her green figs: the vines in flower yield their sweet smell. Arise, my love, my beautiful one, and come. (2:13)

There the springtime is eternal, and it allies itself very well with the fruits of autumn and with the heat of summer. The Bridegroom, by these flowers and by these fruits, marks three seasons rather clearly, but he does not speak of winter, because, as was said, when the soul arrives in this new land, it finds that winter—not only on the exterior but also on the interior—has passed. There is no longer any winter for a soul that has reached God, but there is a composition of three seasons, which are found all united in one and immortalized by the loss of winter, because before the interior winter arrives, the soul has passed through all the seasons of the spiritual life, but after the interior winter, it returns into a continual spring, summer, and autumn. The sweetness of spring does not at all preclude the force of the summer or the fertility of autumn, as the heat of summer does not at all diminish the beauty of the spring or the fertility of autumn; and the fruit of autumn does not at all bother the pleasantness of spring or the heat of summer. O fortunate land! How happy are those who have the joy of possessing you! We are all ordered with the Bride to leave ourselves in order to enter there. It is promised to us all, and the one who possesses it and to whom it belongs, by the right of his eternal birth, and because he acquired it at the price of his blood, invites us insistently to go there. He gives us all the means for that; he attracts us by his pressing inspirations, so why don't we run?

My dove in the clefts of the rock, in the hollow places of the wall, show me your face, let your voice sound in my ears: for your voice is sweet, and your face comely. (2:14)

My dove, says this Bridegroom, my pure, chaste, and simple dove, you who are concentrated in the depths of yourself, as in the hollow places of a wall, and who is hidden there in my wounds, which are the clefts of the living rock, show me your face. But what do you say, O Bridegroom? Your Beloved, is she not completely turned toward you? How is it that you tell her to show you her face? She is as if completely hidden within you; do you not see her? You want to hear her voice, and she is mute for all others but you. O admirable invention of divine wisdom! This poor soul, thinking that to correspond to her Bridegroom she must do as before, to recollect and center down further inside herself, does this with all her might, but this is detrimental. Here, he calls her to the outside, even to her highest; he wants her to leave herself, and this is why he says to her, *show me your face*, so that I hear this voice from the outside, and turn yourself toward me because I have changed position. He assures her that her voice is very sweet, very calm, and very tranquil and that she conforms herself to the language of the Bridegroom, whose voice is not one that must be understood by the volume of its speech. *Your face*, he adds, *is comely*. The highest part of your soul is already beautiful, and it has all the advantages of beauty; you are only missing one thing, which is to go outside of yourself.

If the Bridegroom does not attract his Lover outside with so much force and sweetness, she will never leave herself. It seems that as much as she found herself recollected before and centered in herself, she now feels equally drawn to the outside, and even with more force. For more forces are truly necessary to draw the soul outside of itself than to make it center within. The sweetness she tastes inside by savory recollection also invites it there, but to leave this interior sweetness to find only exterior bitterness, that is very difficult. Besides, by the act of recollecting, she lives and possesses herself, but by leaving herself, she dies and loses herself.

Catch us the little foxes that destroy the vines: for our vineyard has flourished. (2:15)

The faithful Lover asks the Bridegroom to take away the little foxes, which are a number of little faults that begin to appear, because they spoil this interior vine which, she says, has flourished, and this is what makes this vine more agreeable and what makes her love it all the more, hoping to see the fruit there soon. What will you do, poor soul, to abandon this vine, to which you are attached without knowing it? Ah! The Master himself will put little foxes there, which will ravage it and destroy the flowers and cause a strange damage. If he had not used them that way, you are so in love with yourself that you would never come out of there.

My beloved to me, and I to him who feeds among the lilies. (2:16)

Oh, the inestimable happiness of a soul that is completely and unreservedly for her Beloved, and to whom the Beloved is all things! The Lover is very drunk with the goodness and the caresses that the

Bridegroom gives her to oblige her to come out of herself, so that she believes herself already to have arrived at the pinnacle of happiness and to the highest degree of perfection, and she believes that the marriage must soon be consummated. She says that her Beloved is hers, to dispose as it pleases him; and that she is also entirely his, regarding his whole will; and that he takes his rest in her, among the lilies of her purity. He nourishes himself with her graces and her virtues; he lives upon innocence and purity, so as to nourish us from it; he invites us to eat with him the meat that pleases him the most, as he makes known from his words, in another passage, *Drink and eat, my friends* (Song 5:1); *Nourish yourselves with the good food I give you, and your soul being fattened by it will be delighted* (Isa 55:2).

Till the day break, and the shadows retire. Return: be like, my beloved, to a roe, or to a young hart upon the mountains of Bether. (2:17)

The soul, beginning to notice that she no longer sees the Word, believes that he has only hidden himself for one night, or rather that he has fallen asleep in his place of rest. She says to him then, O my dear Bridegroom, since I am under the same roof with you and you are so close to me, return to me a little, letting me perceive you! How I enjoy your sweet embraces, until the day comes and I am more certain of your presence, and the shadows of faith are dissipated by the sweet light of vision and clear enjoyment! Then, remembering the passing union that she felt before, she tells him, pass quickly, if you like, like a little bounding roe, but let it be upon the mountain, so that I can enjoy this central union that was so sweet and so advantageous to me, when you made me feel it.

CHAPTER 3

In my bed by night I sought him whom my soul loves: I sought him, and found him not. (3:1)

The soul, seeing that the Bridegroom is not according her the grace that she expected, after having accorded it to her at a time when she was not expecting it, is astonished by this very difficult absence. She looks for him in the depths of herself, which is her little bed, and during the night of faith, but alas! She is very surprised no longer to be able to find him. She had some reason to look for him there, since this was where he had manifested himself to her and had given her the most vibrant sentiment that she had ever felt of what he is. But, O Lover, you cannot find your Bridegroom there! Do you not know that he ordered you no longer to look for him in yourself, but rather in himself? You will no longer find him outside of himself; come out of yourself as fast as you can in order to belong only to him, and he will let himself be found there. O admirable device of the Bridegroom! When he is most passionate for his Beloved is when he flees with the most cruelty, but it is a loving cruelty, without which the soul would never leave herself and consequently would never lose herself in God.

I will rise, and will go about the city: in the streets and the broad ways I will seek him whom my soul loves: I sought him, and I found him not. (3:2)

O miracle operated by the absence of a God! How often had he invited his Lover to get up from her rest, and yet she could not do it? He urged her with the most tender words in the world, but she was so drunk from the peace and the tranquility she was tasting that she could not leave from there. O faithful soul, the rest that you taste in yourself is only a shadow of rest, at the price of that which you will find in God. It was nevertheless impossible to make her get up, but as soon as she no longer found her Beloved in the bed of her repose, Oh, she says, I will rise now; this bed of repose, which had been before a paradise, is now hell for me, since my Beloved is absent; and with him hell would be a paradise for me. This city, this world that I hated before, will be nonetheless the place of my seeking. For this soul, not yet fully instructed, however passionate she might appear—and rightly passionate about the possession of his sovereign good and her final end—testifies here to the sentiments of a child. She is so weak that it is impossible at first for her to look for God in himself; although she does not find him in her depths, she looks for him in all creatures, in a thousand places where he is not. And being thus spread out on the outside, she amuses herself with the creature, under the pretext of looking for the creator. She looks everywhere because her heart loves, and she can only find rest in what she loves, but she finds nothing because God has not gone out from her to be sought in other creatures. He wants to be sought in himself, and when she will have arrived in him, she will discover there another truth, the beauty of which will ravish her, which is that her Beloved is everywhere and in everything, and that everything is himself, without her being able to distinguish anything from him who is in all places without being enclosed in any.

The watchmen who keep the city, found me: Have you seen him, whom my soul loves? (3:3)

As I saw that I was not finding my Beloved in any mortal creature, I looked for him among the happy spirits who guard the city. And they found me because they are always on guard. These are watchmen whom God has established upon the walls of Jerusalem, who are never silent, day or night (Isa 62:6). I asked them then for news of my Beloved, the one for whom I burn with ardor, but although they possess him for themselves, they could not give him to me. It seems to me that I see Mary Magdalene, who, not finding Jesus in his tomb, looks for him everywhere, asking angels and men (John 20:1–13). But no one can give word of the Beloved other than himself.

When I had a little passed by them, I found him whom my soul loves: I held him: and I will not let him go, till I bring him into my mother's house, and into the chamber of her who bore me. (3:4)

The soul, having left herself and having surpassed all creatures, meets her Beloved, who shows himself to her with new charms. This persuades her that the fortunate moment of the consummation of the marriage is near, and that the permanent union is soon going to be created. In her transport, due to the happiness that she possesses, she exclaims, I have my Beloved, I have found him, I am holding on to him, and I will no longer let him go, because she believes that she can hold him and that he only took himself away from her due to some fault she committed. I will hold on to him so strongly, she continues to say, and I will attach myself to him with such faithfulness that I will no longer let him go, until I bring him into my mother's house—into the bosom of God, which is the chamber of her who bore me, since he is my principle and my origin. But, what are you saying, innocent soul? Is it not his part to guide you there, rather than yours to lead him there? Love believes that everything is possible, as it persuaded Mary Magdalene that she could take away the body of her Lord (John 20:15). The passion that she has to go there makes her say that she wants to bring him there, without considering that she must be there with him and clothed by him.

I adjure you, O daughters of Jerusalem, by the roes and the harts of the fields, that you stir not up, nor awake my beloved, till she please. (3:5)

The Bridegroom, full of compassion after this first trial of his Bride (or at least the first strong and intimate trial), since she started to arise and come outside, makes her, for a time, part of his essential union again. Thus, this poor soul is made so happy from this good, which appears infinitely greater than before, because it has cost her more, that she sleeps, faints, loses herself, and seems dead in the arms of love. One can see by this that, although the soul suffers a lot in looking for her Beloved, in any case her pains are shadows of pains in comparison with the happiness of the possession of this adorable object. This is why Saint Paul said that pains, even the greatest in this life, cannot be compared with the glory that will be revealed to us (Rom 8:18). Her Beloved does not want anyone to awaken her because this awakening will prevent her death and will delay her happiness.

Who is she that goes up by the desert, as a pillar of smoke of aromatic spices, of myrrh, and frankincense, and of all the powders of the perfumer? (3:6)

The friends of the Spouse, seeing her adorned with such perfections and filled with such graces, by an effect of this visit of the

Bridegroom, show their astonishment by these words: *Who is she who goes up by the desert, like a little aromatic smoke?* The Lover is so strongly purified in the arms of her Bridegroom that she leaves there like a subtle vapor that the fire of love has almost consumed. She is like a vapor that stretches high because of her righteousness and justice, and a subtle vapor, to show that she is already all spirit. This vapor is composed of the choicest odors of all virtues, but it is necessary to notice that the odors of which this vapor is composed are gums ready to be melted and powders that are not solid at all. Solidity and consistency in herself are no longer her state. And from where does this vapor so straight and so fragrant rise? It rises from the desert of faith. And where does it go? It wants to go rest in its God.

Behold threescore valiant ones of the most valiant of Israel, around the bed of Solomon? (3:7)

Our Lover, feeling already very disengaged from herself, believes that there is only one thing left to do, and this is true. But alas! There are obstacles to overcome before succeeding here. This is to go to God, who is the bed of rest of the true Solomon. But in order to arrive there, it is necessary to pass through sixty of the strongest valiant men of Israel. These valiant warriors are the divine attributes, which encircle this royal bed and prevent access to those who are not entirely annihilated. They are the most valiant of Israel because it is by these attributes that Israel, which refers to the contemplative, finds its strength, and it is also by them that the strength of God is manifested to men.

All holding swords, and most expert in war: every man's sword upon his thigh, because of fears in the night. (3:8)

All are armed with their swords, in order to fight forcefully against this soul, which, by a secret presumption, wants to attribute to itself what belongs only to God; that is what makes them say with a common voice, who is like God? Divine righteousness is the first that arrives to fight and destroy the self-righteousness of the creature, and then comes strength to strike down man's own strength, making him enter by the experience of his extreme weakness into the strength of the Lord and teaching him no longer to remember anything but the righteousness of God alone.

Providence declares itself against human foresight, and it is so with all the attributes. They are all armed because it is necessary that the soul be destroyed in all these things to be admitted into Solomon's bed, and thus to be the spouse so that the marriage takes place and is consummated. These valiant warriors always have their swords at their sides. This sword is nothing other than the most intimate and penetrating word of God, but the efficient word that, while uncovering the most secret presumption of the soul, destroys it at the same time.

This word is the uncreated Word, which only manifests itself in the depth of the soul to bring about there what it expresses. It no sooner declares itself than, like a thunder bolt, it reduces to ashes that which opposes its passage. This divine Word, while incarnating itself, used itself up—*For he spoke and it was done* (Ps 33:9)—and it imprinted in its humanity the characteristics of its omnipotence. It entered into the abasement of the creature to destroy its elevation, and into its weakness to knock down its strength; and it took the form of the sinner to strike down self-righteousness. It does the same in the soul—it abases it, it weakens it, it covers it with misery. But why does the scripture say that they are all armed in this way because of fear of the night? This means that, as the sense of self holds the soul in darkness and causes it all its disastrous nights, the divine attributes thus arm themselves against it, so that it does not usurp in any way what belongs only to God.

King Solomon has made himself a litter of the wood of Lebanon: (3:9)

The Son of God, the King of Glory, made himself a litter of the humanity to which he is united by his incarnation, with the plan of resting there eternally and making it like a chariot of triumph on which he wants to be carried with radiance and magnificence for the view of all creatures. This royal seat is made of the wood of Lebanon because Jesus Christ is descended, by flesh, from the patriarchs, prophets, and kings, all eminent in their holiness and their character. The Word of God is thus in man, as if on the throne of his majesty. As Saint Paul says, God was in Jesus Christ, by whom he reconciled the world in his grace (2 Cor 5:19).

In each soul Jesus Christ makes himself a throne that he decorates with much magnificence to make it the place of his residence as well as of his rest and his eternal delights, and a place to reign as a sovereign after having acquired it by the price of his blood and sanctified it by his graces. For just as God reigns in Jesus Christ, so Jesus Christ reigns in pure hearts, where he no longer finds anything at all that resists him or displeases him, in order to prepare his kingdom for us and make us participants in his royalty, as the Father had prepared his kingdom for him and communicated his royalty to him (Luke 22:29–30). This litter of the King of Kings therefore is made from the wood of Lebanon. This is the natural depths of humans, which serve as the base and the foundation of the spiritual edifice, and these depths imitate well the height and the value of the trees of Lebanon, since they draw their origin from God himself and they are made in his image and likeness. The Bride of this song is given as the model of this august throne for all the other lovers of the celestial Bridegroom so as to move them toward the pursuit of the same happiness. She herself describes the throne of the Bridegroom, having received a new light in order to know him with more penetration, in the essential, although passing, union by which she just has been gratified. This is why she adds,

He made its pillars of silver, the seat of gold, the going up of purple: the interior he covered with charity for the daughters of Jerusalem. (3:10)

The pillars of the holy humanity of Jesus Christ are of silver, his soul with its powers and his body with its senses and all its parts being of a completed purity, well represented by the most brilliant and the purest silver. Its support, which is the divinity itself, in which Jesus Christ subsists in the person of the Word, is clearly expressed by the support of this mysterious seat all of gold because often in the scripture, gold is taken to be God himself.[4] The step of this divine litter is decorated in purple, which expresses very well that although the bosom of God the Father, which is the dwelling of the Word, was acquired by his eternal generation and he can have no other, and although he made himself man by the decree of the divine justice to which he had voluntarily submitted himself, he was only able, however, to go back up to his Father in order to enter in the fullness of his glory by the purple of his blood: *Since it was necessary that Christ endure great pain and die so that he enter into his glory* (Luke 24:26). The interior of this place of triumph is decorated with very costly ornaments, which are well expressed under the name of charity, as being the greatest and the most precious of all. And are not all the treasures and the fullness of divinity in Jesus Christ (Col 2:3–9)? It is to him that the Holy Spirit was given without measure (John 3:34). The Holy Spirit therefore fills the interior of the majestic throne, since he is the love of the Father and of the Son and also the love by which God loves men, and since he is the union of the divine persons, he is also the knot that links pure souls with Jesus Christ. But the divine Solomon made all that in consideration of the daughters of Jerusalem, who are his elected ones, for whom he did all and suffered all.

In the sanctuary that God raises in his Lover, there are in the same way pillars of silver, which are the gifts of the Holy Spirit, established on divine grace, which is like pure and shiny silver, which serves as their source of material and foundation. Its support is made of gold, because a soul that merits serving as the throne and royal bed of Jesus Christ must no longer have any support other than God alone, and it must be entirely rid of all created support. Its step is all of purple because if *one can only enter into the kingdom of heaven by many afflictions* (Acts 14:22), and if *one can only reign with Jesus Christ after having suffered with him* (2 Tim 2:12), then this is all the more true for those who are called to the first places in the interior kingdom and for the souls who, in this life, will be honored by the wedding with the celestial Bridegroom, as opposed to the common Christian who leaves this world well on the way of salvation, but charged with many debts and imperfections. It is incredible how necessary it is for these chosen souls to be devoured by crosses, reproaches, and reversals. Thus, all the inside is covered with charity, since these living thrones of the Most High, being full of love, are also adorned with all the fruits and ornaments of love. These are good works, merits, the fruits of the Holy Spirit and the practice of the most pure and solid virtues. This is your calling, O daughters of Jerusalem, interior wives, souls of contemplative prayer! This is also what the King of Kings, the King of Peace, has merited for you and offers to you, if you are willing to love him. It is on this rich foundation that the Bridegroom and the Bride base the magnificent praises that they are going to give each other in the following chapters.

Go forth, you daughters of Zion, and see King Solomon in the diadem, with which his mother crowned him in the day of his wedding, and in the day of the joy of his heart. (3:11)

Jesus Christ invites all interior souls, who are the daughters of Zion, to go forth from themselves and their imperfections to contemplate King Solomon, crowned with the crown of glory, crowned by God himself. The divine nature holds the place of the mother in relation to the human nature; it is she who crowns it and who is, all together, his crown. She thus crowns Jesus Christ on the day of his wedding with a glory as sublime as it is infinite and immortal. But what is the wedding day for the Lamb? It is the day on which he ascended to heaven, where he was received at the right hand of his Father, the day of eternal joy. Look at him, daughters of Zion, with all his divine honors, because he wants to share them with you.

CHAPTER 4

How beautiful you are, my love, how beautiful you are! Your eyes are doves' eyes, besides what is hidden within. Your hair is like flocks of goats, which come up from Mount Gilead. (4:1)

Although the Bridegroom cannot yet let the Lover into the nuptial bed, which is the bosom of his Father, he does not, however, stop finding her very beautiful and more beautiful than ever, because her faults are no longer notable sins and are scarcely offenses, but rather are faults that are in her nature, still hard and contracted, which has an incredible pain for being stretched in order to be lost in God. She is therefore very beautiful, both in the interior and exterior, and more beautiful than ever, although she does not believe it, due to that fact that she was prevented from being received in God. This is what makes the Bridegroom assure her she is very beautiful, even without what is hidden from her, which is much more beautiful than all that appears on the outside and all that one can express or even imagine. Your eyes, by your faithfulness, righteousness, and simplicity, are like those of doves. This righteousness is on the outside as well as the inside. The virtue of simplicity, so recommended in the scriptures, makes us act, with regard to God, incessantly, without hesitation, directly, without reflection, and sovereignly, without a multiplicity of plans, of motives, or of practices, but uniquely in order to please God. Also, when simplicity is perfected, one acts on it by habit, without even thinking about it. To act simply with a neighbor is to act with naïveté, without pretense, with sincerity, without disguise, and with freedom, without constraint; those are the eyes and the heart of the dove that charm Jesus Christ. Your hair, which represents the affections that are born in your heart and are your adornment, are so far removed from the things of the earth that they grow higher than the most excellent gifts, in order to arrest themselves in me alone. They resemble in this the goats that go up on the most inaccessible mountains.

Your teeth like flocks of sheep, that are shorn which come up from the washing, all with twins, and there is none barren among them. (4:2)

The teeth represent the understanding and the memory, which serve to chew and ruminate on the things one wants to understand. These powers have already been purified, as well as imagination and fantasy, so that there is no longer any confusion. They are aptly compared to shorn sheep, due to the simplicity that they have acquired by their union with divine persons, where they have had removed their excessive tendency and even ability to reason and to act with reflection and trouble, as they did before. But, although they are divested of their operations, they are not sterile or fruitless because of that. On the contrary, they yield double the fruit, and a fruit very pure and perfect, because the powers are never more fertile than when they are lost in relation to the creature and flow into God from their depths.

Your lips are like a scarlet lace: and your speech sweet. Your cheeks are like a piece of a pomegranate, besides that which lies hidden within. (4:3)

The lips represent the will, which is the mouth of the soul because it presses and kisses strongly, and with affection, what it loves. And since the will of this Lover only loves her God, and all her affections are for him, the Bridegroom compares her to lace dyed scarlet, which signifies the affections reunited in a single will, which is all charity and all love, with all the strength of this will being reunited in its divine object.

Your word, he adds, *is charming*, because your heart has a language that none other than I can hear because it speaks only to me. Your cheeks are like a quarter of a pomegranate. The pomegranate has several seeds that are all enclosed in one rind; in the same way your thoughts are as if reunited in me alone by your pure and perfect love. And all that I have described here, which belongs to the powers, is nothing compared to the value of that which is hidden in your profoundest depths.

Your neck, is like the tower of David, which is built with bulwarks: a thousand bucklers hang upon it, all the armor of valiant men. (4:4)

The neck is the strength of the soul; it is well compared to the tower of David, because all the strength of this soul is in its God, who is the house of Jesus Christ and David. This great king protests in so many places in his psalms that God alone is his support, his refuge, his strength, and, especially, the tower of his strength (Ps 61:3–4). The bastions and the ramparts that surround it are the total abandonment that this soul has made of itself to its God. Confidence, faith, and hope have fortified it in its abandonment. The weaker it is in itself, the stronger it finds itself in God. One thousand shields are ready there to defend it against as many visible as invisible enemies, and it is armed with such strength from God that it does not fear a single attack as long as it remains this way, because here its state is not yet permanent.

Your two breasts like two young roes that are twins, which feed among the lilies. (4:5)

The Bride[5] receives here the facility to help souls, designated by her breasts, but she does not receive it with all the fullness that will be communicated to her later; this facility is only implanted in her, like a seed of fertility, the abundance of which is marked by the young roes that are twins. They are twins because they come from a single source, which is Jesus Christ; they feed among the lilies, since they are nourished by the purity of doctrine, among the examples of the same Jesus Christ.

This passage is explained further in chapter 7, verse 3.

Till the day break, and the shadows retire, I will go to the mountain of myrrh, and to the hill of frankincense. (4:6)

The Bridegroom interrupts the praise of his Lover to invite her to follow him toward the mountain where myrrh grows and up to the hills where frankincense is picked. Until the time, he says, that the day of new life begins to appear, when you should be received in my Father, and the shadows that hold you in the darkness of the most naked faith retire and disappear, I will go to the mountain of myrrh, because you will only find me henceforth in bitterness and in the cross. However, this will be for me a mountain with a very agreeable odor, since the odor of your sufferings will mount toward me, like incense, and it will be by them that I will take my rest in you.

You are all fair, O my love, and there is not a spot in you. (4:7)

Until the soul became completely melted into bitterness and the cross, although she was beautiful, she was not yet completely beautiful; but since she has melted under the weight of trouble and afflictions, she is all fair, and there is no remaining stain or deformity in her. She will be disposed by this to permanent union, if her nature, still hard and contracted, strict and limited, does not prevent this happiness. This quality is not a stain that is in her or anything that offends God; it is only a defect of nature, taken from Adam, which her Bridegroom will gently destroy. But for her, since the cross has completely disfigured her in the eyes of men, she is completely beautiful in the eyes of her Bridegroom; and since she possesses no more beauty, she has found true beauty.

Come from Lebanon, my spouse, come from Lebanon, come: you will be crowned from the top of Amana, from the top of Senir and Hermon, from the dens of the lions, from the mountains of the leopards. (4:8)

The Bridegroom calls her here by the name of Bride and orders her to hurry in letting herself be consummated, destroyed, and annihilated, and then to accept the spiritual marriage. He calls her to be married and crowned. But, O Bridegroom, shall I say it? Why invite a Bride so strongly and so continually to a wedding for which she is very impassioned? You call her from Lebanon, although she is in Jerusalem! Is it because you sometimes give the name of Lebanon to Jerusalem, or else is it to mark, by the height of this famous mountain, the elevation to which she has arrived in your eyes? She has scarcely any more of the road to travel before being united with you in an immortal knot, and when she appears to approach your bed, she is pushed away from it by sixty strong men. Is there not some cruelty in drawing her so forcefully, although with such sweetness, to possess a good that she values more than a thousand lives, and, when she is close to her possession, to rebuff her so rudely? O God, you order, you call, you give the disposition of the state before giving the state, as one gives an exquisite liquid drop by drop, so as to make it more desirable. Oh, what do you not make this soul suffer through the delay of what you promise her? *Come*, he tells her, *my Bride*, because there is now only one more thing to do in order to be so in reality. Until now, I have called you my Beautiful, my Beloved, my Dove, but I have not yet called you by the name of Bride. Oh, how sweet this name is! But the possession of it will be sweeter and more charming! *Come*, he says again, *from the top of the highest mountains*; this means from the pure practice of the most eminent virtues, indicated by the mountains of Amana, of Senir, and of Hermon, which are close to Mount Lebanon. However exalted all this might appear to you, and although it might in fact be so, it is still necessary to go higher and bypass all things to enter with me into the bosom of my Father and to rest yourself there without an intermediary and by the loss of all means, the immediate and central union only coming into being above all created things. But come also from the dens of lions and from the mountains of leopards because it will only be through the cruelest persecutions of men and of demons, like so many ferocious beasts, that you will be able to arrive at so divine a state. It is time to raise yourself higher than ever above all of that, since you are ready to be crowned with the attributes of my Bride.

You have wounded my heart, my sister, my spouse, you have wounded my heart with one of your eyes, and with one hair of your neck. (4:9)

You are my sister, since we belong to the same Father, and you are my Bride, since I have already married you, and there is little left before our marriage is consummated. *My Sister, my Bride.* Oh, words too sweet for a soul afflicted by the beauty that she loves, and by which she is so tenderly loved, which does not let itself be possessed! *You have wounded my heart,* he says to her, *you have wounded my heart.* You have inflicted on him, O Bride, a double wound. One is by the look of your eyes, as if he has said, what wounded and charmed me about you is all your most intense unhappiness, all your disgrace, and your most extreme woes; all this has not caused you to take your eye off me in order for you to behold yourself. You were not even looking at the wounds that I caused you to receive or those I was inflicting on you myself—as if they had not touched you at all. For your pure and righteous love kept you focused uniquely on me and did not permit you to consider yourself or your own interest, but only to envision me with love as your sovereign object. But alas! this afflicted Lover would say, how have I regarded you, since I do not know where you are?

She does not know that her gaze has become so purified that, being always direct and without reflection, she is not aware of it and does not notice that she has not stopped seeing. Moreover, from the moment that it can no longer be seen and one forgets oneself, as well as all creatures, it is necessary that one look at God, and the interior gaze rests on him. The other wound, says the Bridegroom again, is inflicted on me by the union presented by your carefully braided hair. This marks rather clearly that all the affections of the Lover were reunited in God alone, and that she has lost all her will in that of her God. In this way the abandonment of her whole self to the will of God by the loss of all self-will as well as the righteousness with which she applies herself to God without returning to herself any more are the two arrows that have wounded the heart of her Bridegroom.

How beautiful are your breasts, my sister, my spouse! your breasts are more beautiful than wine, and the sweet smell of your ointments above all aromatic spices. (4:10)

The Bridegroom, predicting all the conquests his Bride will achieve for him and how much milk he will get from her breast to nourish innumerable souls, admires her more because, it is necessary to remark, the farther the Bride advances, the fuller her breasts become. The Bridegroom always fills them more for her, which makes him say: *Your breasts are beautiful!* They ravish me and charm me. They are more beautiful than wine because they have wine and milk, wine for the strong and milk for the children. The smells by which you draw souls to me infinitely surpass all perfumes. There will be an odor in you that they will only know when they are advanced, an odor that will draw them and will make them run after you in order to come to me, and they will be led to me by you. This secret odor will surprise those who do not know this mystery. However, their experience will force them to say, I do not know what you have that draws me; it is an admirable odor, from which one can hardly defend oneself, although one does not penetrate it; it must be the ointment of the Spirit, which only Christ the Lord can communicate to his wives.

JEANNE GUYON

Your lips, my spouse, are like a dripping honeycomb, honey and milk are under your tongue; and the smell of your garments, like the smell of frankincense. (4:11)

As soon as the soul has reached the joy of being received forever in her God, she becomes a mother and nurse. Fertility is given to her; she is put into the state of the apostolic life, and from that moment the lips of this person are like a honeycomb that drips continually in aid of souls. These are only lips and not words, because it is the Bridegroom who speaks for his Bride, and the lips of his Bride serve as the organ by which he expresses his divine Word.

Honey and milk, he says, are under the tongue that I give you; it is I who put this honey and this milk under your tongue, and I who make them flow through you in aid of souls, according to their grasp. The Bride is all honey for those who must be won by the sweetness of consolations. She is all milk for souls becoming simple and childlike. The odor of your virtues and of your good works, which serve you like clothes and to which you no longer cling, since the sense of self is banished from you, flows everywhere, like very fragrant incense.

My sister, my spouse, is a garden enclosed, a garden enclosed, a fountain sealed up. (4:12)

The sacred Bridegroom only acts as the panegyrist of his Bride in order to make us see what he wants us to become, by following her example. *My Sister and my Bride*, he says, *is an enclosed garden*, both on the outside and on the inside. Since there is nothing inside of her that is not entirely mine, there is no longer anything outside of her either, or in any of her actions, that is not for me. She is not the proprietor of a single action or of anything else that might be; she is enclosed everywhere, and there is nothing in her for herself or for any other creature. She is also a fountain, since she is intimately united with me, the spring from which she must spread water over all the earth, but she is a fountain that I keep sealed, in such a way that not even one drop will get out, except by my order. And thus the water that she will distribute will be very pure and not mixed, as it is coming out from my spring.

Your plants are a paradise of pomegranates with the fruits of the orchard. Cypress with spikenard. (4:13)

Your fertility will be so spread out that it will resemble a delicious garden full of pomegranates, where the union with the source renders you useful to everyone. The spirit of God will communicate itself through you to diverse places, as one sees with the pomegranate, which represents souls united in charity, communicating its energy to all the seeds that it encloses. It is true that the principal sense of this passage regards the church, but no one would believe how great a fruit the well-annihilated soul would produce in aid of men, as soon as it was applied to help them. There are fruits of all sorts in this garden, with each soul having, along with the qualities common to the others, its own particular character. One excels in charity, and this is the pomegranate; another is known for its sweetness, and this is the apple; another distinguishes itself by suffering and by the odor of its good example, and this is the cypress; and yet another distills devotion, recollection, and peace, and this is the spikenard. And all are helped by the annihilated Bride, according to their needs.

Spikenard and saffron, sweet cane and cinnamon, with all the trees of Lebanon, myrrh and aloes with all the chief perfumes. (4:14)

He continues to put together a portrait of particular qualities of souls, of whom, as the pure result of his goodness, he has made his Bride the mother. And in explaining the characteristics of others, he makes them see, at the same time, that they are all enclosed in his Lover, as in the principle of communication by which they are distributed.

The fountain of gardens: the well of living waters, which run with a strong stream from Lebanon. (4:15)

The fountain of the gardens is the Bridegroom himself, who is the source of grace, which makes the spiritual plants spring up, turn green, grow, and bear fruit. The Bride is like a well in which living and life-giving waters are enclosed. Waters run from the Bridegroom through the Bride, descending impetuously from the height of divinity, represented by Mount Lebanon, to inundate the earth. This refers to all the souls that truly want to enter into the interior kingdom, and tolerate the work, in the hope of harvesting fruits from it.

Arise, O north wind, and come, O south wind, blow through my garden, and let its aromatic spices flow. (4:16)

The Bride invites the Holy Spirit, the Spirit of life, to come and breathe in her, so that this garden so full of flowers and fruit might spread its odor for several souls to use. It is also the Bridegroom who asks that the resurrection of this Bride happen soon and that she take up a new life, by the breath of this life-giving Spirit, the one who will reanimate and revive this annihilated soul, so that the marriage might be perfectly consummated.

CHAPTER 5

Let my beloved come into his garden, and eat the fruit of his apple trees. I come into my garden, O my sister, my spouse, I have gathered my myrrh, with my aromatic spices: I have eaten the honeycomb with my honey, I have drunk my wine with my milk: eat, O friends, and drink, and be inebriated, my dearly beloved. (5:1)

The Bride, as her Beloved told her, is a beautiful garden, always full of flowers and fruit. She insistently begs him to come there to enjoy its delights and to eat its fruits, as if she were saying, I only want beauty or fertility for you. Come, therefore, to your garden, possess everything there, eat from it, and use it in aid of chosen souls, without which I do not want any of it. The Beloved agrees to what his Bride desires. He truly wants to eat everything, but he wants the Bride to be present, so that she can be a witness as he nourishes himself first with what he wants to have his friends eat. *I have gathered*, he says, *my myrrh;* but it is for you, O my Bride, because it is your dish, which is only bitterness, because there is always suffering in this mortal life. This myrrh, however, is never alone; it is always accompanied by very pleasing aromatic spices.

The odor is for the Bridegroom, and the bitter myrrh is for the Bride. As for me, says this Bridegroom, I have eaten all the sweetness that there was; I have drunk the wine and the milk; I have nourished myself from the sweetness of your charity. As delighted as he is by the generosity of his Bride, he orders all of his friends and his children to come and nourish themselves and quench their thirst through his Bride, who is a garden full of fruits and watered with milk and honey. A soul of this strength has what is necessary to provide for the spiritual needs of all sorts of people and can give excellent advise to all those who address themselves to her.

This can also be very well explained by the fact that the church invites Jesus Christ to come eat the fruit of the apple trees, which is nothing other than to gather the fruit of his merits by the sanctification of his predestined ones, such as he will do in his second coming. The Bridegroom therefore responds to his very dear Bride *that he has come into his garden*, when he was incarnated, and *that he gathered his myrrh with his aromatic spices*, when he suffered the bitterness of his passion, which was accompanied by infinite merits and whose odor would go all the way up to God his father. *I have*, he adds, *eaten my honeycomb*. This is to be understood of his actions and teaching because he practiced what he preached; and he ordered us to do nothing more than he did first, meriting for us, by these very things that he practiced, the grace of that which he asks of us. In the same way the life of Jesus Christ was like a honeycomb, the divine order and sweetness of which constituted his nourishment and his happiness in light of the glory that his father received from it and the utility that came back from it to men. *I have drunk my wine with my milk*. What is this wine that you have drunk, O divine Savior, and from which you were so strongly inebriated that you forgot yourself? This wine was the excessive love that he bore for men, which made him forget that he was God, in order to think only of their salvation. He was so inebriated that it is said of him by a prophet that he will be satisfied by opprobrium, so strong was his charity. He drank his wine with his milk when he drank his blood in the Last Supper, which, under the appearance of wine, was virginal milk. This milk was the flowing of the divinity of Jesus Christ into his humanity. This divine Savior invites all his chosen, who feel like nourishing themselves as he did, by suffering, opprobrium, and indignities, and by the love of his examples and of his pure doctrine, which will be for them delicious wine and milk. The wine will give them the strength and the courage to do what is ordered for them, and the milk will charm them by the sweetness of the doctrine that is taught to them. We are therefore all invited to listen to and to imitate Jesus Christ.

I sleep, and my heart watches; the voice of my beloved knocking: Open to me, my sister, my love, my dove, my undefiled: for my head is full of dew, and my locks of the drops of the nights. (5:2)

The soul who waits up for her God feels that, although her exterior appears dead and as if stunned and lifeless, like a sleeping body, nevertheless her heart always has a secret and unknown vigor, which holds it to God. Moreover, truly advanced souls often feel surprising things, which happen only at night and while half asleep. It seems that God operates in them more during the night and in sleep than during the day. The soul, in this sleep, truly hears the voice of her Beloved, who just came to knock on her door. He wants to be heard. *Open to me, my Sister;* I am coming to you, my love, whom I have chosen to make my Bride over all others, my dove in simplicity, my all perfect, my all beautiful and stainless. Consider that my head is full and still dripping with what I suffered for you during the night of my mortal life and that I wiped away for your love the drops of the cruelest persecution of the night. I come therefore to you in this way, so as to make you a part of my opprobrium, my indignities, and my confusions! Until now you have been part of the bitterness of my cross, but you have not been part of the indignity and confusion of my cross. The one is very different from the other; you will have a terrible experience of this.

I have put off my garment, how shall I put it on? I have washed my feet, how shall I defile them? (5:3)

The Bride, seeing that the Bridegroom speaks of making her a part of his indignities, fears much, and as much as she had been courageous and intrepid in accepting the cross, she is now afraid of the abjection with which she is menaced. Many want to bear the cross, but hardly anyone wants to carry the infamy of the cross. When this infamy is proposed to this soul, she fears two things: one is being clothed again in what had been removed from her, so as to know herself and her natural faults; the other is becoming defiled with the affections of creatures. I have, she says, taken off myself, my faults, and what remained of the sinner Adam in me: how can I ever put them on again? And yet it seems to me this is only thing that can cause abjection and confusion; if creatures scorn me without my having caused it by my own fault, I will make this a pleasure and a glory, hoping that this will glorify my God and make me even more agreeable in his eyes. I have washed and purified my affections in such a way that there is nothing inside of me that does not belong to my Beloved. How could I defile them again by commerce with creatures? O poor blind one, against what do you defend yourself? The Bridegroom only wants to test your fidelity and see if you are completely within his will. He appeared guilty; he was covered with confusion, filled with opprobrium, and numbered among the transgressors, he who was innocence itself (Isa 53:3–12); and you who are criminal, you would not tolerate appearing as such. Ah! You will be truly punished for your resistance!

My beloved put his hand through the key hole, and my bowels were moved at his touch. (5:4)

The Beloved, in spite of the resistance of his Bride, puts his hand through a little passage that is still open for him, which is what remains of abandonment, in spite of the repugnancies that the soul feels in abandoning itself so excessively. A soul of this degree bears a depth of submission to the entire will of God, such that she cannot refuse him anything. However, when God explains his particular designs, and, using only the rights that he has acquired over her, he asks her for the last renunciations and the most extreme sacrifices—ah!—this is when all of her bowels are moved, and she truly finds a pain that she did not expect to see. This pain comes from something to which she was attached without knowing it. At this touch all of her nature quivers because it is a painful touch. And this is the most deeply felt ache of the soul, like that which the most patient of men would feel, when, having suffered inconceivable pain without complaint, he could not stop himself from crying out at this touch from the hand of God. Ah! Out of grace, my friends, forget all my other faults, which horrify you! Only have pity for me regarding one thing, that the hand of God touched me (Job 19:21). In the same way the Bride feels herself quiver all over with this touch. How jealous you are, O divine Bridegroom, that your Lover should do your will completely, since a simple excuse, which appears so just, offends you so strongly! Can you not prevent a Bride so dear and so faithful from having such resistance to you? But it was necessary for her consummation. The Bridegroom allows this fault in his Bride, so as to punish her and to purify her at the same time from the attachment that she had to her purity and her innocence and from the repugnance that she felt to taking off her self-righteousness, because, although she knew the righteousness was from her Bridegroom, she was nonetheless attaching herself to it, and she was appropriating something from it.

I arose up to open to my beloved: my hands dropped with myrrh, and my fingers were full of the choicest myrrh. (5:5)

The soul has no sooner recognized her fault than she repents of it and is raised up by a renewal of abandonment and an extension of sacrifice. This is not, however, without pain and bitterness; the inferior part and all of her nature are seized with sadness and fear. All her actions are rendered more painful and more bitter from it, the strongest bitterness that she has ever felt.

I opened the bolt of my door to my beloved: but he had turned aside, and was gone. My soul melted when he spoke: I sought him, and found him not: I called, and he did not answer me. (5:6)

It is as if this soul were saying, I lifted the barrier that prevented both my total loss of self and the consummation of my marriage, because this divine marriage can only be consummated when the complete loss of self happens. I have therefore taken away this barrier by the most courageous abandonment and the purest sacrifice ever. I have opened up to my Beloved, believing that he would enter and would heal the pain that he had caused me by his touching me. But alas, this stroke would be too gentle if he were to apply the cure so quickly! He hides, he flees, he goes away, he only leaves this afflicted Lover the wound that he inflicted on her, the pain of her fault, and the dirtiness that she feels from rising. The goodness of the Bridegroom is so great, however, that, although he is hiding, he does not cease to offer great graces to his friends, all the greater if the deprivations are longer and harder, as he did to his Bride, who will find herself with a new disposition that will be very advantageous to her, although she does not recognize it as such. Her soul melted and liquefied as soon as her Beloved spoke, and, by this liquefaction, she loses her hard and shrunken qualities, which were preventing the consummation of the spiritual marriage. In this way she becomes entirely ready to flow back to her origins. *I sought my Beloved and found him not;* I called him, but he did not offer me a single word. Oh, inconceivable affliction!

The keepers that go about the city found me: they struck me: and wounded me: the keepers of the walls took away my veil from me. (5:7)

Unfortunate Bride! Never has any such thing happened to you before because until now your Bridegroom watched over you. You had rested securely in his shadow; you were assuredly in his arms, but since he has separated himself from you for your fault, ah! what has happened to you? You believed yourself to have suffered a lot through such tests as he had already made of your fidelity, but they were small things compared to what you have left to suffer. What you have suffered with him was only the shadow of suffering, and you must not expect less. Did you think that you were marrying a God ripped with wounds, pierced with nails, and stripped of everything without being treated the same way? This soul finds herself battered and wounded by all those who have kept watch over the city, those who until now had not dared attack her but watched over her incessantly, taking their time to strike her. Who are these keepers? They are the ministers of the justice of God. They wound her, and they take her veil, so dear to her for her own righteousness. O unfortunate Bride, what will you do in so pitiful a situation? The Bridegroom will no longer want you after so sad an accident, which carries with it the abjection of having been mistreated by soldiers and covered with wounds, to the point of having left your veil in their hands, although it was your principal ornament. If you still continue to seek your Beloved, people will say that you are crazy to present yourself to him that way. Moreover, if you stop seeking him, you will die from languor. Your state is certainly deplorable.

I adjure you, O daughters of Jerusalem, if you find my beloved, that you tell him that I languish with love. (5:8)

True love does not have eyes to look at itself. This afflicted soul forgets her wounds, although they still bleed. She no longer remembers her loss. She does not even speak of it; she thinks only of the one she loves. And she looks for him with a degree of strength proportional to the number of obstacles in her possession. She addresses herself to interior souls and says to them, O you to whom my Beloved will undoubtedly show himself, I order you, by him, to tell him that I languish with love for him. O most beautiful of women, do you not want them to tell him of your wounds and what you have suffered in searching for him? No, no, answers this generous soul, I am overpaid for my pains, since I have suffered them for him and I prefer them to the greatest goods. Only say one thing to my Beloved—that I languish with love for him. The wound that his love has made in the bottom of my heart is so strong that I am insensible to all exterior sufferings. I even dare say, in comparison to it, that they are refreshing to me.

What manner of one is your beloved of the beloved, O you most beautiful among women? What manner of one is your beloved of the beloved, that you have so adjured us? (5:9)

The daughters of Jerusalem do not cease to call this Lover *the most beautiful among women* because her most painful wounds are hidden, and those that appear even give luster to her beauty. These other girls are astonished to see a love so strong, so constant, and so faithful in the middle of such trials. They ask: *What manner of one is your beloved?* He must be, they say, of an unequaled merit to possess this sort of Lover. Although these girls are spiritual, they are not yet in a state of understanding such a strong and naked path. If this Bride had been thinking about herself, she would have said: Do not call me beautiful (Ruth 1:20). She would have used some word of humility. But she is incapable of all that; she only has one aim, which is the search for her Beloved. She can only speak of him; she can only think of him. And even if she saw herself accelerating toward an abyss, she would not perform any reflection. That which she previously performed, due to the fear of becoming defiled, cost her dearly, since it caused for her the absence of her Bridegroom. Instructed in this way by her disgrace, she can no longer consider herself, and even if she were as hideous as she is beautiful, she could no longer think about it at all.

My beloved is white and ruddy, chosen out of thousands. (5:10)

My Beloved, says this soul, is white by his purity, by his innocence, and by his simplicity. He is ruddy by his charity and because he wanted to be made crimson and colored with his blood. He is white by his candor and ruddy by the fire of his love. My Beloved is chosen out of thousands, meaning out of all. I have chosen him and have preferred him to all others. His Father has chosen him, among all the children of men, as his only Son and beloved, in whom he is well pleased (Matt 3:17). Thus, if you want to know, O young hearts, who is the one I love so passionately, he is the one whose beauty surpasses that of all children of men, because grace is spread over his lips (Ps 45:2). He is the one who is the spark of eternal light, the unstained mirror of the majesty of God and the image of his goodness (Wis 7:26). Judge if I am right to give him all the preference of my love.

His head is as the finest gold: his locks as branches of palm trees, black as a raven. (5:11)

By the hair that covers his head, one must understand the holy humanity, which covers and hides the divinity. This same hair, or this humanity stretched on the cross, resembles the branches of the palm tree because there, dying for men, it achieved victory over their enemies and will make them merit the fruit of redemption, which we had been promised by his death. Thus, the heart of the

149

palm opened because the church was born from the heart of its Bridegroom. There the adorable humanity appears black as a raven, for it appears not only covered with wounds, but also charged with sins and with the blackness of all men, although it is whiteness and purity without equal. There, where Jesus Christ seemed a worm and not a man, the opprobrium of men and scorned by the people (Ps 22:6), how black was he? This blackness nevertheless did not stop it from revealing its beauty because it only had the charge of unburdening everyone of this blackness.

His eyes like doves upon brooks of waters, which are washed with milk, and sit beside the plentiful streams. (5:12)

She continues to hold up the perfections of her Bridegroom; all his riches and his grand qualities are the joy of the Lover in the middle of her miseries. His eyes, she says, are so pure, so chaste, and so simple, his understandings so purified of all that is material, that they are like doves. They are not doves of an ordinary beauty, but doves washed in the milk of divine grace that, having been given to him in abundance, communicated all the treasures of the wisdom and knowledge of God to him (Col 2:3). He is among brooks of waters in the little souls who, although little advanced, do not cease to be agreeable because of their smallness, especially once they learn to make use of it. But he makes his continual residence among these abandoned souls, among these swift and rapid waters that do not stop for anything in the world and which rise up with more force and run with more impetuousness when presented with the least obstacle.

His cheeks are like beds of aromatic spices set by the perfumers. His lips are like lilies dripping choice myrrh. (5:13)

The cheeks of the Bridegroom represent the two parts of his soul, upper and lower, which are in an order so admirable that nothing could exceed them, as they give off an inconceivable odor. And as the cheeks are united with the head, so also this noble and beautiful soul is united with divinity. The beds full of aromatic spices signify the powers and the interior senses of his holy humanity, which are all in a perfect order. It is assuredly a talented perfumer

150

who chooses and arranges them well, since it is the Holy Spirit that gave so beautiful an order to the entire interior and exterior of Jesus Christ. His lips are well compared to lilies. But these are red lilies, which are common in Syria and of a rare beauty. What lips could be more vermillion, more aromatic, and more beautiful than those that spread the word of the Spirit and of life, and the knowledge of eternal life? From these same lips drip excellent myrrh, since the doctrine of Jesus Christ carries penance, the mortification of passions, and continual renunciation.

His hands are turned and as of gold, full of hyacinths. His belly as of ivory, set with sapphires. (5:14)

His hands signify interior and exterior operations, with the interior ones being all of gold, since they do not reach for anything except to give back to God his Father all that he receives from him. Also, his hands are themselves fashioned and turned, to signify that he receives nothing from his Father that he does not give back to him and that he retains nothing, because he is extremely faithful to return his kingdom to the hands of God his Father (1 Cor 15:24). They are also full of hyacinths because each one of his interior operations distinguishes itself by the most eminent degree of the virtue to which they belong, especially of religion toward his Father and of mercy toward men. His exterior operations are all distributive, liberal, and open in aid of men. His hands are made to be turned; they cannot retain anything. They are full of the most reserved grace and mercy, which he communicates and distributes unceasingly to his poor creatures. His humanity, represented by his belly, is compared to ivory because everything in it is very pure and very solid, since everything there is united to God and dependent on his divinity. It is also adorned and embellished with all possible perfections, which glisten in it like so many precious stones.

His legs like pillars of marble, that are set upon bases of gold. His form as of Lebanon, excellent as the cedars. (5:15)

All the lower part of the body, spoken of here under the name of the legs and the feet that support them, is taken singularly for the flesh of the Savior, and it is well designated by marble, due to its incorruptibility. For even though it succumbed to death for a few hours, all the while being seated on a golden base, which means united hypostatically to divinity, it was not at all reduced to corruption (Acts 2:31). And this entire august sanctuary, upheld by the Word of God, which gives him his incorruptibility, will last eternally. His beauty is immense and so great that it equals that of Mount Lebanon, which is very expansive and extremely fertile, since all the cedars, which are the saints, are planted on it. But although all the saints are planted in Jesus Christ, he is nevertheless elected like them, as a man, being the first predestined. And he is elected for all men, because no one is elected who was not elected in him and by him. It is he who merited their election, all having been predestined to conform to the glory of Jesus Christ, so that he might be the first born of many brothers (Rom 8:29).

His throat most sweet, and he is all lovely: such is my beloved, and he is my friend, O you daughters of Jerusalem. (5:16)

The good qualities of mediocre things are sufficiently expressed by ordinary praises, but some subjects are so far above expression that one can only praise them by avowing that they are above all praise. Such is the divine Bridegroom, who by excess of his perfections renders his Bride mute even when she tries to praise him more forcefully in order to attract hearts and minds. Her passion makes her break out in some praise of the kind that she finds most suited to her Bridegroom. But once no longer carried away by her love, she is ashamed of having wanted to express a merit that is inexpressible. She condemns herself to a sudden silence, which seems to put disorder in a discourse that she uttered as much to vent her passion as to invite her companions to love the one for whom she is so strongly impassioned. Furthermore, her silence is preceded by these words only: *His throat is most sweet.* As the throat serves to express the voice, she makes evident that he is the expression of divinity, and, as God, he is above all attributes and all qualities. If he is accorded some of these, it is to accommodate the weakness of the creature who cannot explain this in any other manner. Then, letting herself continue to be transported by him, she adds, *he is all lovely,* as if she was saying, O my companions, do not believe what I told you regarding my Beloved, but desire to judge it by your own experience. Taste how he is sweet, and then you will be in a state to understand the righteousness and the strength of my love. He is still desirable not only because he is the desire of the eternal hills (Gen 49:26) and the one that the nations desire (Hag 2:7), but also because our hope is to participate in his glory according to our weakness, since he can be imitated by everyone, albeit not in all his perfection. It is, O daughters of Jerusalem, the one who has all his rare qualities, infinitely more than I would know how to describe, whom I love, whom I seek, and for whom I am so impassioned. Judge if I am not right to love him.

Where has your beloved gone, O you most beautiful among women? where has your beloved turned aside, and we will seek him with you? (5:17)

This soul, in her abandonment and in her sorrow, becomes a great missionary. She preaches with such eloquence about the perfection of the one whom she loves, about his infinite sweetness and about his pleasantness, so that she makes her companions want to look for him along with her and to know him. O vanquishing love, when you flee more forcefully, then you achieve more conquests! And this soul, who is like an impetuous torrent due to her violent love, drags with her all she meets. Oh, who would not want to see and to seek so desirable a lover? Young hearts who spend time so uselessly in creaturely amusements, why do you not take up this search? Oh, you would be infinitely happy!

CHAPTER 6

My beloved has gone down into his garden, to the bed of aromatic spices, to feed in the gardens, and to gather lilies. (6:1)

O fortunate Lover, after having looked so much for your Beloved, you finally have news of him! You had said so often that you would hold on to him so much that you would no longer let him leave. However, you have let him go farther than ever. Alas! she says, I was reckless; I did not consider that it was not for me to retain him. It is up to him to give himself and to withdraw himself as he likes, and I must only want his will and be indifferent to his comings and goings. I avow that my love was self-interested, although I did not know it. I preferred, over his own pleasure, the pleasure that I had in loving him, seeing him, and possessing him. Ah! if I was fortunate enough to see him again, I would never act that way. I would let him come and go at his will, and this would be the means to lose him no more. I know, however, that he has gone down to the garden, this Beloved, and that he is in my soul, but he is so much there for him that I no longer want a part of it. He is in the profoundest depths, in the supreme part where that which is most aromatic is found. This is where God lives; it is the source and the seat of all virtues. He comes there in order to nourish himself of all that belongs to him because there is no longer anything that is mine or for me. He takes his innocent pleasures in this garden that he himself planted, cultivated, and made bear fruit by his living warmth. Let him gather his lilies; let all purity be for him; let him take all the pleasure and all the advantage from it.

I to my beloved, and my beloved to me, who feeds among the lilies. (6:2)

As soon as the soul is entirely lost to herself, she is completely disposed to be received in the nuptial bed of the Bridegroom, where she is no longer simply introduced to him but rather is tasting the sacred and the chaste delights of the kiss of his mouth that she had desired at first, and that she possesses at present by the essential union by which she just was gratified. She cannot stop herself from expressing her happiness by the words: *I to my beloved, and my beloved to me.* O inexplicable honor! I cannot say it otherwise than to say that I am completely and unreservedly for my Beloved, and that I possess him without any obstacle, hindrance, or restriction. O Bride worthy of the jealousy of the angels! You have finally found your Beloved, and although you are no longer so rash as to say that you will keep him, or will no longer let him leave, in any case you have him in a more solid manner than ever. You have him so as to lose him no longer; who would not congratulate you for such a great honor? You are so strongly for your Beloved that nothing prevents you from losing yourself in him; since you have been melted by the heat of his love, you have been allowed to flow into him, as if returning to your own end. Ah! says this incomparable Bride, if I am always for my Bridegroom, he is also all for me! For I feel once again his goodness; he gives himself to me in a way as ineffable as it is new. He pays back my pain with the most tender caresses. He nourishes himself still among the lilies of my purity. The lilies of the soul, which please him much more than those of the flesh, represent the general loss of the sense of self—a soul without a sense of self is a virgin soul. The lilies of the body are the integrity of the senses.

You are beautiful, O my love, sweet and comely as Jerusalem: terrible as an army set in array. (6:3)

The Beloved, having found his Bride completely free of a sense of self, all prepared for the consummation of the marriage, and to be received into him by the permanent and durable state, admires the beauty of this soul. He tells her that she is beautiful and charming; he finds in her a certain sweetness and an attractiveness that approaches the divine. *You are*, he says to her, *comely as Jerusalem*, in that, since you have lost that which was yours in order to devote it entirely to me, you are adorned and embellished with all that is mine, and you have a part in all that I possess. I find you all ready to be my dwelling place, as I want to be yours; you will be in me, and I will be in you. But if you have such attraction and such sweetness for me, you are, on the contrary, terrible to the devil and to sin, like an army ready for battle. And without fighting you will cause your enemies to flee because they fear you as much as me, since you have become one same spirit with God (1 Cor 6:17), by the loss of yourself in me. O poor souls who fight continually throughout your life and only win very small victories, although they cost you many wounds, if you give yourself to God for good and let yourself be his, you will be more feared and more terrible than an infinite number of men armed for combat and already set in array.

JEANNE GUYON

Turn away your eyes from me, for they have made me flee away.
Your hair is like a flock of goats, that appear from Gilead. (6:4)

One would not believe the scrupulousness of the love of God and the extreme purity that he asks of souls who are his wives. What constitutes the perfection of one state is the imperfection of another. Before, the Bridegroom would rejoice infinitely because his Bride never turned her gaze away from him above, but today he does not want her to look at him. He says that the gaze of the Bride will make him flee. Ah! from the moment the soul starts to flow into her God, as a river into its origin, she must be completely lost and submerged in him. She must then even lose the perceptible vision of God and all distinct knowledge, as little as it might be. There is no longer any vision or discernment where there is no longer any division or distinction, but instead a perfect mixture. In this way the creature could not look at God in this state without seeing her very self and noticing at the same time the operations of his love. But all this must be hidden and covered from her view, so that, like a seraphim, she must have veiled eyes, in order no longer to see anything or seek anything in this life. That is, she is not to want to see anything or to look for any discovery by herself, which she cannot do without infidelity. But that does not prevent God from making her discover and understand whatever he pleases. Only the heart remains uncovered because it cannot love too much.

When I speak of distinction, I do not mean the distinction of some divine perfection in God himself, because this has been lost for a long time, since, from the first absorption, the soul only has a subjective view of God working within her, which is confused and general, without distinction of attributes or of perfections. And although the Lover might have spoken of the grandeur and sovereign qualities of her Beloved, she only would have done it to win souls, without her needing any of these distinct views for herself. And this is only given to her according to the need to speak of it or to write of it. The distinction of which I want to speak is of God and of the soul. Here the soul must no longer and can no longer make the distinction between God and herself. God is she and she is God, since, by the consummation of the marriage, she is flowing back to God and finds herself lost in him, without being able to distinguish herself or find herself again. The true consummation of marriage makes the mixture of the soul with her God so great and so intimate that she can no longer distinguish herself or see herself, and it is this mixture that deifies, so to speak, the actions of this creature, having arrived at a state as high and as sublime as this one here. For they emanate from an entirely divine principle, due to the unity that just was knitted between God and this melted soul flowing back to him, God becoming the principle of the actions and the words of this soul, although she gives birth to them and produces them on the outside.

The marriage of the body, by which two people are one same flesh (Gen 2:24), is only a weak figure of this here, by which, in the terms of Saint Paul, God and the soul are only one spirit from now on (1 Cor 6:17). People are so pained to know at exactly what time the spiritual marriage happens; this is easy to see from what has been said. The engagement or mutual promises are made in the union of the powers, when the soul gives herself entirely to her God, and her God gives himself entirely to her, with the intention to admit her into his union; this is an agreement and a reciprocal promise. But alas, there is still a road to follow, and there is much to suffer before this union, so desired, can be granted and consummated! The marriage takes place when the soul finds herself dead and expired in the arms of the Bridegroom, who, seeing her more disposed, receives her in his union. But the consummation of the marriage only happens when the soul is so melted, annihilated, and distant from herself that she can totally, unreservedly, flow into her God. Then this admirable fusion of the creature with her creator takes place, which reduces them into unity, so to speak, although with an infinite disproportion, such as a drop of water is to the sea. Although having become the sea, she remains, all the while, a little tiny drop of water, in spite of the fact that she is proportionate, in the quality of the water, with all the sea and ready to be mixed with it so as to make only one sea.

If ever a few saints or authors have established this divine marriage in states that are less advanced than those I describe, it is because they were taking engagement for marriage and marriage for consummation. And while speaking with the freedom of mind, they were not always distinguishing exactly these degrees, so that one attributes often the divine union to states that are only the first steps of the interior path. All the souls who have had the favor of engagement believe themselves brides, so much so that the Bridegroom himself refers to them with this name, as we have seen in this song. There is only the experience and the divine light, which can make us know this difference.

The Bridegroom still compares the thoughts of his Bride, designated by her hair, to the goats that have appeared and not to the goats who have stopped. This is because the mind of these consummated people is so clean and so empty of all thoughts that those that come only appear for a few moments and for as much time as it is necessary for the effect that God intends for them.

Your teeth like a flock of sheep, which come up from the washing, all with twins, and there is none barren among them. (6:5)

The Bridegroom repeats to his Bride that which he has said before, to make her see that she presently has, very truly and in free use, what she only had before as a seed. Her teeth are her powers, which have become so innocent, pure, and clean that they are perfectly washed. The sheep that they resemble are not sheared like the first ones, because facility with the use of the powers, in an admirable manner and without confusion, is restored. This is because the memory only recalls things that are necessary, according to the spirit of God, without disordered forms, and at the necessary time. They are no longer sterile, having a double fecundity: one, to do much more than they did before, and the other, to do it better.

Your cheeks are like the bark of a pomegranate, beside what is hidden within you. (6:6)

As the rind is the least part of the pomegranate, which encloses in itself all its goodness, so it is that what appears externally from the soul of this degree is very little compared to what is hidden. The inside is full of the purest charity and of the most reserved graces but covered with a very common exterior. This is because God takes pleasure in hiding souls whom he wants for himself. Men are not worthy of knowing them, and the angels admire and respect them, although under an exterior that is the simplest in the world. In this way, those who would only judge according to appearance would believe them to be the most common, although they are the delights of God. These are not at all the ones who shine in the world by miracles or by extraordinary gifts; all this is too little for them. God reserves them, and he is so very jealous of them that he does not expose them to the eyes of men. On the contrary, he seals them with his seal, as he himself says that his Bride is the sealed fountain (Song 4:12), of which he is himself the seal. But why does he keep her sealed? It is because love is strong as death and jealousy is as hard as hell (Song 8:6). Oh, how well this expresses what I advance because, as death takes away everything from the one whom it holds, so love rips everything from the soul and hides it in the secret of a living sepulcher. The jealousy of God is as hard as hell, in that there is nothing he would not do to possess his brides fully.

Someone will object to me, stating that this soul is not so hidden, since she helps her neighbor. But I respond that this is what covers her with the most abjection, with God using this to render her more unworthy due to the contradictions that she must endure. It is true that those who address themselves to her, and who are in a state to receive some participation in the grace that is in her, feel its effects. But, beyond that, these people are also exceedingly hidden. Ordinarily, God permits the common exterior of the chosen soul to scandalize even those who have a part of their graces, until they often separate themselves from her after God has drawn from her the effect that he intended. In this the Bridegroom treats his Bride like himself. All those whom he had won for his Father, were they not scandalized by him (Mark 14:27)? Let us examine a little the life of Jesus Christ; nothing was more common, as far as the exterior is concerned. Those who do the most extraordinary things are copies of the saints, of whom Jesus Christ said that they would do greater works than he did (John 14:12); these souls here are other Jesus Christs. This is why we notice fewer of the traits of the saints in them. But as for the characteristics of Jesus Christ, if we examine closely, we will see them very clearly there. Jesus Christ, however, is a scandal to the Jews and seems a folly to the Gentiles (1 Cor 1:23). In their simplicity these people often scandalize those who, attached to legal ceremonies rather than to the simplicity of the Bible, only look at the rind of the pomegranate without penetrating the inside.

Oh, you who use them in this way, pay attention to the pomegranate to which the Bride is so well compared, which has a very unworthy rind, although what it encloses is the most excellent of all fruits and even the most agreeable to see and to taste. This is the admirable order of charity that the Bridegroom began to put in the heart of his Bride when he introduced her into his cellars, and which finds itself completed with the pomegranate being fully ripened.

There are threescore queens, and fourscore concubines, and young maidens without number. (6:7)

The Bridegroom says that there are souls chosen among all, like queens, and others who participate in his singular favors, although they do not have the quality of the sovereign ones, as well as a score of young hearts who belong to him in a common way and who start to sigh after his union. But this soul surpasses all in the affection that he has for her. O God, to what happiness have you raised your Bride! He has a few of them who appear like queens, held above the others by the splendor of their virtues. There are several others of them to whom you give part of your caresses, but this Bride alone is more to you than all of the others put together.

One is my dove, my perfect one is but one, she is the only one of her mother, the chosen of her that bore her. The daughters saw her, and declared her most blessed: the queens and concubines, and they praised her. (6:8)

Although the first sense of this verse refers to the divine Mary and of the universal church, as there is, however, nothing attributed to the church as the mystical body that is not attributed proportionately to souls as its members, especially when they are perfectly pure, we can also say that there are souls that God elects for himself in each century in a very singular fashion. God says, therefore, that this soul in whom the marriage has been perfectly consummated by her total annihilation and by her entire loss is a dove in simplicity and that she is unique in that there are few who resemble her; she is also unique because she is reduced in God into the perfect unity of her origin. She is perfect, but with the perfections of

God himself. And because she is exempt from all sense of self and removed from her hard, shrunken, and narrow nature, from that moment, by her entire flowing back, she has entered into the innocence of God. She is perfect in her depths by the loss of all searching for herself. It is necessary to remark that, although the Bridegroom might have given some compliments before now to his Bride, he had not yet said (until she had entirely flowed back into her divine unity) that she was unique and perfect, because these qualities are only found in God when one is entirely consummated there by the permanent and durable state.

She is the only one of her mother, in that, having lost all the multiplicity of her nature, she finds herself alone and separated from all that is natural. The wisdom that engendered and produced her in order to lose her in its bosom is uniquely pleased by her. The most inward looking souls have seen her because God ordinarily permits such persons to be known a bit, sometimes giving a little discernment of their state to other very spiritual souls who are delighted by this knowledge and who, admiring their perfection, declare them fortunate. The queens, who are these elevated souls esteemed by everyone, as well as the common souls inferior in merit, give them equally grand praise because they feel the effects of the grace that is communicated to them. Although this seems contradictory to what was said above,[6] there is, however, no contradiction, because what is said here is understood of the apostolic state of Jesus Christ, where he was received at one moment as a king and savior, and where a little later in the same place he was made to die like a criminal.

Who is she that comes forth as the morning rising, fair as the moon, bright as the sun, terrible as an army set in array? (6:9)

These are the choirs of the Bridegroom's companions, who admire the beauty of his Bride. *Who is she*, they say, *that comes forth*, little by little, for it is necessary to know that the soul, although having reached God, raises herself little by little and perfects herself in this divine life until she arrives to her eternal journey. She raises herself up in God imperceptibly, like the dawn, until she comes to her perfect day and her consummated noon, which is the glory of heaven. But this eternal day starts from this life. *She is fair as the*

161

moon because she draws all her beauty from her sun; she is pure and brilliant, like the *sun*, because she is united to Jesus Christ, in order to be a participant in his glory and to be lost with him in God. *But she is terrible* to the demons, to sin, to the world, and to self-love, *as an army set in array.*

I went down into the garden of nuts, to see the fruits of the valleys, and to look if the vineyard had flourished, and the pomegranates budded. (6:10)

This soul is not so well established in her state in God that she does not still cast some looks back on herself; this is an infidelity, but one that is rare and that only comes from weakness. The Bridegroom permitted his Bride to commit this slight fault, so as to instruct us through this of the harm that self-reflection causes in the most advanced states. She is, therefore, returning for a moment to herself under the best pretexts in the world; it was in order to see there the fruits of her annihilation, and to see if the vineyard was flourishing, if it was advancing, and if her charity was fertile. Does not this seem very just and very reasonable?

I knew not: my soul troubled me for the chariots of Aminadab. (6:11)

I was doing this, she says, without thinking about it and without believing I was doing harm or displeasing my Bridegroom; however, no sooner had I committed this fault than my soul was troubled by the chariots of Aminadab, meaning by thousands and thousands of reflections that were running through my head, like many wretched chariots that were going to cause me to be lost, were it not for my Beloved's hand, which was supporting me.

Return, return, O Shulammite: return, return that we may behold you. (6:12)

The return of the Bride is as prompt and sincere as her fault was slight and unforeseen; due to this it was not witnessed by her companions. What they only noticed in her, which surprised them strangely, was that hardly had she stopped to declare to them the loving things and the beauties of her Bridegroom before she disappeared from their eyes because she was admitted right away to the wedding of the Lamb. This raised her so much above herself and all creatures that the other souls, losing her entirely from sight, beseeched her to come back to them, so that they could contemplate her in her glory and in her joy, just as when they saw her in her trouble. *Return,* they tell her, *O Shulammite, Temple of Peace,* return to teach us, both by your examples and your words, the path that we must follow to attain the happiness that you possess. Come back to be our guide, our support, and our consolation. Finally, come back to take us with you.

CHAPTER 7

What will you see in the Shulammite but the companies of camps? How beautiful are your steps in shoes, O prince's daughter! The joints of your thighs are like jewels, that are made by the hand of a skillful workman. (7:1)

The Bridegroom responds in place of the Bride to those who press her with such insistence to turn herself to them, while not accepting that they are interrupting her in the innocent pleasures that she tastes around him, just as he had already testified to them so many times, imploring them not to wake her up. He tells them, therefore, why do you ask my Bride, with such urging, to turn herself to you, so that you might look at her? What will you see in her, now that she is one same thing as me, but the companies of a camped army? She has the grace and beauty of a company of young virgins because the chaste kiss that I gave her has infinitely augmented her purity. She has also at the same time the strength and the terror of an army because she is associated with the most holy Trinity. She participates in the divine attributes that are armed in order to combat and destroy all the enemies of God on her behalf. O prince's daughter! O daughter of God! cry the young girls; your steps are beautiful, both on the inside and on the outside! The steps of the inside are very beautiful, since she can always advance in God, without ceasing to rest herself. It is the ravishing beauty of this advancement to be a true rest, without rest preventing advancement, or advancement rest. On the contrary, the more one rests, the more one advances, and the more one progresses, the more tranquil is the rest. The steps on the outside are also full of beauty because this soul is completely ordered as if being driven by the will of God and by the order of providence. Her steps cause her to be admired in her shoes because all her steps are taken by the will of God, from which they no longer leave. The joints of the thighs mark the admirable order of her actions, which are performed with an entire subordination of the inferior part to the superior part, and of the superior part to the gaze of God. This skillful worker has forged and melted this soul in the furnace of love.

Your navel is like a round bowl never wanting cups. Your belly is like a heap of wheat, set about with lilies. (7:2)

The navel is taken as the capacity of the soul to receive, or the passive disposition, which is stretched and enlarged until infinity since it is flowing back into God—not only in order for her to receive divine communications, but in order to conceive and to mother many of the souls of Jesus Christ. It is round because it receives a lot and cannot retain anything, only receiving in order to pour out. It is, at the same time, both ready to receive and prompt to distribute, participating in this in the qualities of her Bridegroom. It is always drinking from the water of the spring that runs from divinity, and the most reserved graces are given to her to distribute to others. Your belly, meaning your spiritual fertility, is so abundant that it is like a heap of wheat; it germinates, grows, bears fruit, and nourishes like wheat, and it always has these qualities. But it is set about with lilies as the mark of a complete purity.

Your two breasts are like two young roes that are twins. (7:3)

It would be insufficient for this Bride to mother souls for her Bridegroom, if he had not given her something with which to nourish them. Also, the Bridegroom speaks here of her breasts to mark that she is not only mother but also nurse. In effect, she has something to give her children with such abundance that her breasts are always full, although she empties them incessantly and there is not one moment when she does not open them in aid of someone. And although they nurse without ceasing, they do not at all diminish. On the contrary, their abundance is all the greater as she distributes more grace, such that the measure of their emptying is that of their fullness. And they are very justly compared to twin roes, to make us understand that she draws what she gives from God, because just as the little twins are attached to the breast of their mother, so also the Bride is always attached to her God, from whom she draws what she communicates to others.

Your neck like a tower of ivory. Your eyes like the fish pools in Heshbon, which are in the gate of the daughter of the multitude. Your nose is like the tower of Lebanon, that looks toward Damascus. (7:4)

The neck signifies strength. It is of ivory because the purity of the strength consists of being in God, and this makes the strength of the Bride completely pure. This strength is a tower where the soul is sheltered from all danger, and from where she discovers the approach of her enemies. By the eyes the understanding is expressed, and since this power was lost in God, it has become a pool, a source of all good and a remedy of all evils. God uses this mind, which has been willingly lost for his sake, for a thousand great things that serve the good of the neighbor. Are these pools at the gate of the daughter of the multitude? The daughter of the multitude is none other than imagination and fantasy, which trouble and spoil the clarity of the mind, before the mystical division is effected in it. But here that is no longer so, because one is no longer troubled by fleeting and troubling senses, God having put a gate, so to speak, between the mind and the senses. The nose is the symbol of prudence. This prudence has become like a tower of Lebanon because it is strong and invincible, being providence itself and the prudence of God that the soul has received in consideration of its simplicity, which has made her lose all human prudence. This heavenly prudence only ever looks at one side. She only sees the divine moment of providence, and what comes to her from moment to moment constitutes all her foresight. Prudence without prudence, you surpass that of the most prudent men!

JEANNE GUYON

Your head is like Carmel: and the hairs of your head like the purple of the king bound in the channels. (7:5)

The upper part is like a mountain elevated to its God, and the hairs, which represent all the gifts with which she has been gratified, belong so much to God that the Lover has nothing else left to herself. If she has some good or some honor, it is all for God. These are the same goods as her Bridegroom's, in the same way that everything that decorates and embellishes this upper part is royal purple, since it is a participation in the same ornaments with which the king is adorned. But this purple is bound in the channels, as much to perfect more and more the vivacity of its color by the graces that flow from heaven for it, as because it is in the soul as in a channel of distribution that receives all the graces of her God without resistance, but who lets them at the same time flow back to him, without retaining anything for herself. Or else she serves only as a channel in order to give free passage to the waters of graces, so that they flow into the spiritual gardens.

How beautiful you are, and how comely, my dearest, in delights! (7:6)

God, seeing his own perfections in his Bride as in a mirror that represents them with fidelity, lets himself be ravished with the beauty contemplated in his Bride, and he says to her, *O my dearest, how beautiful you are* in my beauty, and how my beauty is beautiful in you! You create all my delights, as I create all those of my Father. For, representing me actively and naturally, like a beautiful mirror that changes nothing in the object that is presented by it, you give me infinite pleasure; you are beautiful and ravishing, since you are adorned with all my perfections. But if you create my delights, I also create yours, and our pleasures are shared.

Your stature is like that of a palm tree, and your breasts like clusters of grapes. (7:7)

Your stature, which means all your soul, is the same as that of the palm tree, due to its straightness. Far from the favors that I give you making you stoop over, on the contrary, just like a beautiful palm tree, you are never more upright than when you are carrying most of them. The female palm tree has two qualities: one of them is being even straighter when it is the most charged with fruits; the other is producing no fruit except under the shade of her male palm tree. Thus, this beautiful soul has two qualities: one is never to curve toward herself for any grace that she might have received from God; the other is not to produce the least action by herself, however small it might be, but to do all of them in the shade of her Bridegroom, who makes her do them each in its time. Her breasts are very aptly compared to a cluster of grapes. Although the grape is full of liquid, this is not for itself, but it gives what it encloses to the one who squeezes it. This soul is of this sort. The more she is squeezed and oppressed by persecution, the more she communicates and is indulgent to those who wrong her.

I said: I will go up into the palm tree, and will take hold of its fruit: and your breasts will be like the clusters of the vine: and the odor of your mouth like apples. (7:8)

The young virgins, having heard the comparison that the King of Glory just made of his Bride to a palm tree, transported by the desire to participate in his graces, cry out all in the same voice, or else with just one of them explaining the passion of all the others, I want to climb the palm tree to pick the fruits; I want to be the disciple of this excellent mistress of all perfection. And if this mother so rich and so wise deigns to accept me as her daughter, I will feel the effect of the ointment of the Bridegroom that is in her. The fruit of her word will be for me like a cluster of grapes with an exquisite sweetness, and the purity of its maxims will embalm me with its odor.

Your throat like the best wine, worthy for my beloved to drink, and for his lips and his teeth to ruminate. (7:9)

One of the young girls of Zion continues to praise the Bride. She understands, by the throat, the interior of the soul. It is a wine because all is liquid there and all flows back to God without being stopped in its own consistency. It is a wine for God's drinking, since he receives this soul in himself, changing her and transforming her into himself. He makes her his pleasure and his delight. He ruminates on her and savors her, so to speak, losing her more and more and transforming her into himself, in a manner always more admirable. This wine is truly worthy of the mouth of God, since she alone is capable of making it, and this is also worthy of the soul, since it is her sovereign happiness and her final end.

I to my beloved, and his turning is toward me. (7:10)

The Bride certifies that what the girls say is true, avowing it to them and even confirming it. Since, she says, the ardent love of my Beloved has entirely devoured me, I have been so very lost in him that I can no longer find myself, and I must say, with still more truth than the other times, that I totally belong to my Beloved, since he changed me into himself. Thus, he would no longer know how to reject me, and I also no longer fear to be separated from him.

O love, you no longer reject such a soul! And one can say that she is forever confirmed in love, since she has been consummated by the same love and changed in it. The Beloved, no longer seeing anything in his Bride that is not of him or from him, no longer turns away his gaze or his love from her, as he can never cease to look at himself or to love himself.

Come, my beloved, let us go forth into the field, let us abide in the villages. (7:11)

The Bride can no longer fear anything because all has become God to her, and she finds him equally in all things. She no longer has anything to do with means or with being closed up and shut in; she has entered into an excellent participation in the immensity of God. All that is said of this ineffable union is understood with all the essential differences between the creator and the creature, although with a perfect unity of love and of mystical recollection in God alone. She no longer fears losing him, since she is not only united to him, but also changed in him. This is why she herself invites him to go out of the enclosure of the house or of the garden. Let us go, my love, she says, let us go to everyone to make conquests for you.

There is no longer any place too little or too big for me, since my place is God himself, and everywhere I am, I am in my God.

Let us get up early to the vineyards, let us see if the vineyard flourishes, if the flowers are ready to bring forth fruits, if the pomegranates flourish: there will I give you my breasts. (7:12)

She invites her Bridegroom to go everywhere, because then she is put into action. And as God is always acting outside and always resting inside, so too is this soul, who is confirmed inside in a perfect rest but completely active on the outside. What she had done a little while ago with faults, she does now with perfection. It is no longer herself or the fruits that are in her that she regards, but she sees all in God. She sees in the fields of the church a thousand good acts that are to be done for the glory of her Bridegroom, and she works there with all her might, according to the occasions that providence provides her and to the total extent of her vocation.

But explain to us, O admirable Bride, what do you mean to say when you say that you will give your breasts to your Bridegroom? Is it not he who makes them fertile and who fills them with milk? Ah! she means that being in a perfect freedom of spirit and breadth of the soul, since she has no sense of self in working for his glory, she will give him all the fruit of her breasts and will have him drink the milk with which he fills them. He is the source as well as the end into which she wants to empty them.

The mandrakes give a smell. In our gates are all fruits: the new and the old, my beloved, I have kept for you. (7:13)

Admirable unity! All is shared between the Bridegroom and the Bride. As she no longer has anything that belongs to her, she also shares all the goods of her Bridegroom. She no longer has material goods or interest in her own things, and this is why she says that the beginning and advancing souls, designated by the mandrakes, have spread their smell. This reaches us. My Beloved, she says to him, all that I have is yours, and all that you have is mine. I am so naked and stripped of all, that I have kept, given, and reserved all sorts of fruits for you, all sorts of actions and productions, whatever they might be, without any exception at all. I have given you all my works, such as the old ones that you have performed in me from the beginning, and the new ones that you may perform at any moment in me. Moreover, I have nothing that I have not given to you—my soul, with all its powers and its operations, my body with its senses and all that it can do. I have consecrated everything to you. Just as you have given them to me to keep, conserving their use for me, so do I guard them all for you in such a way that both the ownership and the use is all for you.

CHAPTER 8

Who shall give you to me for my brother, sucking the breasts of my mother, that I may find you without, and kiss you, and now no man may despise me? (8:1)

The Lover asks that the union go to a deeper level. Although the transformed soul is in a permanent and durable union, she is nevertheless like a bride who applies herself to the needs of the house and who must come and go, but without ceasing to be a bride. But apart from that, there are moments where the celestial Bridegroom pleases himself by hugging and caressing his Bride more strongly. This is therefore what she is asking at this moment. Who will give me, she says, the one who is my Bridegroom and my brother, since we suck together the breasts of our mother, who is the divine essence. Since he has hidden me with himself in God, I unceasingly suck the breasts of divinity with him. But in addition to this honor, which is inconceivable, I want to be alone outside to enjoy his sweet embraces, by which he makes me recollect in him and buries me more and more in him. She asks for one more grace, which is only accorded late, and it is that the outside be transformed and changed like the inside. This is because the inside has been long transformed before all the outside is changed. In this way, for a time, certain slight weaknesses remain, which serve to cover the grandeur of the grace and do not displease the Bridegroom. However, they are like a kind of weakness that draws in some way the scorn of creatures. Let him transform me on the outside then, she says, so that no one might scorn me any longer. That which I ask is for the glory of God, and not for my own gain, no longer being in a state to look at myself.

I will take hold of you, and bring you into my mother's house: there you will teach me, and I will give you a cup of spiced wine and new wine of my pomegranates. (8:2)

The soul that finds itself so tightly united to her God feels two things. The first is that her Bridegroom is in her, as much as she is in her Bridegroom. Just as an empty vase at the bottom of the sea would be filled with the same water by which it is surrounded and would contain, without understanding, that in which it would be contained, in the same way the soul who is carried by her Bridegroom carries him as well. And where does she carry him? Only where she can go. She carries him into the bosom of her Father, which is the house of her mother, since it is the place of her origin. The other thing that she feels is that he instructs her there, letting her penetrate his secrets, which are only revealed to the favorite Bride, to whom he teaches all the truths that she must know, or of which he wants to give her knowledge by an excess of his love. O admirable knowledge, taught with little noise, in the ineffable and always eloquent silence of divinity. The Word speaks incessantly in this soul and teaches her in a manner to shame the greatest doctors. But in proportion as he teaches the soul by insinuating himself more and more in her and enlarging incessantly her passive capacity, so this faithful soul has the Bridegroom drink of her wine mixed with sweetness and the sweet and sour of her pomegranates, which produces charity in her, continually rendering back to him all that he gives her with entire purity. This is only the ebb and flow of communications, the Bridegroom giving to the Bride and the Bride rendering to the Bridegroom. O incomparable Bride, how to say it? You have a part in the commerce of the most holy Trinity, since you receive incessantly and you render perpetually back what you receive.

His left hand under my head, and his right hand will embrace me. (8:3)

God, as we have already said, has two arms with which he holds and embraces his Bride; one is his all powerful protection, with which he holds her, and the other is the perfect charity with which he embraces her. This sacred embrace is nothing more than the enjoyment of himself and the essential union. When the Bride says here, *He shall embrace me*, she is not speaking of a thing that must happen and that has not yet come, since she has had this divine embrace in the nuptial kiss, but rather as a thing that will be always present and always future because its duration will extend into eternity.

I adjure you, O daughters of Jerusalem, that you stir not up, nor awake my love till she please. (8:4)

As there are three sorts of interior slumbers, the Bridegroom also beseeches three times, at different moments, that his Beloved not be awakened. The first is in the union of the powers, where she has a slumber of violent ecstasy, which spreads to all of her senses. He begs then that she not be awakened because this slumber is also the season in which he helps to detach the senses from the objects to which they attach themselves impurely, so as to purify them.

The second is the slumber of death, where she expires in the arms of love. He does not want her to be awakened until she wakes herself up through the effect of the voice of the all-powerful God, who calls her from the tomb of death to spiritual resurrection. The third is the slumber of rest in God, permanent and durable. It is a rest of ecstasy, of a sweet and continual ecstasy, which no longer causes any alteration to the senses, the soul having passed into her God by the happy departure from herself. It is a rest from which she will never be diverted. He does not at all want any of his lovers to be troubled or upset in any rest, but rather to be relinquished there by others, since they sleep in his arms.

The first rest is a promised rest, for which one gives a deposit and collateral; the second rest is a rest given; and the third is a confirmed rest that will never be interrupted again. It could be such a rest absolutely; however, although freedom abides, it would be in vain that the Bridegroom would say, *till she please*, as if she would ever again not want it. But after a union of this nature, it would be from the most extreme ingratitude and infidelity that she would ever want that. However, the divine Bridegroom who, by praising his Bride himself and accepting that she be praised in his presence, wants at the same time always to instruct her further. In order to make her understand that only a vain complacency in oneself and the scorn of others can give entry to a rather deplorable ruin, in the following verse, he is going to place again before her eyes the lowness of her origin and the misery of her nature, so that she will never depart from her humility.

Who is this that comes up from the desert, flowing with delights, leaning upon her beloved? Under the apple tree I raised you up: there your mother was corrupted, there she was deflowered that bore you. (8:5)

The soul rises little by little from the desert because her very self is a desert after she abandoned it. It is no longer only the desert of faith, but it is the desert of herself. She is bursting with all sorts of delights because she is flowing and as full as a basin overfilled with water from the spring. She overflows on all sides, in order to make others a part of it. She is no longer relying on herself. This is why she no longer fears the abundance of her delights. She no longer fears being knocked over, since her Beloved, who spreads them in her bosom, carries them himself, with her, allowing her to walk, leaning on him. Oh, admirable advantage of the loss of these created supports! One receives God alone as support in exchange for them.

Under the apple tree I raised you up. I got you out of the mystic death, truly delivering you from your own corruption, and from being corrupted and spoiled by what your mother had communicated to you by her sin. For all the operations of God in the soul only aim at two things: one, to deliver it from its current malice and of the malignancy of its corrupt nature; the other, to render it to its God as pure and clean as it was before Eve let herself be seduced. Eve, in her innocence, belonged to God without any sense of self, but she let herself be violated, withdrawing herself from her God to be a prostitute to a demon. In this way we have all participated in the unhappiness of this prostitution. We come into the world like illegitimate children who no longer have a trace of their true father. They can only be recognized as belonging to God when they are made legitimate by baptism, but although they are made so, they do not let go of something from this unfortunate fornication. They still have a malign quality opposed to God, until God, by long, strong and frequent operations, takes away this malign quality, drawing the soul from itself, taking away all infection from it, giving it back an innocent grace, and losing it in him. This is what he calls raising her up from the same place where her mother, who is human nature, was corrupted.

Put me as a seal upon your heart, as a seal upon your arm, for love is strong as death, jealousy as hard as hell, its lamps are fire and flames. (8:6)

The Bridegroom invites the Bride to put him as a seal upon her own heart because, just as he is the source of life for the soul, he must be its seal. It is he who prevents her from ever leaving such a happy state. She is then a sealed fountain that no worker can open or close except himself. He wants her to put him also as a seal on her exterior and on her operations, so that everything is reserved for him and nothing moves except by his order. She is then the enclosed garden for her Bridegroom, whom he closes and nothing opens, and he opens and nothing closes (Rev 3:7). *For love*, says the Bridegroom, *is strong as death*, in order to do what he wants with his Lover. He is strong as death since he made her die in everything so that she might live in him alone. *But jealousy is as hard as hell.* This is what makes him close up his Bride in this way. He wants so much that everything should be for him that, if by some infidelity as difficult as grievous, she simply retired from her dependency, she would be from that moment rejected by him, as if in hell, by the excess of his indignation. The lamps that he lights are ardent lamps with a fire that lights by burning, and that burn while lighting. O Lamb, who opens and closes the seven seals! Seal your Bride so well that she may never leave except by you and for you, since she is acquired by you in an eternal marriage.

Many waters cannot quench charity, neither can the floods drown it: if a man should give all the substance of his house for love, he shall despise it as nothing. (8:7)

If the many waters of afflictions, contradictions, miseries, poverties, and obstacles could not extinguish charity in such a soul, one must not believe that the rivers of abandonment to providence might do this, since these are the ones that conserve it. If one had enough courage to abandon all one possesses and all of oneself so as to have the pure charity that is only acquired by the loss of all the rest, we must not believe that, after so generous an effort to acquire a good that one esteems more than all other things, and which effectively is worth more than the universe, this person might come to scorn it, to the point of taking back all that has been left behind. This is not possible. God, by this, makes us understand the certainty and the consistency of this state and how difficult it is for a soul who has arrived there ever to leave.

Our sister is little, and has no breasts. What shall we do to our sister in the day when she is to be spoken to? (8:8)

The Bride is so happy with her Bridegroom that all is shared between them. She speaks to him of the affairs of other souls and treats him informally, as if it was a question of domestic affairs. What will we do, she says, to this soul, still little and tender, who is our sister due to her purity and simplicity? (She is speaking of all similar ones in the person she is designating.) What will we do with her the day I must start to communicate with her? She does not yet have breasts, or enough of a disposition for the divine marriage. She is not at all in a state to help others. In what way will we act with her? It is thus that the wives must consult Jesus Christ on behalf of souls.

If she is a wall: let us build upon it bulwarks of silver: if she is a door, let us join it together with boards or cedar. (8:9)

The Bridegroom responds to her, if she is already like a wall, waiting through strong passivity, let us start to build upon her bulwarks of silver for her defense against the enemies of this advanced state, which are human reason, reflection, and the subtlety of self-love. But if she is still only like a door, only beginning to depart from her multiplicity and to enter into simplicity, let us adorn her with graces and virtues, which should have the solidity and the beauty of cedar.

I am a wall: and my breasts are as a tower since I am become in his presence as one finding peace. (8:10)

The Bride, delighted by the instruction and the promise that she just received from the mouth of her Bridegroom, gives herself as an example of the success of this guidance. I am myself, says she, a wall of this strength. My breasts are like a tower, which can serve as asylum and defense for many souls, and which holds me in assurance, since I have appeared before you as one who finds peace in God, no longer to lose it ever again.

The peaceable had a vineyard, in that which has people: he let out the same to keepers, every man brings for its fruit a thousand pieces of silver. (8:11)

It seems, O my God, that you have taken pleasure to anticipate all doubts and objections that could be formed. One could say that this soul, who no longer possesses and who no longer operates anymore by herself, no longer has any merit. You are, O God, this God of peace who has a vineyard, of which you entrust principal care to your Bride, and the Bride is this vineyard itself. She is situated in a place that is called *people*, because you have rendered your Bride fertile and the mother of innumerable people. You have committed your angels to look after her, and she brings a big profit back to you, O God, and to the soul herself. You give her the freedom to use it and to taste the fruits of it; she has the advantage of no longer being in the state of nearly losing you or of displeasing you and, however, still to be in one of not ceasing to profit and to merit.

My vineyard is before me. A thousand are for you, the peaceable, and two hundred for them that keep its fruit. (8:12)

The chaste Bride no longer says, as before, *I have not cared for my vineyard.* It was then a vineyard with which people wanted to burden her against the will of God. But as for this one here, which is committed to her by her Bridegroom, ah, she takes admirable care of it! All that is from God's order agrees very well with all sorts of works, either interior or exterior, and all is done with a marvelous ease, since the person who is charged with it is allowed great liberty.

The fidelity of the Bride is worthy of admiration because, although she may guard and watch over the cultivation of this vineyard so exactly, she nevertheless lets all come back to the Bridegroom and gives to the guards a fair wage, without asking anything for herself. Perfect charity does not know what it means to think of its own interests.

You that dwell in the gardens, the friends listen: make me hear your voice. (8:13)

The Bridegroom invites his Bride to speak on his account and to enter truly into the apostolic life by teaching others. *You,* he says, *O my Bride, who dwells in the gardens,* in the flowerbeds always blooming with divinity, where you have not ceased to be since winter has passed, you have been in the gardens, which are equally beautiful for the variety of the flowers with which they are adorned and for the bounty of fruits of which they are full. I say to you, O my Bride, whom I hold incessantly with me in these gardens of delights, leave, for a moment, the rest full of sweetness and of silence that you taste there and *make me hear your voice.* The Bridegroom, by these words, asks his Bride two equally admirable things. One is that she leave, for his sake, this profound silence, in which she was until now, because, as in all the time of faith and of the loss of God, she has been in a grand silence, since this was necessary to reduce her depths into the simplicity and unity of God alone. Now that she is entirely consumed in this unity, he wants to give her this admirable harmony of knowing multiplicity and unity, which is a fruit of the consummated state of the soul, without the multiplicity preventing the unity or the unity preventing the multiplicity. He wants her to join the word to the speechlessness of the depths, which is the state of unity. The exterior praise of the mouth is an imitation of what must be accomplished in glory, where, after the soul will have had several centuries absorbed in this ineffable and always eloquent silence of divinity, she will receive her glorified body, which will give sensible praise to the Lord. In such a way, after the resurrection, the body will have its own praise, which will be an augmentation of happiness and not an interruption of the peace of the soul.

Even in this life, when the soul is consumed in unity and this unity can no longer be interrupted by exterior actions, the mouth of the body is given a praise, which belongs just to it. And an admirable agreement is created between the silent word of the soul and the sensible word of the body, which constitutes the consummation of praise. The soul and the body render a praise conforming to what they are. The praise of only the mouth is not praise, as God says through his prophet: This people honor me with their lips but their heart is very far from me (Isa 29:13). The praise that comes purely from the depths, being a silent praise, and all the more silent since it is more complete, is not an entirely perfect praise, since the person, being composed of soul and body, must combine one and the other there. The perfection of praise is that the body might have its own, which is of a manner such that, far from interrupting the profound and always eloquent silence of the depths of the soul, on the contrary it augments it. And the silence of the soul in no way prevents the word of the body from issuing praise, conforming to what it is, to be given to its God. In this way the consummation of the prayer, both in time and in eternity, is done in relation to this resurrection of the exterior word, united with the interior.

But as the soul, who is accustomed to deep and ineffable silence, fears to interrupt it, sometimes this makes it painful to take up this exterior word again. And this is what forces her Bridegroom, so as to make her lose this imperfection, to invite her to have him listen to her voice. *Make me*, he tells her, *O my Bride, hear your voice!* It is time to speak, to speak to me with the mouth of the body in order to praise me in the manner that you have learned during this admirable silence. There is, moreover, a completely ineffable inner word, God rendering to the soul the freedom to speak to him sometimes, according to his will, with much happiness.

He invites her to speak to souls of interior things, and to teach them what they must do to please him. It is a principal function of the Bride to instruct and teach the inner life to friends of the Bridegroom, who do not have as much access to him as his Shulammite. This is therefore what the Bridegroom desires of her, both that she should speak to him with the heart and the mouth, and that she should speak to others on his behalf.

Flee away, O my beloved, and be like to the roe, and to the young hart upon the mountains of aromatic spices. (8:14)

The soul, who no longer has any interest other than that of her Bridegroom, neither for herself nor for any other creature, and who can desire nothing but his glory, seeing something that dishonors him, says to him, *Flee, O my Bridegroom!* Leave these places that have for you only an unpleasant odor. Go to these souls who are on mountains of aromatic spices, who have risen above the corrupt vapors, spoiled by the malice of the temporal world. These are mountains of aromatic spices, due to the smell of exquisite virtues that you have put in them. And it will only be in these souls that you will find true rest.

The soul who gets to this degree enters into the interests of divine justice, in regard both to herself and to others, in such a way that she cannot want anything for herself, or for anyone else, other than what this divine justice would like to give her in time and in eternity. The Bride also has the most sincere charity ever toward her neighbor, only serving this person for God and in God's will. But although she might be totally ready to be an anathema for her brothers and sisters, like Saint Paul (Rom 9:3), she works for nothing else but their salvation. She is nevertheless indifferent to success, and she cannot be afflicted either by her own loss, or by that of any other creature, from the perspective of God's justice. What she cannot tolerate is for God to be dishonored, because God has ordered charity in her since the time she has entered into the purest dispositions of perfect charity.

One must not believe that a soul of the degree of this Bride would be zealous in any way for the sensible presence and the sweet and continual enjoyment of the Bridegroom. It was a perfection that she had before to desire ardently this charming passion because it was necessary to make her begin and go to him. But now it is an imperfection that she should not allow, her Beloved possessing her perfectly in her essence and in her powers, in a manner very real and invariable, above all time, and all means, and all places. From now on, she is no longer only sighing after distinct and noticeable moments of pleasure, besides which, she is on such an entirely self-less path with respect to all things that she would no longer know how to fasten a desire upon anything at all, not even the joys of

Paradise. This state is even the mark that she is possessed in her depths. It is why she witnesses here to the Bridegroom that she is quite content that he might go where he pleases, that he might visit other hearts, that he might win them over, that he might purify them, that he might consume them in all the mountains and the hills of the church, and that he might take delight in aromatic souls embalmed with graces and virtues. But for herself, she would have nothing more to ask of him, or nothing to desire of him, unless it be he himself who leads her in this movement, not that she scorns or rejects the divine visits and consolations. No, she has too much respect for and submission to God's operation. But these sorts of graces are hardly any longer in season for such an annihilated soul as she, who is established in the pleasure of the depths, and, having lost all her will in God's will, she can no longer desire anything. This is well expressed in the agreeable figure, *Flee away, O my beloved; and be like to the roe, and to the young hart upon the mountains of aromatic spices.*

The indifference of this soul is so great that she can lean neither toward the side of pleasure, nor toward the side of deprivation. Death and life are the same to her, and although her love is incomparably stronger than it ever has been, she cannot, however, desire Paradise, because she lives in the hands of her Bridegroom, like things that are not at all. This must be the effect of the most profound annihilation.

Although in this state she is more ready than ever to help souls, and she serves with extreme care those whom her Bridegroom sends to her, she is, however, incapable of desiring to help others and can only do it through a specific order from providence.

THE LIFE OF MADAME J. M. B. DE LA MOTTE GUYON WRITTEN BY HERSELF

PART ONE: YOUTH
From Her Birth Until Her Leaving France

1.1—To Make the Goodness of God Understood

[1.] Since you would like me to write to you¹ about a life as miserable and as extraordinary as mine, and since in the first attempt I appeared to you to have made too many omissions to leave it the way it was, I want with all my heart to obey you, to do what you want of me, although the work seems somewhat painful to me in my current state, which does not allow me to reflect much. / Nevertheless, with God having given me to you in such an admirable and real manner, I believe it would be a crime to refuse you such a thing. //²

I would so wish to be able to make you understand the goodness that God has had for me and the excess of my ingratitude, / *the disorder in which I lived for some years*, // but it would be impossible for me to do this, as much because you do not want me to write of my sins in detail as because I have forgotten many things. I will try, however, to fulfill my duty in a way that minimizes error as much as possible, relying on the assurance that you give me never to show it to human eyes and to burn it when God has brought about the effect that he envisions for your spiritual good, for which I would sacrifice all things, being persuaded as I am of the designs that God has for you, as much for your sanctification as for that of others. But I assure you at the same time that you will only arrive there through

181

much pain and work and by a path that will appear to you totally contrary to your expectations. If you are convinced that God only establishes his great works on nothingness, then you will not be surprised by any of this. He seems to destroy in order to build; he does it in this way so that this temple that he destines for himself, built even with much pomp and majesty but built nonetheless by the hand of men, might be so destroyed that there no longer remains a stone upon a stone. This is the frightful debris that will serve the Holy Spirit in making a temple that will not be built at all by the hand of men, but by his power alone.

[2.] Oh, if you could understand this mystery, as profound as it is, and conceive the secrets of God's guidance, which is revealed to the little ones but hidden from the great and wise of the earth who imagine themselves to be the counselors of the Lord and to penetrate the depth of his ways, who persuade themselves that they have attained this divine *Wisdom, unknown to those who live*³ still for themselves and in their own actions. This wisdom is *hidden* even from *the birds in the air* (Job 28:21), meaning those who, by the liveliness of their illumination and by the force of their elevation, nearing heaven, think themselves to penetrate the height, the depth, the width, and the vastness of God. This divine wisdom is not known even by those who pass in the world for extraordinary people, enlightened and educated. From whom will it be known and who will be able to tell us this news? Perdition and death—these are the ones who have assuredly heard with their ears the sound of his glory. It is thus by dying to all things and by being truly lost in regard to them, in order to pass into God and subsist only in him, that one has some understanding of true Wisdom.

[3.] Oh, how little one understands of his ways and the guidance that this Wisdom has for his most chosen servants! Hardly does one discover something of it than, surprised by the difference between the truth and the ideas that one had formed for oneself regarding true perfection, one cries out with Saint Paul: *Oh, the depth of the riches of the wisdom and of the knowledge of God! How incomprehensible are his judgments, and how unsearchable his ways!* (Rom 11:33). You do not judge things as men judge them, who call the good evil and the evil good, who regard as true justice things that are abominable before God, with which, according to his prophet

(Isa 64:6), he no longer has anything to do, as if they were *dirty rags*—who even *judges*, with rigor, these acts of *justice* (Ps 7:8; Ps 9:4) done from a sense of self, which, just like those of the Pharisees, will be the source of his indignation and anger and not the object of his love and the subject of his recompense. He assures us of this himself when he says, *unless your righteousness abound more than that of the scribes and Pharisees, you shall not enter into the kingdom of heaven* (Matt 5:20). Who among us comes close to the Pharisees in righteousness? And who, in doing many fewer good works than they would do, is not one hundred times more ostentatious than they were? Who among us is not truly comfortable, finding herself righteous in her own eyes and in the eyes of others, and who does not believe that it is sufficient to be just in this way in order to be so in the eyes of God? However, let us see the indignation that Jesus Christ as well as his precursor [John the Baptist] demonstrated against these types of people, Jesus Christ being the one for whom sweetness was so infinite that it was the perfect model of all sweetness, but a sweetness innate and coming from the heart and not like these acts of feigned sweetness, in which the heart of a hawk lies under the appearance of a dove. Jesus Christ, I say, had only a sour attitude for this type of person with a strong sense of self, and he seemed to dishonor them publicly. He portrays them as appalling, while he regards sinners with mercy, compassion, and love; he declares that he has only come for the sinners, as it is the sick who need a physician (Mark 2:17), and that, being the Savior of Israel, he has, however, come only to save the lost sheep of the house of Israel. O Love, it seems that you are so jealous of the salvation that you yourself give that you would prefer the sinner to the righteous one!

It is true that this poor sinner, seeing himself only as scornful, is basically constrained to hate himself. Finding himself an object of horror, he throws himself impetuously into the arms of his Savior; he plunges with love and confidence into the sacred bath of his blood, out of which he leaves white as snow. It is then that, all confused by his disorders and all full of the love of the one who, alone having been able to cure his evils, has had the charity to do this, he loves all the more as his crimes have been the more serious, and his understanding is so much the greater as the debts that have been remitted are the more abundant. While the righteous man, relying on the great number of works of justice that he presumes himself to have done, seems to hold his salvation in his own hands and regards heaven as recompense due to his merit, he damns all sinners with the rancor of his zeal. He makes them believe the entrance to heaven is closed to them, and he persuades them that they must only look upon it as a place to which they no longer have any right, while he believes himself to have the opening all the more assured so that he flatters himself with deserving it all the more. His Savior is almost useless for him; he goes along so loaded with merit that he is overwhelmed by its weight. Oh, let him rest a long while overwhelmed under this glorious charge, while these sinners made naked of everything are carried with speed by the wings of love and confidence into the arms of their Savior, who freely gives them what he has infinitely earned for them!

[4.] Oh, how they first love themselves and have little love of God! They love themselves and admire themselves in their works of righteousness, which they estimate as the cause of their happiness. They are, however, no sooner exposed to the rays of the divine Sun of righteousness than he uncovers all iniquities in them and makes them appear so dirty that their hearts ache, while he pardons Magdalene, empty of all righteousness, *because she loves much* (Luke 7:47), and her love and her faith take the place of all righteousness. How, then, does it happen that the divine Paul, who knew these great truths so well and who described them so admirably, assures us that *the faith* of Abraham *was imputed unto him as righteousness* (Rom 4:22)? This is perfectly fair because it is certain that this holy patriarch performed all of his actions through a great, strong righteousness. Oh, how he did not see them as such, and, being entirely disengaged from all sense of self and empty of love for them, his faith was only founded on the salvation to come, which his Savior was supposed to bring! He *hoped* in him *even against hope* (Rom 4:18), and this faith was imputed to him as righteousness, meaning pure, simple, clear righteousness—righteousness merited by Jesus Christ and not self-righteousness controlled by the self and regarded as if from the self.

[5.] This, which might appear extremely distant from the topic about which I first proposed to write, will not fail to lead you there imperceptibly. And it will make you see that, in order to do his work, either God uses converted sinners for whom past iniquity serves / as a continual abyss and // a counterweight, or God destroys and reverses this sense of self-righteousness and this temple built by the hands of men in such a manner that there does not remain a stone upon a stone that has not been destroyed because all these works are built only on shifting sand, which is the support of the created world and of these same works, instead of being founded on the living rock of Jesus Christ. All that he has come to establish by coming into the world happens by the overthrow and destruction of the same things that he wanted to build. He established his church in a way that seemed to destroy it. What a way to establish a new law and to accredit it, when the legislator is condemned by the experts and the powerful ones in the world as a villain who finally dies at the gallows! Oh, if we knew how much self-righteousness is opposed to the ways of God, we would have eternal grounds for the humiliation and defiance of that which presently constitutes our sole support!

[6.] This supposed, you will not have trouble conceiving the designs of God in the graces that he had made to the most miserable of creatures; you will even easily believe them. These are all graces—by this I mean gifts that I have never merited, on the contrary, of which I have rendered myself very unworthy. But God, by an extreme love of his power and a just jealousy of the attributions that men make to other men of the good that God puts in them, wanted to take the most unworthy subject that there ever was in order to show that these bounties are the effects of his will and not the fruit of our merit, and that it is his own wisdom to destroy that which was superbly built and to build that which is destroyed, using *weak things to confound the strong* (1 Cor 1:27). But if he uses vile and scornful things, he does it in a manner so astonishing that he makes them the object of all creatures' scorn. It is not by seeking men's praise for them that he uses them for the salvation of these same men, but by making them the target of their insults and an object of loathing. This, therefore, is what you will see in the life that you have ordered me to write down.

In Chapters 2 and 3, Guyon describes her birth, frequent childhood ill-nesses, and early religious experiences. She is placed intermittently in con-vents (mostly Ursuline) for her care and education, starting when she is two years old. She describes a neglectful mother and a doting father at home. She closes Chapter 3 with a description of her stay at a Dominican convent at the age of ten, during which she contracts smallpox.

1.4—Religious Vocation?

[1.] After having spent about eight months in this house, my father removed me from there. My mother kept me with her. For a time she was very happy with me; she loved me a bit more because she found me to her liking. She did not stop always preferring my brother to me, which was so visible that everyone disapproved of it because when I was sick and I found something to my liking, my brother would ask for it, although he was feeling fine, and it would be taken away from me to be given to him. One day he made his sword red in the fire, then burned my arm in front of my mother, without her saying anything. Another time he made me get up on the top of the carriage then threw me to the ground. He thought to kill me. I only had some bruises with no cuts, though, because in every fall I have ever taken, I have never had any notable injury. It was your helping hand, O my God, that sustained me. It seemed that you would bring about in me what you say through your royal prophet—that you put your hand under the just so that, in falling, they do not get injured in any way (Ps 36:24). At other times he would hit me, and my mother would never say anything to him about it. This conduct embittered my natural temperament, which would have been sweet without it. I neglected to do good, saying that I was none the better for it. O God, it was not therefore for you alone that I would do good, since I would stop doing it because they did not think better of me for it. If I had known how to make use of the crucifying guidance that you held forth to me, I would have taken that path, and, far from straying, this would have served to make me return to you. I was jealous of my brother because on every single occasion I would notice the different way my mother treated him and me. In whatever he did he was always good, and I was always bad. My mother's servants courted my mother by caressing my brother and mistreating me. It is true that I was bad, for I had fallen back into my first faults, getting angry and lying. Even with all these flaws I did not fail to give alms voluntarily, and I loved the poor. I would regularly pray to you, my God, and I was always pleased to hear about you and to do good readings.

[2.] I do not doubt at all that you are astonished by so oppositional a conduct and such a long string of fickleness; such grace and such ingratitude astonishes, sir, but you will be all the more astonished with what follows when you see that these ways of acting get stronger with age, and that reason, far from correcting such unreasonable practices, only served to strengthen and broaden my sins. It seemed, O my God, that you were redoubling your graces just as much as my ingratitude was increasing. What was happening inside of me is what happens during the siege of a village. You were besieging my heart, and I wished only to defend it against your attacks. I would put up fortifications in this miserable place, redoubling my iniquities each day to prevent you from taking it over. When it seemed that you were going to be victorious over this ungrateful heart, I would make a counterattack. I would put up levies to stop the flow of your goodness and to prevent the passage of your graces. Nothing less than you was necessary to break them, O my Divine Love, you who, by your sacred fire, were stronger than death itself, to which sin has reduced me so much and so often.

I cannot tolerate it when they say that we are not free to resist grace. I have had only a long and disastrous experience with my freedom. It is true that there are free and gratifying graces that do not need the freedom of man, since they are received unbeknownst to man, who is not aware of them at all before receiving them. In truth, I wanted good so feebly that the least attack would set me back. When I was no longer in such a situation, I no longer thought about evil, and I opened my ears to grace. But if the least thing were to set me off, then I would close all the avenues of my heart in order not to hear your secret voice, which was calling me, O my God, and far from fleeing this situation, I sought it out and let myself go with it.

[3.] It is true that our freedom is really disastrous for us. In order to return to what I was considering before, I was saying that you offered to me, O my God, a crucifying guidance for making me return to you, which I did not know how to use, for I had been in torment since my tender youth either due to sickness or persecutions. The girl who took care of me would hit me while dressing me and would only make me turn by hitting me. Everything was orchestrated to make me suffer. But instead of making me turn toward you, O my God, I became troubled and my spirit became bitter. My father knew nothing of all this, because his love for me was so great that he would not have tolerated it. I loved him a lot, but at the same time I feared him so much that I did not speak to him of anything. My mother would often complain to him about me, but he did not have any response for her, except, "There are twelve hours in the daytime; she will be converted." This manner of discipline was not detrimental for my soul, although it made my mood, which was sweet, much more bitter. But what caused my total downfall was that, not being able to endure those people who mistreated me, I sought refuge with those who embraced me in order to corrupt me.

[4.] My father, seeing that I was growing up, put me with the Ursulines during Lent in order for me to receive my first communion at Easter, when I was supposed to be over eleven years old. He put me in the hands of his daughter, my very dear sister, who took great care to prepare me as much as possible to perform this act. I no longer dreamed, O my God, of anything other than giving myself to you for good. I often felt the tug of my good inclinations against my bad habits. I would even perform some penance. Since I was almost always with my sister, and the students I joined who were boarding in the older class were reasonable, I became reasonable along with them. It was surely a kind of murder to raise me badly, because I had a natural tendency strongly leading to good, and I loved good things. A reasonable conduct agreed with me. I let myself easily be won over through sweetness, and without using force my sister would make me do all she wanted me to do without any resistance to her wishes. Examples of bad behavior were so offensive to me that when I was in church with my friends and around them, I could not pray. My sister, noticing this, isolated me, and then I prayed with much devotion. Finally, on Easter Day I received my first communion, which was preceded by a general confession. The confidence that I had in my sister was so great that

I had her write it for me, / and since there was one sin that I wanted to hide from her because of the shame that I had, I never confessed it; this simple fault caused me such pain that I was hesitant to tell her about it. //

I took my communion with much joy and devotion. They let me stay until Pentecost in this house, but since my other sister was the teacher of the second class, she asked that I be in her class for a week. / This request appeared quite reasonable because the week that she was teaching her class my paternal sister was not there; however, // the two very opposed manners of my sisters released me from my first fervor. I no longer felt this new ardor, O my God, that you had me taste in my first communion. Alas! It hardly lasted because I fell more rudely, for my evils were more frequent. I was taken away from religious life.

[5.] My mother, seeing me so big for my age and more to her liking than usual, no longer dreamed of anything other than making me up, showing me to company, and dressing me up. She had some inopportune indulgence in this beauty, which you had put in me, O my God, only to praise and bless you, but was a source of pride and vanity for me. There were several proposals, but since I was not twelve years old, my father did not want to hear them.

***

The adolescent Guyon is very distressed for having missed the visit of a missionary, her cousin, Philippe de Chamesson-Foissy (1632–1674). This event occasions her intensified interest in spiritual practice.

[8.] I would close myself up all day long to read and perform contemplative prayer. I would give all that I had to the poor, even taking laundry home to do it for them. I would teach them the catechism, and when my father and my mother were gone, I had them eat with me and would serve them with great respect. During this time I read the *Works* of Saint Francis de Sales and the *Life* of Madame de Chantal. It was then that I became familiar with how contemplative prayer was performed. I begged my confessor to teach me how to do it, and since he would not do so, I tried to do it alone as best I could. I could not succeed at it, which appeared to me then to be the result of my inability to imagine anything by myself, and I was convinced that one could not perform contemplative prayer without being formally trained and without thinking about it a lot. This difficulty caused me a lot of pain for a long time. I was very diligent, though, and I would pray fervently to God that he give me the gift of contemplative prayer. All that I saw written about the life of Madame de Chantal enchanted me, and I was childlike enough to believe that I needed to do all that I saw there. All the vows that she had taken, I would also take, like that of always trying to attain perfection and to do the will of God in all things. I was not yet twelve years old, but I took on this discipline nevertheless, according to my strength. One day when I read that she had put the name of Jesus on her heart in order to follow the advice of the Bridegroom—*Put me as a seal upon your heart* (Song 8:6)—and that she had taken a hot iron with which she then engraved this Holy Name, I remained truly afflicted from not being able to do the same. I decided to write this sacred and adorable name in capital letters on a piece of paper, and I attached it to my skin in four places with ribbons and a large needle, and it stayed attached this way for a long time.

[9.] I thought about nothing except becoming a nun, and I very often went to the Sisters of the Visitation in order to plead with them to receive me, because the love that I had for Saint Francis de Sales did not let me consider any other community, although my confessor had more inclination toward the Benedictines, whose merit I did not then know. I avoided staying at my house, therefore, in order to go to this monastery. This was easy for me because almost all day long I remained closed up in my room, which belonged to my brother, who no longer occupied it since he was away at school. So they thought I was in my room when I was really at the monastery. / I truly believe that this very regular retreat made my mother very accustomed to being without me and caused some of my future evils. I would very often sneak out, as I have said, to go to the Visitations' [monastery]. // I would make very strong pleas for them to receive me, and although they might have very much desired to have me, and they might have considered this a momentary advantage, they never did dare to grant me entry to their house, as much because they greatly feared my father as because, however they might have loved me, I was extremely young, being barely twelve years old. At this time one of my father's nieces, to whom I have strong obligations, was at our house. She was truly virtuous, and fortune, which had not been favorable to her father, made her dependent on my father in certain ways. She discovered my plan and my extreme desire to become a nun. Since my father was absent for a time and my mother was sick, and I was under her care, she dreaded being accused of having been the cause of this thought in me, or at least the cause of having entertained it. For my father dreaded it so strongly that, although he might not have wanted to stop me from my true vocation for anything in the world, he could not hear about my becoming a nun without shedding tears. My mother would have been more indifferent to this. My cousin went to find my confessor to tell him to forbid me from going to the Visitations' [monastery]. He did not dare to do this at all for fear of making that religious community turn against him because they already believed me to be one of theirs. When I went to confession, he did not want to absolve me for saying that I was going to the Visitations' alone and by twisted ways. I was so innocent that I believed myself to have committed a terrible crime, because no one had ever refused me absolution. I returned so affected by it that my cousin could not help me get over it. I did not stop crying until the next day, when I went that morning to find my confessor. I told him that I could no longer live without absolution; I begged him to give it to me. There was no penance that I would not have performed to obtain it. He gave it to me straightaway. I still wanted to become a nun, and I would try to convince my mother so that she might take me there. But she did not want to do this for fear of angering my father, who was absent, and she would always give in to him upon his return. Since I saw that I could not obtain anything, I copied the signature of my mother, and I made up a letter in which she asked these ladies to receive me, excusing herself due to her sickness for not having brought me herself. But the mother superior, who was a relative of my mother and who knew her writing well, immediately discovered my innocent trick.

Guyon discusses the close relationship between the frequency with which she prayed and her advancement or retreat in virtue in Chapter 5. In Chapters 6 and 7 she details her marriage at the age of fifteen to Jacques

Guyon, who was twenty-two years older than she was. Her opinions and actions are strongly repressed in her new household, owing especially to a troubled relationship with her mother-in-law. She struggles with pride and vanity and endures a difficult pregnancy.

1.8—Meeting and Interior Awakening

[1.] Finally, after much listlessness I once again regained my normal health, and I lost my mother; so many things happened during this time that I am leaving out because they will be of no use to you for getting to know me or for your own needs. This was a continuous period of daily encounters with the cross and with occasions for vanity. My mother died like an angel, and although the attachment she had for my brother was her biggest fault, God, who wanted to start in this life to recompense her greatest acts of charity and her good actions, gave her such a grace of detachment, although she was only sick eighty hours, that she said that she was leaving my brother without any grief. Meanwhile, I was still following my personal routine of contemplative prayer, which I never missed doing two times a day. I kept vigil over myself, continuously improving myself, and I did many works of charity. I went to the homes of the poor and helped them through their illnesses. I did the good that I knew how to do, according to my inspiration, attending church regularly and remaining before the holy sacrament, putting myself through this in perpetual adoration. O my God, you increased my love and patience in the same measure as you increased my sufferings. The temporary advantages that my mother procured for my brother over me, for which I had no grief, did not stop causing me to feel the pain of the cross, for the entire household was against me. I was sufficiently sick during this second pregnancy and at the same time sick from a doubly high fever. However, I was still weak, and I was not yet serving you, my God, with the vigor that you would give me soon after. I truly would have wanted to attach my love for myself and for creatures to you because I was so unfortunate that I always found some others who would love me and whose approval I could not stop myself from seeking, not because I loved them, but because until then I only loved a little and in a feeble way, except for the love that I had for myself.

[2.] You permitted, O my God, that Madame de Charost,[4] who had been exiled, came to my father's house. He offered her lodging, which she accepted, and she stayed for some time. This lady was of a singular piety and of a great interior. Since I saw her often, and she demonstrated friendship for me because she noticed that I wanted to love God, and since, moreover, I was engaged in outer works of charity, which served me well, she noticed that I had the virtues of an active and diverse life but that this life did not at all include the simplicity of contemplative prayer, as hers did. She would say a word about this path sometimes, but since the right time had not yet come, I did not understand her. She served me more by her example than by her words. I saw something on her face that signaled the strong presence of God to me, and I noticed in her what I had never yet seen in anyone. I tried to force my head and thoughts to give me the continual presence of God, but I gave myself a lot of pain, and I hardly advanced. I wanted to have through effort what I could only acquire by ceasing all effort. This good lady charmed me by her virtue, which I saw was well above what was normal. She, seeing my attention going in multiple directions, would often tell me something, but it was not time, so I would not hear it. I would speak about this to my confessor, who would tell me the exact opposite. And since I used to tell her what my confessor had said, she did not dare to explain herself to me.

[3.] My father's nephew, of whom I have spoken,[5] who had gone to Cochinchina with Monsieur d'Héliopolis, arrived. He was coming to back to Europe in order to take some priests there. I was excited to see him because I remembered the good that his first passage brought me. Madame de Charost felt no less joy than I to see him because they got along well together and enjoyed the same interior language that was also known by the Benedictine prioress named Geneviève Granger,[6] one of the holiest young women of her time. I hardly knew her. The virtue of this excellent relative charmed me, and I admired his continual act of contemplative prayer, without being able to understand it. I forced myself to meditate continually, to think unceasingly about you, O my God, to say prayers and short, fervent recitations. But I could not give myself, through these various things, what you yourself give and what is only felt in simplicity. I was surprised when he would tell me that he did not think of anything during contemplative prayer, and I considered with wonder what I could not understand. He would do everything he could to attach me more strongly to you, O my God. He would assure me that if he was happy enough to endure being a martyr, as he was in effect already doing, he would offer it to you to obtain the great gift of contemplative prayer for me. We would say the Office of the Holy Virgin together—often he would stop short because the violence of the attraction would close his mouth—and then he would stop his vocal prayers. I did not yet know what all that was. He had an incredible affection for me. He understood me to be very far from the corruption of the century, to have a repulsion for sin at the age when others only begin to taste its pleasures, for I was not yet eighteen years old. This, coupled with the fact that he could see the bad that I would have been able to do in the world if I were of that tendency, gave him a soft spot for me. I scorned my faults with much candor because I always was clear about these. But since the difficulty that I would find in correcting them entirely would wear down my courage, he supported me and exhorted me to tolerate myself. He really would have liked to give me another method of contemplative prayer that would have been more effective in breaking me of this habit, but I would not give in to that.

[4.] I believe that his prayers were more effective than his words, for he was no sooner outside of my father's house than you had compassion for me, O my divine love. The desire that I had to please you, the tears that I shed, the great labor that I undertook, and the little fruit that I reaped moved you to compassion. In one moment, by your grace and by your goodness alone, you gave me what I would not have been able to give myself through all of my own efforts. I would not say anything to this lady about what I was suffering, and she would have thought me very happy. She would tell me sometimes, "Your mother-in-law seems quite severe, and she frightens me." I would tell her that she was a good, very charitable person. It is true that my crosses must be attributed more to providence than to my mother-in-law because, besides her natural severity and certain things that are typical of people who do not perform contemplative prayer, she had good qualities. But when it pleased you, O my God, to cause a soul to suffer, you used everything for that purpose. Since I was truly imperfect, I needed all of these scissor cuts to tailor me to your divine wishes. This was the state of my soul when, by a goodness as great as I was unworthy, without considering either the graces that I had rejected or my sins, not to mention my extreme ingratitude, and seeing me paddle with such fatigue and without any help, you sent, O my divine Savior, the favorable wind of your divine act, in order to make me move with full sails on this sea of afflictions. The thing happened as I will explain.

[5.] I would speak often to my confessor of the pain that I had at not being able to meditate, imagining nothing. Subjects for contemplative prayer that were too lengthy were useless to me, and I did not understand anything. Those that were very short and full of unction suited me more. This good father did not understand me, and I believed that it was because I could not make myself understood. Finally, God let a good, very spiritual monk of the Order of Saint Francis[7] come to where we were. He wanted to go to another place so as to shorten his route and so as to make use of the availability of water, which would have eased the pain of going on foot, but a secret force made him change plans and required him to pass by the place where I was staying. He readily saw that there was something for him to do there. He speculated that you had called him there, O my God, for the conversion of a man of considerable means, for which he had already worked during a trip that he had taken to this spot. He resolved to himself to attack this without giving up, but his efforts were as useless as the first time. It was the conquest of my soul that you wanted to accomplish through him. O my God, it seems that you were forgetting all the rest to think only about this ungrateful and unfaithful heart. As soon as this good monk arrived in this country, he went to see my father, who was extremely happy. For my father, being yours as much as he was, felt a very great pleasure in seeing people who loved you purely, O my God! My father loved me with an extreme tenderness, and the death of my mother had even augmented his affection for me because, due to this, I was responsible for performing certain duties that I would not have done for him if my mother were still alive.

He thought he was dying when my second son was being born. They hid his suffering from me, but my father, in spite of the joy that he had at going to see God, could not prevent himself from feeling sad that he was dying without seeing me. He asked incessantly for his daughter because, although my brother was with him, this did not satisfy him. The duchess of Charost, who was still at his home, truly gave much helpful assistance, and when she would come to see me I would say to her that I was surprised that my father had not come to see me. She had me understand that his leg hurt. I accepted this as true. But with an indiscreet person having told me he was sick, I got up in spite of all my pain and went to see him. He experienced extreme joy at seeing me. I found him so changed, his tongue so heavy, that I was very worried about him. He got well—not completely, but enough to give me new signs of his affection. He had many crosses to bear because of my brother. He confided in me, although I would tell him nothing of my afflictions, which would have pained him. I would only tell him of one thing, which was my sincere desire to love you, O my God, and the pain of not being able to do this according to my desire. The speed with which I got up after the birth to see my father caused me to have a serious illness. My father, as I have said, truly loved me and only me. He believed himself unable to give me any more solid sign of affection than to arrange my meeting this good monk. He told me what he knew of this holy man and said that he wanted me to see him. At first it was difficult for me because I had never gone to see any monks before. I believed that I should use the occasion to observe the most rigorous rules of behavior. At the same time, I held the insistence of my father as an absolute commandment. I believed that there could be no harm for me if I only did this to obey him.

[6.] I took one of my relatives with me, and I went there. From far away he saw me. He was quite confused because he was very clear that he should see no women, and the solitude of five years from which he was emerging made them seem a bit strange to him. He was then truly surprised that I should be the first to address him, and what I told him augmented his surprise, as he explained to me later that my appearance and my manner of saying things had confused him, so that he did not know if he was dreaming. He only came forward a little, and I believe that if he had not feared to offend the house from which these clergy were drawing almost all of their subsistence—not to mention that his house had been established by the family—without this fear, I say, he would not have come forward. It was a long time before he spoke to me. I did not know how to interpret his silence. I did not stop talking to him and telling him in a few words of my difficulties with contemplative prayer. He responded right away: *It is, Madame, that you are looking outside for what you have inside. Get accustomed to looking for God in your heart, and you will find him there.* After finishing these words, he left me, saying that he was going to look for some writings to give me. He has told me that it was surprise that made me not notice his trouble.

[7.] The next day, he was once again astonished when I went to see him, and I told him the effect that his words had had on my soul. For it is true that, for me, they were an arrow that pierced right through my heart. At that moment I felt a very profound wound, as delicious as loving, a wound so sweet that I desired never to be healed from it. These words put into my heart what I had been seeking for so many years, or rather, they made me discover what was there, which, however, I could not enjoy due to not knowing about it. O my Lord, you were in my heart, and you were only asking me for a simple returning inside to make me feel your presence. O infinite goodness, you were so close, and I was running here and there looking for you, and I was not finding you. My life was miserable, and my happiness was inside of me; I was in misery in the midst of riches, and I was dying of hunger near a prepared table and a continuous feast. O ancient and new beauty, why did I meet you so late?[8] Alas! I was looking for you where you were not, and I was not looking for you where you were. It was from not hearing the words of your gospel when, speaking of your kingdom on earth, you say: *The kingdom of God is not at all here or there, but the kingdom of God is within you* (Luke 17:21). I felt this strongly right away because from then on you were my king, and my heart became your kingdom, where you would command as sovereign and where you would do all your will. For what you do in a heart when you come there as king is the same as what you did when you came into the world in order to be king of the Jews. *It is written*, says this divine king, *at the beginning of the book that I will do your will* (Heb 10:7). This is what he writes first at the entrance of the heart into which he comes to reign.

[8.] I told this good father that I did not know what he had done to me, that my heart was completely changed, that God was there, and that I no longer had trouble finding him. For from this moment a new experience of his presence in my depths was given to me, not by thinking or by putting my mind to it, but as a thing that one possesses truly in a very sweet manner. I felt these words of the Bride of the Song of Songs: *Smelling sweet of the best ointments. Your name is as oil poured out: therefore young maidens have loved you* (Song 1:3). For in my soul I felt an unction that, like a healthy balm, would heal all of my wounds in an instant and would even spread so strongly through my senses that I almost could not open my mouth or my eyes. I did not sleep at all that night because your love, O my God, was not only like a delicious oil for me, but also more like a devouring fire that was lighting such a fire in my soul that it seemed to need to devour all of it in an instant. I was suddenly so changed that I was no longer recognizable either to myself or to others, and I no longer found either faults or repugnancies; all appeared to me as if consumed like straw in a great fire.

[9.] This good father could not decide to take responsibility for directing me, although he saw such a surprising change as coming straight from God. Several reasons led him to refuse this. The first was my outer appearance, which made him apprehensive. The second was my great youth, for I was only nineteen years old. And the third was a promise that he had made to God never to take on the direction of a single person of my gender unless Our Lord might charge him with it by a specific providence. Thus, he told me, because of my insistence to him that he take me under his care, that I should pray to God about this and that he would also do the same. As he was in contemplative prayer, he heard God say: *Fear not to take charge of her; she is my Bride.* O my God, let me tell you that you were not thinking about what you said. What! your Bride, this terrible monster full of rubbish and iniquity who had only offended you, abused your grace, and repaid your goodness with ingratitude? Afterward, this good father told me that he would be pleased to direct me.

[10.] Nothing was easier for me than to perform contemplative prayer; the hours seemed only like minutes to me, and I was unable not to do it. Love would not let me have an instant of rest. I would tell him, "O my love, this is enough; let me be." My contemplative prayer was, from the moment of which I have spoken, empty of all forms, distinctions, and images. Nothing passed from my prayer into my head, but it was a contemplative prayer of joy and of being possessed in the will, where the taste for God was so great, so pure, and so simple that it would draw and absorb the other two powers of the soul into a profound recollecting without action or words. However, I sometimes had the freedom to say some words of love to my Beloved, but afterward all was taken from me. It was a contemplative prayer of savory faith that excluded all distinction because I did not have any vision either of Jesus Christ or of divine attributes. Everything was absorbed into this savory faith in which all distinctions were lost to give love a more expansive place to love without motives or reasons to love. This sovereign of the powers, the will, would devour the two other powers and take all distinct objects away from them in order better to unite them with it. This was so that the distinct, by not arresting them, would not take away the unifying force from them and would not prevent them from losing themselves in love. They might subsist in their unknown and passive operations, but this general light is like that of the sun, absorbing all distinct lights and putting them into darkness from our perspective because the excess of its light surpasses all others.

1.9—Contemplative Prayer beyond Ecstasy

[1.] This, then, is how I first gained knowledge of contemplative prayer, which is truly beyond ecstasy and ravishing, visions, and so on, because all these graces are truly less pure.

Visions are in the lesser powers, in contrast to the will, and their effect must always terminate at the will. Thus, they must be lost in the experience of what one sees, knows, and understands in those states without which the soul would never arrive at perfect union. What the soul would have, what it would even name as union, would be a union mediated and flowing from the gifts of God in all the powers. But this union is not God himself, which means that it is very important to prevent souls from stopping at visions and ecstasy, because this would arrest them nearly all their lives. Moreover, these graces are very prone to illusions because whatever has form, image, and distinction can be counterfeited by the devil as easily as perceptible tastes can be. But whatever is detached from all forms, images, distinctive traits, and beyond anything of the senses, the devil cannot go there.

[2.] Of these types of gifts, the least pure and perfect and the most subject to illusion are visions and ecstasy. Ravishing and revelations are not like this quite as much, although there are similarities.

[3.] The vision is never of God himself, or of Jesus Christ, as those who have it imagine it to be. It is an angel of love that, according to the power that is given to it by God, shows a representation of itself to the soul. / *It seems to me that the apparitions that are believed to be of Jesus Christ himself are a bit like the sun that paints itself in a cloud with such vivid colors that he who does not know this secret believes that it is the sun itself, but it is only its image. Jesus Christ paints himself in this way in the intellect, and these are called intellectual visions, which are the most perfect; or these are made by angels, which, being of pure intellect, can be imprinted and appear in this way. Saint Francis of Assisi, very enlightened on visions, never attributed the imprinting of his stigmata to Jesus Christ himself, but to a seraph who, being an effigy of Jesus Christ, imprinted them on him. The imagination is also imprinted with phantoms and holy representations. There are also corporal ones. And both kinds are the most vulgar and the most subject to illusion.* //

Saint Paul refers to these sorts of things when he says that *Satan himself transforms himself into an Angel of Light* (2 Cor 11:14). What ordinarily happens when one makes a case for visions is that one values them and stops there because all these things arouse vanity in the soul or at least prevent it from seeking the uniquely unknown that is above all type of vision, knowledge and light, according to how Saint Denis explains it.[9]

[4.] *Ecstasy* comes from a palpable taste—that is, a spiritual sensation—where the soul lets itself go too far and faints due to the sweetness that it finds there. The devil offers these types of sensual sweetness in order to make the soul begin to hate the cross, to make it sensual, and to make it vain and self-loving, to arrest it with the gifts of God, and to prevent it from following Jesus Christ by renouncing and being dead to all things.

[5.] *Distinct interior words* are also very subject to illusion. The devil forms many of them, and while they might be from a righteous angel, for God does not speak at all in this way, they do not always mean what they seem, and one rarely understands what is said in this way. For when God forms these types of words delivered by angels, he understands things in his own way, and we take them in our own way, and it is we who are mistaken.

[6.] The *immediate* word of God is nothing more than the expression of his Word in the soul, the substantial word, living and functioning, which has no sound or articulation. Accordingly, it is written: *Dixit, et facta sunt.*[10] This is the word that is never for a moment mute or fruitless; the word that never ceases in the depths of the soul when the depths are so inclined, and which returns to its origin as pure as when it left; the word in which there is never hatred; the word that makes Jesus Christ become the life of the soul, since it is nothing other than himself as Word; the word that has an admirable efficacy, not only in the soul by which it is received, but also in other souls to which it communicates itself as a divine seed that makes them bear fruit for eternal life; the word always mute and always eloquent; the word that is none other than yourself, O my God, the Word made flesh; the word that is the kiss of his mouth and the immediate and essential union that you are, infinitely raised above these created, limited, and intelligible words. In order to return to my subject I will continue to say that

[7.] *revelations of the future* are also very dangerous, and the devil can imitate them through auguries, as he would do in earlier times in pagan temples, where he made oracles. Although they might be from God through the ministry of his angels, it is necessary to go beyond them without being arrested by them, because we do not understand what they signify, true revelations always being very obscure. Moreover, this engrosses the soul very much, preventing it from living in total abandonment to divine providence, giving it false assurances and frivolous hope, preoccupying the spirit with future things, and preventing it from dying and going beyond all things to follow Jesus Christ naked and deprived of all things.

[8.] The *revelation of Jesus Christ* of which Saint Paul speaks is very different from that type (Gal 1:6). It is manifested in the soul when the eternal word is communicated to it; revelation makes us become other Jesus Christs on earth by a participation that makes him continually express himself in us (Gal 2:20). This revelation is always true, and the devil cannot imitate it.

[9.] Raptures come from another principle. God attracts the soul strongly to make it leave itself and lose itself in him, and of all the gifts about which I have written, this one is the most perfect. But the soul, still being arrested by its own sense of self, cannot go beyond itself, attracted as it is by one side and held back by the other. This is what brings about raptures or flights of the spirit, which are more violent than ecstasy, and even at times raise the body from the earth. However, what humans admire to such an extraordinary degree is an imperfection and a fault in the creature.

[10.] *True rapture* and perfect ecstasy are brought about by total annihilation in which the soul, losing all sense of self, passes into God without effort and without violence as into a place that is totally natural and its own. Since God is the depth of the soul from the moment that the soul is detached from all the selfish concerns that would arrest it in itself or in other creatures, it passes infallibly *into God*, where it *lives hidden in Jesus Christ* (Col 3:3). But this ecstasy is only brought about by a naked faith that is dead to all created things, even to the gifts of God, which, being of creatures, prevent the soul from melting into the only begotten. This is why I say that it is very important to have overcome all these gifts, however sublime they might appear. For as long as the soul dwells there, it does not truly renounce itself and thus never passes into God himself. Although the soul might be sustained by these gifts in a very sublime way, by lingering with these gifts it might lose the real pleasure of the giver, which would be an inestimable loss.

[11.] You put me, O my God, in a very uncluttered, very firm, and very stable state by an inconceivable goodness. You took possession of my will, and there you established your throne so that I should not let myself flee from these gifts or shrink away from your love. You put me immediately in your union of the powers and in a continual attachment to you. I could do nothing but love you with a love as profound as it is tranquil, which would absorb all other things. Those souls who are taken in this way have the greatest advantage, and they have the shortest way to go. It is true that when you advance them so much, O my God, they must expect heavy crosses and cruel deaths, especially those who are touched first by much faith, abandonment, pure love, disinterest, and love whose only interest is to be with God without returning to themselves. These were the dispositions that you immediately put into me, along with a desire to suffer for you so vehement that I was completely languishing in it. I was initially disgusted by all creatures; everything other than my love was intolerable to me. The cross that I had carried until then with resignation became my delight and the object of my pleasure.

1.10—Austerity, Divine Love, and Union in Charity

[1.] I was writing all this to this good father, who was full of joy and astonishment at it. O God, what penance did not the love of suffering make me perform! I would undertake all the austerities that I could imagine, but all this was too weak to take away the desire that I had to suffer. Although my body was very delicate, the instruments of penance were ripping me up without causing any pain, as far as I could tell. Every day I would punish myself for a long time with long needles that drew a lot of blood and were killing me, but they did not satisfy me, and I regarded them with scorn and indignation because they could not bring me contentment. And as I only had a little strength, and my chest was extremely delicate, my arms would become weary and my voice hoarse without my hurting myself. I would wear horsehair and iron-needled belts. The former seemed to me like an act of self-love, and the latter would give me extreme pain when I was putting them on and taking them off, but when I was wearing them, they would not hurt me at all. I cut myself with brambles, needles, and nettles, which I would keep on myself; the pain of these used to make me weak at heart and entirely sleepless, without my being able to stay seated or reclined due to the thorns that stayed in my skin. It was one of these latter ones that I would use when I was able to find them because they satisfied me more than any other. I often kept absinth in my mouth, and I would put bitter apples in my food, although I would eat so little that I am astonished that I was able to survive. I was always sick and languishing. If I walked, I would put stones in my shoes. This was, O my God, what you inspired me to do right away, while depriving me of all the most innocent satisfactions. All that would please my taste was refused to it; all that would give it the most pain was provided. My heart, which until then was so delicate that the least dirtiness would raise incredible effects in it, would no longer dare to show revulsion toward this and soon saw itself forced to take what made it cringe so much and for such a long time that not a single revulsion remained. My taste, which until then could tolerate eating virtually nothing, was forced to eat without discernment, without it even appearing that it was still in a state to choose.

[2.] There are two things that I would not tell you if you had not forbidden me to hide anything from you. It is that I had such disgust for spittle that when I would see or hear someone spitting, I would want to vomit and would have other strange effects from it. It was necessary for me, one day when I was alone and when I noticed some of it, the most disgusting that I had ever seen, to put it in my mouth and on my tongue. The effect that this had on me was so strange that I could not get over it, and I had such violent upheavals in my heart that I believed this was going to break some vein in me, and I was going to vomit blood. I did this for as long as my heart was repulsed by it, which was a rather long time, because I could not overcome such things.

[3.] I was not doing this for practice, or to study, or with forethought. You were continually in me, O my God, and you were so demanding and severe that you would not let me avoid the least thing. When I would think of doing something, you would stop me right away and make me, without thinking, do all your will and all that was repulsive to my senses, until they were so supple that they did not have the least inclination or the least revulsion. Due to what I have just said, it was necessary for me to eat pus and to lick bandages. I would apply bandages to all the wounded who would come to me and give remedies to the sick. This mortification lasted a long time, but as soon as my heart no longer felt any revulsion, taking the most horrible things as the best, the thought of doing this was entirely taken away from me, and I have no longer thought about it since. For I was doing nothing myself but would let myself be taken to my king, who governed all as sovereign.

[4.] I had spent several years performing elementary austerities, but through these practices, my senses were subjugated in less than one year. Nothing deadened them as quickly as refusing them everything that pleased them and giving them everything that repulsed them. The rest do not do as much to deaden them, however great the austerities might be, if they are not accompanied by what I have just said, and the rest always leave the senses vigorous and never deaden them. But this, accompanied by recollecting, completely rips the life from them.

[5.] When the good father of whom I have spoken would ask me how I loved God, I would tell him that I loved him more than the most passionate lover loved his mistress. Yet this comparison was still improper, since the love of creatures can never reach that degree either in strength or in depth. This love was so continual, and occupied me always and so strongly, that I could think of nothing else. This touch so profound, this wound so delicious and loving, was inflicted on me during the feast of Mary Magdalene 1668, and this father, who was a very good preacher, was asked to preach at my parish, which was under the patronage of Mary Magdalene. He gave three admirable sermons on this subject. I noticed at that time the effect these sermons were having on me, which was that I almost could not hear the words and what was said. They made such an immediate impression on my heart and absorbed me so strongly in God that I could neither open my eyes nor hear what was being said. To hear your name mentioned, O my God, or your love, was capable of putting me into profound contemplative prayer, and I felt that your word was making an impression directly on my heart and that it was causing all its effect without the intervention of the process of reflection or of the mind. Since then I have always felt this, although in a different manner, according to the different degrees and states that I was passing through. This was so perceptible to me that I could hardly pronounce vocal prayers any longer.

[6.] In the place where I was, this absorption in God absorbed all things. I could no longer see the saints or the Blessed Virgin without God, but I saw them all in him, only being able to distinguish them from him with difficulty. Although I loved certain saints tenderly, such as Saint Peter, Saint Paul, Saint Mary Magdalene,

Saint Theresa, and all those who cultivated the interior life, I nonetheless could not distinguish them all or invoke them outside of you.

[7.] On August 2 of the same year, only a few weeks after my spiritual wound, it was the feast day of Our Lady of the Angels in the convent where this good father, my director, was. In the morning I went to obtain indulgences and was truly surprised when I saw that I could not go through with it. I tried for this with all my effort, but in vain. I stayed more than five hours straight in the church without moving forward at all. I was penetrated by a stroke of pure love so strong that I could not make myself cut short with indulgences the pain caused by my sins. If these indulgences had caused pains and crosses, I would have won. I was telling you: "O my love, I want to suffer for you. Do not cut short my pains; this would be to cut short my pleasures. I only find them by suffering for you. Indulgences are good for those who do not know the price of suffering, who do not like the fact that your divine justice satisfies, and who, having a mercenary soul, fear displeasing you less than they dread the pain that is attached to sin." But fearing that I was misunderstanding and committing an error by not obtaining any indulgences, for I had never heard it said that this might be possible, I was making new efforts in order to win them. But it was useless. Finally, no longer knowing what to do, I said to Our Lord, "If it is necessary to obtain indulgences, transfer the pains of the other life into this one here."

As soon as I had returned to my room, I wrote about my disposition and my sentiments to this good father with such ease and such a fluent manner in explaining myself that, while preaching that day, he made the third point of his sermon by saying word for word what I had written, without changing it or diminishing or adding a single thing, as if it were the word of God that he repeated two times. My surprise was not small when I heard him preach what I had written to him.

[8.] I left all company, and I renounced games and diversions, dancing, and useless walks forever. It had been two years since I had stopped having my hair done. I was very well dressed, however, because my husband wanted it this way. My sole diversion was to steal some moments to be alone with you, O my only love; all other pleasure was for me a pain and not a pleasure. I did not lose your presence, which had been given to me by an infusion as divine as it was continual, not, as I had myself imagined, by an effort of the head or by forcing myself to think about you, but through the depths of my will, where I felt the real pleasure of the beloved object with ineffable sweetness. However, this did not happen as it did later, by an essential union, but by a true union of the will that made me taste through a happy experience that the soul is created to rejoice in you, O my God. This union is the most perfect of all those that operate in the powers. Its effect is greater as well, because the unions of the other powers clarify the mind and absorb the memory, but if they are not accompanied by this one, they are hardly useful because they cause only fleeting effects. The union of the will carries with it, in essence and in reality, what the others only have in distinction, and moreover, it submits the soul to its God, conforms it to all his desires, and little by little causes the death of all its own will by means of the charity of which it is full. It has become united little by little in these depths and loses itself there, as regards what it has brought about through its sense of self and its nature.

[9.] This loss happens in this way, and it is called the *annihilation of the powers*, which cannot be understood as a physical annihilation. This would be ridiculous, but they appear annihilated as far as we are concerned, although they remain always subsistent. This *annihilation* or loss of the powers happens in this manner: as charity fills and lights up the *will*, just as we have said, this *charity* becomes so strong that little by little it overcomes all activity of this will in order to subject it to that of God, so that when the soul is docile, letting itself be consumed and purified by him and emptied of all sense of self and all that is opposed to God's will, little by little it finds itself empty of all self-will and placed in a holy indifference in order to want only what God wants. This soul could never consummate itself by acts of will, even if it worked at continual resignation, because all these are acts of the self, which, although quite virtuous, always cause the will itself to subsist, consequently keeping it multiple, distinct, and dissimilar to that of God. This is unlike when the will stays submissive and only suffers freely and voluntarily, bestowing its cooperation. The will's cooperation is its submission to let itself be overcome and destroyed by the activity of charity, which, while absorbing the will in itself, consumes it in that of God, first purifying it of all reservation, dissimilarity, and sense of self.

[10.] It is the same with the other two powers, where, by means of charity, the two other theological virtues are introduced. *Faith* takes such strong possession of the *understanding* that it makes the latter falter in reasoning to all distinct enlightenment, to all clarity and particular illuminations, even if they are the most sublime—such as might cause visions, revelations, ecstasy, and so forth—which shows how contrary visions, revelations, ecstasy, and so forth are to this and how they prevent the loss of the soul in God, although by these it may appear lost there for a few moments. But this is not a true loss since the soul that is lost in God does not find itself again. It is instead a simple absorption if the thing is through the will, or amazement if it is through the intellect, rather than a loss. I say, therefore, that faith causes the soul to lose all distinct light and absorbs it, by surmounting it, to put it in the light of faith that is above all light. This light is a general and indistinct light, which appears dark from the perspective of the soul that is itself enlightened by it, because its excessive clarity causes one to be unable either to discern or know, just as we cannot distinguish the sun and its light, although thanks to this light we discern objects so perfectly that it prevents us from deceiving ourselves.

[11.] One sees the sun absorb in its general light all the little distinct lights of the stars, which, like these visions, and such, can be discerned very well due to their being circumscribed. However, by making themselves distinguishable they cannot put us in the truth or make us see objects as they are. On the contrary, they would instead make us misunderstand by their false glow. Similarly, it is this way with all other lights that are not those of passive faith, of the infused light, or of the gift of faith from the Holy Spirit, which has the power to disabuse the mind by obscuring the distinct lights of reasoning to put it in the light of truth. This light, although less satisfying for it, is, however, a thousand times more sure than all others and is properly the true light of this life until Jesus Christ, eternal light, raises himself in the soul and lights it with himself, he *who enlightens every man that comes into this world* due to a new life in

God (John 1:9). This is revealed, but I let myself get carried away with the spirit that makes me write.

[12.] *Memory* in the same way finds itself little by little surmounted and absorbed by *hope*, and finally all is lost little by little in pure charity, which absorbs all the soul into it by means of the will, which, as the sovereign of the powers, has the power to lose the others in itself, just as charity, queen of virtues, reunites all the other virtues in itself. And this reunion that then takes place is called unity, central union, because everything finds itself reunited by will and charity in the depths of the soul and in God, our final end, in accord with the words of Saint John: *He who abides in charity, abides in God and God in him* (1 John 4:16).

This union of my will to yours, O my God, and this ineffable presence were so strong and so sweet all together that I could not want either to resist them or to defend myself against them. This cherished possessor of my heart made me see all the way to my least faults.

1.11—Purification

[1.] My senses were, as I have said, in continuous mortification, and I was not giving them any freedom. For it is necessary to know that to make them die entirely, they must not be given any release for a time, until they become entirely dead. Without this they are in danger of never dying, such as happens to persons who are happy to do great exterior austerities, and who nevertheless give their senses certain reprieves, as they say they are innocent and necessary. And they cause their senses to live by doing this because these are no austerities, however great they might be, that make the senses die, as we have seen with those very austere people who feel them revolt all their lives. What destroys them more is generally to refuse them all that can please them and give them all that is disagreeable to them, and to do this without ceasing and as long as it is necessary to make them lose their appetite and their repugnance. If one intends at that point to give them some relief, one would cause the same effect as if there were a person who was condemned to die of hunger to whom one gave a little food from time to time under the pretext of fortifying the person a little. One would prolong the suffering and prevent the person from dying. It is the same with the death of the senses, of the powers, of the mind itself, and of the will itself, because if one does not rip all sustenance from them, however little it might be, one keeps them until the end in a dying life, which is very aptly named mortification. Saint Paul has perfectly distinguished this when he says, *Always bearing about in our bodies the mortification of Jesus Christ* (2 Cor 4:10), which is, in effect, the dying state. But then, in order to make us see that it must not end there, he adds, we are dead and our *life is hidden with Jesus Christ in God* (Col 3:3). We can never lose ourselves in God except through total death.

[2.] The one who is dead in this way no longer needs mortification. But all this has passed away for him, and all is made new (cf. 2 Cor 5:17). And, still, a great mistake is made by people of good will who, having acquired the extinction of their senses by this continual death without relief, remain stuck there all their lives, without stopping the work through a perfect indifference, taking equally the good and the bad, the sweet and the sour, in order to enter into more useful work, which is the mortification of the mind itself and of the will itself, starting with the loss of their own actions, which never takes place without deep contemplative prayer. Neither will the death of the senses ever be complete without profound recollection joined with mortification, because without this the soul's remaining always turned toward the senses keeps them invigorated. In place of this, by recollection, the soul remains separated from them and contributes in this way, however indirectly, to their death more than anything else.

[3.] The more you would increase my love and my patience, O my God, the stronger and more continual my crosses would become, but love made them light to me. I will not give any more detail because it is easy to judge this on the basis of what I have already written. I will only add in what follows what I have not said. O poor souls who consume yourselves with superfluous cares, if you were looking for God in yourselves, you would soon find the end of your pain, since its excess would cause your delight. In the beginning, the love, insatiable for mortification and penance, made me invent all sorts of them, but what was admirable was that, without my paying any attention, soon a mortification would have no more effect on me. Love made it stop working for me in order to make me undergo another that was applicable to me because this love was so subtle and so enlightened that it saw my smallest faults. If I was thinking to speak, it made me see this as a fault, and it made me keep silent. If I was keeping silent, it would find a fault in this. In all my actions it found faults, in my manner of acting, in my mortifications, in my penances, in my alms, in my solitude; ultimately, it found fault in everything. If I was walking, I would notice a fault in my way of walking. If I was saying something to my advantage—pride. If I was saying, "Well! I will not talk too much about myself, neither for good nor bad"—sense of self. If I had been too recollected and reserved—self-love. If I was happy and open, I would be condemned. This pure love always found something to take back and took extreme care to let nothing pass for this soul. It is not that I paid attention to myself, for I was little concerned with myself because my attention toward him, by way of the path of adherence, was continual. I kept vigil over him without ceasing, and he kept continual vigil over me and led me by the hand of his providence in such a way that he made me forget everything. And although I might have felt these things, I did not know how to explain them to anyone. He took away all regard for myself so much from me that I could not examine myself in any way. As soon as I saw myself needing to do this, all thought of myself was taken away from me, and I applied myself to my sole object, which was no longer a distinct object for me but a sweeping and entire clarity. It was as if I had dived into a river of peace. I knew by faith that it was God who possessed my whole soul in this manner, but I was not thinking about it, just as a bride seated near her bridegroom knows that it is he who embraces her without her saying a word to herself and without it occupying her thoughts.

[4.] Going to confession caused me great pain because as soon as I thought to return to myself in order to examine myself, love would seize me with all the force of its unction and recollecting, so that I could no longer look at myself or think about myself, but I was completely absorbed in a love as strong as it was sweet. It was necessary, therefore, to present myself this way at the feet of the priest. It was then, O my God, that you gave me the gift of what you wanted me to say. Had I said it, love had made me so dependent that

I would no longer have been able to open my mouth to pronounce a single word. But this was done with such unction and sweetness that I could only adhere to him. I could hardly understand anything about what the priest was saying. But when he pronounced absolution, I felt something like a flowing of grace and a strong unction. I stayed there so full of love that I could not even think of my sins in order to feel regret. I would not have wanted to displease my dear Bridegroom. Before had he wounded me in this way, I would cry so bitterly at the least faults. But it was not in my power to give myself a disposition other than the one that he put in me. Although I said that I could not do this, it must not be thought that God assaults our freedom. In no way! But he asks us for it with such lures, and he makes us do things with such strength of love and sweetness, that he inclines our heart where he wants. And this heart follows him very freely and with such pleasure and sweetness that it is unable not to do it. The attraction is much freer since it is infallible.

[5.] Although Love might treat me this way, it must not be thought that it leaves me unpunished. O God, with what rigor do you punish your most faithful and most cherished lovers! I am not talking here about exterior acts of penance. They are too weak to punish the least fault in a soul whom God wants to purify radically. On the contrary, they serve rather to relieve and refresh. But the manner that God uses to punish the least faults in chosen souls is so terrible that it is necessary to have felt it in order to understand it. All that I could say would hardly cover the experience of these souls. It is like an interior burning and a secret fire that, coming from God himself, purifies the fault and does not cease to cause an extreme pain until the fault is entirely purified. It is like a bone dislocated from its normal place, which does not cease to cause an extreme pain until it is entirely relocated. This pain is so awful that the soul places itself in a hundred different positions in order to satisfy God for its fault. It would like to rip itself apart rather than suffer such torment. Often one goes quickly to confession in order to be rid of such great torment and multiplies confession without any cause and eludes the designs of God.

[6.] It is then very important to know how to make use of this pain, and the advancement or delay in the soul's development depends almost entirely on this. It is therefore necessary, in this painful, obscure, and confused time, to aid the designs of God and suffer this devouring and crucifying pain in all of its vastness as long as it lasts, without adding to or diminishing it in any way, carrying it passively, without wanting to satisfy God either by acts of penance or by confession, until the pain passes. This, which appears to be nothing, is what is the most awful to bear passively and the most painful to accommodate—and one would not believe that inconceivable courage is necessary.

Those who have not felt this will have trouble believing me. However, nothing is so true. And I have heard this said by a soul who is truly great but has never arrived entirely to God in this life, due to this soul's lacking the courage to let itself be entirely purified by the devouring fire of justice. It had never been able to let itself bear this pain for more than one-half hour without going to rid itself of it by confession. You have instructed me, O my God, in another way. And you have taught me that one must not perform penance or confession unless you are satisfied yourself. O cruel lovable one, unmerciful and sweet exactor, you made me bear this pain not only several hours, but several days, according to the nature of my fault. An unnecessary expression or a hasty word was punished rigorously. And I saw very well that if I had put my hand in the work under the pretext of holding up the Ark, I would have been punished like Uzzah (2 Sam 6:6–7). It was necessary for me to suffer without stirring in the least possible way. I had much pain from letting God perform this operation to its full extent.

[7.] I understand as I write this that this fire of exact justice is the same as that of purgatory, because it is not a material fire that burns souls, as some claim, saying that God enhances their activity and their natural capacity through this. This exacting divine justice burns these poor souls in this way so that by purifying them they are rendered ready to enjoy God. All other fire would be refreshment. This fire is so penetrating that it goes all the way to the substance of the soul and can alone purify it radically. And as these souls are detached from their bodies, nothing distracts them from the pain, and this fire devours them and penetrates them in a terrible way, according to the different degree of each one's impurity. And it is this impurity that causes the vehemence of the fire and its duration. Those who claim that souls desire to leave this fire hardly understand their situation. They remain in peace, all passive in their suf-ferings, without wanting to shorten them, because they are so strongly absorbed in God that, although they suffer in an extreme way, they cannot turn back to themselves in order to see their suf-fering, this return being an imperfection of which they are inca-pable. God ministers to them according to his wishes through the prayers that are offered for them and allows his saints and his church to cut short their torments and diminish the activity of this fire. O God, how true it is that you are *a consuming fire* (Heb 12:29).

[8.] It was therefore in this loving and altogether rigorous pur-gatory that you purified me of all that had been in me that was con-trary to your divine will. And I let you do this, although I suffered indescribable pains, sometimes for several days. I may well have wanted to perform some extraordinary acts of penance, but it was necessary just to keep doing the daily ones, such as love made me do. This pain ordinarily would take away the power to eat. I would force myself violently, however, so that nothing would be apparent and so that no one would notice a continual preoccupation with God on my face. For since the attraction was so strong, it extended to my senses so as to give me such a sweetness, modesty, and majesty that people in the world were even noticing it, and that increased their love for me, as I will explain later.

In the next chapters Guyon speaks about her growing spirituality under the guidance of Mother Granger, in spite of times of spiritual dryness and confessors who judge her negatively. She and her two children are stricken with smallpox, which takes the life of her youngest child and disfigures both her and her eldest child. Family life becomes more difficult. As she cultivates her spiritual practice, servants spy upon her to see if she is pray-ing excessively. While she receives support and encouragement from Mother Granger, others treat her with contempt, and her husband and mother-in-law continue to mistreat her and turn her child against her.

1.18—Father La Combe—Swiftness and Charity

[1.] It had been eight or nine months since I had contracted smallpox when Father La Combe[11] passed by my home. He came to my residence to give me a letter from Father de la Mothe,[12] who

214

asked me to see Father La Combe, saying that he was a good friend. I hesitated a lot about whether to see him because I truly feared meeting new people; however, the fear of offending Father de la Mothe persuaded me to do it. This conversation, which was brief, made him desire to see me again. I felt the same leading[13] on my side because I believed either that he loved God or that he was completely ready to love him, and I wanted everyone to love him. God had already used me to win three monks from there over to him. Father La Combe's eagerness to see me again made him come to our country house, which was only a half-league[14] from town. Providence used a little accident that happened to him to give me the means to talk to him. For after my husband, who enjoyed his intellect a lot, had talked with him, he started to feel bad and went into the garden. My husband told me to go find him for fear that something might have happened to him. I went there. This father said that he had noticed a recollecting and such an extraordinary presence of God on my face that he said to himself, "I have never seen a woman like this one." And this is what made him want to see me again. We got along well, and you permitted me, O my God, to tell him things that opened the way to the inner life for him. God gave him such grace through this miserable channel that he confessed to me that since then he has gone on to become changed into another man. I held high esteem for him because it appeared to me that he was of God, but I was far from predicting that I would always go to the place where he would be.

[2.] My disposition at this time was continuous contemplative prayer, as I have said, without knowing it. My only feeling was of great rest and great savoring of God's presence, which appeared to me so intimate that it was more in me than myself. The feelings were sometimes stronger and so penetrating that I could not resist them, and love took all freedom away from me. Other times it was so dry that I only felt the pain of absence, which was all the more rude since his presence had been so strongly felt by me. I believed myself to have lost love because on the occasions when love was present, I forgot my pains so much that they seemed only a dream to me. And in the absence of love it seemed that it was never supposed to come back because it appeared to me that it was always my fault that it had left me, and that was what made me inconsolable.

If I had been able to persuade myself that it was a state through which it was necessary to pass, I would not have had any pain at all, because the love of God's will would have made all things easy for me. For the distinctiveness of this contemplative prayer is to impart a great love of God's order, a sublime faith, and a confidence so perfect that one would no longer know how to fear any peril, any danger, any death, any life, any spirit, any thunder; on the contrary, one rejoices. And it even imparts a great relinquishing of self, of one's interests, of one's reputation, a forgetfulness of all things.

[3.] They would accuse me of being at the center of all in the house that was badly done, spoiled, or broken. At first I would say the truth, that it was not me. They continued, and I responded nothing more, so they accused me not only of causing the problem, but also of having lied. They said this to those who would come by the house, and afterward, when I was alone with these people, I would not disabuse them of it. I have often heard certain things said in my presence to my friends that were capable of making them lose their esteem for me, but I would never talk to them about these false accusations. Love wanted the secret and to suffer everything without justification. If I had the chance to commit the infidelity of justifying myself, this would not succeed and would bring me new crosses both outside and inside. But in spite of all that, I was so in love with the cross that my heaviest cross would have been not to have any at all. You would sometimes take away the cross, O my God, to make me more aware, and it was then that you doubled my esteem, my taste, and my desire for it, which went sometimes to such an excess that it would devour me. When the cross would be taken away from me for some moments, it seemed to me that it was due to the poor use that I had made of it and that some infidelity had deprived me of such a great good, because I never knew its value except in its loss. O good cross, my cherished delight, my faithful companion, as my Savior was only made incarnate to die in your arms, should I not be conformed to him in this, and will you not be the means by which I will be united to him forever? I would tell you often, O my love, "Punish me in any other way, but don't take away the cross."

[4.] Although love of the cross was so great in me that it would make me languish when the cross was absent, it would no sooner return to me, this lovable cross, object of my prayers and of my hopes, than it would hide its beauties from me to let me see only its rigors, in such a way that the cross was for me a strange sensation. And no sooner would some fault happen than God would deprive me of the cross once again. And then it would appear to me in all its beauty, such that I could not console myself for not having given it the welcome it deserved. I felt myself then burn with love for it. The lovable cross would return with a force proportionate to the vehemence of my desire. I could not reconcile two things that appeared so opposed to me: to desire the cross with such ardor and to bear it with such pain. These alternations made it a thousand times more discernible, because little by little the spirit became used to the cross, and when the spirit starts to bear the cross strongly, the cross is taken from it for a little while so that its return surprises the spirit and overcomes it. Moreover, when one bears the cross with a constant force, one leans on it and gets used to it to an extent that it no longer hurts so much because the cross has something that is noble and delicate and causes a great relief to the soul.

[5.] The crosses that you would send me, O my God, were made by means of your providence so as not to have this effect. Your all-wise hand would accompany them in such a way that, either by changing them often or by augmenting them, they always were new to me. Oh, you know so well, my God, how to weigh crosses in the admirable economy that you keep. You alone know how to crucify in a way conforming to the reach of the creature. You always give new and unexpected crosses. Interior crosses were going in lock step with exterior ones, and they were rather similar. Your dreaded absences would make me die of pain when you had given me, O my God, the strongest proofs of your love. And when my heart was only thinking about loving you, you would allow some unexpected fault to appear, and then you would bring about such long and rude absences that it seemed as if you might never return. And when my soul would start to resign itself and know that this state was more advantageous to it than one of abundance, because it would nourish itself through its sense of self and it was not making use of these states as it should, then you would return more strongly, and my joy was as great as my pain had been strong. I believe that if God were not holding this trial, the soul would never die to itself because self-love is so dangerous that it attaches itself to, and gets used to, everything.

[6.] In this confused and crucifying time what would cause me more pain inside and outside was an incredible facility for understanding. And when something would slip out of my mouth or when one of my responses was a little too brisk, which served to humiliate me quite a bit, they would say that I was in mortal sin.

Guidance less rigorous than this was forbidden for me, O my God. For I was so prideful, so sharp, and of a temperament so naturally contrary, wanting always to win and believing my reasons always better than those of others, that if you had wanted to spare me the blows of the hammer, you would never have polished me to your liking. For I was so vain that I was ridiculous. I could not have been reduced with any fewer crosses. Applause made me unbearable. I had the fault of praising my friends with excess and blaming others without cause. I would like with all my heart to make others know my wretchedness. It seems to me, my God, that it serves admirably as the shadows on the canvas that you have the goodness to make of me. The more criminal I was, the more I owe you, and the less I can attribute any good to myself. Oh, how blind are men who attribute to man the holiness that God imputes to him! I believe, my God, that you have saints who, after your grace, owe a lot for their fidelity. As for me, my God, I am obligated to you alone, and it is my pleasure; it is my glory; I do not know how to say it too often.

[7.] I was doing quite weighty acts of charity. You had given me, O my God, a love for the poor so great that I wanted to provide all their needs to them. I could not see them in their misery without reproaching myself for my abundance. I would deprive myself of what I could in order to help them. What I was served for the best meals was cleared away by my order and taken to them. There were hardly any poor in the area where I lived who did not feel the effects of the charity that you had given me for them. It seemed, O my God, that you only wanted alms from me. Those who had been refused by others were coming to me. I would tell you: "O my love, it is your property; I am only the tenant. I must distribute it according to your wishes." I found a good way to relieve them without having myself found out because I had a person distribute my alms in secret. When it was families who were ashamed, I would send alms to them as if I owed it to them. I clothed those who were naked, and I had girls taught how to make a living, especially those who were beautiful, so that being occupied and having enough to live on, the chance of falling into disgrace was taken away. You would even use me, O my God, to get them out of their troubled states. There was one of them of quality and beauty who died in a very holy way. I furnished milk for the little children, and, particularly around Christmas, I increased my acts of charity for the little children in honor of the child Jesus, who is the center of my love. I would go to see the sick, to console them, and to make their beds. I would apply ointments and dress their wounds, and I would shroud the dead. I would secretly furnish artisans and merchants enough to sustain their shops. One could hardly carry charity further than Our Lord made me carry it according to my state, when married and widowed. I would visit the poor at times when I could not be seen. I would go in the rain. Nothing was difficult for me. I would follow the holy sacrament with much devotion, when it was carried to them.[15]

[8.] Our Lord, in order to purify me further from the mixture of his gifts with my own self-love that I might make, gave me a very strong interior test. I started to feel that the virtue that had been so sweet and so easy for me became an insufferable weight, not that I did not love it extremely, but I found myself powerless to practice it in the way I had learned. The more I loved it, the more I forced myself to acquire some virtue that I saw missing in me, and I would fall, it seemed to me, into what was contrary to it. / There was only one thing regarding which you have always provided a visible and sensible protection for me, and that is chastity. You would give me a very great love of it and would put its effects in my soul, taking away, even in my marriage, through providence, illnesses, or other things, what might weaken it even innocently, and this grace would grow measurably as my widowhood was approaching. This happened in such a way that, in order to preserve me, your providence was constant, to the point of waking me up as soon as the devil wanted to suggest some illusions. These illusions would fall away without leaving any impression on my senses, and I did not have any at all for quite a number of years. This grace was given to me at the spiritual marriage about which I will speak shortly. I want to speak about this to a greater extent because, from the second year of my marriage, God took away all sensual pleasures from my heart, so that marriage was in every way a very rude sacrifice for me. It often would seem to me that I was as unfeeling as if I was without a body. For more than eighteen to twenty years it has seemed to me that my heart and my spirit are so separated from my body that it does things as if it were not doing them at all. If it eats or engages in recreation, it happens with such a separation that I am astonished by it. It is as if this is happening to someone else and with an entire deadening of the vigor of feeling for all its functions. I believe that I have said enough to make myself understood.//

Guyon meets Jacques Bertot through Mother Granger, but communication between Guyon and Bertot is not easy.[16] While Guyon is on a trip to Paris, her father dies, an event of which she had experienced a strong premonition. She returns after he is already buried. Her young daughter then dies, making this a period full of trials for her. She begins to cultivate spiritual growth in others and to travel and make pilgrimages. Another child is born, a son. Mother Granger dies. Another pregnancy ensues. There are problems with her brother that threaten the financial well-being of Guyon's husband, requiring legal action. Chapter 21 describes how she meets a Jansenist priest and formed a strong and distracting desire for his attention and company. As a result, she loses the sense of God's presence and "falls into a purely natural state," accompanied by frustration and despair. Chapter 22 recounts the period leading to the death of Guyon's husband, during which he becomes even more hostile toward her, until his last days, when he tries to counsel her about how to manage her financial affairs upon his death. Mother Granger comes to her in a dream to comfort her. In Chapter 23 she experiences a profound sense of spiritual loss and desolation, and she breaks off relations with the Jansenist priest. She nonetheless continues to struggle with exterior vices and attachments. She employs a clergyman, sent by Bertot, as her son's tutor. The Jansenist priest accuses her of having an improper relationship with this tutor and issues calumnies against her. She loses favor with Archange Enguerrand, the Franciscan who introduced her to Mother Granger earlier, as well as Bertot. She has to flee her home with her children for a brief period. Finally, accusations of improper conduct surface against the Jansenist priest, which put an end to this period of personal trial. Father La Combe helps her during this period of spiritual trial by writing letters to her. The idea comes to her to travel to Geneva for the first time.

1.28—The God-Peace

[1.] It was on this happy day of the feast of Mary Magdalene that my soul was perfectly delivered from all these pains. It had begun to start up a new life with the first letter from Father La Combe.[17] But it was like a dead man being resuscitated who is not yet delivered from his shrouds. Yet in one day I was in perfect life. I found myself raised up above nature as much as I had been rigorously held captive under its weight. I found myself astonished by this new liberty and by seeing this restoration, with as much magnificence as purity, of that which I had believed was forever lost. What I possessed was so simple, so immense, that I could not express it. It was then, O my God, that I found in you, in an ineffable manner, all that I had lost. You gave it to me with new benefits. My trouble and my pain were changed into a peace that, to explain myself better, I will call God-Peace. I would say that the peace that I had before this time was truly the peace of God, the peace gift of God, but it was not the God-Peace that he possesses in himself, which is only found in him.

[2.] Although my joy was extremely great, I was not allowed to give way to it. The memory of my past misery prevented me from enjoying myself and from taking part in nature in any possible way whatsoever. As soon as it wanted to do or to taste something, the spirit made it forgo all. I cannot explain the empire that the spirit then had over nature, except to say that it is like a famous conqueror who was being held captive by the enemy that he came to vanquish and was being made to do what the other wanted and had no more resistance in himself. I was very far from exalting myself or attributing anything to myself in this new state because my experience made me truly see and feel what I was.

[3.] I saw clearly that it was a change in state that would last some time, but I did not believe my happiness to be as great and as immutable as it was. If one judges a good by the work that preceded it, I let mine be judged by the work that I needed to undertake before having it. O Paul, you say that *the sufferings of this time are not worthy to be compared to the glory to come* (Rom 8:18). This is true even in this life, where, I can say for having experienced it, all the work that one endures in this life would be nothing compared to the happiness of possessing you in yourself in the manner that my soul did. One day of this happiness would even be compensation along with interest for several years of suffering. Although it was only in its rising dawn, this did not prevent it from being such as I describe. All ease with which to do good was made greater for me than before, but in a manner so free and so absent of discomfort that it seemed to have become natural for me.

[4.] At the beginning this freedom had less breadth, but the more I advanced, the greater the freedom became. I had the chance to see M. Bertot for a moment. I told him that I believed my state truly to have changed, without telling him about it in detail, or about what I was feeling, or what had come before. I had very little time to speak to him since he was preoccupied with something else. You permitted, O my God, that he said no to me, maybe without thinking about it. I believed him because grace made me believe what people would tell me, in spite of my illumination and my experiences, such that when someone would tell me the opposite of what I thought, no other thought was allowed to remain in my mind, which remained in such submission to what it was told that it did not have a single contrary thought or reflection. This caused me no pain because every state was indifferent to me. However, I felt a certain beatitude to be increased in me. I was entirely delivered from all pain and all inclinations that I believed to have been toward sin. It seemed that I did all sorts of good without a sense of self or a return, and if a return presented itself, it was immediately dissipated. It seemed to me as if a curtain was drawn that covered this thought and made it no longer appear. My imagination was entirely focused so that I had no more trouble with it. I was astonished by the clarity of my mind and by the purity of my heart.

[5.] I received a letter from Father La Combe, who wrote to me that God had made him understand that he had great designs for me and that during the *memento*[18] it had been said to him, "You will dwell in the same place." He did not know any more, and God did not let him know anything more in particular. I always had the thought of Geneva deep in my heart, without explaining it to any-one. I did not stop to think about it or about what Father La Combe had told me about God's designs on my soul. I received all of this with complete indifference, without wanting either to worry about it or to think about it, waiting for everything, O my God, from your all-powerful will. Since my misery was still so close, I even feared that it was the ruse of a demon who, while amusing me with the thought of a good thing that I did not have, would make me lose the one that I possessed by drawing me away from my state. This fear was sweet, peaceful, and infused with confidence and hope. The more miserable I considered myself, the more I saw myself in accord with your designs, O my God, and the more it seemed that, with my misery, my incapacity, and my nothingness being unable to rob God of anything he did, he alone would have all the glory of his works. I would say to you, "O my Lord, take the miserable and the dull-witted to do your works, since you would be given all the glory, and man would attribute nothing to himself. If you took a person of great virtue and enhanced her with talents, some works might be attributed to her, but if you take me, it will be clearly seen that you are the sole author of what you do." I remained this way, without thinking about it any longer or worrying the least bit in the world, persuaded as I was that if you wanted something of me, my God, you would furnish me with the means. I waited, however, with a very firm will to execute your orders whenever you might make them known to me at the expense of my own life. You took away all my crosses and you gave me such a great facility with all things that I was surprised by it. I began to dress wounds; you were making me heal the most incurable. When surgeons did not want to work on them anymore or when they wanted to cut off the parts infected with disease, it was then that you made me heal them. I became so free that I could have stayed in church all day, although I felt nothing perceptible, and I also had no distress at not being there, finding everywhere, in an immensity and a very great vastness, the one whom I no longer possessed but who had destroyed me in him.

[6.] Oh, how I truly felt what you unquestionably say in your gospel, repeated by the four evangelists, and even said two times in one of the Gospels, that *he who loses his life for me will find it, and he who saves his life will lose it* (Matt 10:39; 16:25). O happy loss, which a happy necessity compelled in me! When I believed myself the most lost and without resources, it was then that I found myself the most saved; when I no longer noticed anything about myself, I found everything in my God; when I lost every good, I found all kinds of goods in him; when I lost all created supports, and even divine ones, I found myself in the happy necessity of falling into the purely divine and of falling there through everything that I believed would distance me further from it. In losing all gifts, I found the giver; in losing God in me, I found him in himself, in the immutable, no longer to lose him. O poor creatures who spend all your lives taking the gifts of God and who believe yourselves through this to be the most favored and the happiest, I pity you nonetheless, if you do not go to my God through the loss of these same gifts! How many souls spend all their lives this way and believe themselves prodigies! There are other people who, being destined by God to die to themselves, spend all their lives in a dying life and in strange agonies, without ever entering into God by total death and loss, because they always want to retain something under good pretexts and never lose themselves in all the expanse of God's designs. This is why they never enjoy God in fullness, which is a loss that will only be understood perfectly in the other life.

[7.] O my Lord, what happiness did I not taste in my little solitude and in my little household, where nothing would interrupt my rest! As I was in the country for a long time, and as the young age of my children did not require too much of my energies, given that they were in good-enough hands, I withdrew myself all day long into the woods, where I spent as many happy days as I had had months of pain, for it was there that I gave freedom to the pain to destroy me. This was also where, at the beginning, I gave love the space to consume me. And then I let myself get more lost in an infinite and incomprehensible abyss. I could say nothing about what was happening in me due to my being too pure, too simple, and too outside of myself.

[8.] You treated me, O my God, like your servant Job, giving me back double what you had taken from me and removing my crosses. You gave me a marvelous facility to please everybody, and what is more surprising is that my mother-in-law, who until then had always complained about me in spite of whatever care I took to make her happy, without my doing anything to make her happy and against her own nature, which was not to be happy with anything, admitted that no one could be more pleased with me than she was. The people who had most criticized me expressed pain for it and became my panegyrists. My reputation was reestablished all the more than before, when it seemed the most lost. I stayed in a complete peace, both inside and outside. You did that, O my God, in order to make the sacrifice that you were preparing me to make both more painful and more perfect. For if it had been necessary for me to die during the time of persecution, it would have been a relief and not a sacrifice. I also might never have been able to resolve to leave my pains behind. Without a doubt, I would always have feared to get down off the cross by myself and be unfaithful to it. It seems to me that no one could be as happy as I was both on the inside and on the outside.

Since the cross had always been my faithful companion and friend, from time to time little pains at no longer needing to suffer revealed themselves, but they were absorbed just as quickly as they appeared into a depth that could not admit any desires. Although my body suffered great pain, there was no longer pain, but instead, depths that beatified all things. It seems to me that my soul had become like the New Jerusalem spoken of in Revelation, where there is no more crying or pain (Rev 21:4). The indifference in me was perfect, and my union with whatever pleased God was so great that I did not find a single desire or tendency in myself. What appeared to me to be the most lost was my will because I did not find it for anything whatsoever. My soul could not incline itself more toward one side or the other. All that it could do was nourish itself with daily providences. It found that another will had taken the place of its own, an entirely divine will, which, however, was so suited to it and so natural that it found itself infinitely more free in this will than it had been in its own.

[9.] These dispositions, which I describe as of a past time so that nothing gets confused, have persisted ever since and are even more firm and perfected at the present time. I could not desire one thing or another, but I was happy with all that happened to me, without paying attention or thinking about it unless someone would ask, "Do you want this thing or that one?" I was astonished that I no longer found in myself that which could desire. It was just as if everything had disappeared from inside of me, and a stronger power had taken its place. I had truly felt in the time preceding my troubles that someone more powerful than I was leading me and making me act. I had only, it seemed to me, the will to submit myself voluntarily to all that it did in me and through me, but now it was no longer the same. I no longer found the will to submit; it was as if it had disappeared or, rather, passed into another will. It seems to me that this powerful effort then did everything that it wanted, and I no longer found that soul that it was leading before with extreme love by its crook and its staff. It alone appeared to me, and it as if this soul had given up its place to it or, rather, had passed into it to become thereafter but one same thing with it.

[10.] O Union of unity, requested from God by Jesus Christ for men (John 17:23) and earned by the same Jesus Christ, how strong you are in a soul that you lose in this way in its God! It is there that after the consummation of this divine union, the soul lives *hidden with Christ in God* (Col 3:3). O happy loss, and all the happier that it is not one of the fleeting losses that ecstasy brings about, which are absorptions rather than losses, since the soul again finds itself soon thereafter, but rather one of the permanent and lasting losses that go on continually losing themselves in an immense sea, just as a little fish would continuously sink down into an infinite sea. But the comparison does not appear apt to me. It is rather like a little drop of water thrown into the sea that continually takes on more qualities of the sea itself.

This soul received without having the power to prefer or to choose. When I speak of power, I do not mean an absolute power but one of the soul that still has preferences and desires. It received what was given to it or done to it with complete indifference. At the beginning it still committed some errors due to haste, but these were as if outside of it, without its knowing its state.

Guyon meets the archbishop of Geneva for the first time, and he speaks to her of working with the New Catholics in Gex. Many support her decision to travel to Geneva, including Bertot and the son of Marie de l'Incarnation. She finds it very difficult to leave her children. Surprisingly, her relationship with her mother-in-law is transformed upon her leaving. She begins

226

to be involved with the New Catholics and suspects that this movement is not to her liking. Bertot dies.

PART TWO: TRAVELS
Being Happy with What Happened Outside France

Guyon puts her affairs in order and sets out with her daughter and servants. She travels to Corbeil, Annecy, and Gex. Although worried about her daughter, who suffered during these travels, she is uplifted by meeting up with Father La Combe. Her brother continues to make accusations against her, and she suffers other distresses, both psychological and physical. The archbishop of Geneva makes La Combe her spiritual director.

2.4—State of Expansiveness

[1.] Before speaking of what is left for me to write, which I would voluntarily suppress if I had anything of my selfhood, as much because of the difficulty of explaining it myself as because there are so few souls capable of such little-known and such little-understood behavior, about which I have never read anything similar, I will still say something about the interior dispositions that I had then, so as to try to make myself understood, which will be rather difficult for me due to their extreme simplicity. If this is useful to you who really want to be among my children, and if it is useful to my children by making them all the more lost and by impelling them to let God be glorified in them in his way and not in their own, I will have found my pain put to good use. And if there is something that they do not understand, let them truly die to themselves, and soon thereafter they will have an experience of it stronger than what I could describe to them, because words never equal experience.

[2.] After I had emerged from the state of misery of which I have spoken, I understood how a state that had appeared to me so criminal, but was only so in my mind, had purified my soul, ripping all sense of self away from it. As soon as my mind was enlightened about the truth of this state, my soul was put into an immense

227

expansiveness. I knew the difference between the graces that had preceded this state and those that have succeeded it. Previously, everything was recollected and concentrated on the inside, and I possessed God in my depths and in the intimate part of my soul. But afterward, I possessed him in a way so vast, so pure, and so immense that there was nothing equal to it. Previously, it was as if God was enclosed in me and I was united to him in my depths, but afterward, I was as if in the abyss of the sea itself. Thoughts and images had been lost, but in a way that was perceived, although only slightly so. The soul would let them fall away sometimes, which is still an action. But afterward, it was as if they had disappeared, but in a way so naked, so clean, so lost that the soul does not perform a single action in itself, however simple and delicate it might be, at least a single action that could be evident to consciousness. The powers and the senses are purified in an admirable way. The mind is of a surprising clarity. I was sometimes surprised that no thoughts would appear. This imagination, previously so disturbed, was no longer disturbed at all in any way. There was no more uneasiness or trouble or preoccupation with memory. All is naked and clear, and God makes the soul know and think as he pleases, without unusual forms disturbing the spirit any longer. This is of a very great purity. It is the same with the will, which, being perfectly dead to all its spiritual appetites, no longer has any taste, inclination, or tendency. It remains empty of all human inclinations, both natural and spiritual. This allows God to bend it where he pleases and as it pleases him. This expanse that does not end in anything, however simple it might be, grows each day in such a way that it seems that this soul, by participating in the qualities of the Bridegroom, participates especially in his immensity. In the past one was as if drawn in and closed up in the inside. Afterward, I felt that a hand truly stronger than the first drew me outside of myself and plunged me without vision, light, or knowledge into God in a manner that I loved, since the more distant the soul had believed itself to be from this state, the more ecstatic it was to find it. How sweet this is for this soul who is understood so much more than it can understand!

[3.] There was something that happened to me at the beginning of this state, something for which I have no name. My contemplative prayer was of an inconceivable nakedness and simplicity, and at the same time it was of an inexplicable depth. I was as if drawn very high outside of myself, and what was very pleasing and surprising to me was that my head felt as if it was violently raised. This was all the more novel as, previously, the first movements of this state were just the opposite, being all concentrated. I believe that, at the beginning of my new life, God wanted me to feel this thing, which, though very gentle, was so strong that my body went faint. I believe, I say, that Our Lord permitted this to make me understand this passage of the soul into God for the sake of other souls. For after it had lasted a few days, I no longer felt this violence, although I have felt ever since that my contemplative prayer is no longer in me in the way that I felt it before, when I used to say, *with me is prayer to the God of my life* (Ps 42:8). It will be difficult to understand what I mean unless a person has felt it. When I would go to confession, I could hardly talk, not due to an interior recollecting or due to what I have written concerning myself when I was at the beginning. It was like immersion; this is a word that I use without knowing if it is right. I was plunged down and raised up. One time, while at confession with Father La Combe in Gex, I felt elevated this way by such a strong force that I believed that my entire body was going to be raised from the ground. Our Lord was using this to convince me about what the flight of the spirit was, which would elevate the bodies of some saints to a great height, and about the difference between that and the loss of the soul in God. Before pursuing what happened to me, I will say more about this.

[4.] The flight of the spirit is much more noble than the simple fainting from ecstasy, although sometimes, and almost always, the flight of the spirit causes weakness in the body, since God is drawing the soul strongly, not to its depths, but to himself, so as to make it pass into him, and this soul has not been purified enough to pass into God without violence. This passing only takes place after the mystical death in which the soul truly leaves itself to pass into its divine object—which I call death, meaning a passage from one thing to another. And this is truly the happy passover of the soul, as well as its passage into the promised land. This spirit, which is created to be united to its principle, has, in order to return there, a propulsive quality so strong that, if it were not stopped by a continual miracle, it would cause the body to move wherever it wanted, due to its impetuousness and its nobility. But God has given it an earthly body that serves as a counterweight. This spirit, therefore, created to be united to its principle without any location, and feeling itself drawn by its divine object, stretches toward it with extreme violence, so that when, for a time, God suspends the power that the body has to retain the spirit, it follows with impetuousness. But since it is not purified enough to pass into God, little by little it returns to itself, and the body, gradually reacquiring its quality, returns to earth. The saints who have been the most consummated in this life have had nothing such as this, and even some of the saints in whom it has taken place have lost it at the end of their lives, staying simple and common like the others, because they had in reality and permanently what they had only had as experiences during the period of the elevation of their bodies.

[5.] It is thus certain that the soul, by death to itself, passes into its divine object, and this is what I felt then. And I found that the farther forward I went, the more my spirit was losing itself in its Sovereign, who drew it to himself more and more. And he wanted at the beginning for me to know this for the sake of others and not for myself. Every day this spirit lost itself more and more, and its principle drew it always more until, by virtue of drawing it, it became so distant from itself that it lost itself entirely from view and no longer noticed itself. But the same love that drew it also clarified and purified it to make the spirit pass into himself, and then transformed it into himself. At the beginning of the new life, I saw clearly that the soul was united to its God without intermediary or location, but it was not perfectly lost. It was losing itself each day, as one sees that a river that is losing itself in the ocean is first unified, then flowing into it, but in such a way that the river is distinguished from the sea for a time, until the point where it is finally transformed little by little into the same sea itself, which, by communicating its qualities to it little by little, changes it so much into itself that it finally becomes the same sea with it. I felt the same things in my soul as God made it become lost in him little by little and communicated his qualities to it, drawing it away from what it had of its own.

[6.] At the beginning of the new life I committed errors, and these errors, which would have appeared as nothing, and which on the contrary would have been virtues in another state, were little instances of self-awareness that were slight and on the surface, a hastiness, hardly an emotion, but so slight as to be almost nothing. I felt at first that this would create a gap between God and my soul. It was like a speck of dust. But since this was only on the surface, the gap seemed more slender than a spider web to me, and then God wanted me to go and purify myself by confession, or else he purified me of it himself. And I saw clearly that this gap was like a veil that did not break the union or alter it at all, but covered it. And this very slight gap demonstrated the distinction between the Bridegroom and the Bride. I do not know if I am making myself understood. The soul suffered from this little gap, but in a peaceful way; it saw that it could truly put the gap in place but not take it away. Little by little each gap was lost, and the more infrequent and delicate the gaps became, the more the union lost itself in becoming united, until the point that there was only one instead of two, and the soul lost itself so strongly that it could no longer distinguish itself from its Beloved or see him. This is what caused it pain afterward. As for confession, it was astonished that it did not know what to say, that it no longer found anything, although it might seem that it would have more faults due to the freedom to speak, to talk, and to do what it did not do before. But this did not cause it any more pain and was not considered a fault by it. An inconceivable innocence, which is not known or understood by those who are still closed up in themselves, is its life. But it is necessary to pick up where I left off.

[7.] Before coming to this state, being thus in the confessional, I felt myself so strongly drawn outside of myself that I felt my body getting weak. My face became covered with sweat. I sat down, but since I felt that this state was growing in a delicious manner, though very pure and spiritual, I withdrew myself. I was overtaken by shivering from my head to my feet; I could not speak or talk for the whole day, and from this moment, or rather from this operation, which lasted three days, my soul was much more lost in its divine object, although not entirely. The joy that the soul then possessed is so great that it feels these words of the prophet-king, *And let the just feast and rejoice before God and be delighted with gladness* (Ps 68:3), but the joy is that it appears to the soul that this will no longer be taken away. It seems that these words of Our Lord are addressed to it: *And your joy no man will take from you* (John 16:22). The soul is as if drowning in a river of peace, and it is so penetrated by it that the soul is only peace. Its contemplative prayer is continual; nothing can prevent it from praying or loving. It feels very truly these words: *I sleep but my heart keeps watch* (Song 5:2), because it feels that sleep does not prevent the Spirit from praying in it. O ineffable happiness! Who would have ever thought that a poor soul that believed itself in its final misery could have found in misery itself a happiness equal to that which it tastes without tasting? This does not mean that it does not sometimes feel pains, which even take away its appetite, and the body, which is not accustomed to this, completely languishes from it. But this pain is so sweet and peaceful that one would not know how to distinguish whether it is a sweet pain or a painful sweetness. Every day the soul feels its capacity growing and getting larger, and what astonishes it is that the light of this state increases that state which it had possessed before without knowing it.

[8.] O happy poverty, happy loss, happy nothingness that gives no less than God himself in his immensity, who is no longer adjusted to the limited manner of the creature, and who is no longer possessed by it, but whom he possesses entirely, drawing it always more from itself in order to be drowned in him. The soul knows then that all states of visions, revelations, assurances are obstacles that do not serve this state, which is far above all this, because the soul accustomed to supports feels pain in losing them, and it cannot arrive here without this loss. Thus, all intelligence is given without any viewpoint other than naked faith. And this is where these words of the Most Holy Saint John of the Cross hold true: *When I wanted to possess nothing* through self-love, *everything was given to me without seeking it.*[19] O happy *fallen grain of wheat* (John 12:24), which produces fruit a hundredfold! The soul is then so passive, regarding both the good and the bad, that it is astonishing. Although previously it might have appeared to be a lot like this, it is not at all the same here, because at present it is reinforced in a surprising manner. It receives either one without any movement of its own, letting either one flow by or be lost as it comes. I do not know if this is the right way of speaking, because it passes through as if without touching.

***

The rest of the chapter speaks about her fall from a horse and the ensuing consequences of that fall. Also, we learn that back in Paris she is becoming more esteemed.

In the next chapters Guyon explains how she renounces her fortune, giving it to her family. The archbishop of Geneva tries to make her a mother superior in exchange for the rest of her fortune. Guyon is not interested in this offer, and as a result accusations of intrigue begin to circulate, implicating Father La Combe for impropriety. These accusations of impropriety grow, and Guyon comes to believe that the archbishop of Geneva is leading these attacks, supported by Guyon's brother.

2.8—Teaching

[1.] My soul was just as I have described it, in an entire abandonment and in a very great contentment in a place of such strong storms. It could do nothing other than to remain in its former indifference, wanting nothing, not even of God, whether grace or disgrace, sweetness or crosses. Previously it would want the cross in such a way that it would become quite languishing. Then, it could not desire the cross or choose it, instead receiving all crosses always with the same spirit and accepting them all indifferently from the hand of love; regardless of their nature, difficult or easy, all were welcome. Certain people came to me to say a hundred outrageous things about Father La Combe, believing by doing this that they would enrage me so I would no longer follow his counsel. The more they told me negative things about him, the more Our Lord raised my esteem for him in my soul. I would tell them, "Maybe I will never see him, but I am quite ready to treat him fairly. It is not he who prevents me from binding myself, but it is the fact that this is not my vocation."[20] They asked me who knew better than the bishop that I was mistaken, that my state was worth nothing. I was indifferent to all this. I could be neither assured nor uncertain; I let myself remain there like a person who has nothing to think or desire, having given God the care of wanting on her behalf, and of executing what he wants and in the way he wants.

[2.] This soul has no sweetness or spiritual taste. These are no longer in season. It remains such as it is, in its nothingness for itself, with this being its place, and in everything for God, without returning to any reflection on itself. It does not know if it has virtues, gifts, and graces in the one who is the author of all this; it does not think about this and can want nothing, and everything that concerns it appears foreign to it. It does not even have the desire to procure the glory of God, leaving to God the care of procuring it for himself, and the glory is for God, as it pleases him.

In this state God sometimes uses this soul to pray for some other soul, but this is done without choice or premeditation, in peace, without desire for success. One might ask what this soul does. It lets itself be led by providence and by creatures without resistance. Its life on the outside is quite common, and as for the inside, it sees nothing there. It has no interior or exterior assurance, and yet it was never more assured. The more hopeless everything is, the more tranquil it is in its depths, in spite of the ravages of the senses and of creatures, which, for some time after the new life, cause some minor clouds and gaps, just as I have said. It is necessary to notice that a gap only exists because the soul is only united immediately, but is not transformed, because as soon as it is mixed and has entirely passed into its original being, there are no more gaps. If it committed sins, it would need to be rejected and vomited out, so to speak. Therefore, it finds no more gaps, not even the most subtle and delicate—I could be confused because I did not mark times often enough; what I have marked was already written in May 1682—I mean the reflections, the slight and superficial sense of self, the current faults, when the soul feels very clearly that these create gaps. The soul clearly feels the impurity that comes from human action; a hasty word or a natural or hasty action causes this fog, but the soul can neither prevent nor remedy this, or even want to, because it has experienced so many times that its own efforts are not only useless but also harmful. They dirty it more due to its state of loss.

[3.] At the beginning of the path of faith the soul uses its faults, being humiliated by them through a simple, peaceful, tranquil turning inward, loving the abjection that comes to it from this. The more it advances, the more this simple action without action becomes simplified, but for this soul this is no longer in question. The soul remains unwavering, immobile, bearing the pain that its fault causes without movement, without any action, as simple as it might be. This is what God requires of the soul from the moment it is very passive, and this is the conduct to which he has held me from the first years, long before the state of death. But whatever fidelity the soul might have to perform no perceptible action to end its pain, there would nonetheless be a nearly imperceptible action that the soul would not recognize at that moment. And it would only recognize it afterward because it will find itself then in a state exempt from this simple, indeed very simple, action. It is impossible to understand me without having this experience. This aspect is very difficult, and the soul only becomes strong in this process without process after having committed many infidelities, because at this point, since the fault is real and the soul feels its impurity, it feels at the same time a secret instinct to rid itself of it; but in this degree here, in addition to the fact that nothing coming from itself would be a remedy, it is only the love of its own excellence that brings it to exert itself. It is necessary for all purification to come from God at the degree of which I speak. It is sometimes necessary to wait in a rest without rest for the Sun of righteousness to dissipate the fog. Following this conduct becomes so natural that the soul does not even want to do anything. It leaves itself prey to the inner burning with an unwavering firmness, and even if it were to see all hell bearing arms, it would not change its conduct. It is then that it correctly says along with the prophet-king: *Even if I see an army arrayed for battle, I will not fear; and his strength will reinforce my courage* (Ps 27:3). It might be a bit afraid in all of its senses, but it stays still and hard as a rock, preferring in its perfect abandonment to be the toy of demons rather than to assure itself, even with a sigh.

[4.] The soul in this state does not voluntarily commit any fault. I believe this to be so because it seems that, having no will for anything whatsoever, great or little, sweet or bitter, for honor, wealth, life, perfection, salvation, eternity, nothing found in it could offend God; therefore, it does not. The imperfections of which I speak are all in nature and not in it. But they are still on the surface and are lost little by little. It is true that our nature is so tricky that it gets involved in things everywhere. But the soul is not impeccable, and its greatest faults are its reflections, which are very harmful to it. It wants to examine itself under the pretext of indicating its state. This is why one must never take pains to speak of one's state or to take any account of it if God is not putting what he wants one to say in one's mind. And further, when the director knows the state of the soul, he does not require it. If he required it, or if actual light were to be given to him on the subject, it would be necessary for this to happen to the soul without turning back and without reflection. The self-gaze is like that of the basilisk, which kills.

[5.] The soul must have the same firmness not to stir from the pain of its faults during temptations as well. The devil truly fears to approach such souls, and he leaves them right away, no longer daring to attack them. He only attacks those who bend or who fear him. Souls led by faith are not ordinarily tested by demons. This is for souls led by illumination. For it is necessary to know that trials are made to fit the state of the soul. Those who are led by illumination, by extraordinary gifts, ecstasies, and so forth, also have extraordinary trials that are brought about by the intervention of demons. For, since they think of everything as assured, the trial itself is understood as an assurance. But it is not the same with souls of naked faith. Since they are led by nakedness, by loss, and by what is most common, their trial is simply common as well, but this is truly more terrible and causes them to be all the more lost. What causes their death is nothing extraordinary; it is only the unbalancing of their own temperament. These are pains that they see as true faults and that do not give them any assurance unless it is an assurance of their complete loss. These two states are found in Saint Paul. He says at one point: *And lest the greatness of the revelations should exalt me, there was given me an angel of Satan, to buffet me* (2 Cor 12:7–8). Here the trial conforms to illumination. But since the great doctor and master of spiritual life must have felt all of these states, he does not stop there. He has another trial that he calls *the sting of my flesh*, so as to show that he had felt everything. He prayed, he says, *three times*, and it was said to him: *My grace is all you need, because virtue is perfected in infirmities* (2 Cor 12:5). All this, although done in order to humiliate him, would nonetheless be reassuring for him. He has felt another state that he calls the body of sin, and this expression is admirable because just as the body only rots after death from its own corruption, so also in this state it seems that the soul only feels the exhalations of the body of sin, meaning of a body corrupted by sin. *Wretched man that I am*, he says, *who will deliver me from this body of death?* (Rom 7:24–25). For I feel that this is a body that carries death in itself, which I would not know how to make alive. And then, convinced of his powerlessness to deliver himself from such a great evil, after having deplored his wretchedness, which is then without assurance, and with an understanding of his powerlessness, he says *wretched man that I am, who will deliver me from this body of death*, this putrid and disgusting body that I carry, although I am alive. He answers himself: *This will be the grace of God by Our Lord Jesus Christ.* And how do you understand that, O Paul? It is that Jesus Christ, by taking the place of the sinful, carnal man in me, by casting off this old man from me, this body corrupted by sin, will clothe me once more because he vanquished death in me when he said: *O death, I will be your death, O hell, I will be your destruction. But the sting of death is sin* (Hos 13:14; 1 Cor 15:55–56). When Jesus Christ vanquishes death in me by his life, and when his life surmounts my death in this admirable duel, there will no longer be any sting in death, since there will be no more sin. And this is when grace will deliver me from this body of sin through Jesus Christ my Savior. I say, therefore, that the same firmness that one must have regarding faults and temptations, in order to give no foothold to the devil, is also necessary regarding gifts and graces.

[6.] In this state everything is so intimate that nothing is noticeable. But if something falls upon the senses, the soul is unshakable in letting the grace come and go, not making any movement, as simple as it might be, either to taste or to know. It leaves everything as if it were happening in another, without taking part in it at all. At the beginning and for a rather long time the soul sees that nature wants to take part in it, and at that point its fidelity consists in restraining it, without permitting the least effusion. But the habit that it took on to restrain it makes the soul stay immobile, as if the thing does not touch it anymore. The soul no longer looks at or appropriates anything, and it lets everything flow into God with purity, just as it left there. Until the soul is in this state, it always sullies God's operation a bit by getting involved, just as streams become contaminated by the places through which they flow, but as soon as these same streams flow into pure places, they then retain the purity of their spring. This destroys nature a lot and chases it from its home, not giving it any refuge. Unless from experience or from God making this guidance known to the soul, it cannot understand or imagine this itself due to its great nakedness. The mind is empty, no longer crossed by thoughts; nothing fills a certain emptiness, which is no longer painful, and the soul discovers in itself an immense capacity that nothing can either limit or prevent. Exterior occupations no longer cause any pain, and the soul is in the state of consistency that cannot be expressed and even less understood.

[7.] Oh, if souls had enough courage to let themselves become lost without having pity for themselves, without looking at anything or leaning on anything, what progress they would make! But no one wants to leave land; at most one advances a few paces. As soon as the sea is agitated, one becomes afraid and weighs anchor and often stops navigating. Love of one's own interest causes all these disorders. It is still important here not to look at one's state, following the advice of the Bridegroom to the Bride: *Turn your eyes away from me, because they make me take flight* (Song 6:5), not only to prevent the loss of courage, but also due to self-love, which has become so rooted that the soul often observes its life and would like to control its empire by a certain complacency toward and preference for its state. Often also, the idea that one adopts of the importance of one's state makes one want to see the same perfection in others. One adopts ideas of others that are too low, and one does not enjoy conversing with people who are too human. It is not the same with the soul that is truly abandoned and truly dead. It prefers to converse with demons by the order of providence than to converse with angels by its own choice.

[8.] That is why it does not know how to choose either a state or a condition, however perfect it might be. It is content with all that it has; this is all that the soul needs in order to be fully happy. It could not feel pain or happiness from the presence of people who belong to God the most and who would seem to be the most necessary for it, and in whom it has complete confidence, because it is fully satisfied and has everything that it needs, although it lacks everything. This is what makes the soul not seek to see or speak to anyone; instead, it receives providences for both. Without these providences what is human always remains, however compelling the pretext that one makes. The soul feels very strongly that all that is done through choice and election, and not through providence, nullifies it and is far from helping it, or at least is not very productive. But what makes this soul so fully contented? It does not know at all; it is content without knowing the reason for its contentment and without wanting to know it. But in a vast, immense way that is independent of exterior events, it is more content in the humiliation of its own wretchedness and in the scorn of all creatures by this order of providence, than on the throne by its own choice. If it needed only to sigh in order to leave this most frightful place, it would not do so.

[9.] O you alone who leads these souls and who can teach these ways so conducive to loss and so contrary to the ordinary spirit of the devotion, which is full of itself and of its own pursuits, lead souls without number there, so that you might be loved purely! Only these souls love you as you want to be loved. All other loves, however great and ardent they might seem, are not pure love, but truly a love mixed with a sense of self. These souls can no longer endure austerities by themselves or desire them, but they perform those they are made to perform with indifference. They have nothing extraordinary on the outside, and their lives are most common. They do not think at all about humiliating themselves, instead letting themselves be as they are, because the state of annihilation where they are is below all humility. Such souls should not be judged by those who are still in a state of perfecting themselves through their own efforts, because they would often take for pride the simplicity with which these people, exempt from a sense of self, speak of all things and of themselves. But they should know that this is not at all the case, that these souls are doing things that delight God, *who delights to be with the children of men* (Prov 8:31), meaning those souls who are childlike and innocent. They are truly far from pride, only being able to attribute nothingness and sin to themselves. And they are so united with God that they no longer see anything except him, and all things in him. They would proclaim the graces of God with the same facility as they would their wretchedness, and they talk of either in an indifferent way, as God permits them to do and as it can be useful for the good of other souls.

[10.] Those reservations that are so good and so holy at a time when Our Lord consecrates all his graces and pains through a profound silence—as one can see from what he did in me—would be acts of selfhood for the souls I have described because these souls are above the self. This passage by Jeremiah is so beautiful: *He will sit down and will hold his peace because he has taken it upon himself!* (Lam 3:28). As long as the soul is still in the solitude of itself, it is necessary for it to content itself with silence and rest. But then it is necessary for it to go beyond and to raise itself so far above itself that it finally loses itself in God and all things with it, and then it no longer knows its virtues as virtues, but it has them all in God as from God without anything in reference or in relation to itself. This is why those who are still in themselves should not measure the freedom of these souls or compare them to their own shrunken acts, although these acts are very virtuous and proper to them. Nonetheless, they need to understand that what brings about perfection in their state would be imperfect for the souls of whom I speak.

[11.] What brings about the perfection of one state always turns into the imperfection and the beginning of the state that follows. It is similar in the degrees of erudition; for example, someone who finishes one class and is perfect in it is imperfect in the one that follows. And it is necessary for this person to stop acting in the way that made him perfect in his own class in order to enter into another, completely different one. Saint Paul says this so well: *When I was a child, I spoke like a child, I acted like a child* (1 Cor 13:11), and this was perfection in the state of childhood, which has one hundred pleasures, but when one has become fully adult, things change to the opposite. Saint Paul speaks of this in still another way when he says something, speaking of the law, which one can apply to laws regarding perfection that one might impose on oneself. *The law*, he says, *was our teacher to guide us to Christ, so that we might be justified by faith* (Gal 3:24). Therefore, this law and this perfection that one imposes on oneself, which Our Lord himself makes us practice, are very necessary to get to Jesus Christ. But when Jesus Christ has become our life, this teacher who was so useful to us becomes useless. And if we still wanted to follow this teacher, we would not let ourselves be led by Jesus Christ enough, and we would never enter into the perfect freedom of the children of God, which is born in the Spirit of God.

[12.] For when one lets oneself be guided by the Spirit of God, he lets us enter into the freedom of his children, adopted in Jesus Christ and by Jesus Christ, *because where the Spirit of God is, there is also freedom*, because he *did not give us his spirit by measure* (John 3:34), for *those whom he predestines to be his children, he has called them and those whom he has called, he has justified*. Therefore, it is he who brings about in them this righteousness that conforms to their call. But for what has he destined these deeply cherished souls? *To be conformed to the image of his Son* (Rom 8:29–30). Oh, this is the great secret of this call and of this justification and why so few souls arrive at this state. It is because such a soul is predestined to conform to the image of the son of God. But, one will say, are not all Christians called to conform to the image of the Son of God? Yes, each one is called to be conformed to it in some respect because if a Christian did not bear the image of Jesus Christ in himself, he would not be saved, since he is only saved by this characteristic. But the souls of which I speak are destined to bear Jesus Christ himself and to conform to him in everything, and the more perfect their conformity is, the more perfect they themselves are. One will see in what follows in my writings how much it pleases God to conform my soul to himself.

[13.] These are the souls in which God engenders his Word. He makes them bear the inclinations of this same Word, without the soul discovering these same inclinations in itself for a very long time. But when light is given, either through speaking or writing, the soul knows very well that, as Jesus Christ led a common and natural life, without anything extraordinary except near the end of his life, such a soul also has nothing extraordinary for a very long time. The guidance of providence followed blindly constitutes its whole path and life, becoming all to all (cf. 1 Cor 9:22), its heart becoming every day all the more vast in order to carry others, however flawed they might be. And it truly sees that when it prefers the virtuous to the flawed, it commits a fault, preferring a certain sympathy to the order of God. Until one is here, one is little suited to help others. It is only then that one starts to help them effectively. This is difficult, and one is pained in surrendering to it at first, because this manner of acting is regarded as a waste of time, a defect, and a whim. But the soul in whom Jesus Christ lives and for whom he is the way, the light, the truth, and the life, clearly sees things in a different way (John 14:6). It no longer finds any creature disagreeable or difficult to tolerate. It bears them through the heart of Jesus Christ.

[14.] This is where the apostolic life starts. But is everyone called to this state? Very few, as far as I understand it. And even for those few who are called to it, few walk there in true purity. Souls with passive illumination and extraordinary gifts, although they might be holy and quite seraphic, do not enter at all onto this path. There is a path of illumination, a holy life where the creature appears quite admirable; since this life is more apparent, it is also more highly regarded by people who are not enlightened. These people have something very dazzling in their lives; they have a fidelity and courage that astonish, and this is what adorns the lives of the saints admirably. But as for the souls who walk on this path under consideration, they are not very well known. God deprives them, weakens them, strips them again and again, thereby taking all support and all hope away from them and making them lose themselves in him. They have nothing great that would be evident. From this it happens that the greater their interior, the less they can speak of it, because as one can see, they only see misery and poverty for a very long time, then they no longer see themselves. The greatest saints, the most interior, are those who are spoken of the least. As for the Holy Virgin, it is true that there was nothing more to say about her after having said that she was the mother of God, her maternity enclosing all the possible perfection of a pure creature. Let us consider Saint Joseph, Mary Magdalene, Saint Scholastica, and so many others; what can we say about them? Nothing at all. Saint Joseph spent a part of his life as a carpenter. What a job for the husband of the mother of a God! Jesus Christ, just the same. Oh, if I could express how I conceive of this state, but I can only stumble! I have gotten away from my story, but I am not mistress of myself to do otherwise.

Father La Combe is taken to Rome to be judged for improper conduct and heresy. He returns from Rome very troubled and discouraged. Guyon is further harassed by her brother. She takes refuge at the Ursuline convent with her daughter, and both suffer health problems. Father La Combe is made to return to Rome for further interrogations, still engineered by the archbishop of Geneva, and Guyon continues to attend to those in need of spiritual guidance and to grow in her own understanding of God's ways. She and La Combe grow deeper in their relationship through their continuing correspondence. At this time, she is also inspired to write Spiritual Torrents.

2.12—Power over Souls

[1.] Our Lord, who truly wanted me to bear him in all his states, making me begin with the first and continue all the way to the last, as I will explain, and who wanted to simplify me entirely, gave me a miraculous obedience regarding Father La Combe. I believe that Our Lord did this to simplify me as much on the outside as on the inside, to make me express the Child Jesus. And my obeying, as the state that I was put in afterward clearly demonstrates, was also a sign and evidence for Father La Combe, for since he had been guided by evidence, he could not leave that path. And in everything that was said to him or that God would make him experience, he always went looking for evidence; that is where he had the most difficulty in dying and why he made me suffer so much. Our Lord, in order to make him enter more easily into what he wanted of him and of me, gave him the greatest evidence of all, which is this miraculous obedience. And to show that it did not depend on me and that God was giving it for him, when he was strong enough to lose all evidence, and God wanted to make him enter into destruction, this obedience was withdrawn from me in such a way that, without paying attention to it, I could no longer obey him. And this was done to make him become more lost and to take the support of evidence away from him, because all my efforts were useless. It was necessary for me to follow from within the one who was my master and who gave me this repugnance to obedience that only lasted as long as was necessary to destroy the support that he and I both would have acquired from my obedience.

But before speaking about this it is necessary to say that this obedience was so miraculous that however extremely sick I might have been, I would get well when he so ordered it, either by word or letter. I had then such a strong instinct for his perfection and for seeing him die unto himself that, far from pitying him, I would have wished all the sufferings imaginable for him. When he was not faithful or when he took things so as to nourish the self-life, I would feel devoured, which surprised me to no small extent given how indifferent I had been up to that point. I would complain to Our Lord, who reassured me with an extreme goodness, and with the extreme dependence that he gave me, which made me become like an infant.

[2.] The girl that my sister had given me to care for fell gravely ill. Our Lord gave her the same dependence on me that I had on Father La Combe, with some differences, however. I helped her as best I could, but I found that I had hardly anything to tell her, except to command her ailment and her disposition, and all that I said to her was done. It was then that I learned what it meant to command by the Word and to obey by the same Word. I found Jesus Christ in myself equally ordering and obeying. Our Lord gave the devil the power to torment this poor girl like Job, and, as if he would not have been strong enough all alone, he was accompanied by five more who reduced her to such a state with her illness that she was on death's door from it. These miserable creatures fled as soon as I approached her bed, and I was not yet gone when they came back with even more furor and told her, *It is for us to have compensation for the evil that she did to us*, speaking of me. Since I saw that she was too exhausted and that her weak body could no longer endure the suffering that they were causing her, I forbade them to approach her for a time. They withdrew immediately, but the next day when I woke up, I had a strong leading to let them find her. I told her, "I am allowing the devil to torment you." They returned with such furor that they reduced her to extremity. After having given them various reprieves and having allowed them to return, I had a strong leading to forbid them from ever attacking her again.

I forbade them to do it; they never returned after that. She still did not stop being sick, until one day when she received Our Lord with such weakness that she could hardly swallow the host. After dinner I had a strong leading to tell her, "Get up and be sick no more." She got up and was no longer sick. The nuns were truly amazed, since they knew nothing of what was happening, and they saw her on her feet after a morning of being in an extreme condition. They attributed her sickness to the vapors.

[3.] As soon as the demons withdrew from this girl, I had the impression that they were enraged with me. I was in my bed, and I told them: "Come to me and torment me if your master permits." But far from doing this, they fled me. I understood right away that demons fear an annihilated soul more than hell, and that individuals led by faith are not the ones whom they attack, for the reasons that I have given. I felt such an authority over the devil in me that, far from fearing him, it seemed to me that I would make them all flee from hell if I were there. It is necessary to know that the kind of soul of which I speak, in whom Jesus Christ lives and operates, does not perform miracles like those who perform them through a power that is in them. These of whom I speak operate through the annihilation of the soul, for as it is no longer anything, nothing of all this can be attributed to it. One must not attribute anything to the soul in any of this. Also, when the leading impels it, it does not at all say, "Be healed in the name of Jesus Christ," because this "Be healed in the name of Jesus Christ" is a power in the person to perform miracles in the name of Jesus Christ, who performs the miracle and who says through this person, *Be healed,* and one is healed, or *let the demons retire,* and the demons retire. When one says this one does not know why one says it, or what it means to say it, but it is the Word who speaks and operates, as it says: *dixit et facta sunt.*[21] One does not speak any prayers before this because these miracles happen without the person meaning to do them and without the soul considering it a miracle. One says quite naturally what one is given to say. Jesus Christ wanted to pray at the resurrection of Lazarus, but he only did it for the sake of those who were present because he says to his Father: *And I knew that you hear me always; but I said it because of the people who stand about, that they may believe that you sent me* (John 11:42). The other servants of God, gratified by the gift of miracles, pray and obtain what they want by doing so. But here it is the Word who uses his authority and who acts through the words of the person in whom he lives and reigns.

[4.] There are two things one must notice about this: first, that the souls of which I have spoken do not ordinarily perform their miracles by giving something or by simply touching, but by the word, although they sometimes accompany it with a touch. It is the all-powerful word. The other thing is that these miracles require consent, or at least no opposition, on the part of those on whom one performs them. Our Lord Jesus Christ asked those good people whom he healed: *Do you want to be made whole?* (John 5:6) There was to be no doubt that the people who came to him for this, or who wanted nothing else, really wanted this. This is the secret of the operation of the Word and of the freedom of man. On the dead or on inanimate objects it is not the same thing; he speaks, and through his speaking it is done. But for this the soul's consent is necessary.

I have felt this several times, and I felt in myself how God not only respects man's freedom, but even the desire for free consent. For when I was saying, "Be healed," or for interior pains, "Be delivered from your pains," if they agreed without any reply, they were healed, and the word was effective. If they resisted under good pretexts, by saying, "I will be healed when it pleases God," "I only want to be healed when he wills it," or in a despairing way, "I will not be healed," "I will not escape this pain," then the word did not have any effect, and I felt this within me. I felt that the power withdrew into me, and I felt what Our Lord says when the hemorrhaging woman touched him, and he asked, *Who touched me?* The apostles told him, *The crowd is around you and you asked who touched you!* It is, responds our Lord, *that divine power left me* (Luke 8:44–46). In the same way in me, or rather through me, Jesus is making this power flow by means of his word, but when this power was not received by the subject, due to a lack of agreement, I felt it suspended in its source, and this caused me a kind of pain. I would almost feel angry with these people. But when there was no resistance, and instead full acceptance, this divine power would have its full effect. One would not believe the delicacy of this divine power, and although it is so powerful over inanimate things, the least thing by man would either completely stop it or restrain it.

[5.] There was a good nun afflicted by violent temptations. She would go to confess to a sister whom she believed very spiritual and in a state to be able to help her. But far from finding help, she was strongly reprimanded. The other, scorning her and treating her harshly because she experienced temptations, would say, "Do not approach me, I beg you, since you are that kind of person." This poor girl, in frightening desolation, came to find me, believing herself lost due to what this sister had said. I consoled her, and Our Lord relieved her right away, but I could not stop myself from telling her that the other one would most certainly be punished and that this other person would fall into a state worse than hers. The other one, feeling very pleased with herself, used this as an opportunity to come find me, and she told me how she had answered the nun's request and added that she was horrified by people who had temptations and that, as for herself, she had never had a bad thought. I told her, "My sister, for the friendship that I have for you, I wish you to have the same pain as the one who came to talk to you, and even more pain." She answered me with a certain pride, "If you asked it of God for me, and if I would ask the opposite of God, I believe that I would be granted my request at least as much as you." I answered her sternly, "If this is my own interest that I seek, my request will not be granted, but if the interest is only God's and yours, he will do it sooner than you think." I told her this without thinking. That same night (we were speaking at night) she entered into a temptation so strong and furious that its like is hardly ever seen. It lasted two weeks with the same strength. It was then that she was able to understand her weakness and what we would be without grace. She first felt an inconceivable hatred for me, saying that I was the cause of her pain. But eventually this served her like the mud for the man born blind who was granted sight (John 9:6–7); she saw very clearly what had brought such a terrible state upon her.

In a passage omitted here, Guyon describes an eight-month illness that reduced her to an almost childlike state.

[7.] Our Lord, however, given the weaknesses of his children, gave me the power of a God over souls, in such a way that through one word, I would put them in pain or in peace according to what was necessary for the good of these souls. I saw that God was making himself obeyed in me and from me like an absolute sovereign, and I would no longer resist him. I took part in nothing. You would perform in me and through me, my God, the greatest miracles, and I was not able to reflect upon it. I felt a candor of soul inside, exempt from malice, which I could not express. Moreover, it was necessary to continue telling my thoughts to Father La Combe or writing them to him, and to help him according to the light that had been given to me. I was often so weak that I could not raise my head to take nourishment, and when God wanted me to write to Father La Combe, either to help him, to encourage him, or to explain to him what Our Lord had made me know, I had the strength to write. Once my letters were finished, I would find myself in the same state of weakness.

Guyon speaks about her deepening connection with Father La Combe, with whom she often communicates in silence. She continues to give spiritual advice, suffers another grave illness, founds a hospital, and begins another period of travel to Lausanne, Turin, and Grenoble, where she offers spiritual guidance to many people.

2.21—Explanations, Commentary, and Short Method

[1.] You were not happy simply to make me speak, my God; you gave me more leadings to write about the holy scripture. There was a time when I no longer read because I did not find any emptiness in me at all needing to be filled, and on the contrary, there was too much fullness. As soon as I would begin to read the holy scriptures, I was led to write down the passage that I was reading and, soon after, to write an explanation of it. In writing down the passage I did not have the least thought about the explanation, and as soon as it was written, I was led to explain it, writing with inconceivable speed. Before starting to write, I did not know what I was going to say. While writing, I saw that I was writing things that I had never known, and light was given to me. At the time of this manifestation,

I saw that I had treasures of erudition and knowledge within me that I did not know I had. Having written, I would not remember anything at all of what I had written, and neither forms nor images were left in me. I could not have used what I had written to help other souls, but when that moment came, Our Lord gave me what I would say to them and all that was necessary for them, without my trying at all.

[2.] In this way Our Lord had me explain all the holy scriptures. I did not have a single book except the Bible, and I only used that, without researching anything else. When I used it, while writing about the Old Testament, passages from the New Testament were given to me to support what I was saying. It was not that I was looking for them, but they came to me at the same time as the explanation. And in the same way in the New Testament, I would use passages from the Old Testament, and they would come to me in the same way, without my looking anything up. I had almost no time to write except at night, because I needed to speak all day long, without any attention to myself, or to speaking or writing, and as little careful of my health or my life as of myself. I only slept one or two hours every night, and along with that I had a fever nearly every day, ordinarily very high, and nonetheless I continued this without discomfort, without worrying about dying or living. The one to whom I belonged without reserve did what pleased him through me without my getting mixed up in his work. You yourself, O my God, used to wake me up, and I had to depend on and obey your will so entirely that you did not want to tolerate the least natural impulse. When it got the least involved you punished it, and it fell away immediately.

[3.] You made me write with such purity that it was necessary for me to stop and start again as you wanted. You made me experience all behaviors; all of a sudden you would make me write, then stop right away, and then start again. When I was writing during the day, I was consistently interrupted, and I often left my words half written, and you would give me what you wanted immediately afterward. What I wrote was not at all in my head, such that I had a head so free that it was in a complete void. I was so disengaged from what I was writing that it was like a stranger to me. It took me one moment of reflection to be punished; I was punished, my writing slowed down immediately, and I remained like an idiot until I was inspired from above. The least joy from the graces that you accorded me was very rigorously punished.

All the faults that are in my writings come from when, not being used to God's operation, I was very often unfaithful at those points, believing myself to do the right thing by continuing to write when I had the time for it, without being moved to do so, because I had been ordered to finish the work. It is therefore easy to see some places that are beautiful and supported and others that have neither refinement nor unction. I have left them the way that they are so as to show the difference between the Spirit of God and the human and natural spirit, being ready, however, to reconcile them according to the present light that is given to me, in case someone orders me to do so.

[4.] What test did you not make of my abandonment before this time? Did you not take hundreds of different forms for me in order to see if I was yours without reserve in every trial, and if I still had some little self-interest? You always found this soul flexible and pliable to your desires. What have you not made me suffer? Into what humiliation have you not thrown me to counterbalance your graces? To what, my God, have you not delivered me, and through what painful straights have you not made me pass? What I did not previously dare to touch with the tip of my finger became my ordinary food. But I had no pain at all from what you did to me. I saw with pleasure and compliance, not taking any more interest in myself than in a dead dog, I truly saw your divine games with compliance. You raised me to the sky and right away threw me in the mud; then, with the same hand, you picked me up from where you had thrown me. I saw that I was the game played by your love and by your will, the victim of your divine justice, and it was all the same to me.

[5.] It seems to me, O my God, that you treat your dearest friends as the sea treats its waves. Sometimes it pushes them impetuously against the rocks, where they break, at other times against the sand or in the mire, and then just as quickly the sea takes a wave to its bosom and clasps it with as much force as that with which it had previously rejected it. This is the game that you play with your friends who do not cease to be one with you, changed and transformed into yourself, although you make a continuous game of rejecting them and clutching them to your bosom, just as a wave that is pushed more impetuously is swallowed up by a deeper trough. O my God, I have so many things to say, but I cannot say anything of the ways of your just and indulgent love because they are too subtle.

[6.] This love is infinitely pleased to make those whom it has rendered one with you the continuous victims of its justice. It seems that these souls are made like holocausts, in order to be burned by love on the altar of divine justice. Oh, there are few souls of this sort! Nearly all souls belong to mercy, and there are plenty of this type. But to belong to divine Justice, oh how rare, but how great this is! These souls are God's alone, without any consideration for or relation to themselves concerning salvation, perfection, eternity, life, or death. All this is nothing for them. Their business is to let divine Justice satisfy itself in them, as Deborah says, with the blood of the dead—meaning, with this soul already dead through love, that this justice satisfies itself through this dead soul and takes vengeance on it for the sins of others. It comes down to this: it satisfied itself with a glory that is in accordance with this attribute, a glory that does not permit the least return to the creature and wants all for itself. Mercy is entirely distributive in aid of the creature, but justice devours and ravishes all, without having any regard for the victim it sacrifices, and it can desire nothing except for itself. This is why it does not spare the victim. But it wants voluntary victims who do not have any aim in their suffering other than itself, just as it has no other aim than itself in causing suffering. It is not that the soul thus devoured by divine Justice pays any attention to this cruel, lovable thing which treats it so ruthlessly. No, it has neither thought nor self-interest. The soul only thinks about these things when it is led to write or speak about them. But this justice so devouring is only nourished by suffering, by opprobrium and ignominies, and with the same hand that struck the author of justice, without him thinking about his own benefit, it strikes just as strongly those who are predestined to be the most conformed to it. But, one asks, how is such a soul supported by this cruelty of the divine Justice? It is supported without support by the same cruelty. The more it is abandoned to God, it seems, the more it is supported by God above all other support, because one must not believe that such a soul has anything for itself that can satisfy it, either on the outside or on the inside—nothing at all. All is rigor without any rigor; all that is given to it is only given for others and to make God known, loved, and possessed.

[7.] My friend started to become jealous of me due to the recognition that was given to me.[22] God permitted this to purify this holy soul again by this weakness and the pain that this caused it. Her friendship changed to coldness and to something more. It was you, O my God, who permitted this, just as I have said. Certain confessors also started to get worked up, saying that it was not my place to get mixed up in helping souls and that some of their penitents were entirely open with me. This was where it was easy to notice the difference between confessors who sought only for God in the guidance of souls and those who were looking out for themselves. The former would come to see me and were so happy about the graces that God accorded to their penitents, without paying attention to the channel that was used. The others, on the contrary, stirred up the city secretly, raising it against me. I saw that they would have been right to oppose me if I had simply been consumed with myself, but besides only being able to do what God wanted me to do, I sought out no one; nonetheless, they came from everywhere, and I received them all indifferently. Sometimes they came to oppose me. There were two monks from the same order as the begging brother of whom I have spoken.[23] One was from the Provinces, very knowledgeable and a great preacher, and the other preached during Lent at the cathedral. They came separately after having studied a large number of difficult issues to test me on them. They did so, and although these were matters far removed from my grasp, Our Lord had me answer as correctly as if I had studied them all of my life. Then, because of what I told them myself about what Our Lord gave me, they went away not only convinced and happy, but even impassioned by your love, O my God!

[8.] I always continued to write, and with an inconceivable speed because my hand could hardly follow the spirit that dictated to it, and during this long work I did not change my conduct at all or use a single book. The copyist, however diligent he might be, could not copy in five days what I would write in one night. What is good comes from you alone, O my God, and what is bad comes from me; by this I mean from my unfaithfulness and from the admixture I introduced into your pure and chaste doctrine without knowing my impurity. At the beginning, I committed many faults, not yet being trained in the operation of the Spirit of God that was making me write. For he made me stop writing when I had the time to write and when I could do so comfortably, and when I seemed to have a great need to sleep, then he would make me write. When I would write during the day, it was with continuous interruptions, because I did not have time to eat due to the large number of people who would come to see me. I had to leave everything as soon as I was asked to. And moreover, the girl who served me in this state of which I have spoken would come to interrupt me for no reason at any moment when the mood took her. I often left the sentence half finished without worrying about whether what I was writing would be followed up or not. The places that might be defective are so only because sometimes I wanted to write since I had the time, so then grace was not the source. If these places were frequent it would be pitiful. Finally, little by little, I got used to following God's ways and not my own.

[9.] I wrote the *Commentary on the Song of Songs* in a day and a half and still received visitors. The speed with which I wrote was so great that my arm became swollen and completely stiff. At night it hurt me terribly, and I thought I was not going to be able to write for a long time. While I was sleeping a soul from purgatory appeared to me who urged me to ask my divine Bridegroom for her deliverance. I did so, and it seemed to me that she was delivered right away. I said to her, "If it is true that you are delivered, heal my arm," and it was healed that moment and was in a state to write. Let me add to all that I have said about my writings that a significant part was lost from the Book of Judges. I was asked to make the book complete. I rewrote the lost passages. Long afterward, having moved to another place, they were found where no one ever would have expected them to be. The old and the new were found to be perfectly the same, which astonished many people of erudition and merit who did the verification.

[10.] A councilor from Parliament who was a model of saintliness came to me. This good servant of God found on my table the method of contemplative prayer that I had written a long time before. He asked me for it, and, having found it much to his liking, gave it to some others who were his friends to whom he believed it would be useful. All of them wanted copies. He took care, along with the good brother, to get them copied; they asked me to arrange it, and I did. I added some things and a little preface, and they had it printed with the title *A Short and Easy Method of Contemplative Prayer*. This was the way that this little booklet, which was used as a pretext to imprison me, was published. This councilor is one of my intimate friends and a great servant of God. This poor little booklet has been reprinted five or six times in spite of my persecution, and Our Lord gives it a very great benediction. These good monks took fifteen hundred of them.

[11.] The good begging brother wrote perfectly well, and Our Lord inspired him to copy my writings, or at least a part of them. He also gave this same idea to a monk of another order, so that each of them took some to copy. He was working hard one night, writing something that he believed urgent because he had misunderstood what had been requested of him, and it was also extremely cold. Since his legs were exposed, they became very swollen, to the point that he could not move. He came to find me, quite sad and fed up with writing. He explained his pain to me and said that he could not do his mission. I told him to be healed, and he was healed at that instant in a way that made him very happy and very willing to transcribe this work, by which he was assured that Our Lord accorded him very great graces. There was also a fine but very inconsistent girl. She had a very bad headache; I touched her, and she was immediately healed.

[12.] The devil became so outraged at me due to these conquests that you were making, O my God, that he riled up some people, who came to see me. There was a fine girl of great simplicity who earned her living through her work, a girl who received very great grace from Our Lord. The devil broke two teeth in her mouth. Her cheek became swollen from a tremendous tumor, and he told her that if she came to see me any longer he would to the same to others. She came to find me in this state and told me in her innocence: "The evil one did this to me because I come to you. He says a lot of bad things about you." I told her to forbid him to touch her, on my behalf. Seeing that he had been caught and that he dared not touch her because he could not do what God had forbidden through me, he told her many insulting things, made frightening poses in front of her, and assured her that he was going to stir up the strangest persecution that I would ever have. I laughed at this because I hardly feared him. Although he might stir up such strange persecutions, I know that he will serve the glory of my God in spite of himself.

2.22—Communications and Suffering for Father La Combe

[1.] This poor girl came to me one day all in tears. She said to me, "O my mother, I have seen such strange things!" I asked her what it was. "Alas!" she said, "I saw you like a lamb in the middle of a pack of enraged wolves. I saw a frightening mob of people in all kinds of robes, of all ages, of all sexes and conditions—priests, monks, married people, girls, and women—with pikes, halberds, naked swords, who were attempting to stab you. You were letting them do so without moving or being surprised, and without defending yourself. I was looking all around to see if there might not be someone to help you and come to your defense, but I did not see anyone." A few days later, those who made a secret plan against me through envy suddenly burst forth like thunder. Written accusations started to circulate everywhere, and I was shown the most frightening letters in the world, which envious people had written about me without knowing me. These people said that I was a witch, that it was through magic that I attracted souls, that everything in me was diabolical, and that if I performed charitable works, it would be with counterfeit money, and they accused me of a thousand other crimes that were all as false as they were unfounded.

[2.] As the storm was growing each day and they were truly saying *Crucifige*[24] to me, just as Our Lord had let me know from the beginning, some of my friends advised me to go away for a time. The almoner of the bishop of Grenoble told me to go and spend some time at Saint Baume and Marseilles and said that they even wanted me there and that there were some very spiritual people there. I would have a fine girl and another ecclesiastic, and during this time the storm would pass. But before speaking about my departure from

Grenoble, I must still say something about the state that I bore in this land.

[3.] I was in such a fullness of God that I was often either lying down or entirely confined to bed without being able to speak. And when I had absolutely no possible means of expressing this fullness, Our Lord did not permit it to be so violent because I could no longer live with this violence; my heart only wanted to pour its overabundance into other hearts. I had the same union and the same communication with Father La Combe, and although he was so far away, it was as if he were nearby. Jesus Christ was communicated to me in all his states. It was then that his apostolic state was the most noticeable. All of God's operations in me were shown to me in Jesus Christ and explained by the holy scripture, such that I bore in myself the experience of what was written. When I could not write or communicate in another way, I was quite languishing, and I felt what Our Lord says to his disciples: *I have Passover dinner to eat with you* (Luke 22:15). Oh, how he delayed its arrival for me! This was the communication of himself through the Last Supper and his passion, when he says, *All is consumed, and rendering his spirit he lowered his head* (John 19:30), because he was communicating his spirit to all people capable of receiving it, and he *remitted it to the hands of his Father* (Luke 23:46) and of his God, as well as his kingdom. It was as if he was saying to his Father: "My Father, my kingdom is that I reign for you, and you for me, over men; this can only be done through the pouring out of my spirit on them. Let my spirit be then communicated to them through my death!" And in this is the consummation of all things. Often the excessive fullness took the freedom to write away from me, and I could not do anything except stay in bed without speaking a word. Although it was this way, I had nothing for myself; all was for others, as nursemaids are full of milk but are not more sustained by it—not that I missed anything, for ever since my new life I have not had a moment of emptiness.

[4.] Before writing about the Book of Kings on everything concerning David, I was put into such a tight union with this holy patriarch that I was communicating with him as if he were present, not in images, forms, or figures, for my soul was too far away from these things, but in a divine manner, in ineffable silence and in perfect reality. I understood this holy patriarch, the grandeur of his grace, God's conduct in him, all the circumstances of the states through which he had passed, and the fact that he was a living figure of Jesus Christ and a pastor chosen for Israel. It seemed to me that all that Our Lord had me do for souls was in union with this holy patriarch and with those to whom he had simultaneously given me a union like the one I had with David, my dear king. O Love, did you not make me see that the admirable and real union between this holy patriarch and me would never be understood by anyone because no one was in a state to understand it?

[5.] It was then that you taught me, O my love, that through this very admirable union I was given the gift of carrying Jesus Christ the Word-God into souls. Jesus Christ is born of David according to the flesh. Oh, how many conquests did you have me make in this ineffable union; my words were effective and had an effect in hearts. It was to educate souls about Jesus Christ. I was in no way the mistress speaking or saying things, because the one who was leading me was making me say them as he wished and as many times as it pleased him. There were souls to whom I was not permitted to say a single word and others for whom there were deluges of grace. But this pure love did not tolerate a single excess or amusement.

Sometimes there were souls who would ask several times for the same things. When they had been told about these things according to their need, and this was only the desire to speak, I could not respond to them, without my paying any attention. Then they would tell me, "You said this last time, do we need to keep to it?" I would tell them yes. And then I came to understand that because a response would have been useless, no response was given to me. Our Lord said, all will pass, but his words will not pass, and there is not one of them that would have this effect. It was entirely the same with those among them whom Our Lord led through the death of themselves, and who would come looking for human consolation. I only had for them what was strictly necessary, after which I could no longer speak. I, however, would have spoken of a hundred indifferent things, because this is what God allows me to do in order to be all things to everyone and not to trouble my neighbor, if not for his word, of which he himself is the dispenser.

Oh, if preachers spoke in this spirit, what fruits would they not produce? There were others among them, as I have said, to whom I could only communicate myself in silence, but a silence as ineffable as it was effective. Those were the rarest, and it is the special characteristic of my truest children. This is—perhaps I have already said this because I can sometimes repeat myself—the communication of the blessed spirits.

[6.] It was there that I learned the true manner of dealing with the saints in heaven—in God himself—and with the saints of the earth. O communication so pure, who will be able to understand you other than the one who knows you? If people were of the spirit one would speak to them in the spirit, but due to weakness it is necessary to return to words. I had the consolation a while ago to hear this read from Saint Augustine, in a completely spiritual conversation that he had with his mother. He complains that it is necessary to return to words due to our weakness.[25] I would sometimes say: "O love, give me hearts big enough to contain such a great abundance." It seemed to me that a thousand hearts would be too few.

I had some insights regarding communication during the Last Supper between Jesus Christ and Saint John. My insights were not from illumination, but from experience. Oh, how truly I felt, O beloved disciple, my divine master's communication to your heart and the manner in which you learned ineffable secrets and how you continued a similar exchange with the Blessed Mother! Oh, let them call this communication an admirable exchange! I was given to understand that this was the language of the nativity, and how the Holy Child communicated to the kings and the shepherds and gave them knowledge of his divinity. It was also in this way that the Virgin Mother, approaching Saint Elizabeth, began an admirable exchange between Jesus Christ and Saint John, an exchange that communicated to him the spirit of the Word and of his holiness, which was so effective that it always persisted.

This is why Saint John the Baptist demonstrated no haste to come and see Jesus Christ after this communication, because they were communicating, though far away from each other, just as they would have near each other. So as to receive these communications more fully, he withdrew himself into the desert, and when he preached repentance, what did he say of himself? He does not say that he is the Word, because he knew very well that this was Jesus Christ, Eternal Word. But he says only that he is a voice.

His voice serves as a passage for the word and carries it forth, so that after being full of communications from the divine Word, he was made into the expression of this same Word, pushing this divine word into souls through his voice. He knew it from the first. He did not need anyone to tell him who he was. And if he was sent disciples, it was not for him but for them, so as to make them disciples of Jesus Christ. He only baptized with water to show what his function was because just as water leaves nothing as it flows, so too the voice leaves nothing. There is only the word, which is expressed. He was thus made to carry the word, but he was not the word. And the one who was the Word baptized with the Holy Spirit because he had the gift of imprinting himself in souls and communicating himself to them through the Holy Spirit. I understood that the created Trinity would not speak within itself in any other way. Saint Joseph and Mary communicated to each other through Jesus; Jesus was the reason and the purpose of their communications. O adorable exchange! It has not been observed that Jesus said anything during his hidden life, although it is true that not a single one of his words will be lost. O love, if everything that you have said and brought about in silence was written, *I do not believe that the whole world could hold the books that would be written about it* (John 21:25).

[7.] All that I felt was shown to me in the holy scripture, and I saw with admiration that nothing happens in the soul that is not in Jesus Christ and in the holy scripture. When I communicated with closed hearts, I suffered great torment. It was like an impetuous stream of water that, not finding any outlet, returns against itself, and I was sometimes at the point of death from it. O God, could I describe or make understood all that I suffered in that place and the mercy that you accorded me? A number of things cannot be mentioned, as much because they cannot be expressed as because they will not be understood. What made me suffer the most was Father La Combe. Since he was not yet convinced, concerning his state, that God was exercising him with crosses and reversals, his doubts and hesitations gave me strange blows. However far from me he might be, I felt his pains and his moods. He was bearing a state of interior death and of the cruelest and most terrible highs and lows that have ever taken place in the world. According to the understanding that God had given me, he was one of his servants presently on earth who was the most agreeable to him. It was impressed on me that he was a selected vessel whom God had chosen to carry his name to the Gentiles, but that he would show how much suffering this same name requires. When in these trials he felt as if he had been rejected by God, he felt at the same time divided from me, and as soon as God would receive him into himself again, he would be reunited with me more strongly than ever. And he would find himself enlightened regarding my condition in an admirable way, God having given him an esteem that went as far as veneration, such that he could not hide his feelings from me. And he repeated to me often: "I cannot be united to you outside of God because as soon as I am rejected by God, I am also from you, and I feel myself divided from you, in doubt and continuous hesitation about what concerns you. And as soon as I am good with God, I am good with you. I know the grace that he accords me in uniting me with you and how dear you are to him and the depths that he has put in you."

[8.] O God, who will ever understand the pure and saintly unions that you make between your creatures! The carnal world only judges carnally, attributing what is the purest grace to a natural attachment. You alone, O God, know what I have suffered in this regard. All the other crosses, however strong, seemed to me shadows of these / *and those that I suffered due to the girl who was with me. What she made me suffer was equal to the torment of purgatory. All grace was communicated to her through me or N. [Father La Combe] but a good bit more through me. When she let herself be destroyed by God, I allowed it willingly, but when she resisted God, and she was concerned with self-preservation, I suffered inexplicable torment, such that all that I could say about it would only be a weak sketch of the truth. I begged her sometimes to go away, but since she did not understand what she made me suffer, she would get hurt by this and would say that it was motivated by hate. In this way I was obligated to tolerate her, although I was susceptible to intolerable torments, such that I would gladly have run into a fire so as to avoid such pain. She would complain to N., saying that I could not tolerate her, and since he believed that was reasonable, he would reprimand me for a lack of charity. And I could not make him understand a state that will always be incomprehensible to those who have not had the experience. O God, who could understand such a strange torment without this? There are so many things to say about what this girl caused me to suffer that I prefer to keep quiet about it. The friendship that she had for me, which was too natural, caused me inexplicable torment. All her exterior faults that were believed to make me uncomfortable would cause me no pain. Although she was maladroit to the point of incessantly doing things that were the exact opposite of what she should do and were what she herself wanted to do, when she did some wrong to me, believing herself to do me some good, she would get very hurt and be inconsolable, but as for me, I would feel no pain. Although she had negative feelings toward me, as evidenced by her losing or breaking things that she held, I never spoke to her about any of these things that only concerned my person and my own interest. I was indifferent to all of this. Along with this, she had all sorts of the most intolerable natural faults. She imagined that all of these faults were the reason why I hardly tolerated her demonstrations of affection. But she was truly mistaken, and what astonished her was that I never reprimanded her for that. Her sense of self, the resistance that she had to God, and the natural inclination she had for me caused all my torment. I was often reduced to staying in bed or seated on the floor with my back against the wall, not being able to move due to the violence of my pain. N., as I have said (God permitting it to be this way), never understood either this state or the other that I will explain shortly, which together were the source of the hardest crosses that I have ever had to bear. The other crosses that I have described were hardly perceptible to me any longer, as much because, as I have said, all that comes to me from the outside can no longer hurt me unless God applies his hand inside to make them perceptible to me, as because I do not care for my honor any more than for my life, provided that my God is pleased. This pain does not depend at all on me, God alone controlling it. What made me still suffer much was a discernment of minds that Our Lord gave me, such that as soon as a person was not doing well, I would have an impression of it on the inside. I would first understand the degrees or states of souls without my being able to do anything else to change the feeling, if one can call a feeling a thing that was in me without me, and concerning which thought and reflection had no role.*

When I would tell N. what God made me understand about people whom he respected, especially those who had extraordinary gifts, and about the self-love that was in them, he would take that for pride and a lack of charity. When I was able to reflect even the least bit, I would see that, according to the ordinary rules of virtue such as I had conceived them before, he was right, but I could not do otherwise. And my torment was very great because if I said, "I will no longer tell him these things, but might I be mistaken?" you would reject me, O my God, and I entered into a strange interior hell. I no longer knew myself, and I was like those who are out of their minds. It was necessary for me to return to my first tranquility. I would cry out either from the heart or the mouth: "Fine, my God, I will continue to tell him and write everything to him," and as soon as I would write or say these things to N., he would get angry, and he would get pained by me due to doubt, defiance, and division. And as soon as he would break off contact with me, I would feel as if someone had split my heart in two. Bodily separation is nothing because, absent or present, all was the same to me, provided that his heart remained faithful to God and he did not separate himself from me, because his union was always a necessary and not a voluntary one. At last I told him everything with my ordinary simplicity, whatever the cost might be, because I could not resist God, and after a lot of torment he knew that I was telling him the truth. But this knowledge was only given to him late, after he had made me suffer.

God always gave me great faithfulness and righteousness in N.'s view. God would sometimes show him this, and he would be inconceivably impressed to see the faithfulness and the righteousness that Our Lord had given me and by which I had suffered. At other times all was hidden from him; he felt only separation and saw only my misery. This lasted a long time, but the more we advanced the more he was assured of our state, with the union becoming stronger and more intimate and the separation more rare. //

Our Lord once made me understand that when Father La Combe became established in his permanent state and had no more inner vicissitudes, he would no longer have them regarding me either, and he would remain forever united with me in God. It is presently this way. I saw that he only felt the union and separation due to his weakness and that his state was not yet permanent. I only felt this because he separated himself, and it was necessary for me to bear all of this. But as soon as the union was without clashes and in perfection, he no longer felt it, nor did I. It happened as if by an awakening to interior conversation in the manner of the blessed.

The union of the soul with God is only felt because it is not entirely perfect. But when it is consummated in unity, it is no longer felt; it becomes natural. One does not feel the union of the soul with the body; the body lives and functions in this union without thinking about it or paying attention to the union. It exists; the body knows it, and all the functions of life that it performs do not permit the body to ignore it. However, one acts without paying attention to all that. It is the same in the union with God, and with certain creatures in him, because what shows the purity and eminence in this latter union is that it conforms to the union with God, and it is all the more perfect in proportion to the increasing consummation of the soul's union with God. If, however, it were necessary to break off this very pure and holy union, one would feel it all the more since it is pure, perfect, and imperceptible, just as one feels clearly when the soul wants to separate itself from the body through death, although one does not feel the union.

[9.] Since I was in the state of childhood of which I have spoken,[26] and Father La Combe was getting angry and breaking off contact with me, I would cry like a child, and my body would become quite languishing, and what was surprising is that I would find myself at the same time both weaker than the little children and strong as God. I found myself quite divine and enlightened about everything and strong under the most difficult crosses, and yet feeling the weakness of the smallest children. O God, I can say that I am perhaps the creature in the world from which you have wanted the greatest dependence. You put me in all sorts of states and different postures that my soul neither wanted nor could resist. I was so strongly yours that there was nothing in the world that you could have required of me that I would not have done with pleasure. O God, I had no interest in myself at all, and if I had seen this being, I would have ripped it up into a thousand pieces, but I no longer saw it. Normally, I did not understand or become aware of my state, but when God wants something from this miserable void, I feel that he is the absolute master and that not only does nothing resist him, but nothing even contradicts his wishes, however rigorous they appear. O love, if there is a heart in the world over which you are fully victorious, I can say that it is this poor heart. You know this, O love, and that your most righteous wishes are its life and its pleasure because it only subsists forevermore in you. I have gone on a tangent, which is ordinarily the case due to interruptions, and I have even had serious illnesses since I started to write, so I leave myself to the one who leads me.

Guyon continues her travels to Marseilles, Genoa, Alexandria, and Verceil, where she joins Father La Combe once again, and then she returns to Turin and Grenoble. Once back in France she learns that her brother has been spreading false rumors about her and Father La Combe. In Grenoble she reunites with her friends and Father La Combe, and prepares for the next stage of her life, knowing that there will be trouble ahead.

PART THREE: PARIS
From Her Return to France Until a Few Years Before Her Death

Guyon describes her arrival back in Paris in 1686 and explains how Father La Combe was set up and duped by his enemies, including Guyon's brother, which leads to his trial. These deceptions include further calumnies that implicate Guyon as well and draw attention to her Short and Easy Method. *La Combe is found guilty and arrested in October 1687. Guyon becomes the target of increasing suspicion and accusations, leading to her first period of imprisonment at the Convent of the Visitation in January 1688, where she undergoes several interrogations. At this time Guyon is also under much pressure to arrange a marriage for her daughter to which she and her daughter were deeply averse.*

3.6—Pressures to Arrange Her Daughter's Marriage

[1.] Until this point I had felt inexplicable happiness and joy from suffering and being held captive. It seemed to me that the captivity of my body made me further taste the freedom of my spirit; the more closed up I was on the outside, the more open and expansive I was on the inside. My contemplative prayer was always the same, simple and nothing, although there were times when the Bridegroom would clasp more strongly and plunge me further into himself. I had lived in this manner until the time that I committed the infidelity of wanting to observe myself in the way that I have described. On the feast of Saint Joseph I was put into a more marked state, which was more in heaven than on earth. I was going to the Calvary that is at the end of the garden, my jailer having received permission to take me there. In this place, where I was always delighted, I remained for a long time, but in a state too simple, pure, and naked to be able to speak about it. The most elevated dispositions are those of which one can say nothing. I am not surprised that nothing is said of the dispositions of the Blessed Virgin or of Saint Joseph. All those that have anything marked are truly weak.

[2.] I understood clearly through this state, which was so far above everything that can be said about it, though it was in the same depths that do not change at all, that there was a kind of new cup to drink—just as Jesus in his transfiguration conversed about his sufferings (see Matt 17:1–9; Luke 9:28–36), and this same transfiguration was like the pledge of what had to be endured and an introduction to the passion, into which Jesus Christ entered internally from that very moment, depriving himself for the rest of his life of the effusions of his divinity upon his humanity in such a way that he was deprived, from this moment on, of all support that he might have had before. And his glory, appearing on his body, worked as if in a last effort to withdraw forever, and before being all closed up in his divinity, it left his humanity in a deprivation as much the greater as the state of glory and joy were the more natural for it, owing to its hypostatic union with the divine nature, and this suspension of glory and of beatitudes was a continuous miracle. Just as from the transfiguration, so far as I can understand, until the death of Jesus Christ, all effusion of beatitude was suspended in order to leave him in pure suffering, I can say that much the same has happened to me, though unworthy of participating in the states of Jesus Christ, and with the disproportion between a little and weak creature and a God and man.

Because the feast of Saint Joseph, who is a saint to whom I am united in a very intimate way, was like a day of transfiguration for me, it seemed to me that I no longer had any qualities of the creature. And since this time a kind of suspension has taken place, such that I have been as much abandoned by God as persecuted by humans. It is not that I had any pain from this abandonment or that my soul had any inclination for other things. This can no longer be the case because it lacks any leaning or inclination whatsoever, but it does not leave this state of abandonment, which is such that I am sometimes obligated to think about whether I have a being and a subsistence.

[3.] I was this way during all of Saint Joseph's Day, and this started to diminish little by little until the day of the Annunciation, which is the day of my heart's joy. On that particular day, however, it was communicated to me that I was about to enter into new sufferings and drink to the dregs of God's indignation. The dream that I had had where all God's indignation was falling on me came to mind again. It was necessary to immolate myself once more. The night of the Annunciation I was in such agony that I cannot express it; the fury of God was complete, with my soul not having any support either from heaven or from earth. It seemed to me that Our Lord wanted to make me feel some of his agony in the garden. This stayed with me until Easter, after which I was put back into my former tranquility, with this difference—that all support is taken away and I am, whether in regard to God or in regard to humans, like that which is no more. I must make an effort to think if I am and what I am, if there are, in God, some creatures and something that subsists.

[4.] Although I might have been treated in the way that I have described and that I will explain later, I have never had any resentment toward my persecutors. I have not at all ignored the persecutions that they have inflicted upon me; God wanted me to see everything and know everything. He gave me interior certitudes that it was so, and I have never doubted them for one moment. But although I might have known them, I had no venom at all against them, and if it had been necessary to give my blood for their salvation, I would have done so and would do it still with all my heart. I never went to confession on their account. There are weak spirits who say that one must not believe that people do what they do. However, did Jesus Christ and the saints pluck out their eyes in order not to see their persecutors? They saw them, but they saw at the same time that they would not have had *any power if it had not been given to them from above* (John 19:11). This implies that, loving the blows that God inflicts, one cannot hate the hand that is used to hit us, even though one truly sees what it is.

Powerful enemies attempt to blackmail Guyon to agree to an unwelcome marriage for her daughter to obtain her own release from the Visitation.

3.7—False Letters

Guyon remains in prison and is transferred to an area in the convent that is virtually uninhabitable. More accusations are leveled against her.

[7.] I fell dangerously ill, and the doctor judged me to be in serious peril. This could not be otherwise, being closed up in a place with air so hot that it seemed like an oven. They wrote to M. the official to have me given the necessary relief and even the sacraments and to permit someone to enter into my room to serve me. He gave no response, and without the superior of the house, who believed that they could not in good conscience let me die without any relief and who told the mother superior to give me some, I might have died without help. For when they spoke of this to Monsignor the Archbishop, he said: "Look at her, truly—sick at being closed up between four walls after what she has done!" and although the councilor asked him about it, he did not want to grant anything. I had a very violent, continual fever, an inflammation of the throat, a cough, and a continuous discharge from my head going to the chest, which, it seemed, would suffocate me. But, O God, you did not want me, since you inspired the superior of the house to give the order to have me seen by a doctor and a surgeon because I would have been dead without the prompt bloodletting that they performed. I believe that few examples of similar treatment will be found. I knew all this and how all of Paris was enraged against me, but I had no pain. My friends feared that I was dying because with my death my memory would remain in opprobrium and my enemies would have the upper hand. They believed that I was already dead, and they were rejoicing over it. But you, O my love, did not want them to rejoice over me. You wanted, after having lowered me into the abyss, to make your mercy shine.

[8.] The day of Pentecost it was put into my mind that there were several martyrs of the divinity under the ancient law because the prophets and so many other Israelites were martyrs of the true God and only suffered in order to support the divinity. In the primitive church martyrs spilled their blood in order to support the truth of Jesus Christ crucified, God and man. Their martyrdom was also bloody. But presently there are martyrs of the Holy Spirit. These martyrs suffer in two ways: first, to maintain the reign of the Holy Spirit in souls; and in the second place, to be victims of the will of God because the Holy Spirit is the will of the Father and of the Son because it is the love of them. These martyrs must suffer an extraordinary martyrdom, not by spilling blood but by being captives of God's will, the puppets of his providence and martyrs of his spirit. The martyrs of the primitive church suffered for the word of God that was announced to them by the interior Word. Present-day martyrs suffer for their dependence on the Spirit of God.

[9.] It is this *Spirit* that is going *to pour out on all flesh*, as the prophet Joel says (Joel 2:28). The martyrs of Jesus Christ were glorious martyrs, Jesus Christ having drunk all confusion and opprobrium, but the martyrs of the Holy Spirit are martyrs of shame and ignominy. This is why the devil no longer exercises power upon the faith of these last martyrs; this is no longer in question. But he directly attacks the domain of the Holy Spirit, opposing himself to the celestial motion in souls and discharging his hate on the bodies of those whose spirits he cannot attack. Oh, the cruelest and most horrible martyrdom of all! Also, it will be the consummation of all martyrdoms. As the Holy Spirit is the consummation of all graces, so will the martyrs of the Holy Spirit be the last martyrs. After this, for a very long time, the Holy Spirit will so strongly possess hearts and minds that it will have made its subjects do, through love, all that will please it, as the devils by tyranny made those whom they possessed do all that they wished. O Holy Spirit, Spirit of Love, do with me all that will please you for all time and eternity! Let me be a slave to your will, and as a leaf lets itself be moved by the will of the wind, I let myself be moved by your divine breath. But as the impetuous wind breaks, uproots, and snaps all that resists it, break all that opposes your empire; break the cedars just as your prophet explains. Yes, the *cedars* will be *broken* (Ps 29:5); all will be destroyed, but *Emitte Spiritum tuum, et renovabis faciem terrae.*[27] It is this same destructive spirit that will renew the face of the earth.

[10.] This is very certain. Send your Spirit, Lord; you have promised it. It is said (of Jesus Christ) that he expired, *emisit spiritum*,[28] marking by that the consummation of his pains and the consummation of the centuries. Also, it is said that he gave up his spirit after having said *consummatum est*,[29] which denotes to us that the consummation of all things will happen through the extension of this same Spirit throughout the world and that this consummation will be that of eternity, which will never be consummated because it will only subsist evermore through the Spirit, life-giving and immortal. Our Lord, by dying, put his spirit back into the hands of his Father, as if to have us know that after this Spirit has left God to come onto the earth, it would return to God and would withdraw itself almost totally from the earth, but it will remain immutable for a long time. This is the Spirit who is, who was, and who will be the will of God and the love communicated to men.

[11.] The reign of the Father was before the incarnation; that of the Son was through the incarnation, according to what is said of Jesus Christ, who came to reign; and after his death, Saint Paul said that he *will hand over his kingdom to God his Father* (1 Cor 15:24), as if this apostle wanted to say through Jesus: "I have reigned, O my Father, in you and through you. You have reigned in me and through me; I will presently hand over my kingdom to you so that we may reign through the Holy Spirit."

In the Our Father, Jesus Christ asks God, his Father, for us that his kingdom may come. Has his kingdom not arrived since Jesus Christ is king? But let us listen to what Jesus himself teaches, *that your will be done on earth as it is in heaven.* It is as if he were asking that his true reign, which must come through that of the Holy Spirit, might come when he, while communicating himself to men, must make his will accomplished through them on earth, as it is done in heaven, without resistance, without delay and infallibly. It will be then, my Father, says Jesus Christ, that our reign will be consummated on earth. It will be then that my *enemies will be made the stool for my feet* (Ps 110:1), and this will be so because the Holy Spirit, by subjecting all wills, will subject all men to Jesus Christ, and all wills being subjected, all spirits will be subjected too. This is what will bring it about that when the Holy Spirit will have renewed the face of the earth, there will be no more idolaters; all will be subjected through the Spirit to the Lord.

[12.] O Spirit, consumer of all things, reduce everything into one! But before that can be, you will be a destructive Spirit. Also, Jesus Christ, speaking of the Spirit that he is about to send, said, *I have not come to bring peace, but the sword* (Matt 10:34). *I have come to cast fire on the earth; and what do I will, but that it be kindled?* (Luke 12:49) *It is necessary to be reborn in the spirit and in the water* (John 3:5); the word is like water that runs, but it is the spirit that makes it fertile. *It is this Spirit that will teach us everything* (John 14:26; John 16:13). As Jesus Christ said, *He will take what is mine* (John 16:14), for it is through the Holy Spirit that the Word is communicated to us, as in Mary, Spirit who teaches through the heart.

Guyon is in a state of uncertainty about her captivity and possible release; all the while the intrigue associated with her case continues to grow. Madame de Maintenon begins to vie for her release, although there is opposition at court.

3.9—Deliverance

[10.] A few days after my release, I was at B[eynes] with M(adame) de Charost;...having heard of M. (abbot of F_),[30] I was suddenly preoccupied with him with an extreme force and sweetness. It seemed to me that Our Lord united me with him as with no other. He asked me to give my consent; I gave it. Thus it appeared to me that almost a spiritual filiation came to be between him and me. I had the chance to see him the next day. I felt inside that this first meeting was not satisfactory to him, that he had no taste for it, and I felt a *je ne sais quoi* that made me intend to pour my heart into his, but I was not finding the corresponding feeling from him, which made me suffer a lot. That night, I suffered extremely due to him. We were enclosed in a carriage for three leagues.[31] In the morning, I saw him; we spent some time in silence, and the cloud blew over a little, but it was not yet what I was hoping for. I suffered for eight entire days, after which I found myself united to him without any obstacle. And since this time I always find that the union grows in a pure and ineffable way. It seems to me that my soul has a complete relationship with his, and these words of David concerning Jonathan, that his soul was bound to that of David (1 Sam 18:1), appear to me appropriate for this union. Our Lord has made me understand the big plans that he has for this person and how dear this person is to him.

3.10—Fénelon—Apostolic State

[1.] I cannot write anything else about myself. I will no longer do so.

I often feel the pain of souls in order to deliver them....

/ *There was one time when I had the opportunity to know that Our Lord had given me M. L.*[32] *like the fruit of my works and of my prison; I found myself too well paid by him for all my pains. Before ever entering into one of his desires, which I cannot truly call desires since they are outside of me, and one more powerful than me controls them, I would say, in a certain languor of love, "Give me children or I will die." I could not doubt having begotten him by Jesus Christ after, being in B[eynes], he was offered to me so that I might accept him. In full knowledge, I could not stop myself from looking at him like my son, and although I did not dare share this with him out of respect, my heart named him in this way, and it was necessary sometimes to let out what I kept inside out of restraint and to write: "O my son, you are my beloved son in whom I am well pleased" (Matt 3:17; Luke 9:35). It was such that if I hesitated on this point because of a tenderness that I carried for him that was all too maternal but very strong, Our Lord would reject me, and I only had access to him when letting go of my tenderness and communicating to him, although from afar, a very strong grace. It seems to me that since he was given to me at B[eynes] I have accepted him, and that I offer myself so as to carry him in my bosom and to suffer for him all that would please love, and that since I have carried him in my bosom, I found him always in me. This was around the feast of Saint Francis in the month of October 1688.*

Since this time, I have never been invited by God to return to my depths without finding him near my heart. But this is in a manner as pure and spiritual as it is real because there is nothing imaginative in me, but all really passes into my depths. Since I was carrying him in this way in my heart, it seemed to me that all the graces that God was making for him passed through me. And I could not doubt it; I felt him closer and more present than the children I had carried in my belly, and of all the spiritual children that God has given me I never had one that was equal to this one. This is an intimacy that cannot be expressed, and unless being made of the same thing nothing could be more intimate. All I had to do was to think of him in order to be more united with God, and when God would hold me tight it appeared to me that the same arms that hugged me also hugged him.

For the first eight days after our first meeting at B[eynes] I suffered a lot because I found something like a confusion between him and me that prevented my heart from spilling into his, but as much as I suffered, I found that this confusion unraveled until finally being cleared up. I found that, with an incomparable sweetness, my heart was spilling into his without my seeing it or without my speaking of it. At the beginning this happened to a lesser extent, then more and more easily, in such a way that I felt that there was a nearly continuous streaming of God into my soul and from my soul into his, like cascades that fall from one basin into the next. This often happened in such a way that I could not talk and would retire to let myself be possessed by God and let him operate in me in to do all that he wanted. There were moments when I was woken with extreme haste, and I found him all ready to receive, so he would receive. But sometimes I felt that he was put into a state of dryness. I would not tell him that. Not being able to speak to him, I would write him something, but it was impossible for me to express clearly what I felt in regard to him. God made me understand the great designs that he had on this soul and how it was dear to him. I was astonished that he was giving me more for him than for all the others combined, and I was made to believe by this that one wanted to advance him a lot and that he would not be given anything except through this miserable channel. I did not dare explain any of this to anyone else. However, I was sometimes so strongly pushed that, in order not to resist, no longer being able to do so in spite of my natural repugnance, I would go beyond this and write him. I hoped for a certain freedom, which was to be able to act with him without difficulty and that he would be able to conceive what I was to him in Jesus Christ, but, the avenues being closed, I was not able to explain myself enough.

I learned that M. L. would be the tutor for the duke of Burgundy, and I sent for him in May 1689. God will use him in a singular manner, but it is necessary for him to be annihilated and extremely diminished.

272

God worked especially to destroy his own wisdom and his own reason, and he used my madness to accomplish his work in him.

I was made to know, beginning in 1680, when God had me see him in a dream, that he gave him to me and he gave me to him, but I only met him in 1688. His face was known to me right away; I looked for it everywhere without finding it. Our Lord had me know that even then he had some attraction to the inner life. I did not yet have a soul to which mine was so completely related. I dreamed of him twice in a fairly short time, where it was confirmed to me with certainty that God wanted to use me and that he wanted to annihilate him in his interior extensively and lead him through his pure will. I wrote to him about this dream artlessly. A few days later—it was nearly the feast of Saint John in 1689—I was made to believe that God wanted to lead him like a child, through smallness, and that it was necessary that I see him sometimes, that it was necessary to nurse him, without which he would always languish, that he would be tested, and that God wanted to annihilate him by this, using for the wisest man the feeblest subject.

You alone understand, O my love, what you have given me for this soul, what I feel and what I would always be ready to do for it. I understood that God wanted me to have full confidence in him, to follow his advice and to ask him things, that he would be the heir of what God had me write, that he might correct it and even burn it, which I do not believe he did; in any case I would leave it absolutely up to him. I was happy to propose this to him, but seeing that he had some repugnance, I waited for the time when God would know how to dispose him, in accord with my understanding of how he wants things. In regard to him, God gives me the simplicity to write to him as God moves me to do this, although I know that, having as much intellect and knowledge as he has, he might find only shabbiness in my expressions and in what I write to him. But all this does not give me pain. I can do it with kindliness, and he will discern what is from God and what is from my shabbiness, the smallness that he will exercise in tolerating me being very agreeable to God, so that what is of God always had its effect, although it is not always perceived. June '89.

Whatever the union that I might have had with Father La Combe, I swear that the one that I have with M. L. is of yet a whole other nature. And there is something in the nature of this union that I have with him that is entirely new to me, having never felt it before. It is the same concerning that which I endure for him. This difference can only ever be understood through experience. I believe that God has given him to me in this way to cultivate him and to make him die through opposition to his natural tendencies. Also, I see clearly that he will not be cultivated by heavy crosses, his state being united and not subject to alternating between pains and joy.

It is necessary then to destroy his own wisdom in all places where it is entrenched, and it is for this that God has destined me. It seems to me that he has chosen me in this century to destroy human reason and to make the wisdom of God reign over the debris of human wisdom and reason itself. The Lord will one day make his mercy burst forth. He will establish the reigns of his empire in me, and the nations will recognize his sovereign power. His spirit will be widespread in all flesh; my sons and my daughters will prophesy, and the Lord will put his sweetness in them. It is I, it is I who will sing, in the midst of my weakness and my baseness, the song of the Lamb, which is sung only by the virgins who follow him everywhere, and he only considers virgins those whose hearts are perfectly selfless. All others are an abomination to him. Yes, in him I will be the despot of those who dominate, and those who are not subjugated for any reason will be subjugated in me through the force of his divine authority, from which they will never be able to separate themselves without separating themselves from God himself. What I bind will be bound; what I loose will be loosed; and I will be this rock fixed to the cross, rejected by all the architects who are the strong and learned. And they may never admit it, but this rock will be used as the cornerstone of the temple that the Lord has chosen to build—this Jerusalem descended from heaven, sumptuous and triumphant, like a bride who leaves the nuptial bed. //

I forgot to say that after the resuscitated state, it was several years before I was in the state that is called apostolic, or with a mission to help others. With all sense of self having been consumed in the purgatory that I had experienced, I then found myself with happiness similar to that of the blessed, with the exception of the beatific vision. Nothing from here touched me, and neither do I see presently anything in heaven or on earth that can trouble me concerning myself. The happiness of a soul in this state cannot be understood without the experience, and these ones, who die without being employed in helping their neighbor, die in supreme happiness, although full of exterior crosses.

But when it pleased God to want to honor me with his mission, he made me understand that the true father in Jesus Christ and the apostolic pastor must suffer like him for men, bear their lethargy, pay their debts, be dressed in their weaknesses. But God does not do these types of things without asking the soul for its consent. But he is truly sure that this soul will not refuse him what he is asking! He himself inclines the heart toward what he wants to obtain; it seems then that he imprints on it his words: "I was happy; I possessed glory; I was God, but I left all that. I was subjected to pain, to scorn, to ignominy, to torment. I became man to save man. If you want to finish what is missing from my passion and for me to extend my quality of redeemer into you, you must consent to lose the happiness that you enjoy to be subjected to miseries, to weaknesses, to carry the languor of those with whom I charge you, to pay their debts, and finally to be exposed not only to all the interior pain from which you yourself have been delivered, but to all of the strongest persecutions. If I had stayed in my hidden life, I would never have suffered any persecution; only those who are employed to help souls are persecuted." The consent to immolation was necessary, then, for entering into all the designs of God on the souls that he destines for himself.

[2.] He made me understand that he was not calling me, as was first believed, to a propagation of the exterior of the church, which consists of winning over heretics, but to the propagation of his Spirit, which is only ever the interior spirit, and that it would be for this Spirit that I would suffer. He does not destine me even for the first conversion of sinners, but for those who are touched by the desire to convert themselves in the perfect conversion, which is only ever this interior spirit. Since this time Our Lord has not charged me with a soul without asking for my consent and, after having accepted this soul in me, without having immolated me to suffer for it.

It is good to explain the nature of this suffering and how it is different from that which one suffers for oneself.

[3.] The nature of this suffering is something more intimate, stronger, and more detached. It is an excessive torment. One does not know where it is, or in which part of the soul it resides. It is never caused by reflection and cannot produce any. It causes neither trouble nor entanglement. It does not purify at all, which is why the soul does not find that it gives it anything. Its excess does not prevent a joy without joy and a perfect peace; it does not take away anything from its expansiveness. One is not ignorant that it is for souls that one suffers, and very often one knows who the person is. One finds oneself at that moment united with the person in a painful way, as a criminal is attached to the instrument of his torment. One often bears the weaknesses that these people should feel, but ordinarily it is a general, indistinct pain, which often has a certain relation to the heart that causes extreme heart pains, but violent pains, as if one was pressing it or piercing it with a blade. This pain, which is completely spiritual, is seated in the same place that is occupied by the presence of God. It is stronger than all corporal pains, but it is so insensible and so removed from feeling that the person who is overcome by it would believe, if capable of reflection, that it does not exist and that she is mistaken. What have I not suffered since God wanted me to share in the apostolic state! But however excessive my suffering has been, and whatever weakness I had in the senses, I have never desired to be delivered from it; on the contrary, charity for these souls increases as the suffering becomes greater, and the love that one has for them grows with the pain.

[4.] There are two kinds of pain: one caused by their present infidelity, the other that exists to purify them and to make them advance. The first squeezes the heart, afflicts it, weakens the senses, and causes a certain kind of agony and something like a tugging, just as if God were pulling from one side and the soul from the other, which could rip the heart in half. This pain is more unbearable that any other, although it is not more profound.

The pain of purification for others is a general, indistinct pain that tranquilizes and unites one to the person for whom one suffers in God. In the end, it is a difference that experience alone can make understood; all people who experience it will understand me. Very often, nothing equals what one suffers for people who are not aware of it or for others who, far from recognizing it, have disdain for those who are consumed for them through charity. All this does not diminish this charity at all, and there is nothing relating to death or torment that one would not endure with extreme pleasure to render them as God wants.

[5.] Divine Justice applied to the soul to make it suffer through purifying others does not cease to cause suffering when it is for an actual infidelity, if this infidelity has not stopped. It is not the same for purification; this happens in intervals, and one experiences relief after having suffered it. One finds that one acquires a certain ease with this soul, which signifies that one has suffered for, purified, and in the present moment put the soul as God wants it. When souls are on this path and when nothing stops them, this all comes together, but when they are stopped, there is something inside that makes it known.

[6.] God's justice causes certain souls to suffer from time to time until the point of entire purification. Immediately after they arrive where God wants them, one no longer sacrifices anything for them, and the union, which had often been covered by clouds, clears up in such a way that it becomes like truly pure air, penetrated everywhere, without distinction, by the light of the sun. As M. was given to me in a way more intimate than any other, what I have suffered and what I will suffer for him surpasses all that can be said; the least separation between him and me, or between him and God, because one is like the other, is like a little speck in the eye that causes extreme pain and does not bother any other spot in the body where it might be put. What I suffer for him is very different from what I suffer for others, without being able to penetrate the cause, unless it is only that God has united me more intimately with him than with any other, and that God has bigger plans for him than for others.

[7.] When I am suffering for a soul, if I merely hear the name of this person said, I feel a renewed extreme pain. Although for several years I might be in a state equally naked and empty of appearance, due to the depth of fullness, I do not stop being full. Water filling a basin and finding itself within the limits of what this basin can contain does not know how to discern anything of this fullness, but when one pours in too much, it is necessary to let some out, or it will burst. I never feel anything for myself, but when one stirs this infinite, full, and tranquil heart with something, this causes the fullness to be felt with such excess that it gushes over the senses. Far from saying or reading certain passages, this is what makes me avoid them. It is not that anything comes to me from exterior things, but just one word can stir the depths. Something said either in truth or counter to truth stirs it in the same way and, were it to last, would make it explode.

[8.] Since one would have trouble reading during the entire time that faith is savory (I understand [that one feels] a certain *je ne sais quoi* that closes the mouth), it might be thought that this is the same thing, but this would be mistaken. One cannot avoid using an expression concerning these last states that might have some signification similar to that concerning former states. This comes from the dearth of terms, and only experience can clear this up because all those who are in states of naked faith combined with support and with some deep savor believe themselves at the point I mention. The first are recollected, or rather feel moved into themselves by reading or by what they are told, toward a certain preoccupation with God that closes their mouths and often their eyes, preventing them from continuing their reading. It is not the same here; it is an overflowing of fullness, a gushing from depths that are satisfied and always full for all the souls who need to draw water from this fullness. It is a divine reservoir where the children of Wisdom incessantly draw what they need when they are truly disposed, not that they always feel what they draw there, but I truly feel it. These things that are written must not be taken literally, because if they are taken in that way, there is almost no consummated state that a soul of a certain degree might not believe itself to have felt, but with patience it will see this infinite difference later for itself. Even souls of inferior degrees will often appear more perfect than these souls consummated in love and through love, because God, who wants them to live with other men and to hide the view of such a great treasure, covers their exterior with apparent weaknesses, which, like foul grime, cover infinite treasures and prevent their loss.

[9.] If God had not entirely separated the exterior of these souls from their interior, they would no longer be able to converse with men. One feels this in the new life; it seems as if there is nothing left other than to die. One finds oneself so far away from the rest of men, and they think so differently from how one thinks that others become intolerable. The soul would then voluntarily say: *O my God, let your servant die in peace according to your promise, since my eyes have seen your salvation* (Luke 2:29–30). The souls arriving here find themselves in a real, consummated perfection, and they ordinarily die in this state when they are not destined to help other souls; but when they are, God divides the depths, which have become divine, from the exterior and delivers that exterior to infantile weaknesses, which holds the soul in a continuous abstraction and a total ignorance of what the soul is, unless these depths about which we have spoken are stirred for the good of others as well. Thus, one finds oneself truly a stranger, but one cannot express how this is so. Exterior weaknesses of these souls serve as a covering for them and even prevent them from serving as a support for others on the road to death to which they lead them. These are all infantile weaknesses. If the souls who are led by these persons would penetrate through this very weak exterior to the profoundness of their grace, they would look at them with too much respect and would not die to the support that such guidance would provide for them. If the Jews could have penetrated through the completely common exterior of Jesus Christ, they would never have persecuted him, and they would have been in continuous admiration of him.

[10.] These persons are a paradox both to their own eyes and to the eyes of all who see them because only the coarse bark is seen, although divine sap nonetheless comes out of it. Thus, those who want to judge them by the eyes of the reason do not know how to go about it. O divine wisdom, O savory knowledge, you flow incessantly from the mouth and the heart of these souls like a divine source that communicates life to an infinity of branches, although only a coarse, mossy bark is seen. *What will you see in the Shulammite, this soul so chosen, all you who consider her*, says the sacred Bridegroom, *except the companies of a camped army?* (Song. 6:13—7:1). *No, you will only see this in her. Do not carry any judgment O you who are not here, and be persuaded that although I might be black, I am very beautiful, that my sun through its burning gazes has decorated me in this way* (Song 1:5) to conserve me for himself and to hide me from the view of all creatures. To attack these souls is to wound the heart of God; to judge them is to judge God. Those who do this are led astray in their judgments, and this is what makes them dare, as the apostle Saint Jude says, to curse holy things and *to blaspheme* the sacred mysteries of the inner life (Jude 1:10).

[11.] The soul in this state is ignorant of itself, as it is unknown to others. When it speaks or writes about this, touching on itself, it does so as it does about divine things. It only speaks or writes about it through the light currently given to it in the present moment, which only lasts for as long as is necessary to speak or write about it, without it being possible to see or to think afterward about what was seen before, unless the present light might render it so. It is like a person for whom one opens a cabinet full of treasures, who sees them while it is open and who stops seeing them when it is shut. Also, this soul is the *sealed fountain* (Song 4:12). The Bridegroom alone opens—no other opens; no other shuts. Such a soul does not care either about honor, or about wealth, or about life, not only concerning the will but concerning real practice. Therefore, it no longer has anything to be careful for. If the soul was not this way, it would not be able to serve souls in the full manner of God's plans. The least caution prevents the effect of grace. Oh, how few souls really want to deliver themselves up for others without any self-interest, ready to do and to suffer for others! The charity of an apostolic soul cannot be understood. It is the charity of Jesus Christ himself. O profoundness of this charity, devoid of zeal and feelings, who could understand you?

[12.] All the greatest crosses come from this apostolic state, if one can call these sorts of things crosses, because hell and all men are stirred up to prevent the good taking place in souls. If Jesus Christ had not left his hidden life, he would not have been persecuted by the Jews and crucified. If God let these hidden souls stay in the secret of his countenance, they would be protected from the persecution of men. But one would endure the wheel and fire itself with a happy heart for a single soul! We must not be astonished if devils stir up all the areas of their dominion against apostolic souls. He knows well that a soul of this sort, if it is listened to, destroys his empire.

All devotions only harm him moderately because he is compensated by the self-love of the sanctimonious for what they make him lose through their regular practices. But there is no benefit from a soul devoted to the truth of God and to his pure love, which lets itself be destroyed by the sovereign domain of God and which, no longer subsisting in itself, gives full power to God to extend his empire even further. The devil can only approach these souls from afar. The rage that animates him against them knows no bounds. Oh, how mistaken is he who judges devotion through exterior actions! In order to be devout, or devoted to God, it is necessary to have neither any choice of nor any preference for esteeming one action over another. One makes up ideas and imagines that a soul that belongs to God in a certain way must be of such and such a kind, and when one sees the opposite of these ideas, one concludes that God is not there at all, and it is often where he is the most. Oh, the sovereign independence of my God!

You would not be God if you did not know how to glorify yourself through what disgraces you in appearance. God has his pleasure in all that renders us supple and small. He does not make a case for any virtue, but for having a soul in his hand in order to elevate it to the clouds and push it into the mud without its changing its situation in the smallest way. A state that depends on some exterior good is truly a virtuous state and not a divine state.

[13.] There are particular saints of the Lord who are not sanctified, like the other saints, by the practice of virtues, but by the Lord himself and by an infinite suppleness. They are truly more the saints of God since they are only saints of and for him. They are saints in his way and not in that of men. O my love, you have so many souls who serve you in order to be holy. Make for yourself a troop of children who serve you because you are holy, who serve you in your way! These are the children for whom you sanctified yourself, and this is enough for them. Oh, what a terrible monster is the sense of self! Yes, my God, let me be at least the toy of your will. Let there be neither virtue nor sanctification for me, but only singing with the church, *Tu solus Sanctus.*[33] I sing the same thing for myself and for those you have given me, so that you might be glorified and sanctified, not in them, but in you and for you. O pure love, to what a point do you reduce your subject!

[14.] The souls of which I speak are incapable of a preference or predilection for anything; instead, they are moved by a necessity, which, not being in them at all, due to their freedom, finds itself in God himself after the sacrifice of this same freedom. They have no natural love, but an infinite charity, applied and stirred more strongly for certain subjects than for others, according to God's design, peoples' need, and the intimacy of the union that God wants them to have with each other. This strong love, which seems even ardent, is not in the powers like the other inclinations, but in this same depth, which is God himself. He governs as sovereign and inclines this same depth indistinguishably from himself toward the thing that he wants one to love, and to which one is united, and this love is him in such a way that it cannot be distinguished from God, although it ends with a particular subject. These depths, stirred toward this person, cause an attraction toward him as toward God. And just as everything that stirs these depths renders God perceptible, which could not otherwise be so, owing to the transformation, so too the innate inclination stirred toward this creature renders God perceptible, but in a stronger, purer manner, more disengaged from the sensible proportionately as the soul is in an eminent degree. One feels something that would seem to relate to this from the beginning of the way, where all that impels us to God causes a perceptible inclination toward God, but these things are in the senses or the powers, according to the degree of the soul. That is not what I mean; this is in the very depths, inaccessible to all others except God himself.

[15.] There is no state thus consummated that a soul at this beginning might not attribute to itself, especially those who go, as the scripture says, from faith to faith (Rom 1:17). Since, as has been said, one has the first fruits of the Spirit from the beginning, and it is the same faith that grows deeper and purifies itself, expands itself, and stretches itself up to perfect consummation, it is rather the same at the beginning and has almost the same effect. The whole difference is that it resides in the powers all along the way until it loses itself in the intimate depths that are nothing other than God himself, who consummates all in his divine unity. Even the interior government, which must be the entire guidance for souls of faith, uncovers itself, from the beginning, for persons destined to an eminent faith. They are more sensitive, more distinct, more in the powers at the beginning, but finally it is this that leads them and impels them to mortify themselves, renounce themselves, speak and keep quiet, detach themselves until it causes their loss within itself in the God-depths. Then it changes its nature and becomes so natural that it loses all that made it distinct outside of God, so that the creature acts as naturally as it breaths; its suppleness is infinite.

[16.] It is good to explain here something that, through lack of experience, could cause souls to make mistakes. It is that the soul, reduced to God and having come to an infinite suppleness through its relationship with God, appears either reserved or as having trouble saying certain things to others. It is no longer a fault that is in it in regard to itself, but this closing up comes from the person to whom one must speak, because God makes known, as if by a premonition, all the dispositions of the soul to whom it is necessary to speak. And although the soul, if one asked, would assert that it has no repugnancy to receive what it would be told, because its will is effectively disposed this way, it is certain, however, that whatever good will it might have, things are repugnant to it, either because they exceed the present range of this person or because secret ideas of reasonable virtue still remain. It is, therefore, the closing up of the person to whom one speaks that causes one's repugnance to talking. Moreover, the exterior state of being childlike has a thousand little things that might pass for infidelities similar to those of people who, through self-love, do not say things that are repugnant to them, but it is easy to see that this is not like that, because they have passed through a state that did not permit them the reserving of a thought, however much it might cost them. It is necessary to judge souls in this state more by what God has made them experience than by what one sees, because otherwise one would judge them in relation to one's own state and not by what they are. What is weak in God is stronger than the greatest strength because this weakness does not come from not having acquired all the strength that is virtuous and understood by reason, but from having infinitely surpassed it. It is lost in the divine strength, and this is what causes these contraries, which ally themselves so well, although they appear unlikely allies, of the divine strength and of the child's weakness, and so forth. Up to the end of 1688.

3.11—In Solitude—Frequenting Saint-Cyr

She is with her daughter and her daughter's family for over two years.

[4.] Some time before the marriage of my daughter, I had met Monsieur La Mothe de Fénelon, as I have already said, and the family into which she had married being among his friends, I had the chance to see him several times. We had some conversations on the subject of the inner life, to which he made many objections. I responded to him with my ordinary simplicity, and I had occasion to believe that he had been happy with these responses. Since the affairs of Molinos[34] were causing a great stir, people had become mistrustful of the simplest things and of the most common terms among those who had written on these matters. This gave me the chance to explain my experiences thoroughly to him. The difficulties that he had with me only served to enlighten him about the basis of my sentiments. Thus, no one has been better able to understand them than he. This is what in the ensuing time served as the cause for the persecution that was leveled against him, as his responses to M. de Meaux[35] have made known to all people who read them without prejudice.

Guyon recounts the events of several years spent at Saint-Cyr and the kindness shown to her by Madame de Maintenon. This period does not last, however, and she becomes the target of renewed suspicions, accusations, and suggestions of heresy. She is made to leave Saint-Cyr.

3.13—Bossuet

[1.] Some of my friends thought it proper for me to see Monsignor the Archbishop of Meaux, who was said not to be against the inner life. I knew that he had read *The Short and Easy Method* and the *Commentary on the Song of Songs* more than eight or ten years ago, and that he had found them very good. This is what made me gladly consent to this. But, O my Lord, how often have I experienced in my life that all that is done through consideration and the human view, however good, turns into shame, confusion, and suffering. I flattered myself at that moment, and I accused myself for my lack of faith, that he would uphold me against those who were attacking me for it, but I was far from knowing him! And how subject to error is that which is not seen in your light and which you do not disclose yourself!

[2.] One of my very highly regarded friends, Monsieur de Chevreuse,[36] brought M. de Meaux to my home. The conversation soon fell on the reason for the visit. They spoke about *The Short and Easy Method*, and this prelate told me that he had read it before, as well as the *Commentary on the Song of Songs*, and that he had found them very good. What I am saying here is not to support these books, which I have submitted with all my heart and which I submit still, but to make a plain relating of all that has happened, as I have been asked to do. Monsieur de Chevreuse gave him the *Torrents*, about which he made some remarks, not condemning things, but about things that deserved clarification.

***

[4.] With M. de Meaux having then accepted the proposal to examine my writings, I had them put into his hands, not only the printed ones, but also all the *Commentaries* on the holy scripture. It was a lot of work for him and required four or five months to have the chance to read it all thoroughly, which he did very carefully at his country home, where he went to be less interrupted. To demonstrate more confidence in him and to show him the deepest recesses of my heart, I had him sent, as I have said, the story of my life, where my most secret dispositions were explored with much simplicity. I asked him for the secrecy of the confessional on this, and he promised an inviolable one. He read everything attentively; he wrote out long excerpts and, after the time that he had requested, arrived at a point to listen to my explanations and to show me his difficulties.

[5.] This was at the beginning of 1694. He wished to see me at the home of one of his friends who lived near the Daughters of the Holy Sacrament. He said mass in this community, and he gave me communion. We dined together. This conference, which according to him should have been secret, was known by everyone. A lot of people sent their requests that he go to the Daughters of the Holy Sacrament so that they could talk to him. He went there, and they took extreme care to warn him, and he appeared to me to be thus warned when he returned that night and he spoke. He was no longer the same man. He had brought all his excerpts and a memoir containing more than twenty articles to which all of his difficulties had been reduced. God helped me in such a way that I satisfied him with respect to all that concerned church dogma and the purity of the doctrine, but there were some places concerning which I could not satisfy him. Since he was speaking with extreme animation, and he barely gave me the freedom to explain my thoughts to him, it was not possible to make him change his mind about some of these articles as I had done with the others. We separated late, and I left this conference with my head so exhausted and in such a great despondency that I was sick for several days. However, I wrote him several letters afterward in which I explained to him these difficulties that had arrested him as best I could, and I received one from him that was more than twenty pages, where it appeared that he had been impeded only by the novelty of the material for him and the little experience he had with interior ways, about which one can hardly judge except by experience.

[6.] I will reproduce most of these difficulties here, as far as memory permits me. He believed, for example, that I was rejecting and condemning as imperfect distinct acts, such as petitions, good desires, and so forth—which I was very far from doing, since the contrary is found throughout all of my writings. How little they wanted to pay attention to them! But since I had felt helpless to perform these discursive acts, a helplessness common to certain souls, regarding which they needed to be warned to be faithful to the Spirit of God, who calls them to something more perfect, I tried, as much as I could, to help them through the straits of the spiritual life, where, for the lack of a guide who has been through this, souls are often impeded and exposed to error concerning what God wants from them. It is easy, it seems, to conceive that a person who locates her happiness in God alone can no longer desire her own happiness. No one can locate all her happiness in God alone except she who lives in God through pure charity. When the soul is there, it no longer desires any happiness other than that of God in himself and for himself. No longer desiring any other happiness, all selfish happiness, even the glory of heaven for itself, can no longer make it happy, nor is it consequently the object of its desire. Desire necessarily follows love. If my love is in God alone and for God alone, without any return to myself, my desire is in God alone, without any relationship to me. Desire in God no longer has the vivacity of a loving desire, which does not enjoy what it desires, but it finds rest in a full and satisfying desire. For God being infinitely perfect and happy, and the happiness of this soul being in the perfection and in the happiness of its God, its desire cannot have the activity of an ordinary desire, which waits for what it desires, but it finds rest in the one that possesses what it desires. Here, then, is the center of this state of the soul and what makes it no longer notice all the good desires of those who love God in relationship to themselves, or of those who love themselves and look for themselves in the love they have for God.

[7.] This does not prevent God from changing dispositions, making the soul feel the weight of its body for some moments, which will make it say: *Cupido dissolve, et esse cum Christo.*[37] At other times, not feeling anything but the disposition of charity toward its brothers, without a return or a relationship to itself, it *will desire to be an anathema and separated from Jesus Christ for its brothers* (Rom 9:3). These dispositions, which appear to contradict each other, fundamentally agree with each other in a way that does not vary at all. Thus, although the beatitude of God in himself and for himself, into which the perceptible desires of the soul have, as it were, flowed and rested, causes the soul to be happy, God does not cease to awaken those desires when it pleases him. These desires are no longer like desires from before, which are in the self-will, but desires stirred and excited by God himself, without the soul thinking about itself, because God, who holds it directly turned toward him, renders its desires, like its other acts, free from reflection in such a way that it cannot see them unless he shows them to it or its words give it some understanding by giving it to others. It is certain that to desire for oneself, one must will for oneself. But with God's whole care being to sink the will of the creature in his, he also absorbs all known desire in the love of his divine will.

[8.] There is still another reason why God takes perceptible desires away from the soul and puts them into the soul as it pleases him. It is that he answers the desires of this soul and the preparation of this heart, in such a way that, the Spirit desiring for it and in it, its desires are prayers and requests. But it is certain that Jesus Christ says in this soul: *I know that you will hear me always* (John 11:42). A vehement desire for death in such a soul would be nearly a certainty of death. To desire humiliations is far below desiring the enjoyment of God; however, when it has pleased God to humiliate me a lot through calumny, he has given me a hunger for humiliation. I call it a hunger in order to distinguish it from desire. At other times he inspires this soul to pray for particular things. It truly feels in the moment that its prayer is not formed by its will but by the will of God, because it is not even free to pray for whom it pleases or when it pleases. But when it prays, it is always answered. It does not attribute anything to itself for this, but it acknowledges that he who possesses it answers himself in this soul. It seems that I conceive this infinitely better than I explain it.

[9.] It is the same as the sensible inclination or even the perceived, which is much less than the sensible. When one body of water is lower than another that is discharging into it, this happens with a rapid movement and a perceived sound, but when both bodies of water are at the same level, the inclination is no longer perceived. There still is one, but it is unnoticeable and imperceptible, so that it is true to say in one sense that there is none. As long as the soul is not entirely united to its God with a union that I call permanent, to distinguish it from passing unions, it feels its inclination toward God. The impetuousness of this penchant, far from being a perfect thing, as less enlightened people think, is a fault in it and shows the distance between God and the soul. But when God unites himself with the soul in such a way that he has received it into himself, where he holds it hidden with Jesus Christ, the soul finds a rest that excludes all sensible inclination and is such that only experience can make it understood. It is not a rest in the savory peace, in the sweetness, and in the deliciousness of a perceived presence of God, but it is a rest in God himself that participates in his immensity—such breadth, simplicity, and clarity has this rest. The light of the sun stopped by mirrors would have something more blazing than the pure light of air; however, these same mirrors, which increase its brilliance, terminate it and remove purity from it. When the ray is terminated by something, it becomes filled with atoms and becomes more distinguishable than when in the air, but it is very far from having its purity and simplicity. The simpler things are, the more pure and vast they are. Nothing is simpler than water, nothing purer, but this water has an admirable breadth due to its fluidity. It also has the quality that, having no quality itself, it takes on all sorts of impressions. It has no taste, and it takes on all tastes; it has no color, and it takes on all colors. The mind and the will in this state are so pure and so simple that God gives them such color and such taste as it pleases him, like this water, which is sometimes red, sometimes blue, ultimately imprinted with the particular color and taste that one wants to give it. It is evident that although one gives this water the diverse colors that one pleases due to its simplicity and purity, it is not, however, true to say that the water in itself has taste and color, since in its nature it exists without taste and without color, and it is this lack of taste and color that renders it susceptible to all tastes and all colors. This is what I feel in my soul; it has nothing that it can distinguish or know in itself or as belonging to itself, and this is what constitutes its purity, but it has all that is given to it and as it is given, without retaining anything of this for itself. If you asked this water what is its quality, it would answer you that it is not to have any. You would tell it: "But I saw you red!" "That is not my nature; I do not even think about what is made of me, about all the tastes and about all the colors that are given to me." It is with form just as with color. Since water is fluid and without consistency, it takes on all the forms of the places where it is put, in a vase either round or square. If it had its own consistency, it would not be able to take all forms, all tastes, and all colors.

[10.] Souls are good for but little as long as they conserve their own consistency. God's whole design is to make them lose all that they have of the self through the death of themselves, so as to move, change, imprint, and act upon them as he pleases. In this way, it is true that they have all forms, and it is true that they have none, and this is the reason that, feeling only their simple, pure nature without singular impression, when they speak or write about themselves, they deny all forms to be in them. For they do not speak according to the variable dispositions into which they are put, to which they do not pay attention, but instead according to the depth in which they exist, which is their continually subsisting state. If the soul could be shown as the face is, I would not want, it seems to me, to hide any blemishes. I submit all of it.[38]

[11.] I still believe that what makes the soul no longer able to desire anything is that God fills its capacity. I will be told that the same thing can be said about heaven. There is this difference, that in heaven not only is the capacity of the soul full, but this capacity is also fixed and can no longer grow. If it grew, the saints would grow in holiness and in merit. In this life, when God has purified a soul by his goodness, he fills this capacity; this is what causes a certain satisfaction. But at the same time, he augments and expands this capacity, and by expanding it he purifies it. This is what causes interior suffering and purification. In this suffering and purification, life is awful; the body is a burden. In fullness, nothing is missing from the soul; it can desire nothing. The second reason is that the soul is as if absorbed in God in a sea of love in such a way that, forgetting itself, it can only think of its love. All care of self is a burden to it. An object that infinitely exceeds the soul's capacity absorbs it and prevents it from turning toward itself. It is necessary to say of these souls what is said of the children of Wisdom: *It is a generation that is only obedience and love* (Ecclus 3:1). The soul is incapable of any reason, view, or thought other than love and obedience. It is not that one condemns the other states—not at all—and I explained myself to M. de Meaux, in a manner, it seemed, so as to leave him no doubt about this.

3.14—Required Clarifications

[1.] I still have a fault; it is that I say things as they come to me, without knowing if I am saying them well or poorly. When I say or write them, they appear clear as day to me, after which I see them as things that I have never seen before, far from having written them. Nothing remains in my mind but a void, which is not inconvenient. It is a simple void, which is inconvenienced neither by a multitude of thoughts nor by their scarcity. This is what caused one of my greatest troubles while talking to M. de Meaux.

[2.] He ordered me to justify my books; I defended myself as much as I could because, having submitted them with all of my heart, I did not want to justify them, but he wanted it. I protested first that I only did this through obedience, condemning that for which I was being condemned with all the sincerity in the world. I had always held to this language, which was more that of my heart than of my mouth. He still wanted me to give him reasoning for an infinite number of things that I had put in my writings, which were entirely new and unknown to me.

I remember, among other times, when I was considering Elihu, the man who spoke for so long to Job when his friends had stopped talking to him. I never knew what I meant to say. M. de Meaux wanted me to say that all this Elihu said in such a long discussion was through the Spirit of God, which did not appear so to me. On the contrary, one sees an astonishing fullness of himself. I will say here in passing that if one will give some attention to the speed with which God had me write things well above my natural capacity, it is easy to conceive that, having had such a small part in it, it is very difficult for me, not to say even impossible, to give a rationale in a dogmatic manner. This is what has always led me to say that I took no part in it, and that only having written through obedience, I was as happy to see everything burned as to see it praised or highly regarded.

There were also errors of the copyists that made the meaning absolutely unintelligible, and M. de Meaux wanted to make me responsible for the errors that he insisted were there, and he overpowered me with the vivacity of his arguments, which were always reduced to the credibility of the dogma of the church, which I did not pretend to dispute with him. He did this instead of peacefully discussing the experiences of one in submission to the church, who only asked to be corrected, supposing that that person did not conform to the rules that it prescribed, which was precisely the topic in question, concerning which this examination had been undertaken.

[3.] He spoke to me of the woman of the Apocalypse (Rev 12:1ff.), as if I had pretended to be her myself. I responded to him that, by this, Saint John understood the church and the Blessed Virgin, that Our Lord was happy to compare his servants to a thousand things that were properly fitting only for him, and that there is nothing in the general church that does not take place, in part, in the individual soul. It is thus an application that is made to the soul, and God knows how to fulfill this application, as when Saint Paul says that he was completing what was lacking from the passion of Jesus Christ (Col 1:24), or when what is said of Wisdom is applied to the Blessed Virgin, but Solomon's intention was only to express Wisdom, and so it goes. It is therefore a comparison that God nonetheless takes pleasure in fulfilling. All that was said of the woman of the Apocalypse, in the sense in which it pleased God to attribute it to me—this fullness, for example—is not in the body but in the soul, as several people who will read this have felt in me. It seems that a torrent of grace is sent out; when the subjects are prepared, this is received in them; when the subjects are not, it is sent back to us. This is what Jesus Christ said to his disciples: those who are children of peace will receive peace; as for those who will not receive, *your peace will return to you* (Matt 10:13). It is that to the letter. One does one's best to explain these things, and not as one wants, but *the sensual man will not understand* (1 Cor 2:14) that which only the spiritual man is given to understand.

[4.] As for the flowing of grace, this was another difficulty for M. de Meaux. I was given to hear the words of Our Lord when the hemorrhaging woman touched him: *A secret power has left me* (Luke 8:46). I have never claimed to make all of this believable. I wrote in order to obey and have said things as they were shown to me. I have always been ready to believe that I was mistaken, if I was told so. God is my witness that I hold on to nothing, and I have always been ready to burn the writings as soon as they were believed to be capable of harm. There is little imagination in what I write because I often write what I have never thought. What I would have wished for M. de Meaux was that he not judge me by reason but by his heart. I had not premeditated any response before seeing him; the plain truth alone was all my strength, and I found myself content that my mistake would be known as the grace of God. My wretchedness might be mixed with his pure light, but can mud tarnish the sun? I was hoping that the same God who once made a female donkey speak could make a woman speak who often knew no more about what she was saying than Balaam's female donkey (Num 22:1–35). These were the dispositions of my heart when I had the conference with M. de Meaux, and, thanks to God, I have never had any other.

[5.] The objections that he made came, I believe, from the little knowledge he had about mystical authors, whom he admitted never having read, and from the little experience that he had with interior ways. He had been struck on certain occasions by extraordinary things that he had seen in certain persons or that he had read about, which made him judge that God had some special ways by which he made them reach great saintliness. But this way of simple faith, little, obscure, which produces in souls, according to the designs of God, this variety of individual leadings by which he guides them himself—it was a jargon that he looked at as the effect of mere imagination, the terms of which were as unknown to him as they were intolerable.

[6.] Another thing for which he reproached me is having put down somewhere that I had no grace for certain souls or for myself. When I spoke of no longer having grace for myself, I did not mean to speak about sanctifying grace, which one always needs, but about gratuitous grace, sensible, distinct, and perceived, which is felt at the beginning of the spiritual life. I meant to say that I was contributing nothing spectacular to the reign of God, except by winning some souls through my opprobrium, through ignominy and confusion. He attributed to the sensible what was purely spiritual, like what I had put in my *Life* of an impression that I had had at Beyne, being with Madame de C(harost).[39] Certainly, it has never been my state to have extraordinary things that overflowed onto the body, and I believe that ordinarily this only happens in sensible love and not in the purely spiritual. But on this occasion, when a passage of the holy scripture had been read on which a very profound light was given to me, the people who were present explained it in the opposite way. I did not dare to speak, and there was a contrast between what I knew was true and what was said, which could not be so. The powerlessness to speak not being removed, the necessity of hearing others speak caused an effect on me that I have only felt this one time, which overflowed onto my body to the point of finding myself feeling sick. This is what Saint John of the Cross says: "They were confusedly speaking a *je ne sais quoi* that kills me and puts me beside myself."[40]

It is true that, when God gave me some souls, I have felt some intolerable and inexplicable pains in my heart. It was an acute impression in the bottom of my soul that I could only understand by this, which is given to me—that Jesus Christ, while having his side opened on the cross, gave birth to the predestined. He had his heart opened to show that they were departing from his heart. He suffered in the Garden of Olives the pain of his separation from the reprobates who would not profit from the blood that he was about to shed for them. This pain was excessive in him and such that God's strength was necessary for bearing it. I have explained this in the Gospel of Saint Matthew.

[7.] M. de Meaux raised still greater objections to me concerning what I had said about my life in the apostolic state. What I wanted to say is that people, such as lay men and women, whose state and condition distance them from helping souls, must not interfere by themselves, but that, when God wanted to use them by his authority, it was necessary that they be put into this state about which I had written.

What had given occasion for it is that a number of good souls who feel the first fruits of the unction of grace—this unction of which Saint John speaks, which teaches all truth (1 John 2:27)—when, I say, they start to feel this unction, they are so charmed by it that they would like to share their grace with everyone. But as they are still not in the source, and this unction is given to them for themselves and not for others, in spilling over outside they lose the sacred oil little by little, like the foolish virgins, while the wise ones preserved their oil for themselves until they were introduced into the chamber of the Bridegroom. Then they can give their oil because the Lamb is the lamp that lights them. That this state is possible, we only have to open the stories of all times to show that God used lay men and women without training to instruct, edify, guide, and make souls arrive at a very high perfection.

I believe that one of the reasons why God wanted to use them in this way is so that the glory would not be stolen from him. *He chose weak things in order to confound the strong* (1 Cor 1:27). It seems that God, jealous of the attribution that is made to men of what is only due to him, might have wanted to make a paradox of these people who are not in a state to take his glory from him. Regarding what concerns me, I am ready to believe that my imaginations are mixed up with divine truth like shadows, which might cover it well but not damage it. I ask of God, with all my heart, that he crush me in the most terrible ways rather than that I should rob him of the least glory. I am only a pure nothing. My God is all-powerful and pleases himself in exercising his power on the nothing.

[8.] The first time that I wrote about my life, it was very short. I had put down my sins in detail and had spoken only very little of God's graces. They made me burn this, and they ordered me absolutely to omit nothing and to write all that came to me without regard for myself. I did it. If there is something too prideful, I am only capable of wretchedness. But I believed that it was more important to obey without self-regard than to disobey and hide God's mercies by a selfish humility. God may have had his designs in this. It is an evil to publish the secret of one's king, but it is well done to declare the grace of the Lord one's God and to raise up his kindnesses by the lowness of the subject on whom he exercises them. If I make a mistake, the fire will purify everything. I do not have any difficulty in believing that I might be mistaken, but I cannot either complain or trouble myself about it. When I gave myself to Our Lord, it was without reserve and without exception, and since I only write through obedience, I am also as happy to write extravagances as good things. My consolation is that God is neither less great, nor less perfect, nor less happy for all of my errors. Once things are written, there is nothing left in my head; I have no ideas at all. When I can reflect, it seems to me that I am below all creatures and a true nothing.

[9.] When I spoke of *binding* and *loosing*,[41] these words must not be taken in the sense in which they are said of the church. It was a certain authority that God seemed to give me to draw souls away from their pains and to return them back there, God permitting that this was found true in these souls. I did not believe myself to be the best, nor that this was done in a manner that reflects on me, which God has never permitted, but I have put things down as they had been shown to me by writing simply and without self-regard.

[10.] M. de Meaux always insisted that I was working to snuff out distinct acts as believing them imperfect. I have never done this, and when I was interiorly positioned in powerlessness to do them, and my powers were as if bound, I put up a fight with all my might, and I only gave up through weakness to God, the strong and powerful. It seems that even this powerlessness to perform reflective acts has not taken the reality of the act away from me. On the contrary, I found that my faith, my confidence, my abandonment were never more alive, nor my love more ardent. This made me understand that there was one kind of direct act without reflection, and I was acquainted with it through a continual exercise of love and faith, which, rendering the soul submissive to all events of providence, becomes the door to a veritable hatred of self, only loving crosses, ignominies, opprobrium. It seems to me that all Christian and evangelical characteristics are given to it.

It is true that this confidence is full of rest, exempt from care and trouble. It can do nothing else except love and rest in its love. It is like a drunken person who is incapable of anything but drunkenness. The difference between these people and the others is that the others eat food in order to nourish themselves, chewing it with care, and those others swallow the substance of it without reflecting on it. I am so far from wanting to snuff out distinct act as being imperfect that, for the few who take the trouble to read my writings, they will notice expressions in many places there that are very distinct acts. It would be easy to show that they then flow out from the source and why at this time one expresses one's love, faith, and abandonment in a very distinct manner, and to show that one does this the same way in canticles or spiritual songs, and that one cannot do this in contemplative prayer unless God impels one.

[11.] It is necessary to notice that acts must be in accord with the state of the soul. If it is multiple, the acts must be multiple; if it is simple, simple ones, either direct or reflective. Patience is an act. The one who receives performs an act, though a less noticeable one than he who gives. The flowing of the soul into God is an act. The one who is moved and acted upon performs acts.

They are truly not acts of the self. Souls are not the source of their acts. It is an act like following a hand that pushes. The agent moves his subject; the moved subject acts by his motor. All of these are acts, but not organized and methodical acts, nor acts of which the cause is the soul, but God. But the acts that God brings about are more noble and more perfect, although more imperceptible. *All who are led by the spirit of God are the children of God* (Rom 8:14). The one who is moved performs an act, which is not properly his own act but an act of allowing himself to be moved without resistance. He who does not admit these secondary acts destroys all the operations of grace as first causes and makes God only secondary and only accompanying our action, which is opposed to the doctrine of the church. The one who lets himself be moved performs an act of submission, and so forth.

[12.] I can say the same thing about requests, for M. de Meaux most tormented me about requests, not only in this first conference, but in those that I had with him at the end of that same year, of which I will speak next. I am putting together here, as well as I can remember, all that related to this examination in order not to do it two times. M. de Meaux wanted me then to make some requests, but what could I request? God gave me more good things than I want; what would I ask of him? He anticipates my requests and my desires. He makes me forget myself so as to think of him. He forgot himself for me, how could I not forget this for him? The one to whom love leaves enough liberty to think of himself hardly loves, or at least, can love more. The one who does not think about himself at all can neither ask nor pray for himself. His love is his prayer and his request. O divine charity, you are every prayer, every request, every action of grace, and yet you are none of that. You are a substantial prayer, which contains all distinct and detailed prayer eminently. O love, you are this sacred fire, which makes your victims pure and innocent without their thinking about their purity. They speak of themselves outside of themselves, in you, as of you, without distinction. I am not surprised, O David, by the way you spoke of yourself as Christ, of whom you were the figure. You had become so much the same thing as him that in the same passages you speak of yourself and of him, without changing style or person. Finally, it seems to me that the exercise of charity contains every request and every prayer, and since there is a love without reflection, there is also a prayer without reflection, and that which has this substantial prayer satisfies all prayers, since it contains everything. It does not break them down due to its simplicity. The heart that waits for God without ceasing attracts God's vigilance over it.

There are two sorts of souls: the ones that God leaves free to think about themselves and the others that God invites to give themselves to him through a forgetfulness of themselves so complete that he reproaches them for their least self-regards. These souls are like little children who let themselves be carried by their mothers, who have no care at all about what concerns them. This does not condemn those who act. These and the others follow their attraction according to the Sprit of grace and the advice of an enlightened director. Let one open the *Treatise on the Love of God* by Saint Francis de Sales; he says the same thing in an infinity of places. I say then that there are spiritual moments of powerlessness, just as there are corporal ones. I do not condemn acts or good practices, God forbid! When I wrote of these things, I did not claim at all to give a remedy to those who are in good form and who have a facility for these practices, but I did it for the many people who cannot perform these distinct acts. It is said that these remedies are dangerous and will be abused. One only has to take away the abuse, and this is what I have worked for with all my might.

[13.] M. de Meaux claimed that there were only four or five people in the world who had these ways of praying and who would have difficulty performing acts. There are more than one hundred thousand in the world; thus, one has written for those who are in this state. I have tried to take away the abuse, which succeeded in making an exaggeration of my terms—that is, for all souls that start to feel certain moments of powerlessness, which is very common, to believe themselves to be at the summit of perfection. And I wanted, while pointing out this last state, to make them understand their distance from it. As for what concerns the core of doctrine, I profess my ignorance. I have believed that my director would take away bad terms and that he would correct what he did not believe good. I would prefer to die a thousand times than to stray from the sentiments of the church, and I have always been ready to disavow and condemn all that I might have said or written that might be contrary to it.

The intervening chapters recount Bossuet's mounting persecution of her, supported by Madame de Maintenon, and the involvement of others such as Tronson. Guyon is very affected by the death of Fouquet, the father of her lifelong friend Madame de Charost. Guyon writes the Justifications *during this time.*

3.17—Interviews at Issy

[1.] I soon noticed a change in M. de Meaux. Although he was very reserved about disclosing his feelings when he was speaking to my friends, he was not the same with people whom he believed disinclined toward me. I had confided the story of my life to him, as I have already said, under the seal of confession. My most secret dispositions were written there. However, I learned that he had shown it to others and had made jokes about it. He wanted to force me to show it to these other men and insisted on this so strongly (although it had nothing to do with the examination in question), that I saw myself obliged to pass it on where he wanted.

I had it given to them. I communicated with the duke of Chevreuse about all that came from M. de Meaux and about how many times I had reason to believe that he only dreamed of condemning me. He had said that this could not be done without the story of my life and that one would see the pride of the devil in it. It was for this reason that he wanted to show it to these other men.

[2.] I asked Monsieur de Chevreuse to have things written down as they were decided by these men, and in order to have proof of what was happening, I asked him with much insistence to be at the conferences. I strongly wished that they would have passed judgment only at the end of the process, and that until that point they would have truly wanted to suspend their judgment, only being able to judge after, being all together and having prayed to God, God at that moment would touch their hearts with his truth, independently of their minds. For, outside of that, when the same grace of those assembled for a question of truth escapes and departs, the mind takes the higher ground, and one no longer judges except by the mind. Moreover, no longer being upheld by the grace of truth that has only its moment, and finding itself carried away by the clamoring crowd of people supported by the credit and authority afforded by favor, while listening to them, the mind obstructs the heart through the continual doubts that it forms. Monsieur de Chevreuse proposed it to these men. Monsieur de Châlons and Monsieur Tronson[42] would have voluntarily consented to it, because these two gentlemen proceeded with all the straightforwardness and good faith imaginable, but M. de Meaux found a way to prevent it. He had made himself so much the master of the whole affair that it was absolutely necessary for all to bend to what he wanted. He was no longer the same as he had been six or seven months before, in the first examination. Since at that point he only engaged in it in a spirit of charity and in the interest of knowing the truth, in spite of his extreme persistence, he had not stopped considering many things that his prejudice would have made him reject. He appeared even sometimes touched by certain truths and to respect things that struck him, although he might not have had the experience. But now it was no longer the same thing. He had a target from which he did not swerve, and since he wanted to deliver a brilliant condemnation, he brought everything that he thought capable of contributing back to that point.

[3.] It was in this same spirit that he wrote a long letter to Monsieur de Chevreuse to prove to him that, according to my principles, the sacrifice of eternity was a real consenting to the hatred of God, and other things of this nature concerning these examinations. It still turns my stomach when I think of this. To agree to hate God! Good God! How can a heart that loves him so passionately mean such a thing? I believe that this rather strong view could cause death. This needs an explanation, and I will give it here much as I sent it to him at the time. Although the soul may be placed in such terrible trials that it does not doubt its reprobation (which is called a holy despair), although it may bear in itself the state of hell (which is a feeling of the pain of the damned), if one were to stir its depths by such a proposition, it would cry out, "Rather a million hells without this hate." But what one calls consenting to the loss of its eternity—this is when the soul in this state of trial believes this certain and then, without any view but its own unhappiness and its own pain, makes the complete sacrifice of its eternal loss, even thinking that its God will be neither less glorious nor less happy. Oh, if one could understand the excess of love (of God) and the hatred of self this creates, and how far one is from having these thoughts in detail! But how would I be heard and understood? Alas, how many times in this state have I asked my God for hell through grace, in order not to offend him! I would tell him, "O my God, hell is the penalty of sin in others; make it prevent all sin in me, and make me suffer all the hell that the sins of all men merit, provided that I do not offend you at all."

[4.] The sacrifices of particular and distinct things only happen in the exercise, as a person who falls in water first makes all efforts to save herself and only ceases her effort when her weakness makes it useless. Then she sacrifices herself to a death that appears inevitable to her. There are anticipated sacrifices, like general sacrifices, which distinguish nothing, unless God proposes to the soul the greatest pains, aches, renunciations, confusions, scorn of creatures, disgraces, loss of reputation, and persecution on the part of God, of men, and of demons, and this without specifying anything in particular about the means that he must use. For the soul never imagines them such as they are, and if he proposed them to it and it could understand them, it would never consent to them. What does God do? He asks for the free will that he has given to it, which is the only thing that the soul can sacrifice as belonging to itself. It makes a sacrifice to him of all that it is, so that he may make of it and in it all that he pleases for time and eternity, without any reserve. This happens in an instant, without the mind working through any of it. But from the beginning of the path of faith the soul bears this innate disposition, that if its eternal loss caused an instant more glory for God than its salvation, it would prefer its damnation to its salvation, and this viewed from the side of the glory of God. But the soul understands that it would be unhappy without sin to glorify its God.

[5.] It makes then a sacrifice of everything that it is, so that he may make of it and in it all that will please him. It feels that the same God who asks for a general consent to pains causes this consent to be given. One gives it as soon as the thing is proposed, and when the sacrifice is sweet and gentle, the exercises that follow it are infinitely cruel, because the soul absolutely forgets the sacrifice that it has made to its God and no longer remembers anything but its misery. Its clouded mind, its hardened and rebellious will, and its pain are inexplicable torments for it.

There are others God causes to make this sacrifice of all of themselves (although it is in general and without any more knowledge of the means than the first) with such strange pains that one can say that it is a mortal agony. The bones are broken, and one suffers a pain that goes beyond imagination in giving oneself up to God. These here suffer less in these trials, and the pain of consent was a good purification for them. But notice that this sacrifice envisages nothing specific other than extreme pain when it anticipates the trial or the purification.

[6.] It is the same with the sacrifice that happens in the trial because then the soul is entirely plunged not only into pain, but also into the experience of its misery, into a feeling of reprobation that is such that the soul roars, if one can say as much. Then, through despair, it makes the sacrifice of eternity, which seems to escape from it in spite of itself. In the first sacrifice the soul only dreams of its trouble and of its pain or of the glory of God, but in this last one it seems that it has lost God, and that it has lost him by its fault, and that this loss is the cause of all miseries. It suffers, in the beginning, from rages and painful despairs; the fear of offending God makes it desire, by anticipation, a hell that it cannot avoid. This violence ceases at the end of the trials, and it is like a person who can no longer cry because she no longer has the strength.

And the pain is more terrible because its violent suffering was a support. But when mortal illnesses arise in this state, in which one believes oneself two fingers away from the real hell by death—for this appears in all its horror—without finding either refuge or means of assuring one's eternity, and heaven seems of brass (I know this from having felt it), then the soul sacrifices itself to God very truly for its eternity, but with agonies worse than hell itself. It sees that all its desire was to please God, and that it is going to displease him for an eternity. However, a certain depth remains for it, which says, but without relieving it, "I have a Savior who lives eternally, and the more my salvation is lost in me and for me, the more it is assured in him and through him," but this only lasts a few moments. What is astonishing it that in this state the soul is so afflicted and so tormented by the experience of its miseries and of the fear of unknowingly offending God that it is happy to die, although its loss might appear certain to it, so as to leave this state and no longer run the risk of offending God, because it believes itself to offend him, although this is not at all the case. Its folly is such and its pain so excessive that it does not consider that by living it can convert itself, and that by dying it loses itself—not at all—because it imagines that there is no more conversion for it. The reason for this is that, never being diverted by a single self-regard or a single consent, its will remaining attached to God and not turning away from him, it no longer finds this will in order to perform acts of pain, of detestation, and the rest; this is what causes it the most pain.

[7.] What is still surprising is that there are souls in whom all these pains are only spiritual, and these are the ones that are the most terrible. To these the body is cold, although the soul sees itself in the will for all evils and in the impossibility of committing them, and these are the ones that suffer the most. If I could say how I felt this strange pain and, with it, the disposition of the body being married but without any correspondence to marriage and without betraying anything about this, one would see well what this pain really is. I call it spiritual hell because the soul believes itself to have the will for all evils without being able to commit a single one of them and without correspondence to the body. Others suffer less in the spirit, and in all ways, and feel very great weaknesses in the body. But I have written so much about this that there is no more to say about it.

[8.] However, I will further add, to respond to the objection of M. de Meaux touching on the sacrifice of purity, that this proposition can never be as he supposed it in anticipation. For the trial precedes the sacrifice. God permits virgins (and it is these to whom this happens most ordinarily) to enter into trials that are all the greater as they are all the more attached to their purity. Seeing that God tries them either by demons in a known manner or by temptations that appear natural to them, it is such a great pain for them that hell without these pains would be a relief for them. Then, they make a sacrifice to God through this same purity that they have preserved to please him with the attachment. But they do it with agonies of death, not that they consent to a single sin—they are more distanced from it than ever—but they bear what they cannot prevent with a resignation and sacrifice of their whole selves. I beg that attention be paid to what these souls so tried by God suffer by inexplicable torments and to the fact that they do not permit themselves a single satisfaction, which would even be impossible to find, while these other miserable ones who give themselves over to all sins suffer no pain, giving their senses what they desire and living in unrestrained debauchery.

It is through people of this character that the persecution brought against me has begun. I have said elsewhere that they were going from confessor to confessor, accusing themselves as if converted from all the horrors of Quietism, and, as they supposed that

I shared in their same feelings, they caused all the indignation of these people to fall upon me, while giving themselves the merit of a true conversion. This is what caused them not only to be left alone while I was ripped apart and persecuted in the strangest way, but they were canonized, so to speak, and left free to spread all the poison of their bad principles, based only on a terrible debauchery without limit. O my God, you see it and suffer for it! I have done all that was possible for me to withdraw a few of them from this unhappy state when providence put me in reach of doing so. I would do it again even if, to withdraw a single one, it must cost me persecution.

[9.] I would notice every day, from what would come back to me from M. de Meaux, that he was becoming more and more distant, and what was worst for the cause in question was that he was becoming set in his ideas, because this fixation established a nearly insurmountable obstacle to the light of truth. What clarifications had I not given during the first conference about requests, desires, and other acts? But nothing penetrated because he wanted to condemn, and I learned from Monsieur de Chevreuse that he still repeated over again those same objections. How not to understand that the perceived desire, being an act and an operation of the self, must die with the other acts, or rather, must pass into God in order no longer to have desires other than those that God gives—and that since one no longer takes up one's own will, one also no longer takes up one's own desires? This does not prevent God from causing one to desire and to will to do what pleases him, and he who makes the soul can move it to desire, although it no longer has desires of its own. For if it had desires of its own, this would be a subsistence of the self and a fixation. But the author who writes of the essential will[43] says all that can be said about this, along with Saint Francis de Sales on the will,[44] for the same reasoning will apply to both. It is that this is neither death nor a loss of desires or of will, but a flowing of these same desires and of this same will into God, for the soul transports all that it possesses with it. When it is in itself, it desires and wills in its own manner; when it has passed into God, it wants and desires in the manner of God. If one does not admit the flowing of the desires into God, one must not admit either any loss of the operation of the self, or of any act of the self or of any will; one is so attached to the other that they are indivisible. In the same way that one no longer resumes one's operations at any time after having left them—as one no longer returns to the womb of one's mother after having left it—in that same way one also no longer resumes one's own desires. But in the same way that one does not leave one's own operations in order to become useless, but in order to let God operate, and operate oneself with his movement, so one lets one's desires flow into God only in order to desire according to his movement and to will through his will. We cannot condemn the one without condemning the other because it is a necessary sequence. After all, I am not the only one who speaks of the loss of the sense of self. If it is condemned in me, the channel is nothing in itself. God will write it in the spirit and in the heart of whom he pleases. This fixation of M. de Meaux caused me infinite pain because, although I might be able clarify from the outside, it is for God to stir the inside, but how can he do this if one remains shut up, even if only by a hair?

[10.] I learned further that one of the great complaints of M. de Meaux was that I would praise myself and was horribly presumptuous. I would willingly ask who is more humble, he who speaks words of humility about himself and says nothing to his advantage (ordinarily these are praised by others and would have trouble tolerating that they might be thought bad were they to say it of themselves) or else simply to say good and bad of ourselves and to take no trouble about whether everyone thinks good or bad of us and whether one describes us in a good or bad way—he who humbles himself or he who is very happy to be humiliated? As for me, I say what I know is good in me because it belongs to my Master, but I feel no pain that none of it might be believed, that I might be decried in the sermon, that I might be libeled in the papers! This does no more to me than when I praise myself, and since I do not correct my apparent pride because I am not ashamed of it, I am also not embarrassed by public outcry, because I think worse of myself than all others might.

Guyon is moved to another place of internment, the Visitation Convent of Saint-Marie in Meaux, where, in spite of her bad public reputation, she is esteemed by the superior and the sisters. Bossuet's behavior shocks the women of the convent. He tricks Guyon with the promise of papers that allow for her release, which he ultimately tries to take back from her. She is released, nonetheless, and Madame de Maintenon is displeased.

3.19—Surprising Blackmail

[6.] Since I had been at Meaux for six months, when I was only engaged to spend three, and moreover my health was very bad, I asked M. de Meaux if he was happy and if he desired anything else of me. He said no. I told him that I would be leaving then, since I had to go to Bourbon. I asked him if he would find it acceptable for me to finish my days with these good nuns because they loved me, and I loved them as well, although the air was very bad for me there. He was very happy with this and told me that it would always be a pleasure to receive me in the future and that the nuns were very happy and very edified by me and that, as for him, he was returning to Paris. I told him that my daughter or some of my friends' ladies-in-waiting would come to fetch me. He turned toward the mother superior and said to her, "My mother, I ask you to receive warmly those who come fetch Madam, either her daughter or those ladies of her friends, to lodge them and have them sleep in your house and to keep them as long as they would like."[45] The dependence of these religious women of Saint Marie on their bishop and their exactitude in following to the letter all that he orders them to do, without overlooking the smallest thing, is well enough known. Two ladies then came to fetch me. They arrived for dinner, they dined, they ate supper, and they went to bed; they dined again the next day at the convent. Then, around three o'clock, we left.

[7.] Hardly had I arrived when M. de Meaux regretted letting me leave his diocese. What made him change, as was learned later, is that, having reported to Madame de Maintenon the terms on which this affair ended, she indicated to him that she was hardly happy with the attestation that he had given me, that this concluded nothing and would even cause an effect contrary to what was proposed, which was to disabuse the people who were disposed in my favor.

He believed then that by losing me, he lost all the hope with which he had flattered himself. He wrote me again to ask me to return to his diocese, and at the same time I received a letter from the mother superior that he was more resolved than ever to torment me and that, whatever desire she had to see me again, she was obligated to have me know that M. de Meaux's feelings conformed to what I knew. What I knew was that he was establishing a high fortune on my persecution, and since he wanted persecution for a person well above me,[46] he believed that by my eluding him, everything was eluding him. Mother Le Picard, in sending me the letter of which I just spoke, sent me a new attestation from M. de Meaux, so different from the first, which he wanted me to send back to him, that I judged that henceforth I could not hope for any justice from this prelate. In effect, from the time he returned from Paris and he reported to the people who were attacking the terms that he established with me, they made him feel strongly that they were not happy with his interrogation and that they were expecting a different result from it in the future than the one which a justification, such as the attestation that he had given me, could cause for me. He resolved, whatever the cost, to withdraw it and to substitute another in its place. He had written to her to withdraw this first attestation and to give me the latter. And if I had left Meaux, she was to send it to me at once so that he might have back the first one that he had given me. The mother, who clearly saw from all the past treatment what I was going to be exposed to if I fell once more into the hands of M. de Meaux, let me know about it through her letter so that I would avoid all discussion with him in the future. However, to keep up the appearance of cordial relations with him, from which I had never turned away, I responded to the mother superior. Without complaining about a trial so bizarre and so full of injustice, I said that I had passed along what M. de Meaux was requesting into the hands of my family, and that after all that had happened, they had such great interest in a document of this nature, which proved my justification, that it was likely that they would not want to give it up. This was all the more the case since what she sent me on behalf of the prelate not only did not serve as my justification, but also seemed to support all that was said against me, not saying anything contrary to it.

[8.] Here is a copy of the said first attestation:

We, Bishop of Meaux, certify to whom it may concern that, by means of the declarations and submissions of Madame Guyon, which we have in our possession, written by her hand, and the prohibitions accepted by her with submission, of writing, teaching, and preaching dogma in the church, or of distributing her printed books or manuscripts or of leading souls in the ways of contemplative prayer or otherwise, together with the good testimony that has been provided to us during the six months that she has spent in our diocese and in the monastery of Saint Marie, we remain satisfied by her conduct and have continued to allow her to take the holy sacraments in which we have found her. We declare, beyond what we have indicated, that we have not found her implicated in any way in the abominations of Molinos or others who are condemned elsewhere, nor have we intended to imply her in the mention that has been made of them by us in the ordinance of April 16, 1695. Given at Meaux, July 1, 1695.

J. Bénigne, B. of Meaux (by Monsignor Ledieu).

Here is a copy of the second:

We, the Bishop of Meaux, have received the present submissions and declarations of the said Lady G(uyon), as well as that of April 15, 1695, and that of July 1 of the same year, and have given her written accounts of it in order to validate the judgment, declaring that she has always received and is receiving without objection the blessed sacraments in which we have found her, as her submission and sincere obedience, both before and since the time that she has been in our diocese, along with the authentic declaration of her faith and the testimony that has been given to us regarding her good conduct for the six months that she has been in the aforementioned monastery, required it. We have enjoined her to make, at suitable times, the requests and the other acts that we have noted in the said articled signed by her, as essential to piety and expressly commanded by God, without which no faithful person could dispense under the pretext of other acts supposedly more perfect or eminent, or whatever other pretext it might be, and we, as a diocesan bishop and by virtue of the obedience that she has voluntarily promised above, have repeatedly prohibited her to write, teach, or preach dogma in the church, or to distribute her printed books or manuscripts, or to lead souls in the ways of contemplative prayer or otherwise, to which she has submitted once more, declaring to us that she would do the said acts. Given at Meaux, the day and year mentioned above.

J. Bénigne, Bishop of Meaux.

[9.] One can judge, by the persistence of M. de Meaux and by the hopes that he had conceived, the effect that such a refusal produced in him. He gave sermons about how I had climbed the walls of the convent to escape. Besides the fact that I climb very badly, all the nuns there were witnesses to the contrary. This has spread so quickly, however, that a lot of people still believe it. A trial of this nature no longer permitted me to put my trust in M. de Meaux's discretion, and since I was made to understand that they were going to push things to the most violent ends, I believed that I needed to leave all that could happen up to God and, however, to take prudent measures to avoid the effects of the threats that were made to me on all fronts. I had several places where I could withdraw, but I did not want to accept any of them in order not to embarrass anyone or to compromise my friends and family, to whom my escape could have been attributed. I made the resolution not to leave Paris, to stay there at some remote place with my ladies, who were very discreet and who generally shielded me from public view. I stayed in this way for five or six months. I spent the days alone, reading, praying to God, working. But at the end of 1695 I was arrested, as sick as I was, and taken to Vincennes. I was kept for three days sequestered with Desgrez,[47] who had arrested me, because the king, full of justice and kindness, did not want to consent to my being put in prison, saying several times that a convent would suffice. They deceived his justice with the strongest calumnies and painted me in his eyes with colors so black as even to make him ashamed of his kindness and his equity, so that he finally consented to having me placed in Vincennes.

3.20—Why Have You Abandoned Me?

[1.] I will not talk about my long persecution here, which made such a stir, by a ten-year stay in all kinds of prisons and an exile almost as long, which is not yet over, and by trials, calumnies, and all imaginable sorts of suffering. There are details too abominable, on the part of various people, which charity makes me cover up, and it is in this sense that *charity covers a multitude of sins* (1 Pet 4:8), and on the part of others who, being seduced by ill-intentioned people, are respectable to me for their piety and for other reasons, although they might show too bitter a zeal for things about which they really do not know. I am keeping quiet for some of these people out of respect and for some of the others out of charity. What I can say is that, of a long series of crosses, of which my life has been full, it can be judged that the greatest were reserved for the end, and that God, who has not rejected me, by effect of his kindness, took care not to leave the end of my life without a greater conformity to Jesus Christ. He was arraigned before all kinds of courts; he accorded me the grace to undergo the same. He suffered the utmost outrages without complaint; he accorded me the mercy of treating them the same way. How could I do otherwise with the vision he gave me of his love and his goodness? In my resemblance to Jesus Christ, I considered as favors what the world considered as strange persecutions. The peace and the joy from within prevented me from seeing those who otherwise would be the most violent persecutors other than as the instruments of the justice of my God, which was always so adorable and so amiable. I was thus in prison as in a place of delights and of refreshment, this general deprivation of all creatures giving me more of a place to be alone with God, and the deprivation of things that seem most necessary making me taste an exterior poverty that I would not have tasted otherwise.

Thus, I considered all these apparently great evils, this disgrace so universal, as the greatest of all things. It seemed to me that it was the work of the hand of God, who wanted to cover his tabernacle with the skin of beasts to hide it from the eyes of those to whom he did not want to show it.

[2.] I have borne mortal sickness, overwhelming illnesses, and pain with no relief. God, not being content with all of this, abandoned me for several months on the inside to the greatest desolation, such as I can only express with these words alone: *My God, my God, why have you abandoned me?* (Mark 15:34; Matt 27:46; Ps 22:1). It was during this time that I was led to take God's side against myself and to practice all the austerities that I could advise myself to undertake. Seeing God and all creatures against me, I was elated to take their side against myself. How could I complain about what I have suffered with a love so detached from all self-interest? Should I be interested for myself presently, after having made such a complete sacrifice of this me and of all that concerns it? I thus prefer to consecrate all these sufferings through silence. If God permitted that one day, for his glory, he might want to make some of it known, I would adore his judgments, but as for me, my side is taken in what concerns me personally.

[3.] Regarding contemplative prayer, I must always attest to the truth of its ways. I have defended my innocence with enough firmness and truth to leave no doubt in the public mind that the calumnies that are made about people whose contemplative prayer is true and whose love is sincere are false and their speeches rash and contrary to all sorts of truth and justice. The stronger the calumny, the more happy and content is the heart that loves God and has a conscience that reproaches it with nothing. It seems that persecution and calumny are weights that push the soul further into God and make it taste inestimable happiness. What does it matter to it that all creatures are raging against it, when it is all alone with its God, and it gives him solid proof of its love? For when God bestows good things upon us, it is he who gives us the marks of his own love, but when we suffer what is one thousand times more terrible than death, we give him proof of the fidelity of ours. Thus, since there is no other way to demonstrate to God that we love him except by submitting to the most terrible pains for his love, we are infinitely indebted to him when he gives us the means.

[4.] But maybe there will be surprise that, not wanting to write any detail of the greatest and strongest crosses of my life, I have written about those that are a good bit less so. Some reasons brought me to this. I believed it necessary to touch on some of the crosses of my youth to show the crucifying guidance that God has always had for me. Regarding the other times that concern a more advanced state of my life, since the calumnies did not concern me alone, I believed myself to be obligated as a matter of conscience to present the details of certain facts to show not only their falsity, but also the conduct of those by whom they were caused, who are the true authors of these persecutions, of which I was only an accidental object, particularly in recent times. For, truly, I was persecuted in this way to implicate people of great merit whom they found outside of their grasp and only vulnerable to attack when their affairs were mixed up with mine. I thought that I should make understood some of the details relating to these sorts of facts, and all the more so because, it being a question of my faith for which they wanted to make me suspect, it seemed important to me to let it be known at the same time how I have always been far from the sentiments that they wanted to ascribe to me. I believed it to be my duty to religion, to piety, to my friends, to my family, and to myself. But as for the bad personal treatments, I believed it necessary to sacrifice them and sanctify them through a profound silence, as I have remarked.[48]

3.21—Final Pages, the Simple and Invariable State

[1.] Since my life has always been consecrated to the cross, I was no sooner released from prison, with the spirit starting to breathe again, than my body was overcome with all sorts of infirmities after so many trials, and I was continually sick with illnesses that often brought me close to death.

In these last times I am only able to speak about my dispositions a little bit or not at all, meaning that my state became simple and invariable.

When I speak here of a fixed and permanent state, as in my other writings,[49] I do not speak of an immutable state that one cannot diminish. I call it permanent and fixed in relation to the states that have preceded it, which are full of vicissitudes and variations. When I speak of the mystical incarnation, I believe that this is what Saint Paul calls the knowledge of Jesus Christ in us (Phil 3:8). All the states of death, of burial, of resurrection, and of the destruction of the old self in order to be made a new creature in Jesus Christ, are also described by Saint Paul (see Rom 6:6; 2 Cor 5:17). I hope that this might serve the little and humble souls that can know from their experience that the states described are true. And I hope that those who do not want to let themselves be guided, governed, and led by Jesus Christ might let them be what they are and might not curse them, and, as Saint Jude says, that they might not blaspheme against mysteries that they do not understand (Jude 1:10).

The base[50] of this state is a profound annihilation, finding nothing nameable in me. All I know is that God is infinitely holy, just, good, and happy; that he holds in himself all that is good, and in me all miseries. I do not see anything below me or anything more disgraceful than me. I recognize that God has accorded me graces capable of saving a world, and that maybe I have repaid everything with ingratitude. I say "maybe" because nothing subsists in me, neither good nor bad. Good is in God; I have only nothingness for a share. What can I say of a state that is always the same, without consideration or variation? For dryness, if I have any of it, is equal to the most satisfying state for me. All is lost in the immensity, and I can neither desire nor think. If one believes some good of me, one is mistaken and wrongs God. All good is in him and for him. If I could have one satisfaction, it would be from what he is and what he will be forever. If he saves me, this would be gratuitous because I have neither merit nor dignity.

[2.] I am astonished that people have some confidence in this nothingness. I have said as much. However, I respond to what is asked of me without embarrassment about whether I respond well or poorly. If I speak poorly, I am not at all surprised by it; if I speak well, I have no intention of attributing it to myself. I go without going, without considerations, without knowing where I am going. I want neither to go nor to stop. Desire and instincts have disappeared; poverty and nakedness are my lot. I have neither confidence nor mistrust, finally Nothing, Nothing. As for the little bit I am made to think for myself, I believe myself to mislead everyone, and I do not know how I mislead them or what I do to mislead them. There are times when I would desire, at the risk of a thousand lives, that God might be known and loved. I love the church; all that hurts it, hurts me. I fear all that is contrary to it, but I cannot give a name to this fear. It is like a child at the breast who, without discerning monsters, turns away from them. I do not look for anything, but I am immediately given very strong expressions and words. But if I wanted to have them, they would escape me, and if I wanted to repeat them, it would be the same. When I have something to say and I am interrupted, everything is lost. I am then like a child from whom an apple has been taken without his having noticed it. He looks for it and no longer finds it. I am vexed for a moment by what has been taken from me, but I forget it right away.

[4.] Nothing is greater than God; nothing is smaller than me. He is rich; I am very poor, and I lack nothing. I have no sense of need about anything. Death, life, it is all the same to me. Eternity, time, all is eternity, all is God. God is Love, and Love is God, and all in God and for God. You might as soon draw light from darkness as something from this nothing; it is a chaos without confusion. All forms are outside of the nothing, and the nothing admits none of them. Thoughts only pass; nothing stops; I can say nothing as a command. When what I say or write has passed, I no longer remember it. It is as if from another person to me. I can want neither justification nor esteem. If God wants one or the other, he will do as he wishes; it does not matter to me. Let him glorify himself through my destruction or in reestablishing my reputation; either one or the other is equal on the scale.

[5.] I do not want to mislead you all or not to mislead you. It is for God to enlighten you and to make you reject or incline toward this nothing, which is not leaving its place. It is an empty beacon. Can someone light a torch there? Is it a false light that could lead to the precipice? I do not know anything about it; God knows it. This is not my business; it is up to you to make this discernment. There is nothing but to extinguish the false light. The torch will never light itself alone if God does not light it. I beg God to enlighten you always to do only his will, because when you scorn me, you do me justice, and I can find nothing to say about it. Here is what I would say about this nothing—that I would like, if I could desire, that it should be forgotten forever. If the *Life* was not written, it would run a great risk of never being written; however, I would rewrite it at the slightest signal, without knowing why or what I wanted to say. O my children, open your eyes to the light of truth! *Amen.*

[1.] I will say again here that God keeps me in extreme simplicity, righteousness of heart, and openness, such that I only notice these things on certain occasions, because without an occasion that stirs this up, I see nothing.

[3.] If someone said something to my advantage, I would be surprised, finding nothing in me. If someone blames me, I know nothing except that I am wretchedness itself, but I do not see where the blame is. I believe it without seeing it, and everything disappears. If someone made me reflect on myself, I would not recognize any good there. I see all good in God. I know that he is the principle of everything and that without him I am only a beast. He gives me a free air and makes me speak to people, not according to my dispositions, but according to what they are, giving me even a natural intelligence with those who have this—and that by an air so free that they are happy about it. There are certain devotees whose language is a babbling to me. I do not fear the traps that they set for me. I do not take any precautions, and everything goes well. Sometimes I am told: "Be careful of what you say to so-and-so!" I forget this immediately, and I cannot be careful. Sometimes I am told: "You have said such-and-such a thing; these people here might interpret it wrongly; you are too simple." I believe this, but I can only be simple. O carnal prudence, how opposed I find you to the simplicity of Jesus Christ! I leave you to your partisans. As for me, my prudence and my wisdom is Jesus, simple and small. And even if I would be queen by changing my conduct, I could not do it. Even if my simplicity might cause me all the pain in the world, I could not leave it.

I beg those who will read this not to be indisposed against the people who, through a zeal perhaps too bitter, have pushed things so far against a woman, and a woman so submitted, because, as

Tauler says: "*God, wanting to purify a soul through sufferings, would throw an infinite number of holy people into darkness and blindness for a time, so that they might prepare this chosen vessel through the reckless and unfavorable judgments that they bear against the soul in this state of ignorance. But finally, after having purified this vessel, he would (sooner or later) lift the blindfold from their eyes, not treating harshly any fault they might have committed through a hidden guidance of his admirable providence. I say, further, that God would rather send an angel from heaven to prepare this chosen vessel by tribulations than to leave it stained and impure.*"[51]

December 1709

(End of *The Life*)

NOTES

Introduction

1. Marie-Louise Gondal, *Madame Guyon (1648–1717): Un nouveau visage* (Paris: Beauchesne, 1989), 14.

2. Pierre Goubert, *Louis XIV and Twenty Million Frenchmen*, trans. Anne Carter (New York: Random House, Vintage Books, 1970), 21.

3. Pope Innocent XII summarized his view of the conflict with an aphorism that became popular: "The Archbishop of Cambrai has erred through excess in the love of God; the Bishop of Meaux has sinned through a lack of love for his neighbor."

4. For a development of this argument, see Michel de Certeau, *The Writing of History*, trans. Tom Conley (New York: Columbia University Press, 1988), 133. A thorough treatment of the identification of sin with crime under Louis XIV is presented in Philip F. Riley, *A Lust for Virtue: Louis XIV's Attack on Sin in Seventeenth-Century France* (Westport, CT: Greenwood Press, 2001).

5. For a thorough analysis of the causes and implications of this phenomenon, see De Certeau, *Writing of History*, Part 2, chaps. 3 and 4.

6. For thorough treatment of Guyon's importance to feminist scholars, see Gondal, *Madame Guyon*; Marie-Florine Bruneau, *Women Mystics Confront the Modern World: Marie De L'Incarnation (1599–1672) and Madame Guyon (1648–1717)* (Albany: SUNY, 1998); and Françoise Mallet-Joris, *Jeanne Guyon* (Paris: Flammarion, 1978).

7. Bruneau, *Women Mystics*, 141.

8. Elizabeth C. Goldsmith, *Publishing Women's Life Stories in France, 1647–1720: From Voice to Print* (Burlington: Ashgate, 2001), 87.

9. Mallet-Joris, *Jeanne Guyon*, 218.

10. Michel de Certeau, *The Mystic Fable*, Vol. 1, *The Sixteenth and Seventeenth Centuries*, trans. Michael B. Smith (Chicago: University of Chicago Press, 1992), ix–x. We follow Smith's usage here, reserving

the term *mystics* (in italics) for the name of the new science described by de Certeau. In accord with Bernard McGinn's definition, the term 'mystics' (without italics) refers more broadly, here, to people participating in "that part of [Christian] belief and practice that concerns the preparation for, the consciousness of, and the reaction to what can be described as the immediate or direct presence of God" (*The Foundations of Mysticism: Origins to the Fifth Century* [New York: Crossroad, 1991], xvii).

11. De Certeau, *The Mystic Fable*, 1:16, his italics.

12. Ibid., 76–77.

13. For a broad historical survey of mysticism in this period, see Louis Cognet, *Post-Reformation Spirituality*, trans. P. Hepburne Scott (New York: Hawthorne Books, 1959), 9–16.

14. Ibid., 16.

15. Ibid. For additional resources, see also William M. Thompson, ed., *Bérulle and the French School*, trans. Lowell M. Glendon (Mahwah, NJ: Paulist Press, 1989); and Regis J. Armstrong and Ignatius C. Brady, *Francis De Sales, Jane De Chantal: Letters of Spiritual Direction* (Mahwah, NJ: Paulist Press, 1988).

16. Louis Cognet, "Ecclesiastical Life in France," in *History of the Church 6: The Church in the Age of Absolutism and Enlightenment*, ed. Hubert Jedin and John Dolan, trans. Gunther J. Holst (New York: Crossroad, 1981), 93–101.

17. De Certeau, *Mystic Fable*, 132.

18. Ibid., 114–15.

19. Guyon, *Life*, 3.14.13.

20. Jacques Bénigne Bossuet, *Instruction sur les états d'oraison. Oeuvres complètes de Bossuet*, vol. 18, ed. F. Lachat (Paris: Libairie de Louis Vivès, 1862–64), 403.

21. Guyon, *Short and Easy Method*, 8.1.

22. Guyon, *Life*, 2.23.

23. Guyon, *Short and Easy Method*, Preface.

24. Jeanne Guyon, *Madame Guyon et Fénelon: La Correspondance secrète, avec un choix de poésies spirituelles*, édition préparée par Benjamin Perrot (Paris: Dervy-Livres, 1982), Letter 41. The theme of "suppleness" is particularly prominent in several of her letters to Fénelon.

25. Guyon, *Short and Easy Method*, Preface.

26. Guyon, *Life*, 2.21.6.

27. On the possibility of illusion in the spiritual life and the need for discernment, see, for example, Guyon, *Correspondance secrète*, Letter 56.

28. See, for example, Guyon, *Short and Easy Method*, Preface; and Guyon, *Life*, 3.13.2.

29. Bruneau, *Women Mystics*, 139–40.

30. Nicholas Paige, *Being Interior: Autobiography and the Contradictions of Modernity in Seventeenth-Century France* (Philadelphia: University of Pennsylvania Press, 2001), 72.

31. Louis Cognet, "Le Coeur chez les spirituels du XVIIe siècle," in *Dictionnaire de spiritualité ascétique et mystique*, ed. Marcel Viller (Paris: Beauchesne, 1937–94), 2302, 2305, quoted in Paige, *Being Interior*, 72.

32. This typology of the soul's powers is not original to Guyon, and its Christian influence can be traced to Saint Augustine's *De Trinitate*. It was widely current in the sixteenth and seventeenth centuries due to its use in popular confession manuals.

33. Guyon, *Short and Easy Method*, 12.1.

34. Ibid., 2.4.

35. Ibid., 4.1–2.

36. Ibid., 6.2.

37. Ibid., 11.

38. Ibid., 12.1.

39. Ibid., 12.5.

40. Guyon, *Correspondance secrète*, Letters 124 and 132.

41. Guyon, *Life*, 2.8.5.

42. Ibid., 2.4.8.

43. Guyon, *Commentary on the Song of Songs*, 1.1.

44. Guyon, *Life*, 1.10.9–12.

45. Ibid., 1.9.

46. Ibid., 1.11.5.

47. Guyon, *Correspondance secrète*, Letter 96.

48. Guyon, *Short and Easy Method*, 17.1.

49. Ibid., 9.1.

50. Guyon, *Correspondance secrète*, Letter 56.

51. Guyon, *Life*, 3.17.3.

52. Ibid., 3.17.6.

53. Guyon, *Short and Easy Method*, 22.2, 22.5.

54. Guyon, *Commentary on the Song of Songs*, 8.4.

55. See Henri Bourgeois, "Passivité et activité dans le discours et l'expérience de madame Guyon," in *Madame Guyon*, ed. J. Beaude et al., 235–67 (Grenoble: Jérôme Millon, 1997). Bourgeois demonstrates Guyon's emphasis on this theme when Guyon claims to write with

direct divine inspiration and to act in direct service of God's apostolic purposes, and in her typology of faith.

56. Guyon, *Life*, 3.10.1.

57. Ibid., 2.22.5.

58. Ibid., 3.7.

59. Ibid., 3.10.1.

60. See, for example, Cognet, *Post-Reformation Spirituality*, 133–35.

61. Quoted in Mallet-Joris, *Jeanne Guyon*, 489.

62. L.-A. Bonnel, *Sur la Controverse de Bossuet et de Fénelon sur le Quiétisme* (Macon: Imprimerie de Dejussieu, 1850), xl–xli.

63. Bruneau, *Women Mystics*, 136.

64. Ronald Knox, *Enthusiasm: A Chapter in the History of Religion with Special Reference to the Seventeenth and Eighteenth Centuries* (New York: Oxford University Press, 1961), 235.

65. Patricia Ward, "Madame Guyon and Experiential Theology in America," *The American Society of Church History* 67, no. 3 (September 1998): 484. For a more thorough treatment of Guyon's reception history among American evangelical and charismatic Christians, see Patricia Ward, *Experimental Theology in America: Madame Guyon, Fénelon, and Their Readers* (Waco, TX: Baylor University Press, 2009).

66. Harris, J. Rendel, *The Influence of Quietism on the Society of Friends*, A Lecture delivered at Bryn Mawr College on April 30, 1900 (Philadelphia: Leeds Press, 1900), 6.

67. Gene Edwards, "Introduction," *Spiritual Torrents*, by Jeanne Guyon (Jacksonville, FL: Seedsowers, 1989), no pagination.

68. Donna Arthur, "Preface," *Experiencing God Through Prayer*, by Jeanne Guyon (Springdale, PA: Whitaker House, 1984), 5.

69. E. J., "Introduction," *Autobiography of Madame Guyon in Two Parts*, by Jeanne Guyon (Chicago: Moody Press, 1917, reprinted 1960), 6.

70. Edwards, "Introduction," no pagination.

71. Jeanne Guyon, *Experiencing the Depths of Jesus Christ*, ed. Gene Edwards (Sargent, GA: Seedsowers, 1975); and Jeanne Guyon, *Experiencing God Through Prayer*, ed. and rev. Donna Arthur (Springdale, PA: Whitaker House, 1984).

72. Guyon, *Short and Easy Method*, Preface.

73. Guyon, *Short and Easy Method*, 23.6. As Louis Cognet points out, the phrase "prayer of the heart" was popularized by the Dominican Alexander Piny, who wrote a book with that title in 1683 (Cognet, *Post-Reformation Spirituality*, 128).

74. Bruneau, *Women Mystics*, 138.
75. Guyon, *Life*, 1.10.9.
76. Bruneau, *Women Mystics*, 176–81.
77. Paige, *Being Interior*, 155–77.

A Short and Easy Method of Prayer

1. From Saint Augustine, Sermon 7 on the First Epistle of John, paragraph 8.

2. The notion of "the simple act" in this passage and in the following paragraph reflects Guyon's rejection of the complete passivity of the advanced soul, a charge frequently leveled against Quietism. The "simple act" is a voluntary, though effortless and unselfconscious, turning of one's attention toward God. Unlike other types of act, the "simple act" can be extended in duration. Further discussion of this controversial idea is presented in the Introduction.

3. The metaphors of uniformity and absorption are probably meant here to communicate a likeness between the spiritually advanced soul and God and a union between the two without the complete loss of individual human identity. Some of Guyon's critics, however, uncharitably interpreted her language as advocacy of a complete deiformity of the person in the highest spiritual state, amounting to identity with God. Such claims had been controversial in mystical writing since the condemnation of Meister Eckhart in the papal bull *In Agro Dominico* in 1329.

Commentary on the Song of Songs

1. The verse numbers in Guyon's commentary on the first chapter of the *Song of Songs* are one less than the verse numbers in most contemporary translations of the Bible. Her 1:1 corresponds to 1:2 in the NRSV, for example, and so on for the rest of Chapter 1. Her numbering corresponds to that of the NRSV starting in Chapter 2.

2. The use of this metaphor (mixing a drop of water into a barrel of wine) to illustrate contemplative union is frequent in the mystical tradition. See, most famously, Bernard of Clairvaux, *Loving God* 10.27–29.

3. In the commentary on 1:7.

4. The Douay-Rheims translation of verse 10 uses the word *seat*, while Guyon's French translation of the verse uses *appui* for the same

word, which we translate here as "support." The subsequent use of the word *seat* translates the French word *siège*.

5. Guyon uses the word *Époux* here, which would normally be translated "Bridegroom," but the context suggests that she must be referring to the Bride.

6. This probably refers to the discussion of the hidden character of the grace in these souls above. See the commentary on 6:6.

Life

1. Tronc indicates this is at the request of Father La Combe (Jeanne-Marie Guyon. *La Vie par elle-même et autres écrits biographiques.* Édition critique avec introduction et notes par Dominique Tronc. Étude littéraire par Andrée Villard. Sources classiques, vol. 29 [Paris: Champion, 2001], 103). All subsequent references to this critical edition of the *Life* will be cited as "Tronc."

2. Following the notation style in Tronc, we begin and end the principal passages that are crossed out or *absent* in the Oxford manuscript with / and //.

3. Perhaps a reference to 1 Cor 2:7 ff.

4. Marie Fouquet, duchess of Charost, was the only daughter of Finance Minister Fouquet under Louis XIV. When her father was disgraced and imprisoned for the rest of his life by the king, the duchess was invited by Guyon's father to come live with his family.

5. This is the cousin mentioned above, Philippe de Chamesson-Foissy.

6. Geneviève Granger was the mother superior at the Benedictine convent at Montargis. She was born in 1600 and died while still ministering to Guyon.

7. This is generally thought to be the Franciscan monk Archange Enguerrand.

8. A reference to Saint Augustine, *Confessions*, 10.27.38.

9. A reference to Pseudo-Dionysius, the anonymous author of *Divine Names, Mystical Theology*, and several other works.

10. Ps 148:5: "He spoke and they were made."

11. François La Combe (1640–1715), who would become not only Guyon's spiritual director in the future but also a close friend.

12. Dominique, Guyon's half-brother and a member of the Barnabite order to which Father La Combe belonged.

13. Guyon uses the term *conduite* (translated throughout this volume as "leading" or "guidance") quite consistently as a spiritual term, suggesting the leading or guidance *of grace*.

14. About one and one-quarter miles.

15. There is a passage added at a later date in the *Life*, but these passages only explain in further detail the points already made. They are therefore not included in this translation.

16. Jacques Bertot (1622–81) became Guyon's spiritual director until his death, although in the last few years of his life he withheld support and guidance from Guyon. He was a friend of Jean de Bernières, a mystic primarily influenced by the French School and Benet de Canfield.

17. This passage refers to a correspondence between Guyon and La Combe, summarized toward the end of *Life* 1.27. She writes to tell him of her feeling of spiritual alienation. He asserts in reply that she remains under the influence of divine grace, though she does not realize it.

18. A prayer of remembrance in the canon of the mass.

19. Tronc notes that this is one of the inscriptions seen on Mount Carmel: "quando ya nolo queria tengolo todo sin querer" (Tronc, 448).

20. Guyon refers here to a request from the bishop of Geneva that she bind herself as superior of a convent in Gex. The request and her refusal are reported in *Life*, 2.6.

21. Ps 148:5. "For he spoke, and they were made."

22. There is no information about who this woman might be.

23. This friar is first introduced in *Life*, 2.18.1, which describes his friendship with Guyon and his status as one of her spiritual "true children."

24. "Crucify."

25. Augustine, *Confessions*, 9.10.24.

26. See *Life*, 2.8.11.

27. Ps 104:30, "Send your Spirit and you will renew the face of the earth."

28. Matt 27:50, "Yielded up his spirit."

29. John 19:30, "It is consummated."

30. This refers to François de Salignac de la Mothe-Fénelon (1651–1715), who was to be Guyon's friend and confidant for the rest of his life. He became the tutor of the duke of Bourgogne the next year, making him the second most important clergyman in France. He was then to fall into disgrace, along with Guyon, during the Quietist Affair.

31. About seven and one-half miles.

32. This also refers to Fénelon.

33. "You alone are holy."

34. Miguel de Molinos (1628–97), a Spanish priest, was condemned in Rome in 1687 for heresy in his teachings of pure love and abandonment to the Spirit, basic principles of Quietism.

35. Jacques-Bénigne Bossuet (1627–1704), archbishop of Meaux, led the long, official examination of Guyon's writings.

36. The longtime friend of Guyon and husband of finance minister Colbert's daughter, both of whom were part of the circle of mystics who were intimate friends of Guyon and who worked tirelessly to obtain her release during her years of imprisonment.

37. Phil 1:23. "I desire to be dissolved and be with Christ."

38. Tronc's critical edition includes several paragraphs at this point from the Oxford manuscript. The Poiret edition moves these paragraphs to the beginning of Chapter 14. For the sake of narrative clarity, we follow the Poiret edition here.

39. This refers to her request to God for spiritual children and her claim that Fénelon was the answer to that prayer, as described in *Life*, 3.10.1.

40. Saint John of the Cross, *Spiritual Canticle*, Stanza 7.

41. See *Life*, 3.10.1.

42. Monsieur de Châlons was a personal friend of Chevreuse, and Monsieur Tronson was a trusted clergyman who was involved in Guyon's interrogations until she was sent to the Bastille. He was thoughtful and prudent in his interrogations, and Guyon appreciated his presence.

43. Benet of Canfield, in his *Rule of Perfection*, Part 3.

44. See Francis de Sales, *Treatise on the Love of God*, Books 6–9.

45. This refers to Mother Le Picard, who was the superior at the Visitation Sainte Marie Convent in Meaux, where Guyon was confined.

46. Fénelon.

47. François Desgrez, a police lieutenant.

48. For narrative clarity, we have followed Tronc's choice in the critical edition of the *Life* and deleted the next three parts (the rest of 5 and the whole of 6 and 7), which belong chronologically to the fourth

part of the *Life*. Guyon repeats the first paragraph of Part 7 in 4.2 and the second paragraph in 4.6.

49. Compare Guyon, *Short and Easy Method*, Chapter 22, and *Correspondance secrète*, Letter 8.

50. *"Fond."*

51. Pseudo-Tauler, *Divine Institutions*, chap. 11.

SELECTED BIBLIOGRAPHY

Dominique Tronc provides a comprehensive, chronological listing of the various French editions of Guyon's primary texts in her 2001 critical edition of *La Vie par elle-même, et autres écrits biographiques.* Patricia Ward provides a comprehensive bibliography of English translations of Guyon's works in her 1995 essay, "Madame Guyon in America: An Annotated Bibliography." Here we list only the most important sources that we consulted in preparing our introduction and the translations.

Primary Sources

Guyon, Jeanne-Marie Bouvier de la Mothe. 1720, 1978. *Les Opuscules spirituels.* Edited by Jean Orcibal. New York: Olms.

———. 1790. *Les Justifications.* Paris: Librairies Associés.

———. 1962. *La Vie de Madame Guyon écrite par elle-même.* Les Cahiers de La Tour Saint-Jacques VI. Paris: Roudil.

———. 1982. *Madame Guyon et Fénelon: La Correspondance secrète, avec un choix de poésies spirituelles.* Édition préparée par Benjamin Perrot. Paris: Dervy-Livres.

———. 1992. "La Cantique des cantiques," in *Jeanne Guyon ou la pensée nue.* Edited with an introduction by Claude Morali. Grenoble: Jérôme Millon.

———. 1992. *Les torrents et Commentaire au Cantique des Cantiques de Solomon.* Edited by Claude Morali. Grenoble: Jérôme Millon.

———. 1992. *Récits de captivité, Inédit.* Texte établi, présenté et annoté par Marie-Louise Gondal. Grenoble: Jérôme Millon.

———. 1995. *Le Moyen court et d'autres récits: Une simplicité subversive.* Texte établi et présenté par Marie-Louise Gondal. Grenoble: Jérôme Millon.

———. 2001. *La Vie par elle-même, et autres écrits biographiques.* Édition critique avec introduction et notes par Dominique Tronc. Paris: Honoré Champion.

———. 2003. *Correspondance Tome 1: Direction spirituelle.* Éditon critique établie par Dominique Tronc. Paris: Honoré Champion.

———. 2004. *Correspondance Tome II: Années de combat.* Éditon critique établie par Dominique Tronc. Paris: Honoré Champion.

———. 2008. *Oeuvres mystiques.* Édition critique avec introduction et notes par Dominique Tronc. Paris: Honoré Champion.

English Translations

Bossuet, Jacques Bénigne. 1698. *Quakerism a-la-mode, or A History of Quietism, Particularly that of the Lord Arch-bishop of Cambray and Madame Guyone....Also containing an Account of the Management of the Controversie (Now Depending on Rome) betwixt the Arch-bishop's book....*London: J. Harris and A. Bell.

Brinton, Howard H, ed. 1946. *A Guide to True Peace, Or the Excellency of Inward and Spiritual Prayer Compiled Chiefly from the Writings of Fénelon, Guyon, and Molinos.* New York: Harper Brothers.

Guyon, Jeanne-Marie Bouvier de la Mothe. 1858. *Letters of Madame Guyon.* Edited by P. L. Upham. Boston: Henry Hoyt.

———. 1897. *The Song of Songs of Solomon, with Explanations and Reflections Having Reference to the Interior Life.* Translated by James W. Metcalf, M.D. New York: A. W. Dennett.

———. 1898. *Autobiography of Madame Guyon.* 2 volumes. Translated by Thomas Taylor Allen. London: Kegan Paul, Trench, Trübner & Co.

———. 1960. *Autobiography of Madame Guyon in Two Parts.* Chicago: Moody Press.

———. 1975. *Experiencing the Depths of Jesus Christ.* Edited by Gene Edwards. Sargent, GA: Seedsowers.

———. 1984. *Experiencing God Through Prayer.* Edited and revised by Donna Arthur. Springdale, PA: Whitaker House.

———. 1987. *The Song of Songs.* Jacksonville, FL: Christian Books Publishing House.

———. 1989. *Spiritual Torrents.* Edited by Gene Edwards. Auburn, ME: Seedsowers.

Secondary Sources

Aegerter, Emmanuel. 1941. *Madame Guyon: une aventurière mystique*. Paris: Librairie Hachette.

Armogathe, J.-R. 1973. *Le Quiétisme*. Paris: Presses Universitaires de France.

Armstrong, Regis J., and Ignatius C. Brady, eds. 1988. *Francis De Sales, Jane De Chantal: Letters of Spiritual Direction*. Mahwah, NJ: Paulist Press.

Balsama, George. 1973. "Madame Guyon, Heterodox..." *Church History* 42: 350–365.

Bayley, Peter. 1999. "What Was Quietism Subversive Of?" *Seventeenth-Century French Studies* 21: 195–204.

Beasley, Faith. 2000. "Altering the Fabric of History: Women's Participation in the Classical Age," in *A History of Women's Writing*. Edited by Sonya Stephens. Cambridge: Cambridge University Press.

Beaude, J., et al. 1997. *Madame Guyon*. Grenoble: Jérôme Millon.

Bonnel, L.-A. 1850. *Sur la Controverse de Bossuet et de Fénelon sur le Quiétisme*. Macon, France: Imprimerie de Dejussieu.

Bossuet, Jacques Bénigne. 1862–1864. *Oeuvres complètes de Bossuet*. Edited by F. Lachat. Paris: Libairie de Louis Vivès.

Brinton, Howard. 1952. *Friends for 300 Years: The History and Beliefs of the Society of Friends Since George Fox Started the Quaker Movement*. Wallingford, PA: Pendle Hill Publications.

Broekhuysen, Arthus. 1991. "The Quietist Movement and Miguel de Molinos." *The Journal of Religion and Psychical Research* 14: 139–143.

Bruneau, Marie-Florine. 1998. *Women Mystics Confront the Modern World: Marie de l'Incarnation (1599–1672) and Madame Guyon (1648–1717)*. SUNY Series in Western Esoteric Traditions. Albany: State University of New York Press.

Bruno, Jean. 1962. "L'Expérience mystique de Madame Guyon," introduction to *La Vie de Madame Guyon écrite par elle-même* in *Les Cahiers de la Tour St-Jacques VI*. Paris: Roudil.

Cholakin, Patricia. 2000. *Women and the Politics of Self-Representation in Seventeenth-Century France*. Newark: University of Delaware Press.

Cognet, Louis. 1959. *Post-Reformation Spirituality*. Translated by P. Hepburne Scott. New York: Hawthorne Books.

———. 1981. "Ecclesiastical Life in France," in *History of the Church 6: The Church in the Age of Absolutism and Enlightenment*. Edited by Hubert Jedin and John Dolan. Translated by Gunther J. Holst. New York: Crossroad.

———. 1937–1994. "Le Coeur chez les spirituels du XVIIe siècle," in *Dictionnaire de spiritualité ascétique et mystique*. Edited by Marcel Viller. Paris: Beauchesne.

Constable, Giles. 1999. "'Love and Do What You Will,' The Medieval History of an Augustinian Precept," *The Morton Bloomfield Lectures IV*. Kalamazoo, MI: Medieval Institute Publications.

Daly, Pierrette. 1993. *Heroic Tropes: Gender and Intertext*. Detroit: Wayne State University Press.

De Certeau, Michel. 1988. *The Writing of History*. Translated by Tom Conley. New York: Columbia University Press.

———. 1992. *The Mystic Fable*, Vol. 1, *The Sixteenth and Seventeenth Centuries*. Translated by Michael B. Smith. Chicago: University of Chicago Press.

De La Bedoyere, Michael. 1956. *The Archbishop and the Lady: The Story of Fenelon and Madame Guyon*. New York: Pantheon Books.

DuBois, Elfrieda. 1986. "Fénelon and Quietism," in *The Study of Spirituality*. Edited by Cheslyn Jones, Geoffrey Wainwright and Edward Yarnold, SJ. New York: Oxford University Press.

Dumas, François Ribadeau. 1968. *Fénelon et les saintes folies de Madame Guyon*. Geneva: Éditions du Mont-Blanc.

Dupré, Louis. 1989. "Jansenism and Quietism," in *Christian Spirituality: Post-Reformation and Modern*. Edited by Louis Dupré and Don E. Saliers, in collaboration with John Meyendorff. Vol. 18 of *World Spirituality: An Encyclopedic History of the Religious Quest*. New York: Crossroad.

Etten, Henry van. 1959. *George Fox and the Quakers*. Translated and revised by E. Kelvin Osborn. New York: Harper Torchbooks.

Fanning, Steven. 2001. *Mystics of the Christian Tradition*. New York: Routledge.

Fénelon, François de Salignac de la Mothe. 1901. *Réponse inédite à Bossuet*. Paris: Librairie Internationale.

Forthomme, Bernard, and Jad Hatem. 1997. *Madame Guyon: Quiétude d'accélération*. Paris: Cariscript.

Fraser, Antonia. 2007. *Love and Louis XIV: The Women in the Life of the Sun King*. New York: Anchor Books.

Gaffney, Edward McGlynn. 1996. "Quietism and Pacifism in American Public Policy: The Triumph of Secular Pacifism in the Religious State," in *War and Its Discontents: Pacifism and Quietism in Abrahamic Traditions*. Edited by J. Patout Burns. Washington, D.C.: Georgetown University Press.

Goldsmith, Elizabeth C. 2001. *Publishing Women's Life Stories in France, 1647–1720: From Voice to Print*. Burlington, VT: Ashgate.

Gondal, Marie Louise. 1989. *Madame Guyon (1648–1717): Un nouveau visage*. Paris: Beauchesne.

Goubert, Pierre. 1970. *Louis XIV and Twenty Million Frenchmen*. Translated by Anne Carter. New York: Random House, Vintage Books.

Grenier, Jean. 1984. *Écrits sur le quiétisme*. Quimper: Callligrammes.

Gwyn, Douglas. 1986. *Apocalypse of the Word: The Life and Message of George Fox (1621–1691)*. Richmond, IN: Friends United Press.

Harris, J. Rendel. 1900. *The Influence of Quietism on the Society of Friends*. A lecture delivered at Bryn Mawr College on April 30, 1900. Philadelphia: Leeds Press.

Hedstrom, Matthew. 2004. "Rufus Jones and Mysticism for the Masses." *Crosscurrents* 54: 31–44.

Heuberger, Jean Marc. 2001. "Les commentaires bibliques de Madame Guyon dans la Bible de Berleburg." *Revue de théologie et de philosophie* 133: 303–323.

James, Nancy. 2007. *The Pure Love of Jeanne Guyon: The Great Conflict in King Louis XIV's Court*. Lanham, MD: University Press of America.

Jantzen, Grace. 1996. *Power, Gender, and Christian Mysticism*. New York: Cambridge University Press.

Jones, Rufus. 1936. *The Testimony of the Soul*. New York: Macmillan Company.

Knox, Ronald. 1961. *Enthusiasm: A Chapter in the History of Religion with Special Reference to the Seventeenth and Eighteenth Centuries*. New York: Oxford University Press.

Kristeva, Julia. 1987. *Tales of Love*. Translated by Leon S. Roudiez. New York: Columbia University Press.

Laude, Patrick D. 1991. *Approches du quiétisme: Deux études suivies du Moyen court et très facile pour l'oraison de Madame Guyon (texte de l'édition de 1685)*. Biblio 17–68. *Papers on Seventeenth Century Literature*, 57–95.

Le Brun, Jacques. 2001. "Présupposés théoriques de la lecture mystique de la Bible: l'exemple de La Sainte Bible de Mme Guyon." *Revue de théologie et de philosophie* 133: 287–302.

Leduc-Fayette, Denise, ed. 1996. *Fénelon, philosophie et spiritualité: Actes du colloque*. Paris: Droz.

Lindberg, Carter, ed. 2005. *The Pietist Theologians: An Introduction to Theology in the Seventeenth and Eighteenth Centuries*. Oxford: Blackwell.

Loring, Patricia. 1997. *Listening Spirituality: Personal Spiritual Practices Among Friends*. Washington, D.C.: Openings Press.

Loskoutoff, Yvan. 2003. "Les Récits de songe de Jeanne Guyon à Fénelon (avec des textes inédits)," in *Songes et Songeurs (XIIIe–XVIIIe siècle)*. Edited by Nathalie Dauvois and Jean-Philippe Grosperrin. Québec: Les Presses de l'Université Laval.

Mallet-Joris, Françoise. 1978. *Jeanne Guyon*. Paris: Flammarion.

McGinn, Bernard. 1991. *The Foundations of Mysticism: Origins to the Fifth Century*. Vol. 1 in *Presence of God: A History of Western Christian Mysticism*. New York: Crossroad.

Millot, Catherine. 2006. *La Vie parfaite: Jeanne Guyon, Simone Weil, Etty Hillesum*. Paris: Gallimard.

Paige, Nicholas D. 2001. *Being Interior: Autobiography and the Contradictions of Modernity in Seventeenth-Century France*. Philadelphia: University of Pennsylvania Press.

Pope, Russell. 1938. "French Quietism: Jeanne Marie Guyon," in *Concerning Mysticism: Being Those Lectures Delivered at Guilford College Library in the Spring of 1938*. Guilford College Bulletin, 21.11: 13–28.

Popkin, Richard. 1992 "Fideism, Quietism, and Unbelief: Skepticism for and Against Religion in the Seventeenth and Eighteenth Centuries," in *Faith, Reason, and Skepticism*. Edited and introduction by Marcus Hester. Philadelphia: Temple University Press.

Randall, Catherine. 2000. "'Loosening the Stays:' Madame Guyon's Quietist Opposition to Absolutism." *Mystics Quarterly* 26: 8–30.

Riley, Patrick. 2002. "Blaise Pascal, Jeanne Guyon, and the Paradoxes of the *moi haïssable*." *Papers on French Seventeenth-Century Literature* 29: 222–240.

Riley, Philip F. 2001. *A Lust for Virtue: Louis XIV's Attack on Sin in Seventeenth-Century France*. Westport, CT: Greenwood Press.

Rivière, Marc Serge. 1991. "The Reactions of the Anti-Voltaire Lobby to *Le Siècle de Louis XIV*: Guyon, Nonnette, Berthier, and Fréron." *Studies on Voltaire & the Eighteenth Century* 292: 217–242.

Salter, Darius. 1985. "Mysticism in American Wesleyanism." *Wesleyan Theological Journal* 20: 94–107.

St. Ville, Susan Monica. 1996. "A Chaos Without Confusion: A Study of the Mystical Discourse of Jeanne Guyon." Ph.D. dissertation. University of Chicago.

Thompson, Phyllis. 1986. *Madame Guyon, Martyr of the Holy Spirit*. London: Hodder and Stoughton.

Thompson, William M., ed. 1989. *Bérulle and the French School*. Translated by Lowell M. Glendon. Mahwah, NJ: Paulist Press.

Treasure, Geoffrey. 2001. *Louis XIV*. London: Pearson Education Limited.

Upham, Thomas. 1961. *Life and Religious Opinions and Experiences of Madame Guyon, Including an Account of the Personal History and Religious Opinions of Fénelon, Archbishop of Cambray*. Originally published by Sampson & Low Co.; transferred to Allenson & Co., Ltd., 1905. Reprinted 1908, 1914, 1920, 1926, 1933, 1940, 1947, 1954. Greenwood, SC: Attic Press.

Ward, Patricia. 1995. "Madame Guyon in America: An Annotated Bibliography." *Bulletin of Bibliography* 52: 107–112.

———. 1997. "Le Quiétisme aux États-Unis," in *Madame Guyon: Rencontre autour de la vie et l'œuvre de Madame Guyon*. Edited by Joseph Beaude. Grenoble: Jérôme Millon.

———. 1998. "Madame Guyon and Experiential Theology in America." *The American Society of Church History* 67: 484–498.

———. 2000. "Fénelon Among the New England Abolitionists." *Christianity and Literature* 50: 79–93.

————. 2009. *Experimental Theology in America: Madame Guyon, Fénelon, and Their Readers*. Waco, TX: Baylor University Press.

Wainwright, Geoffrey. 1976. "Revolution and Quietism: Two Political Attitudes in Theological Perspective." *Scottish Journal of Theology* 29: 535–555.

Winn, Colette, and Donna Kuizenga, eds. 1997. *Women Writers in Pre-Revolutionary France: Strategies of Emancipation*. New York: Garland Publishing.

INDEX

Other Volumes in This Series

Other Volumes in This Series

Other Volumes in This Series

Other Volumes in This Series

Pseudo-Dionysius • THE COMPLETE WORKS
Pseudo-Macarius • THE FIFTY SPIRITUAL HOMILIES AND THE
GREAT LETTER
Pursuit of Wisdom, The • AND OTHER WORKS BY THE AUTHOR OF
THE CLOUD OF UNKNOWING
Quaker Spirituality • SELECTED WRITINGS
Rabbinic Stories •
Richard Rolle • THE ENGLISH WRITINGS
Richard of St. Victor • THE TWELVE PATRIARCHS, THE MYSTICAL ARK,
BOOK THREE OF THE TRINITY
Robert Bellarmine • SPIRITUAL WRITINGS
Safed Spirituality • RULES OF MYSTICAL PIETY, THE BEGINNING OF
WISDOM
Seventeenth-Century Lutheran Meditations and Hymns •
Shakers, The • TWO CENTURIES OF SPIRITUAL REFLECTION
Sharafuddin Maneri • THE HUNDRED LETTERS
Sor Juana Inés de la Cruz • SELECTED WRITINGS
Spirituality of the German Awakening, The •
Symeon the New Theologian • THE DISCOURSES
Talmud, The • SELECTED WRITINGS
Teresa of Avila • THE INTERIOR CASTLE
Theatine Spirituality • SELECTED WRITINGS
'Umar Ibn al-Fāriḍ • SUFI VERSE, SAINTLY LIFE
Valentin Weigel • SELECTED SPIRITUAL WRITINGS
Venerable Bede, The • ON THE SONG OF SONGS AND SELECTED
WRITINGS
Vincent de Paul and Louise de Marillac • RULES, CONFERENCES,
AND WRITINGS
Walter Hilton • THE SCALE OF PERFECTION
William Law • A SERIOUS CALL TO A DEVOUT AND HOLY LIFE, THE
SPIRIT OF LOVE
Zohar • THE BOOK OF ENLIGHTENMENT

The Classics of Western Spirituality is a ground-breaking collection of the original writings of more than 100 universally acknowledged teachers within the Catholic, Protestant, Eastern Orthodox, Jewish, Islamic, and Native American Indian traditions.

To order any title, or to request a complete catalog, contact Paulist Press at 800-218-1903 or visit us on the Web at www.paulistpress.com.